Snow White with the Red Hair

Sorata Akiduki

7

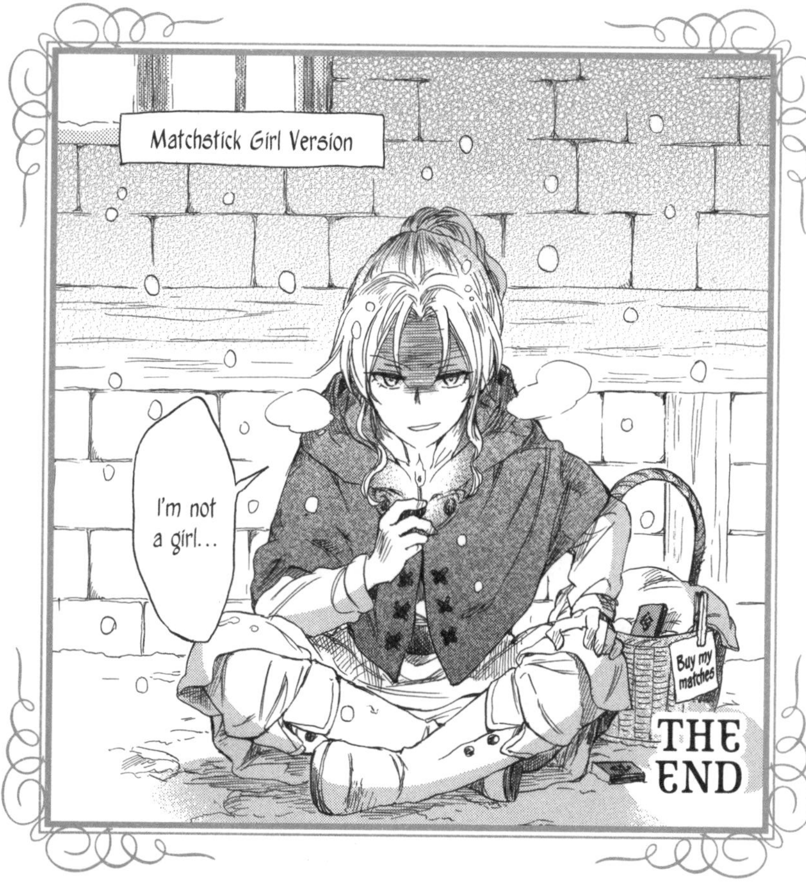
Matchstick Girl Version
I'm not a girl…
Buy my matches
THE END

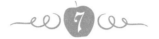

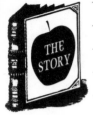

THE STORY

Shirayuki was born with beautiful hair as red as apples, but when her rare hair earns her unwanted attention from the notorious prince Raj, she's forced to flee her home. A young man named Zen helps her in the forest of the neighboring kingdom, Clarines, and it turns out he is that kingdom's second prince! Shirayuki decides to accompany Zen back to Wistal, the capital city of Clarines.

Shirayuki has met all manner of people since becoming a court herbalist, and her relationship with Zen continues to grow, as the two have finally made their feelings known to each other.

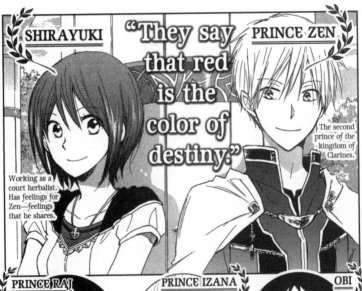

PRINCE ZEN
The second prince of the kingdom of Clarines.
"They say that red is the color of destiny."
SHIRAYUKI
Working as a court herbalist. Has feelings for Zen—feelings that he shares.
OBI
Former assassin. Currently Zen's underling and Shirayuki's bodyguard during her stay in Tanbarun.
PRINCE IZANA
Zen's older brother and the crown prince of the kingdom. Keeping a close eye on Shirayuki and Zen's relationship...
PRINCE RAJ
The so-called idiot prince. Hoping to improve his relationship with Shirayuki!

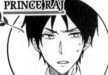

After receiving a banquet invitation from Prince Raj, Shirayuki and her escort, Obi, visit her home kingdom of Tanbarun. She spends the days leading up to the banquet with Raj.

But before she can attend the banquet, a mysterious pretty boy kidnaps her. Shirayuki and the boy are then captured by the Claw of the Sea—an infamous gang of pirates!

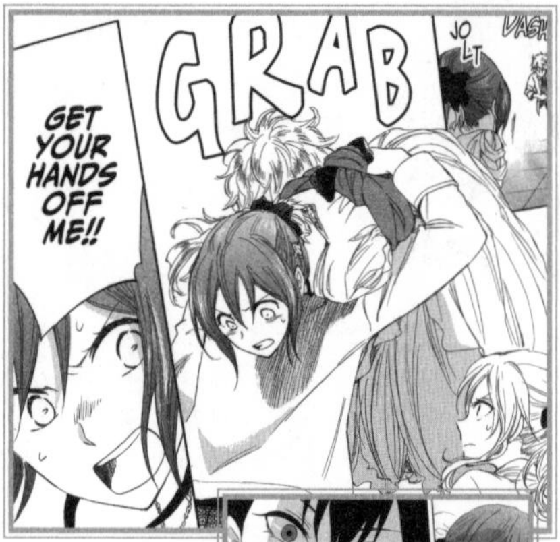
VASH
JOLT
GRAB
GET YOUR HANDS OFF ME!!

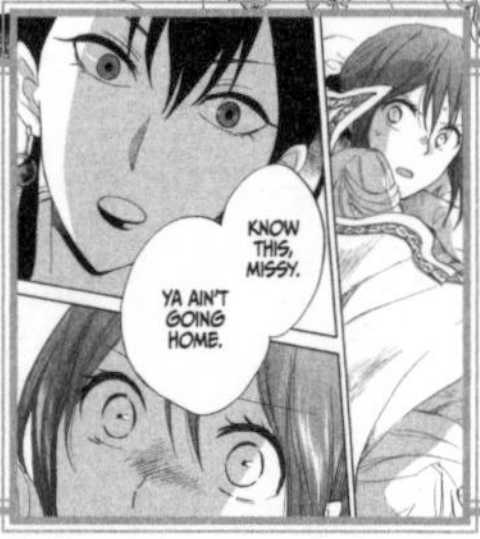
KNOW THIS, MISSY.
YA AIN'T GOING HOME.

Ignoring Izana's orders, Zen races off to Tanbarun. Once there, he rallies his allies, Prince Raj and a group of bandits called the Lions of the Mountain to track down Shirayuki.

Meanwhile, the pirate boss tortures the boy and makes plans to sell off Shirayuki. Just as the two begin to lose hope, the cavalry arrives, with Zen leading the charge!

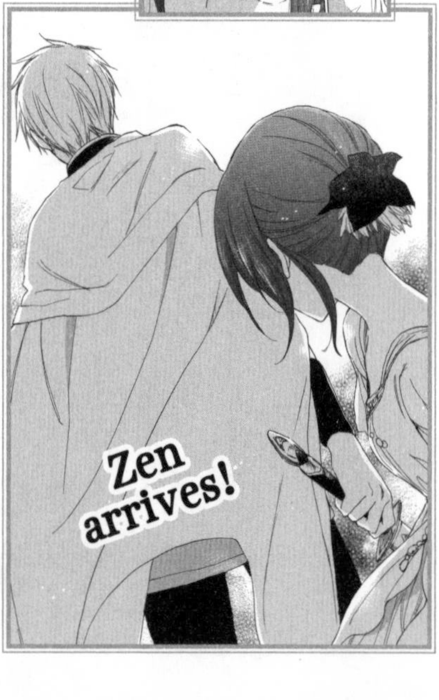
Zen arrives!

Snow White with the Red Hair

VOLUME 7
TABLE *of* CONTENTS

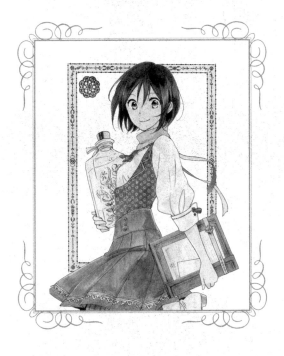

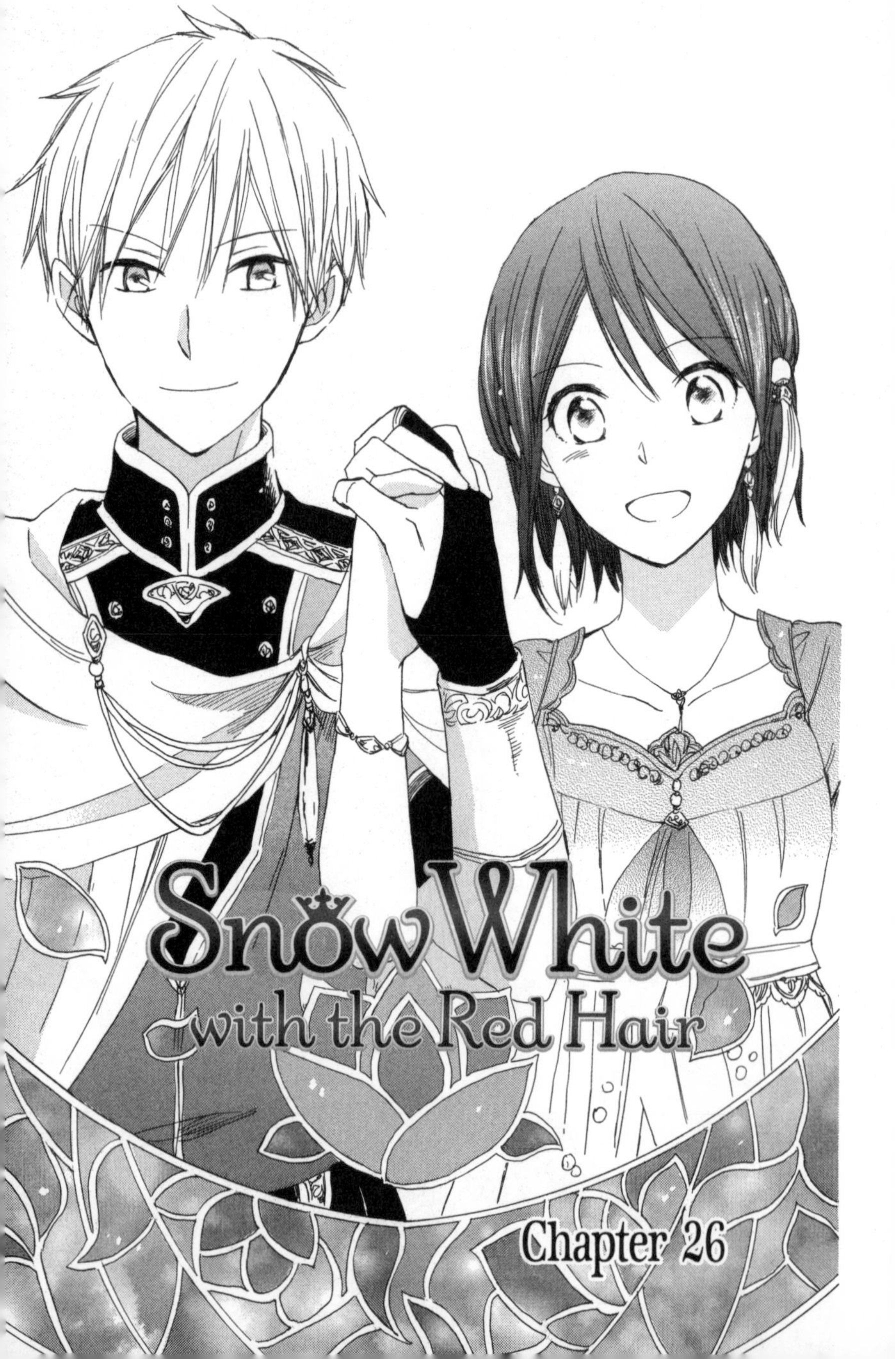
Snow White with the Red Hair
Chapter 26

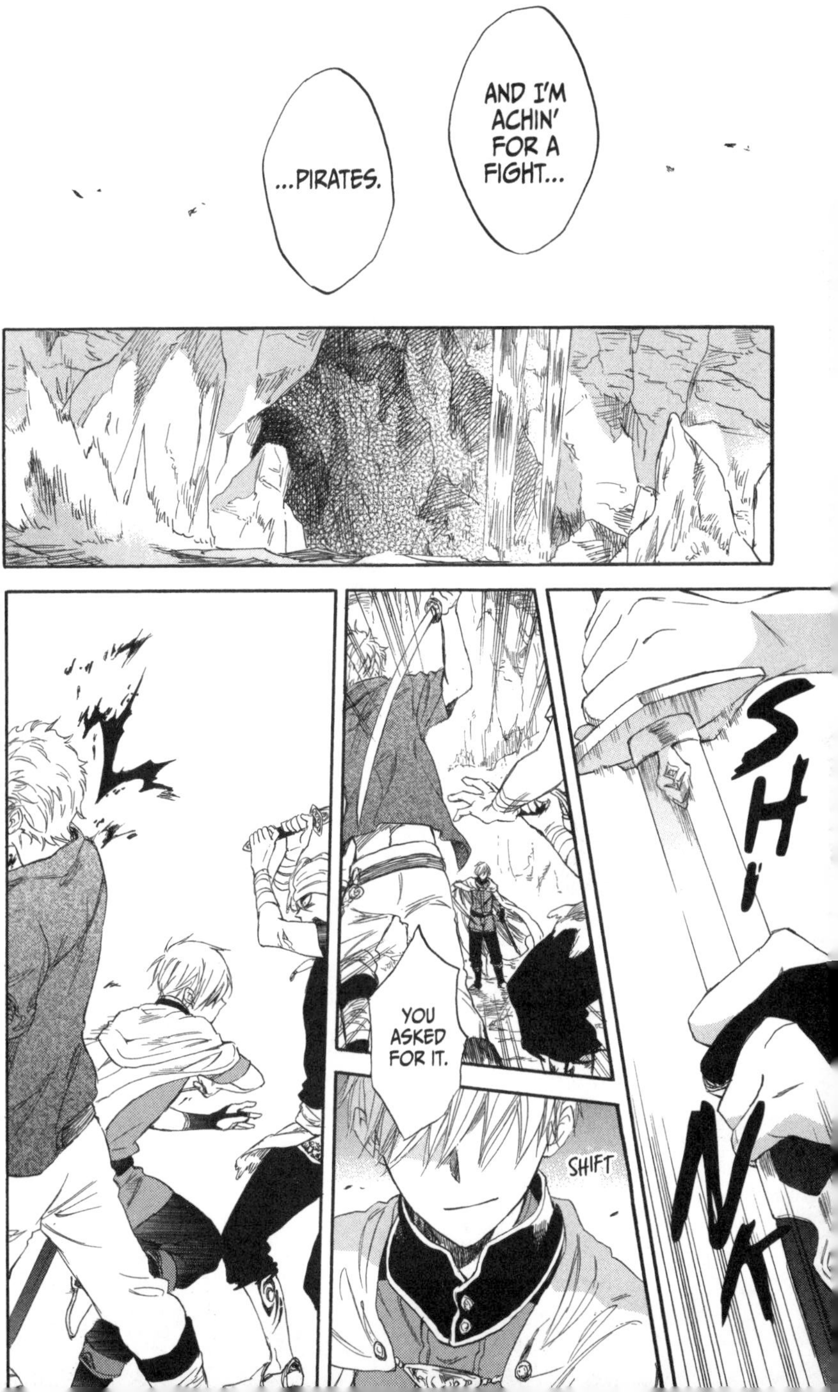
AND I'M ACHIN' FOR A FIGHT...
...PIRATES.
SHINK
YOU ASKED FOR IT.
SHIFT

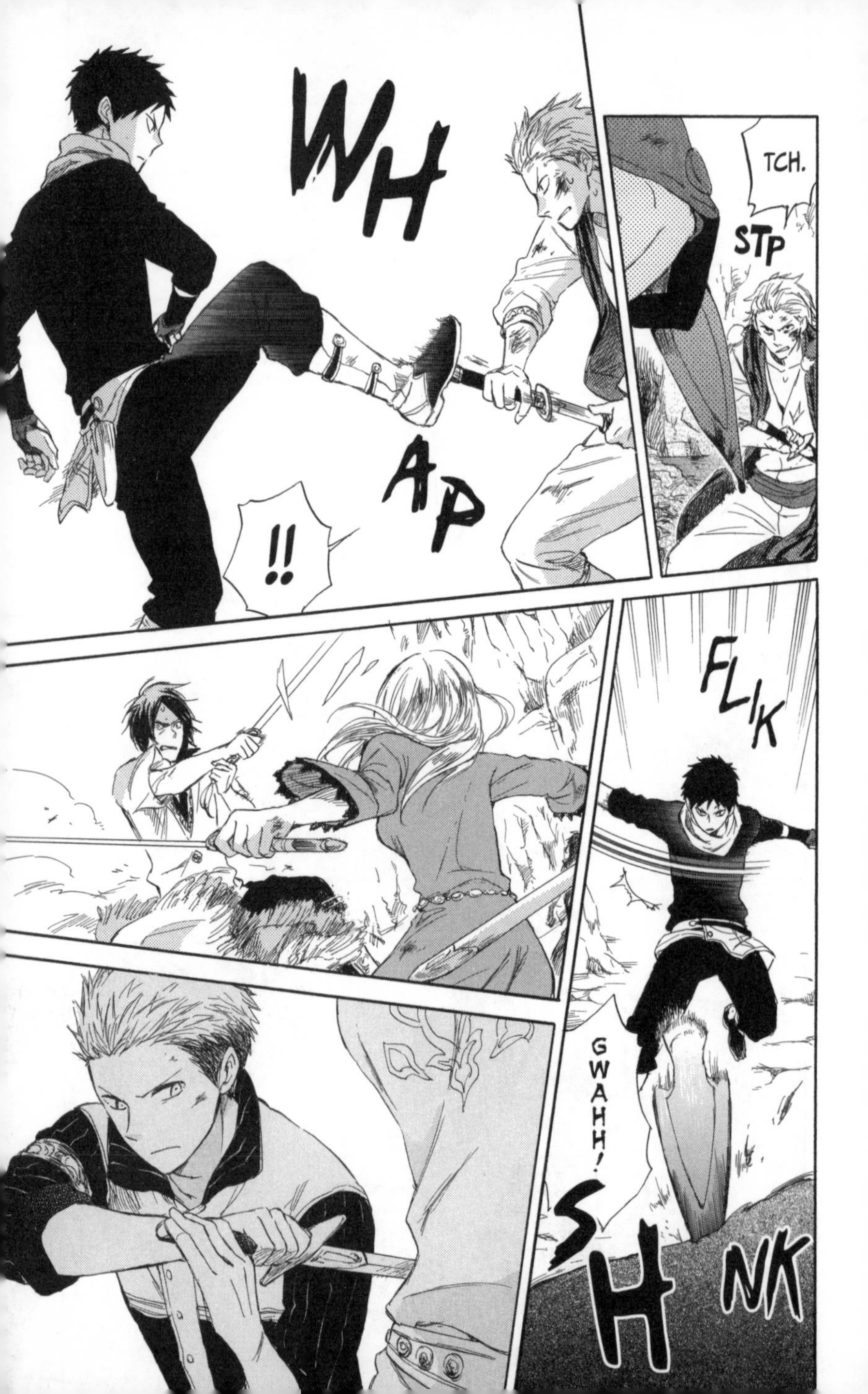
TCH.
STP
WHAP
!!
FLIK
GWAHH!
SHNK

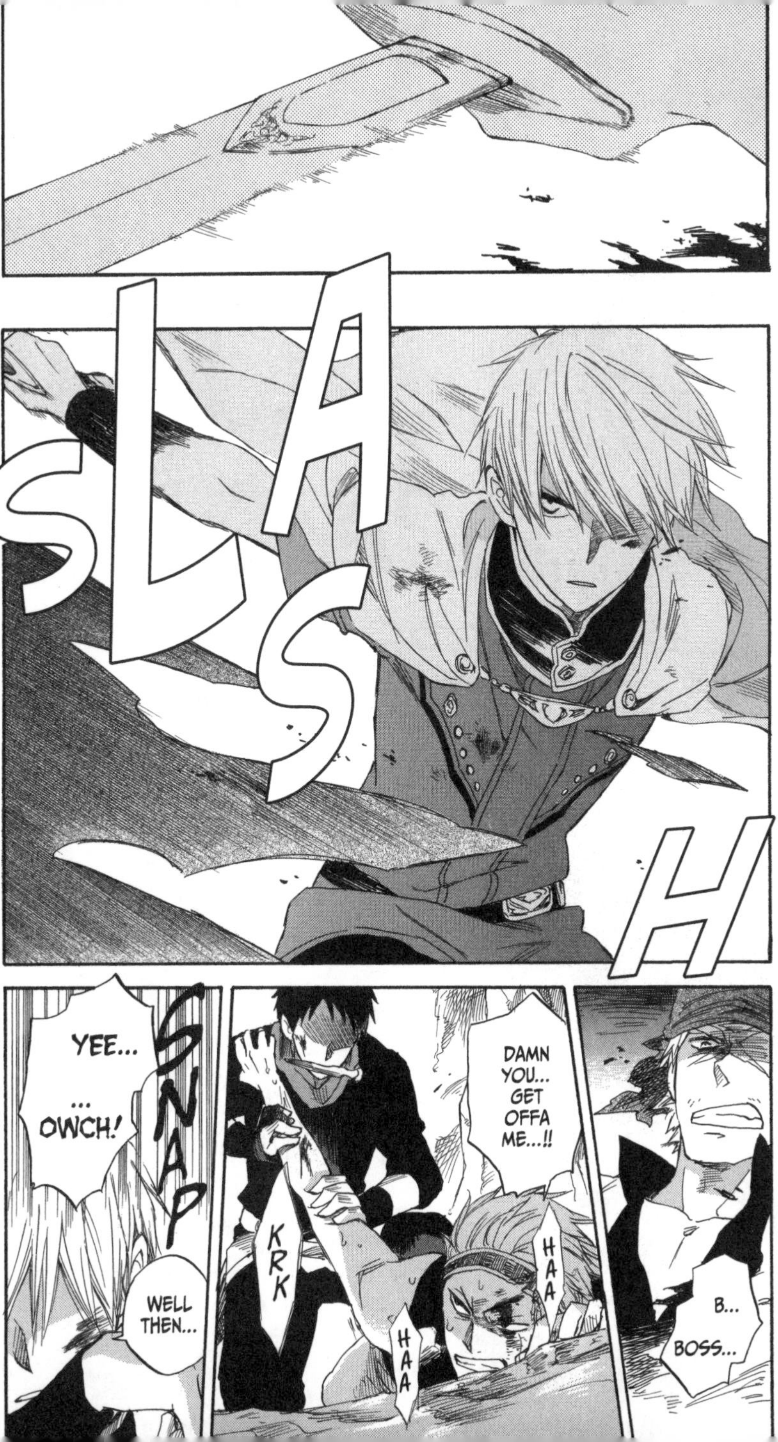
SLASH
B...
BOSS...
DAMN YOU... GET OFFA ME...!!
HAA
HAA
KRK
YEE...
... OWCH!
SNAP
WELL THEN...

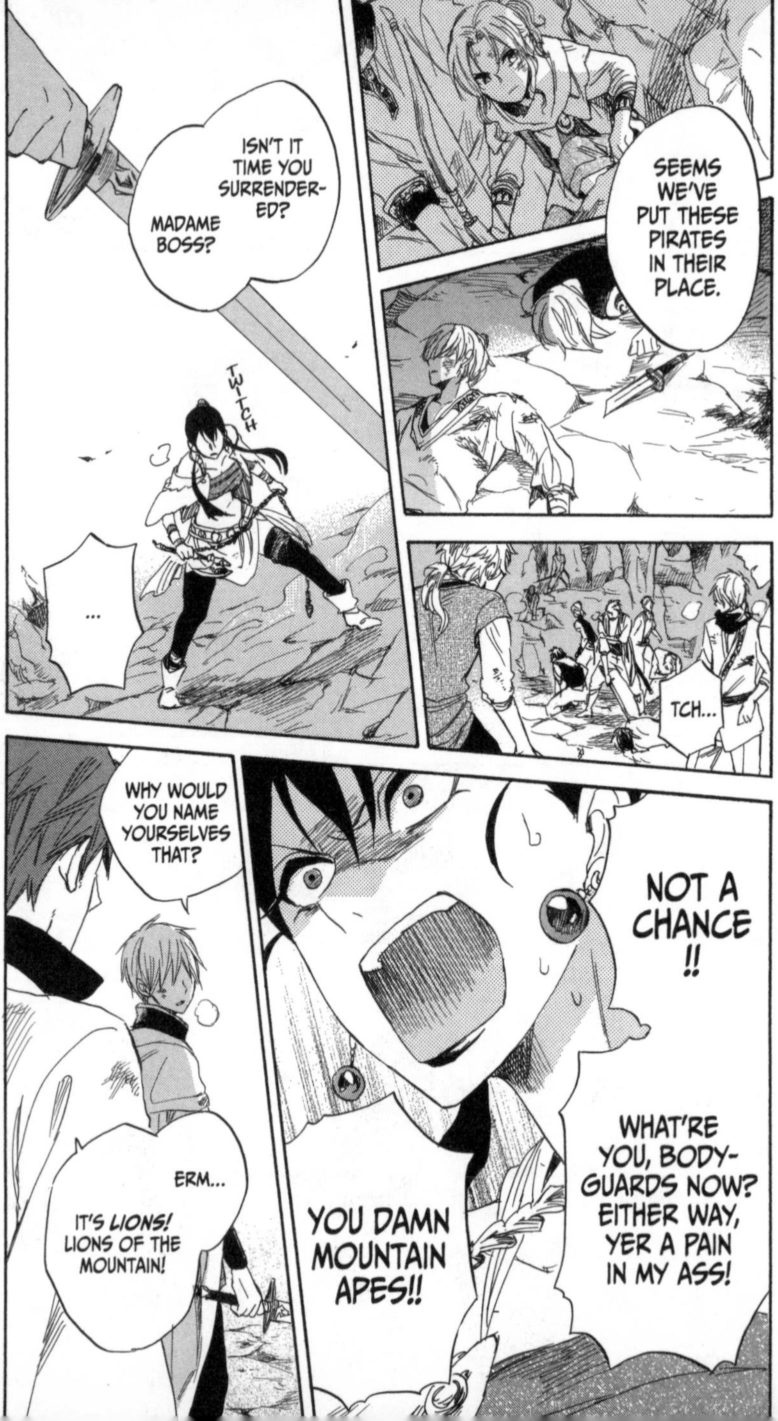
SEEMS WE'VE PUT THESE PIRATES IN THEIR PLACE.
TCH...
ISN'T IT TIME YOU SURRENDERED?
MADAME BOSS?
TWITCH
...
NOT A CHANCE!!
WHAT'RE YOU, BODYGUARDS NOW? EITHER WAY, YER A PAIN IN MY ASS!
YOU DAMN MOUNTAIN APES!!
WHY WOULD YOU NAME YOURSELVES THAT?
ERM...
IT'S *LIONS!* LIONS OF THE MOUNTAIN!

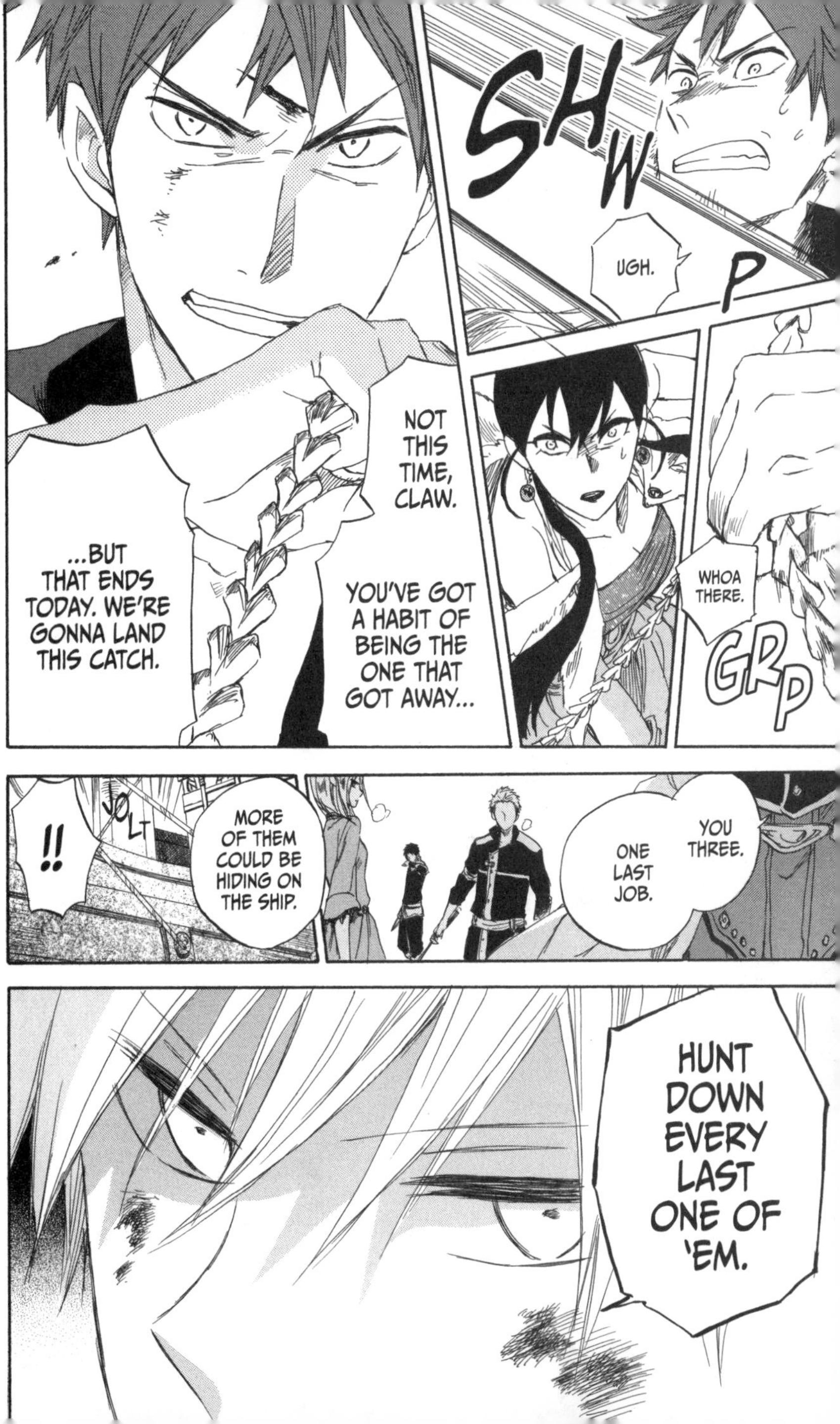
SHWP
UGH.
WHOA THERE.
GRP
NOT THIS TIME, CLAW.
YOU'VE GOT A HABIT OF BEING THE ONE THAT GOT AWAY...
...BUT THAT ENDS TODAY. WE'RE GONNA LAND THIS CATCH.
YOU THREE.
ONE LAST JOB.
MORE OF THEM COULD BE HIDING ON THE SHIP.
!!
JOLT
HUNT DOWN EVERY LAST ONE OF 'EM.

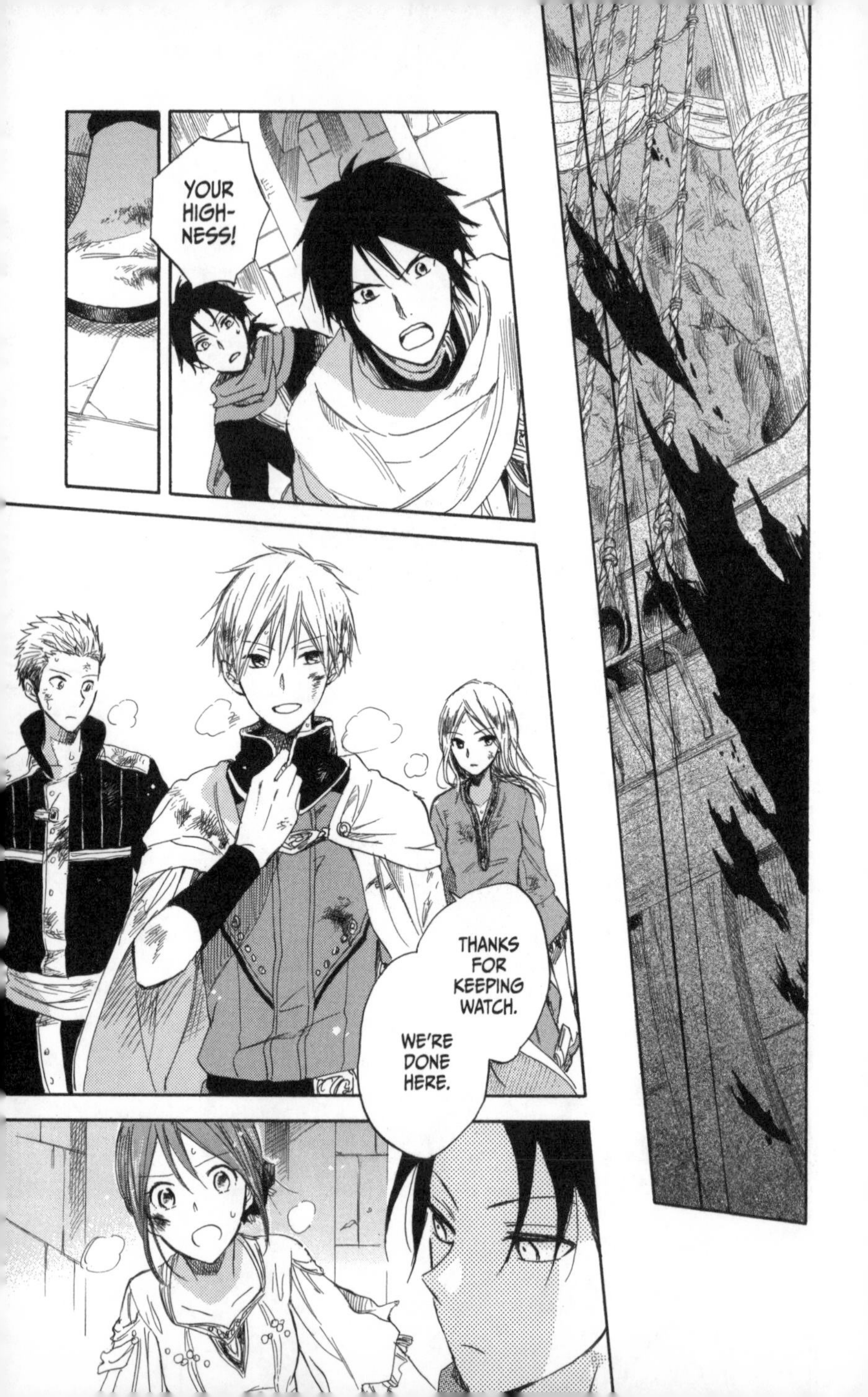
YOUR HIGH-NESS!
THANKS FOR KEEPING WATCH.
WE'RE DONE HERE.

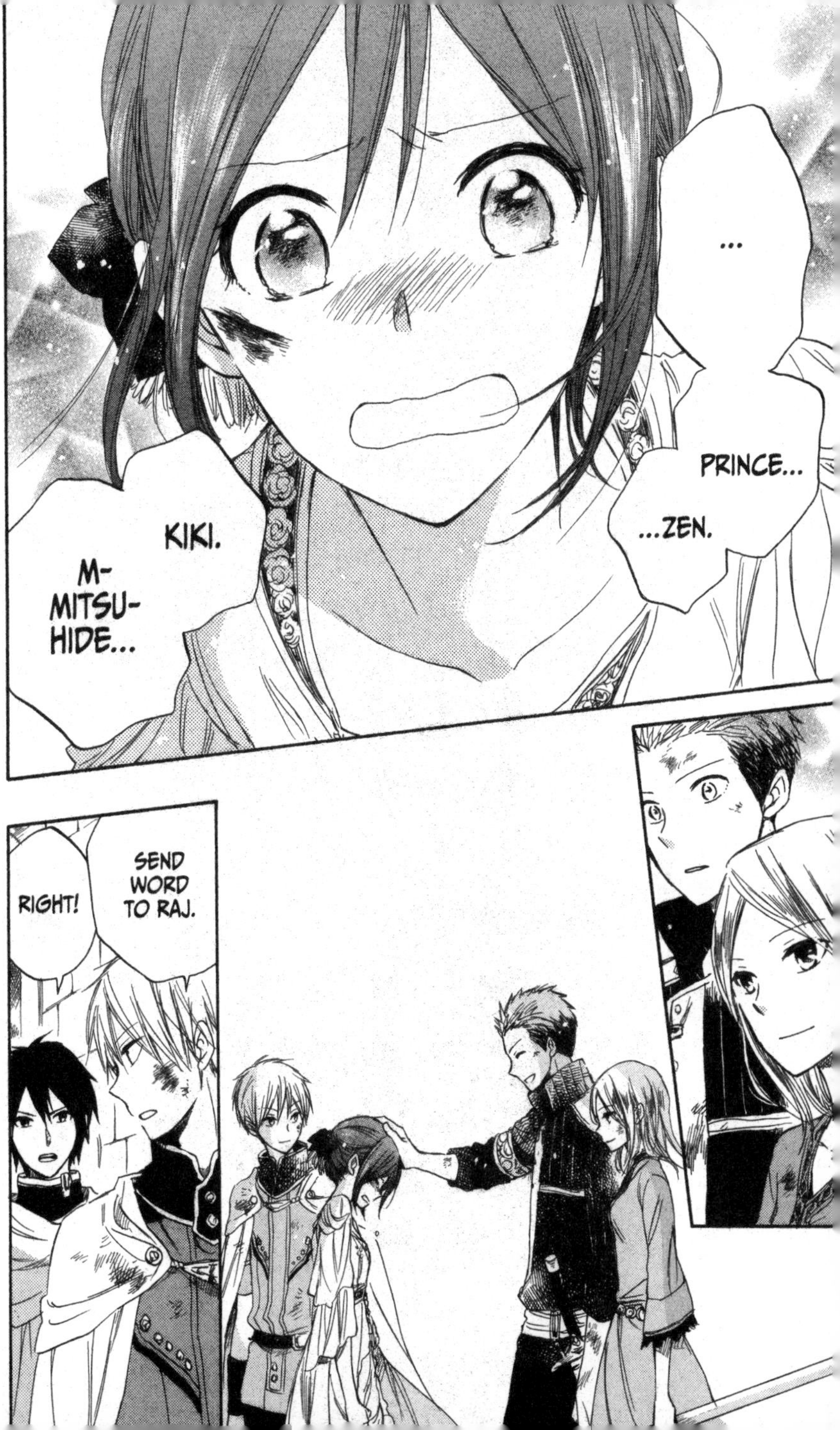
...
PRINCE... ...ZEN.
KIKI. M-MITSU-HIDE...
SEND WORD TO RAJ.
RIGHT!

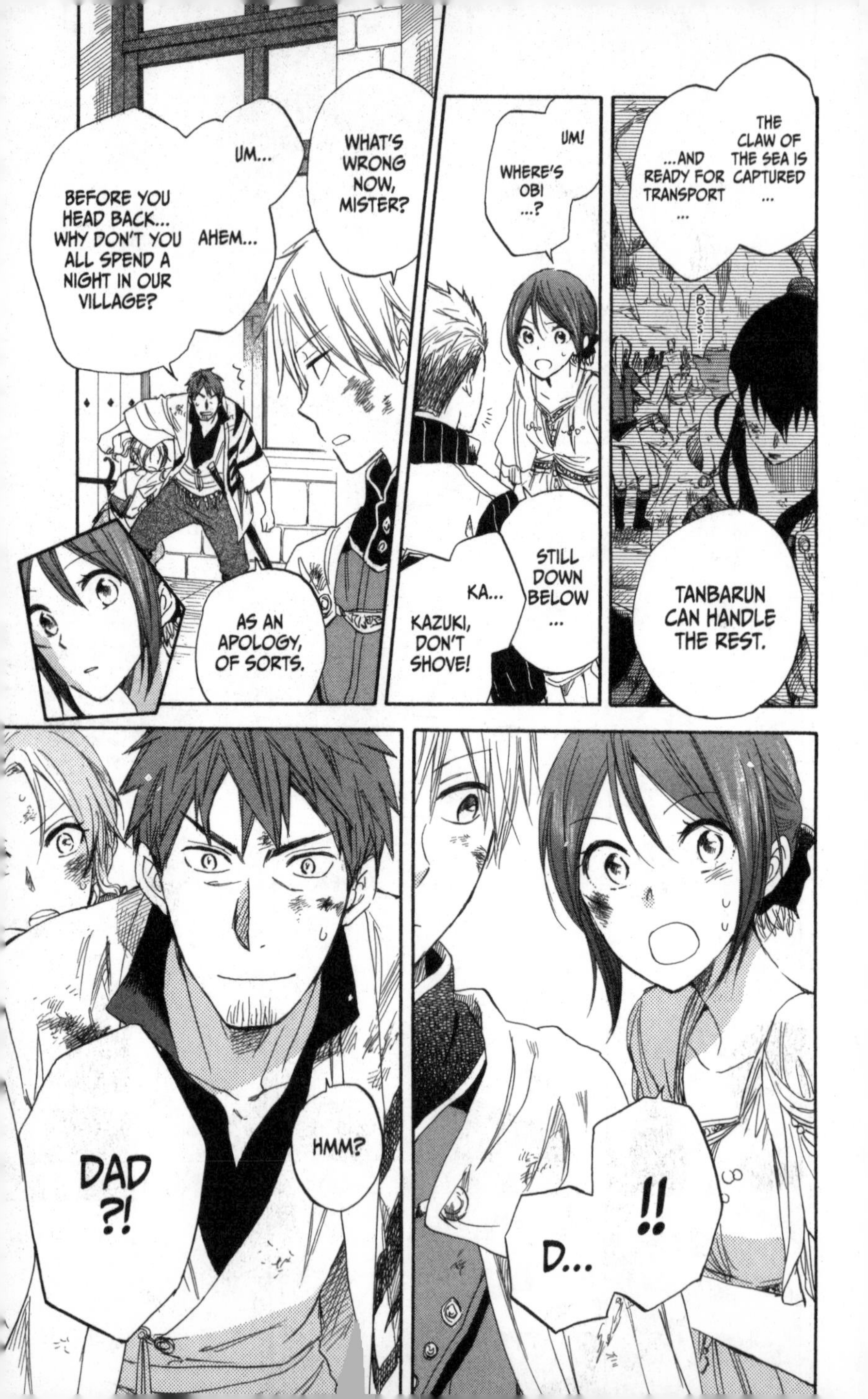
THE CLAW OF THE SEA IS CAPTURED ...
...AND READY FOR TRANSPORT ...
BOSS!
TANBARUN CAN HANDLE THE REST.
UM!
WHERE'S OBI ...?
STILL DOWN BELOW ...
KA...
KAZUKI, DON'T SHOVE!
WHAT'S WRONG NOW, MISTER?
UM...
AHEM...
BEFORE YOU HEAD BACK... WHY DON'T YOU ALL SPEND A NIGHT IN OUR VILLAGE?
AS AN APOLOGY, OF SORTS.
!!
D...
HMM?
DAD ?!

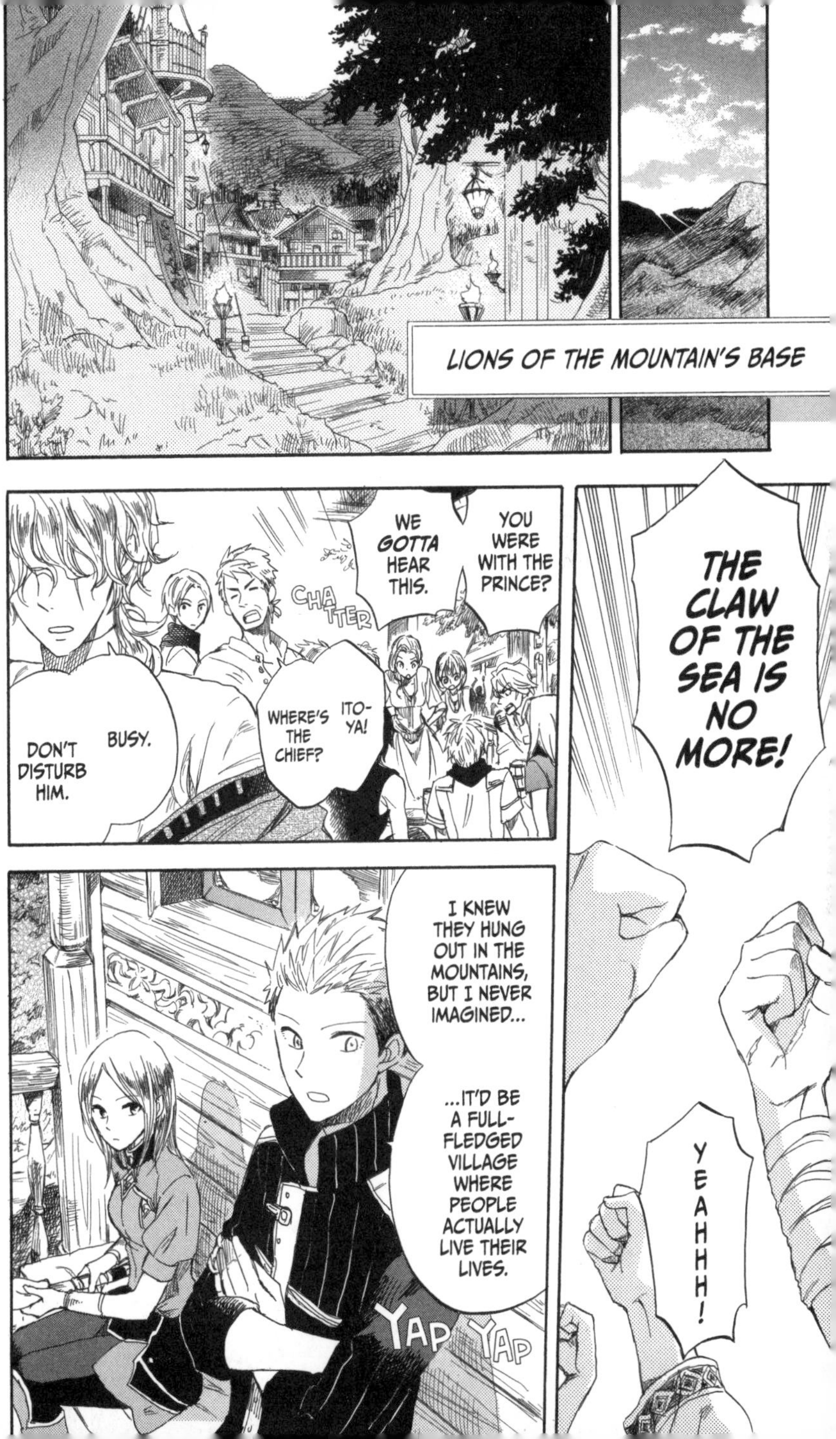
LIONS OF THE MOUNTAIN'S BASE
THE CLAW OF THE SEA IS NO MORE!
YEAHHH!
YOU WERE WITH THE PRINCE?
WE GOTTA HEAR THIS.
CHATTER
ITO-YA!
WHERE'S THE CHIEF?
BUSY.
DON'T DISTURB HIM.
I KNEW THEY HUNG OUT IN THE MOUNTAINS, BUT I NEVER IMAGINED...
...IT'D BE A FULL-FLEDGED VILLAGE WHERE PEOPLE ACTUALLY LIVE THEIR LIVES.
YAP YAP

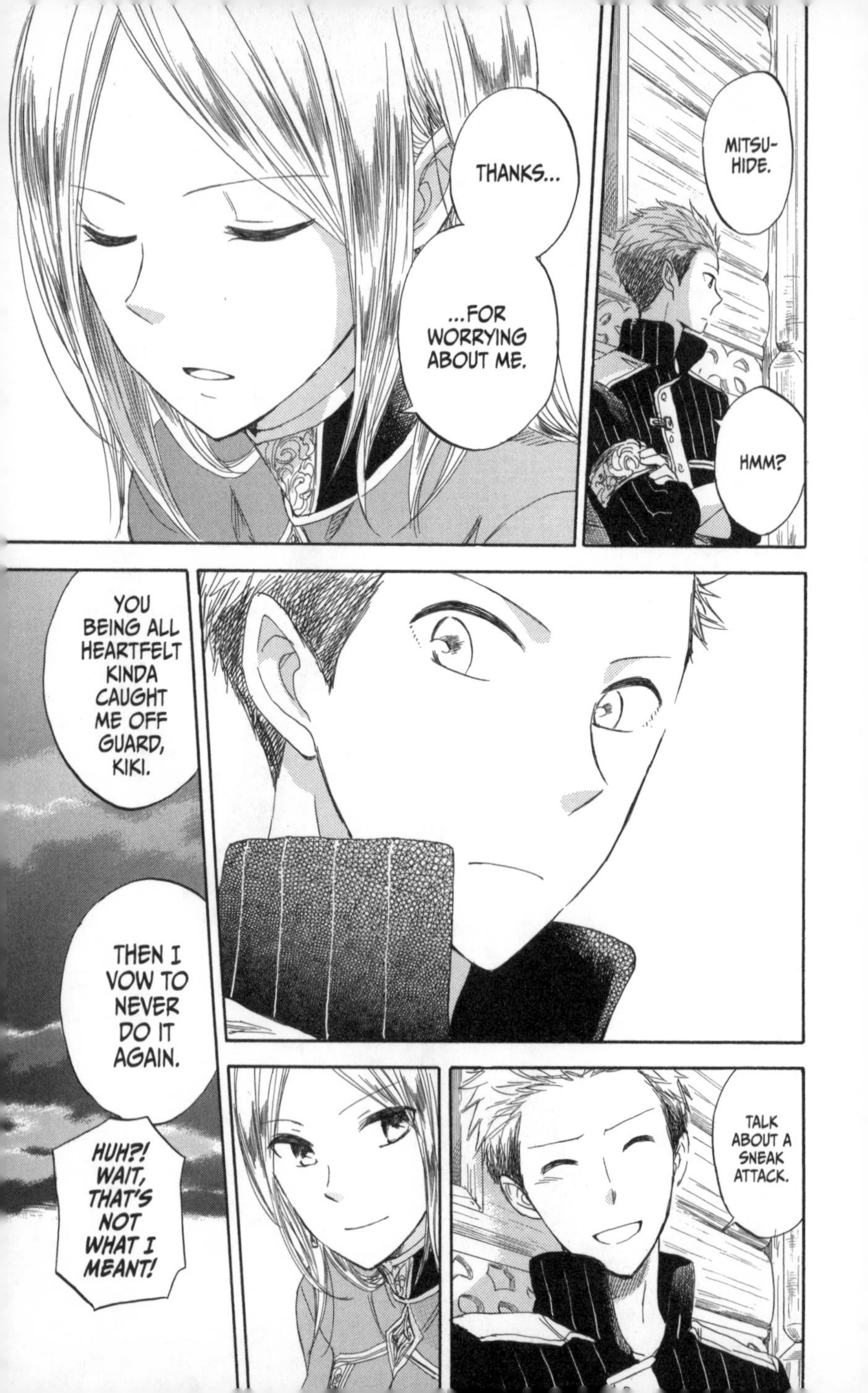
MITSU-HIDE.
HMM?
THANKS...
...FOR WORRYING ABOUT ME.
YOU BEING ALL HEARTFELT KINDA CAUGHT ME OFF GUARD, KIKI.
TALK ABOUT A SNEAK ATTACK.
THEN I VOW TO NEVER DO IT AGAIN.
HUH?! WAIT, THAT'S NOT WHAT I MEANT!

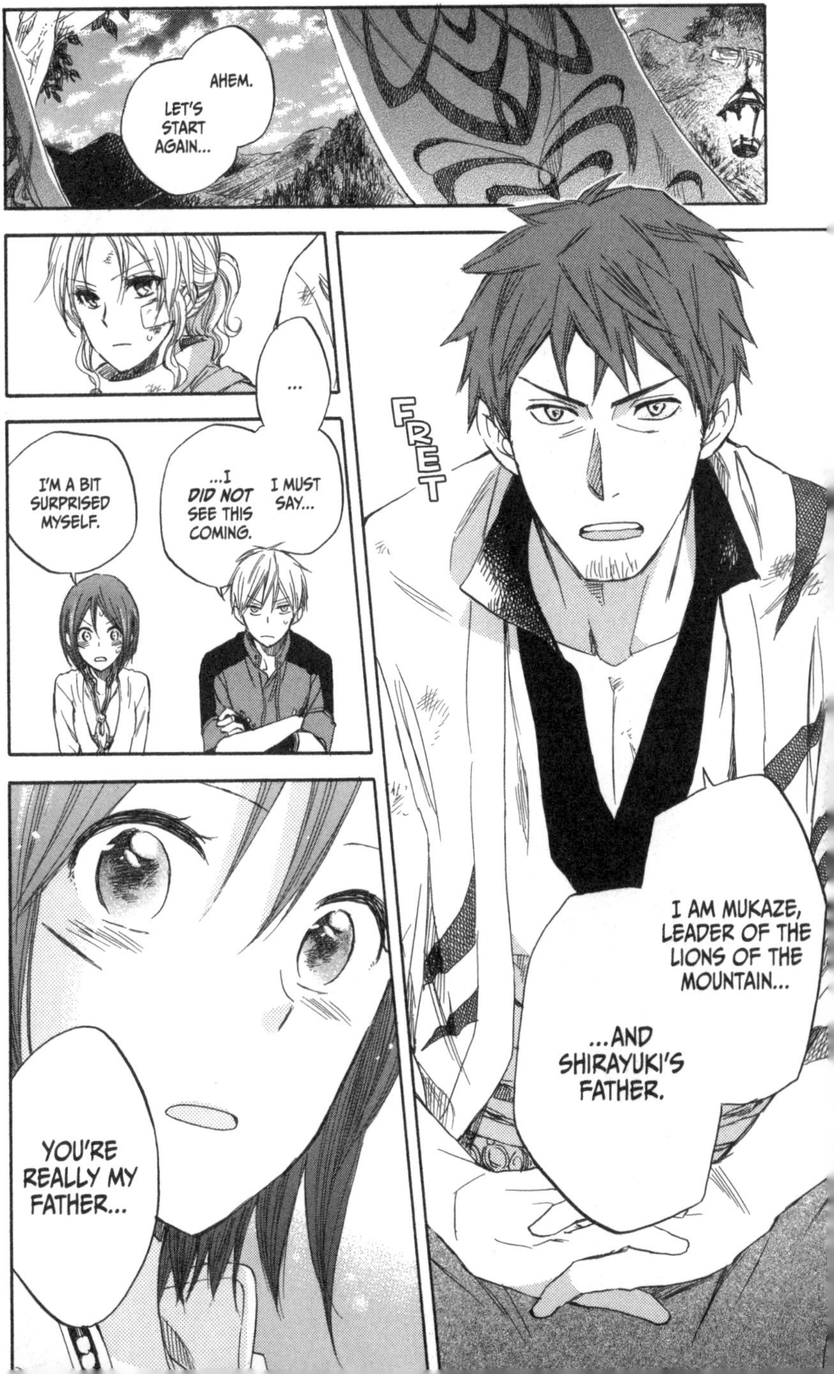
AHEM. LET'S START AGAIN...
FRET
I AM MUKAZE, LEADER OF THE LIONS OF THE MOUNTAIN...
...AND SHIRAYUKI'S FATHER.
...
I MUST SAY...
...I *DID NOT* SEE THIS COMING.
I'M A BIT SURPRISED MYSELF.
YOU'RE REALLY MY FATHER...

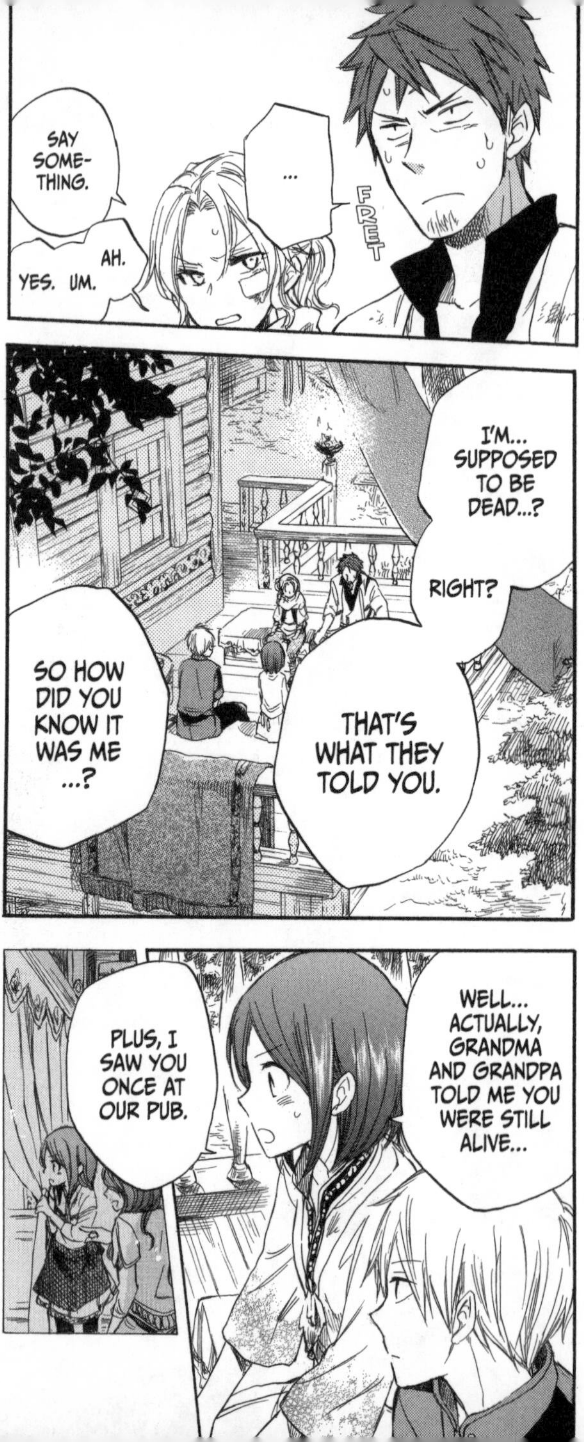
...
FRET
SAY SOME-THING.
AH. YES. UM.
I'M... SUPPOSED TO BE DEAD...?
RIGHT?
THAT'S WHAT THEY TOLD YOU.
SO HOW DID YOU KNOW IT WAS ME ...?
WELL... ACTUALLY, GRANDMA AND GRANDPA TOLD ME YOU WERE STILL ALIVE...
PLUS, I SAW YOU ONCE AT OUR PUB.

1

GREETINGS

Hello, I'm Sorata Akiduki.

Thank you for picking up volume 7 of Snow White with the Red Hair!

Volume

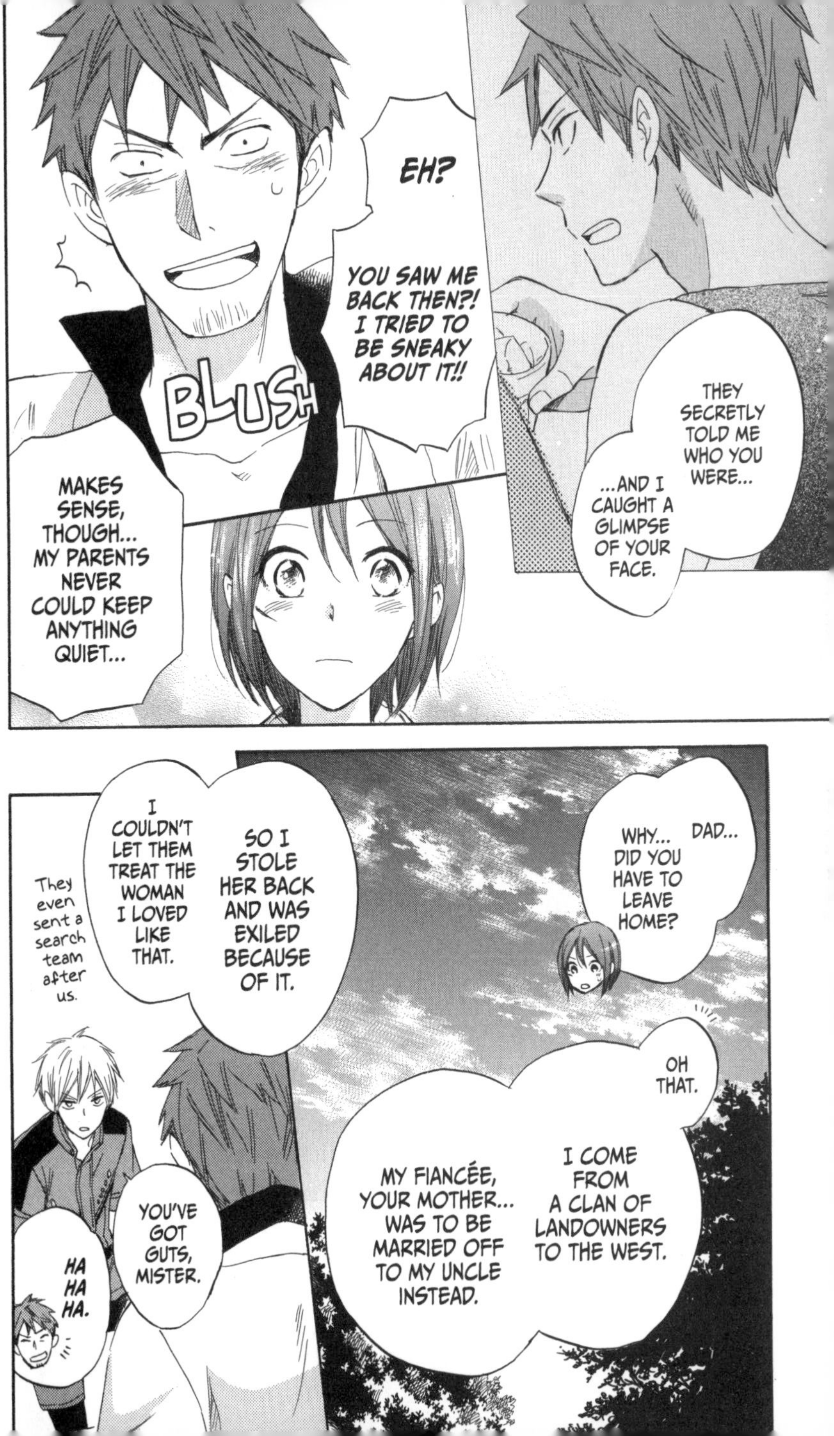
THEY SECRETLY TOLD ME WHO YOU WERE...
...AND I CAUGHT A GLIMPSE OF YOUR FACE.
EH?
YOU SAW ME BACK THEN?! I TRIED TO BE SNEAKY ABOUT IT!!
BLUSH
MAKES SENSE, THOUGH... MY PARENTS NEVER COULD KEEP ANYTHING QUIET...
DAD...
WHY... DID YOU HAVE TO LEAVE HOME?
OH THAT.
I COME FROM A CLAN OF LANDOWNERS TO THE WEST.
MY FIANCÉE, YOUR MOTHER... WAS TO BE MARRIED OFF TO MY UNCLE INSTEAD.
I COULDN'T LET THEM TREAT THE WOMAN I LOVED LIKE THAT.
SO I STOLE HER BACK AND WAS EXILED BECAUSE OF IT.
They even sent a search team after us.
YOU'VE GOT GUTS, MISTER.
HA HA HA.

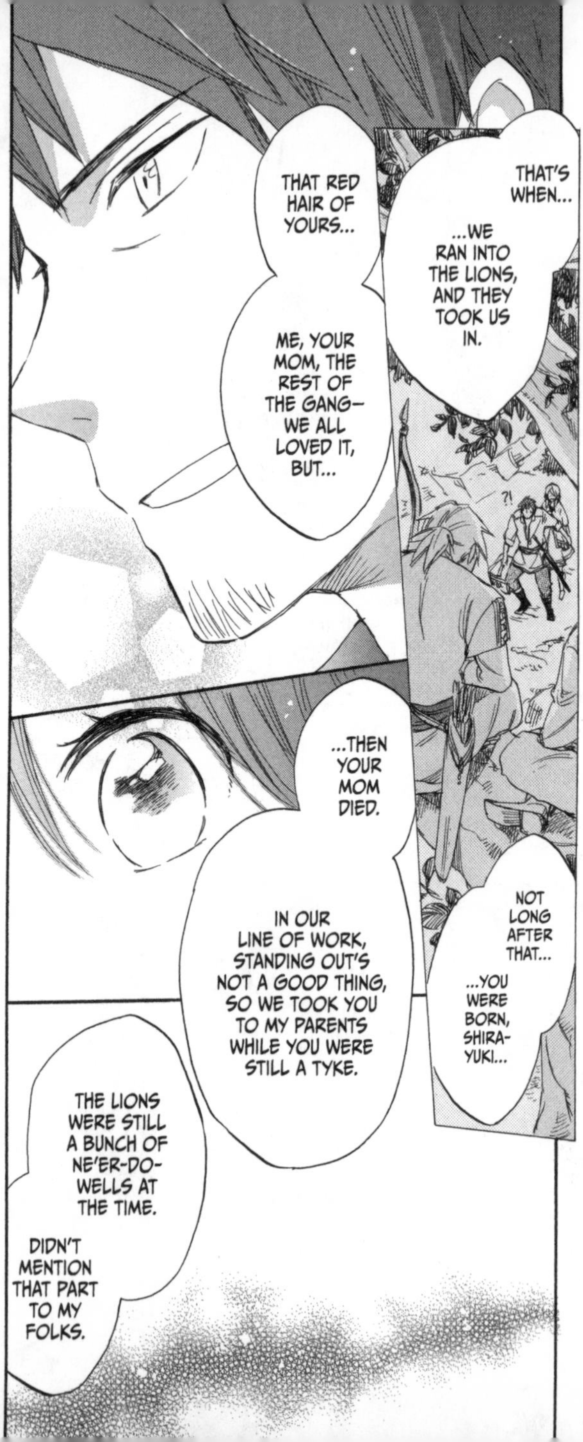
THAT'S WHEN...
...WE RAN INTO THE LIONS, AND THEY TOOK US IN.
NOT LONG AFTER THAT...
...YOU WERE BORN, SHIRA-YUKI...
THAT RED HAIR OF YOURS...
ME, YOUR MOM, THE REST OF THE GANG— WE ALL LOVED IT, BUT...
...THEN YOUR MOM DIED.
IN OUR LINE OF WORK, STANDING OUT'S NOT A GOOD THING, SO WE TOOK YOU TO MY PARENTS WHILE YOU WERE STILL A TYKE.
THE LIONS WERE STILL A BUNCH OF NE'ER-DO-WELLS AT THE TIME.
DIDN'T MENTION THAT PART TO MY FOLKS.

2

PROMOTION

Vahlia no Hanamuko—a compilation of one-shots—released in Japan on the same day as this book.

That makes ten volumes total I've put out. Hooray!

I guess I could think of *Snow White* volume 7 as being my tenth book (since they came out simultaneously), but it's easier to remember that the one-shot compilation is the tenth!

I hope you consider picking that up too.

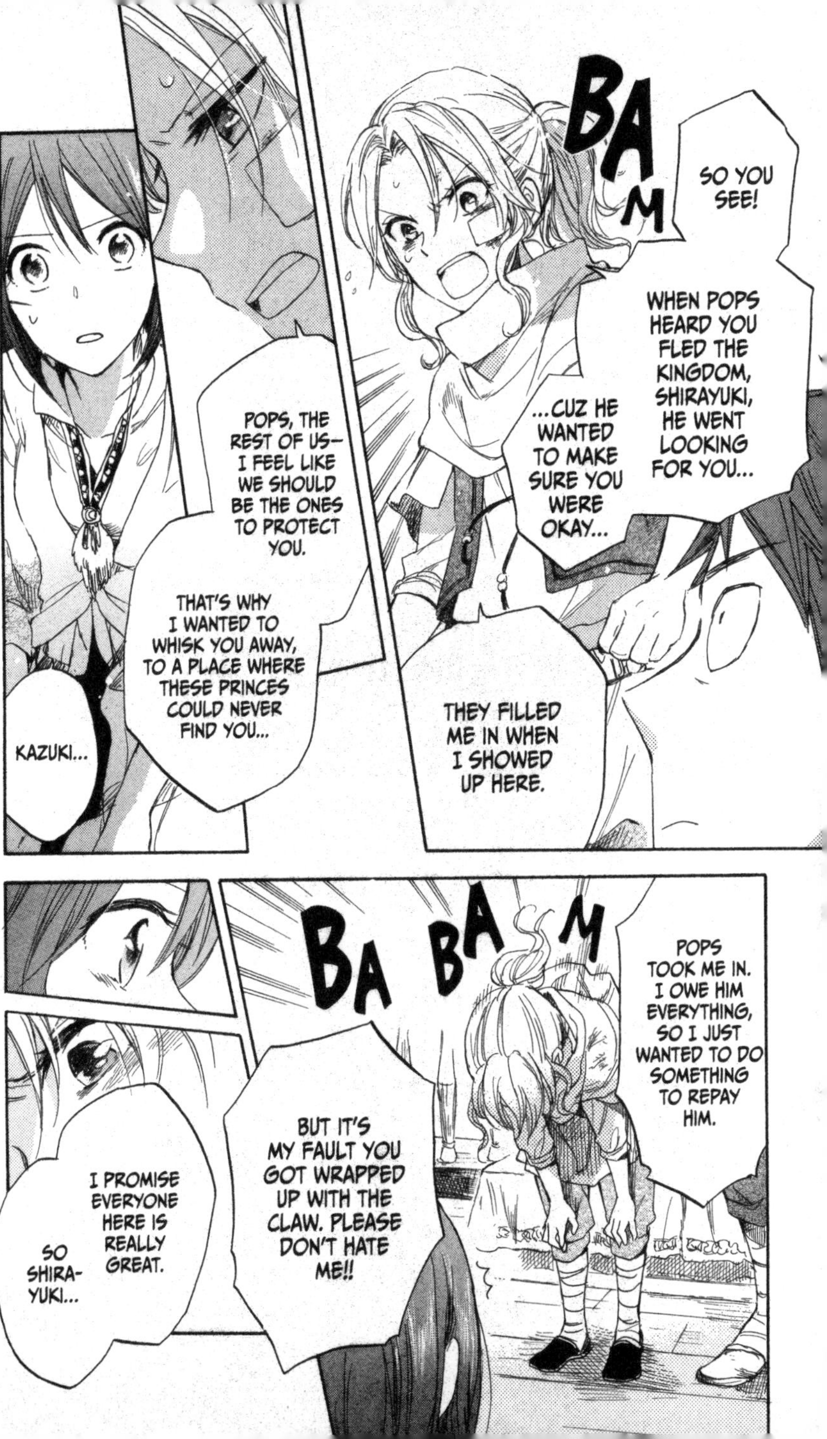
BAM
SO YOU SEE!
WHEN POPS HEARD YOU FLED THE KINGDOM, SHIRAYUKI, HE WENT LOOKING FOR YOU...
...CUZ HE WANTED TO MAKE SURE YOU WERE OKAY...
THEY FILLED ME IN WHEN I SHOWED UP HERE.
POPS, THE REST OF US— I FEEL LIKE WE SHOULD BE THE ONES TO PROTECT YOU.
THAT'S WHY I WANTED TO WHISK YOU AWAY, TO A PLACE WHERE THESE PRINCES COULD NEVER FIND YOU...
KAZUKI...
BA BA BAM
POPS TOOK ME IN. I OWE HIM EVERYTHING, SO I JUST WANTED TO DO SOMETHING TO REPAY HIM.
BUT IT'S MY FAULT YOU GOT WRAPPED UP WITH THE CLAW. PLEASE DON'T HATE ME!!
I PROMISE EVERYONE HERE IS REALLY GREAT.
SO SHIRA-YUKI...

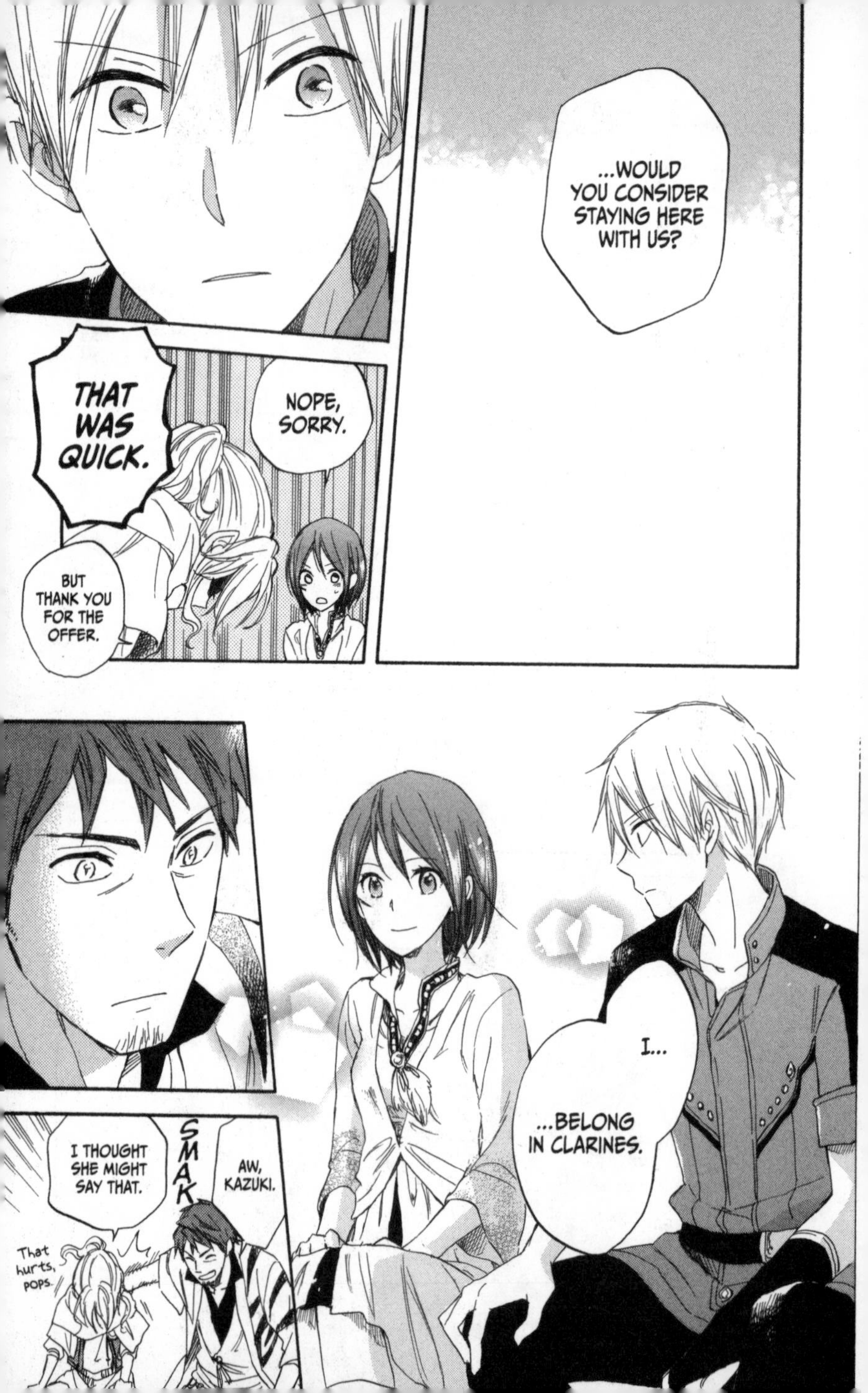
...WOULD YOU CONSIDER STAYING HERE WITH US?
NOPE, SORRY.
THAT WAS QUICK.
BUT THANK YOU FOR THE OFFER.
I...
...BELONG IN CLARINES.
AW, KAZUKI.
SMAK
I THOUGHT SHE MIGHT SAY THAT.
That hurts, pops.

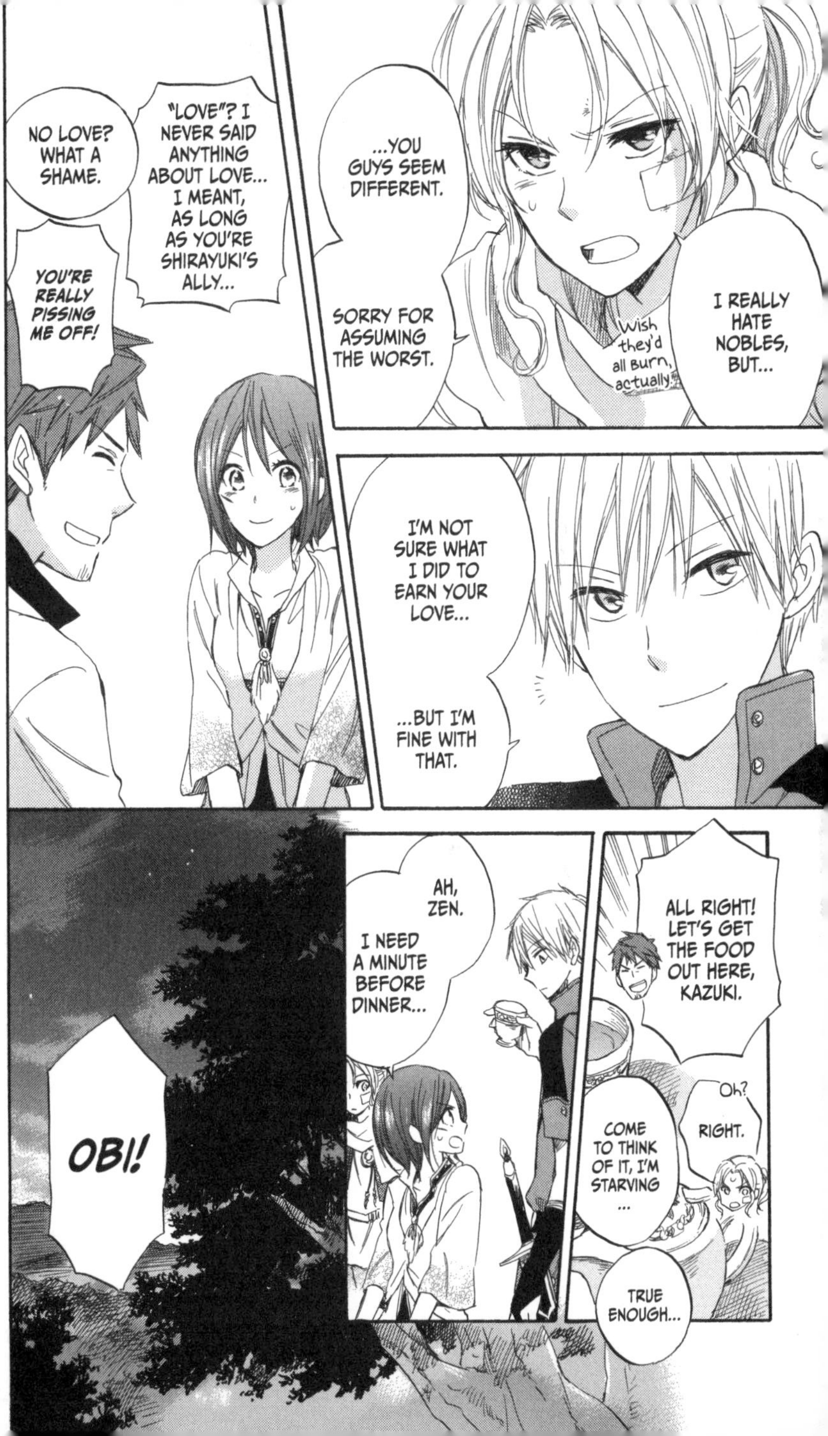
I REALLY HATE NOBLES, BUT...
Wish they'd all burn, actually.
...YOU GUYS SEEM DIFFERENT.
SORRY FOR ASSUMING THE WORST.
I'M NOT SURE WHAT I DID TO EARN YOUR LOVE...
...BUT I'M FINE WITH THAT.
"LOVE"? I NEVER SAID ANYTHING ABOUT LOVE... I MEANT, AS LONG AS YOU'RE SHIRAYUKI'S ALLY...
NO LOVE? WHAT A SHAME.
YOU'RE REALLY PISSING ME OFF!
ALL RIGHT! LET'S GET THE FOOD OUT HERE, KAZUKI.
Oh?
RIGHT.
COME TO THINK OF IT, I'M STARVING...
TRUE ENOUGH...
AH, ZEN.
I NEED A MINUTE BEFORE DINNER...
OBI!

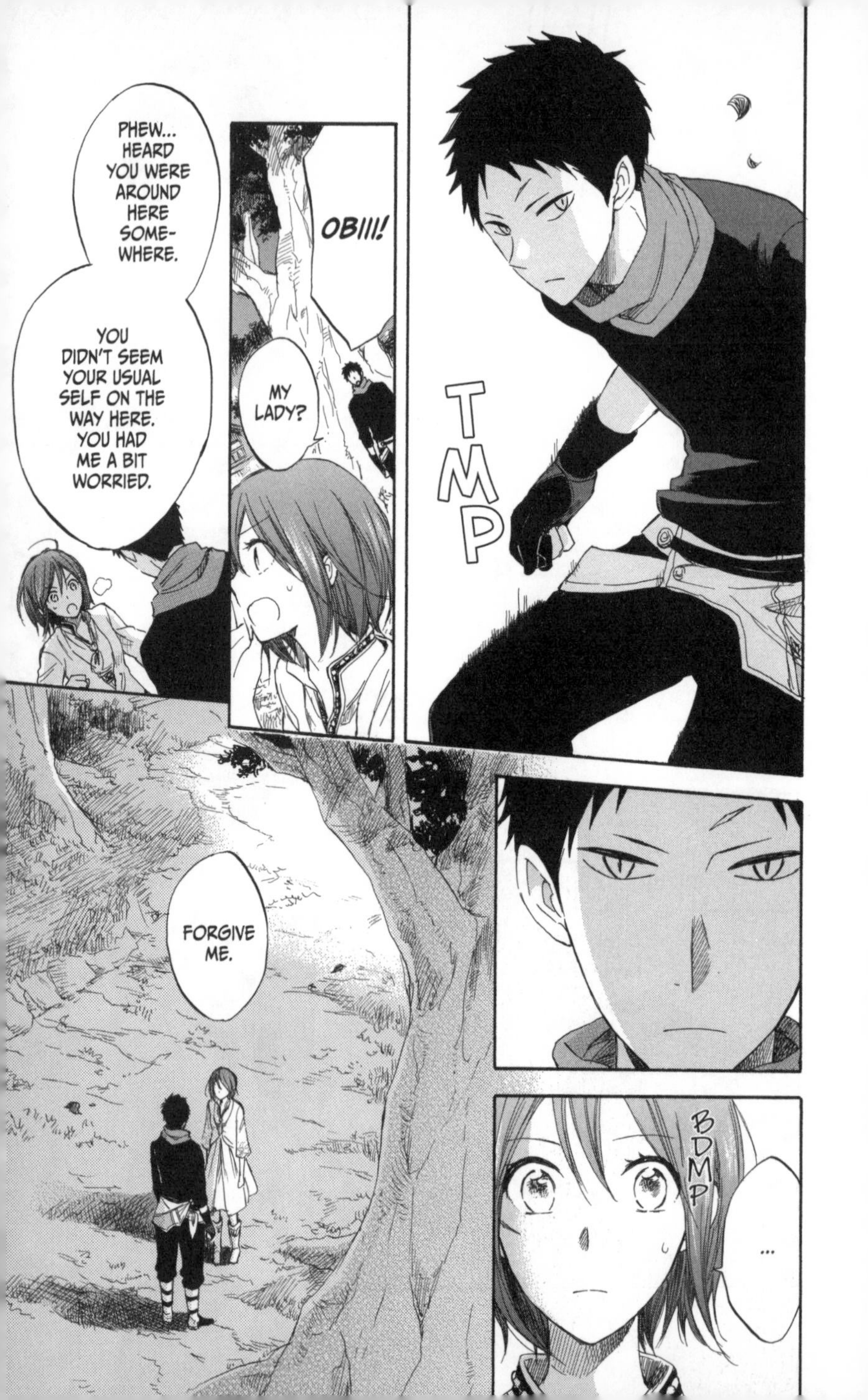
TMP
OBIII!
MY LADY?
PHEW... HEARD YOU WERE AROUND HERE SOME-WHERE.
YOU DIDN'T SEEM YOUR USUAL SELF ON THE WAY HERE. YOU HAD ME A BIT WORRIED.
BDMP
...
FORGIVE ME.

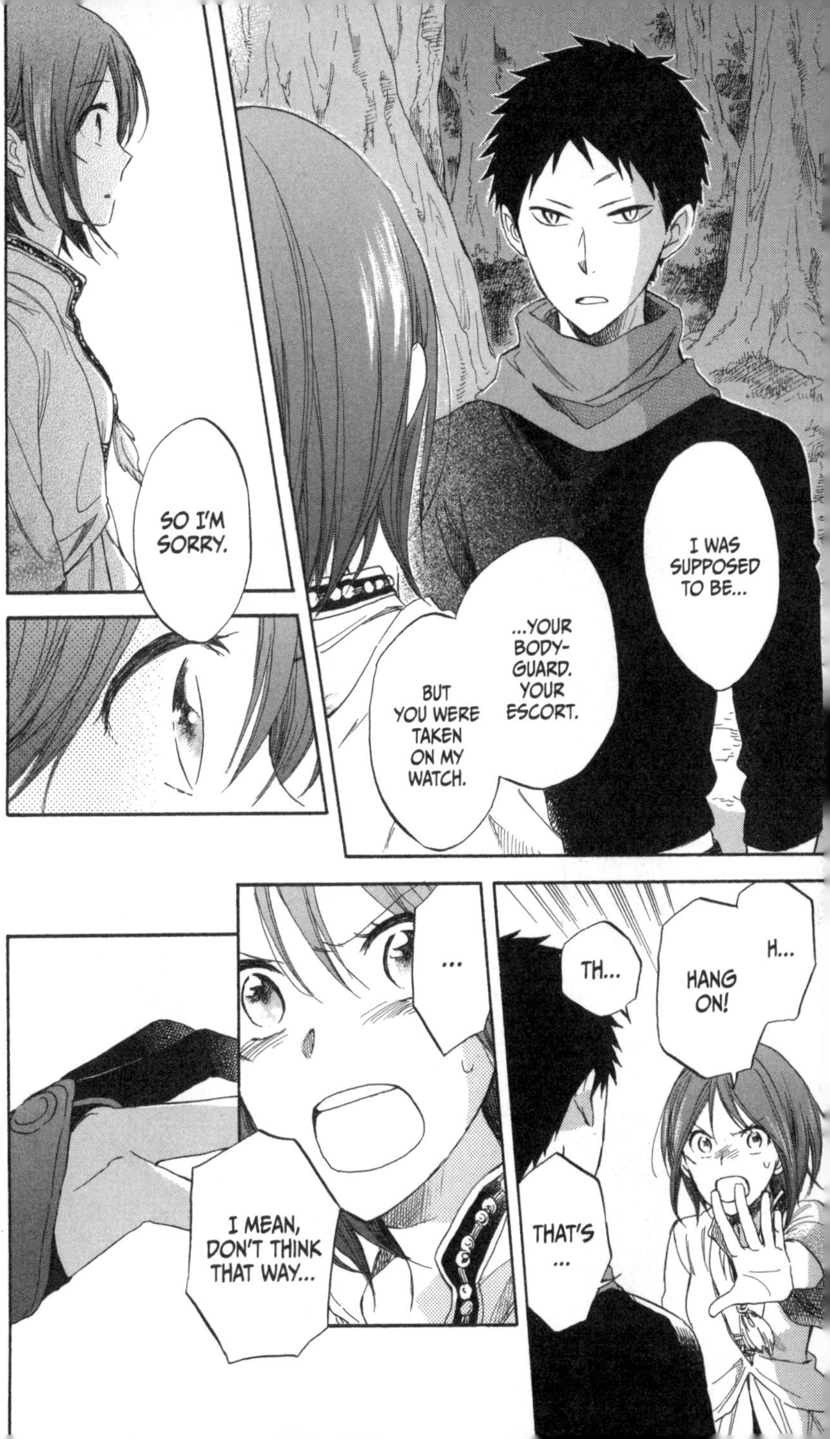
I WAS SUPPOSED TO BE...
...YOUR BODY-GUARD. YOUR ESCORT.
BUT YOU WERE TAKEN ON MY WATCH.
SO I'M SORRY.
H... HANG ON!
TH...
THAT'S ...
...
I MEAN, DON'T THINK THAT WAY...

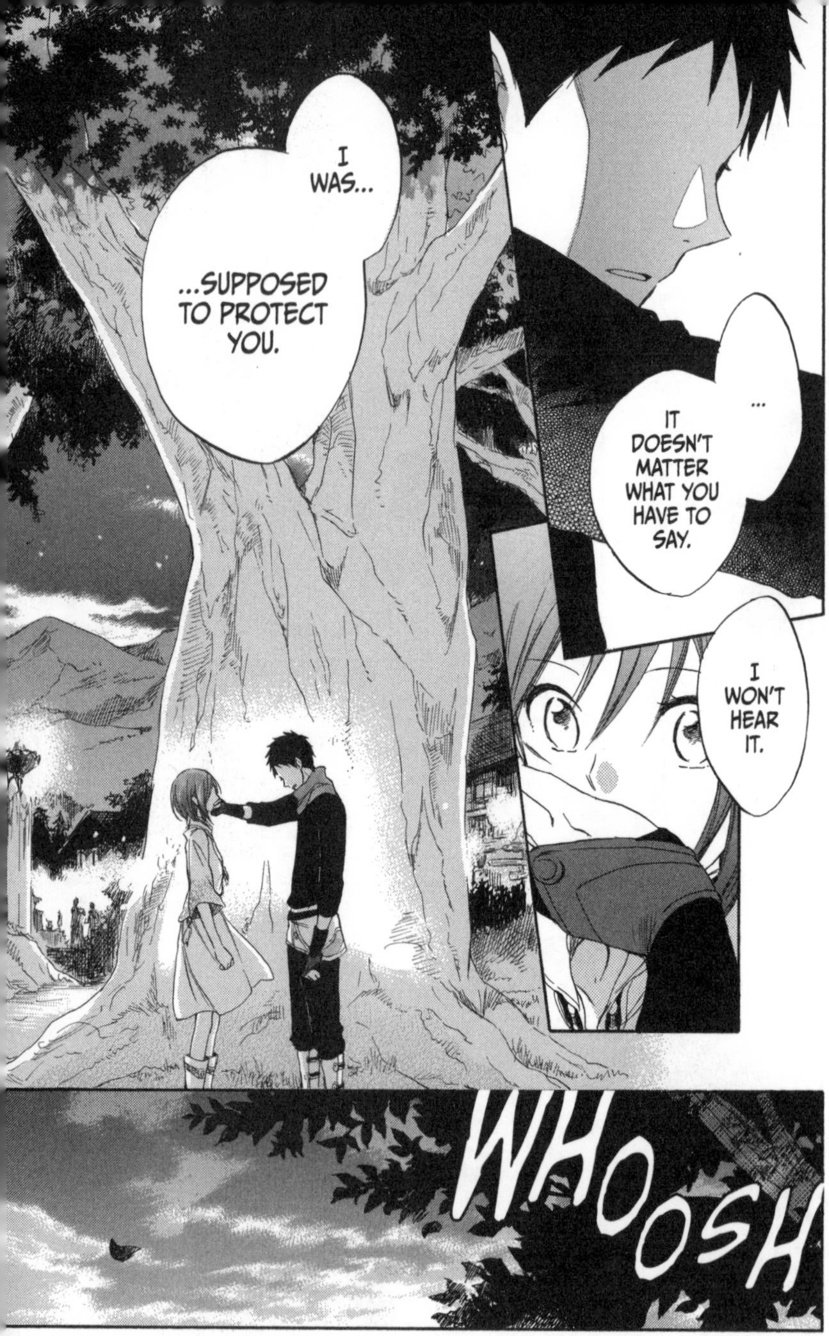
I WAS...
...SUPPOSED TO PROTECT YOU.
...
IT DOESN'T MATTER WHAT YOU HAVE TO SAY.
I WON'T HEAR IT.
WHOOSH

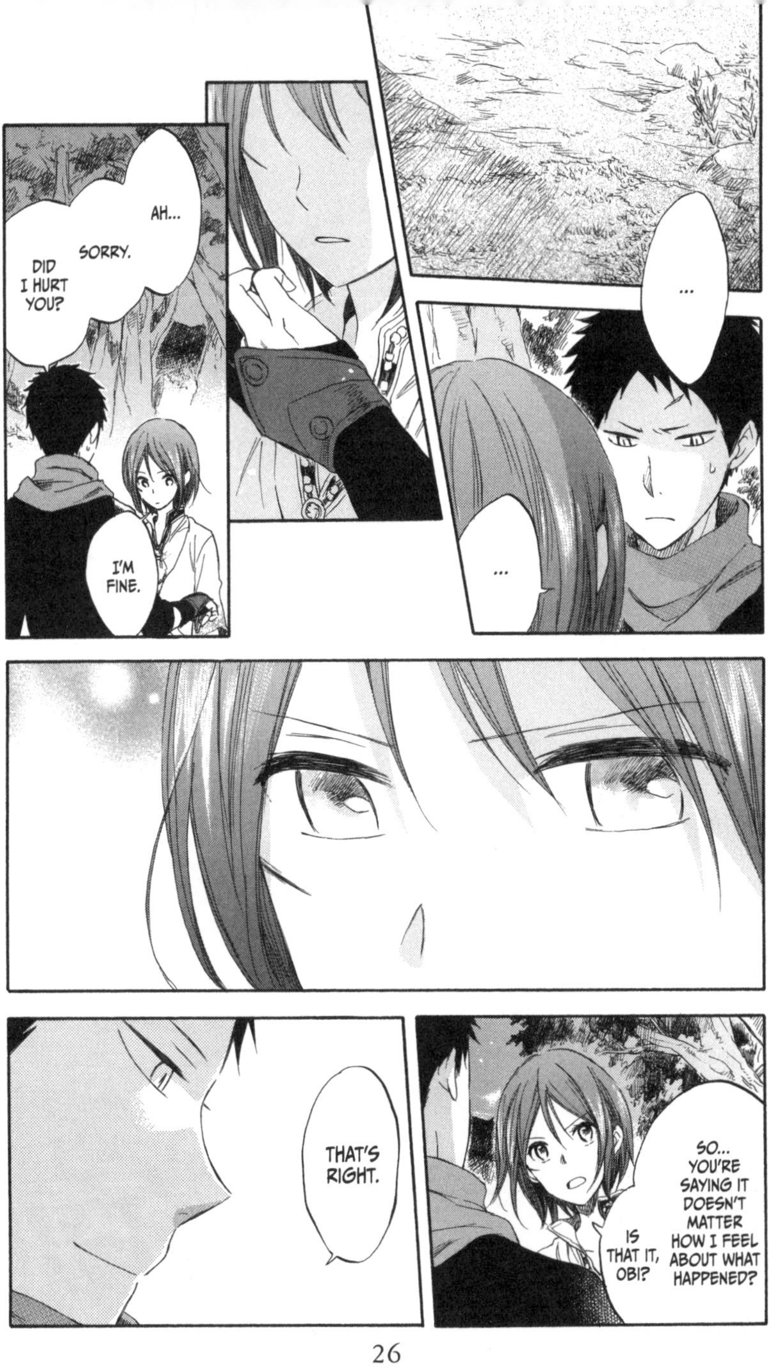
...
...
AH... SORRY. DID I HURT YOU?
I'M FINE.
SO... YOU'RE SAYING IT DOESN'T MATTER HOW I FEEL ABOUT WHAT HAPPENED?
IS THAT IT, OBI?
THAT'S RIGHT.

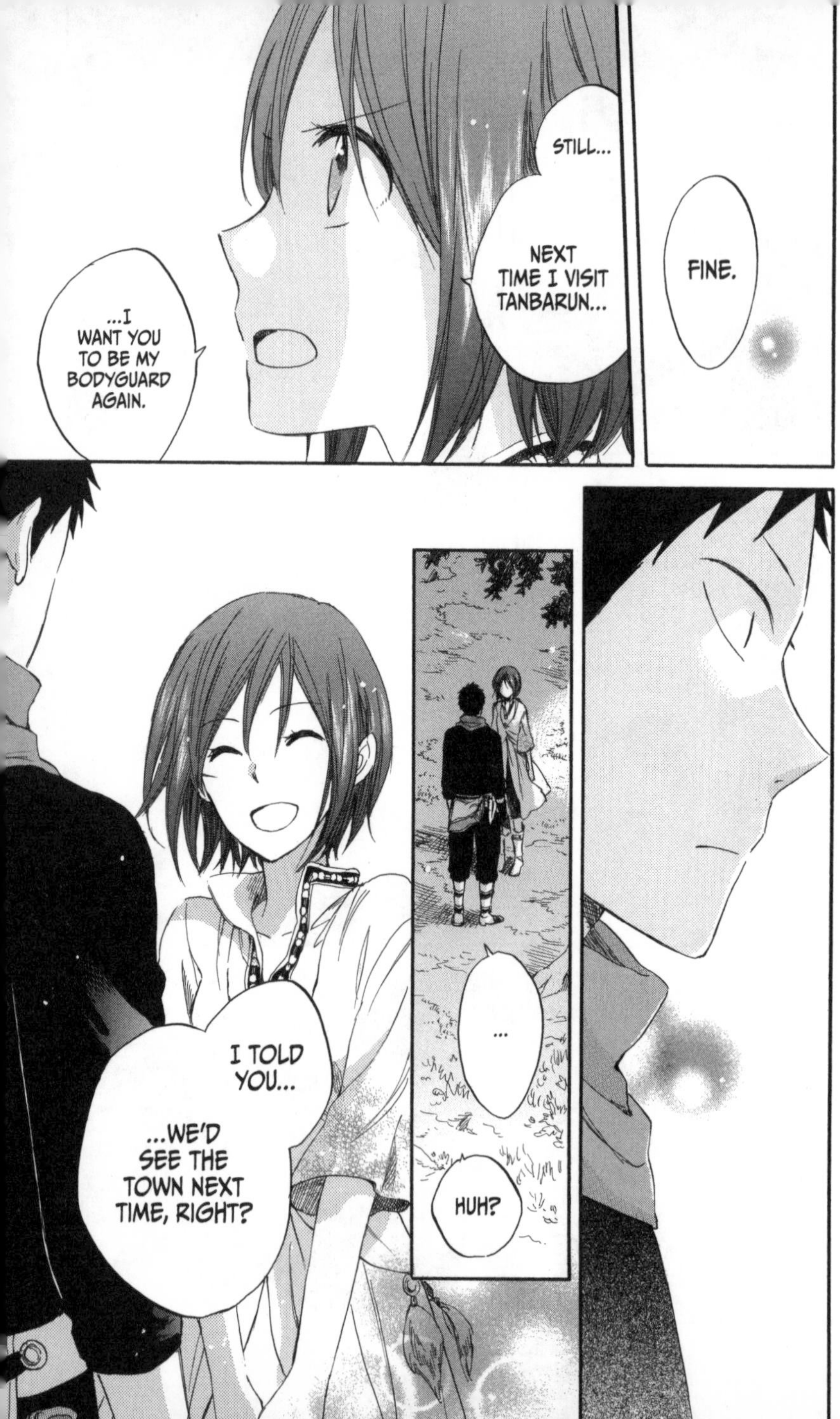
FINE.
STILL...
NEXT TIME I VISIT TANBARUN...
...I WANT YOU TO BE MY BODYGUARD AGAIN.
...
HUH?
I TOLD YOU...
...WE'D SEE THE TOWN NEXT TIME, RIGHT?

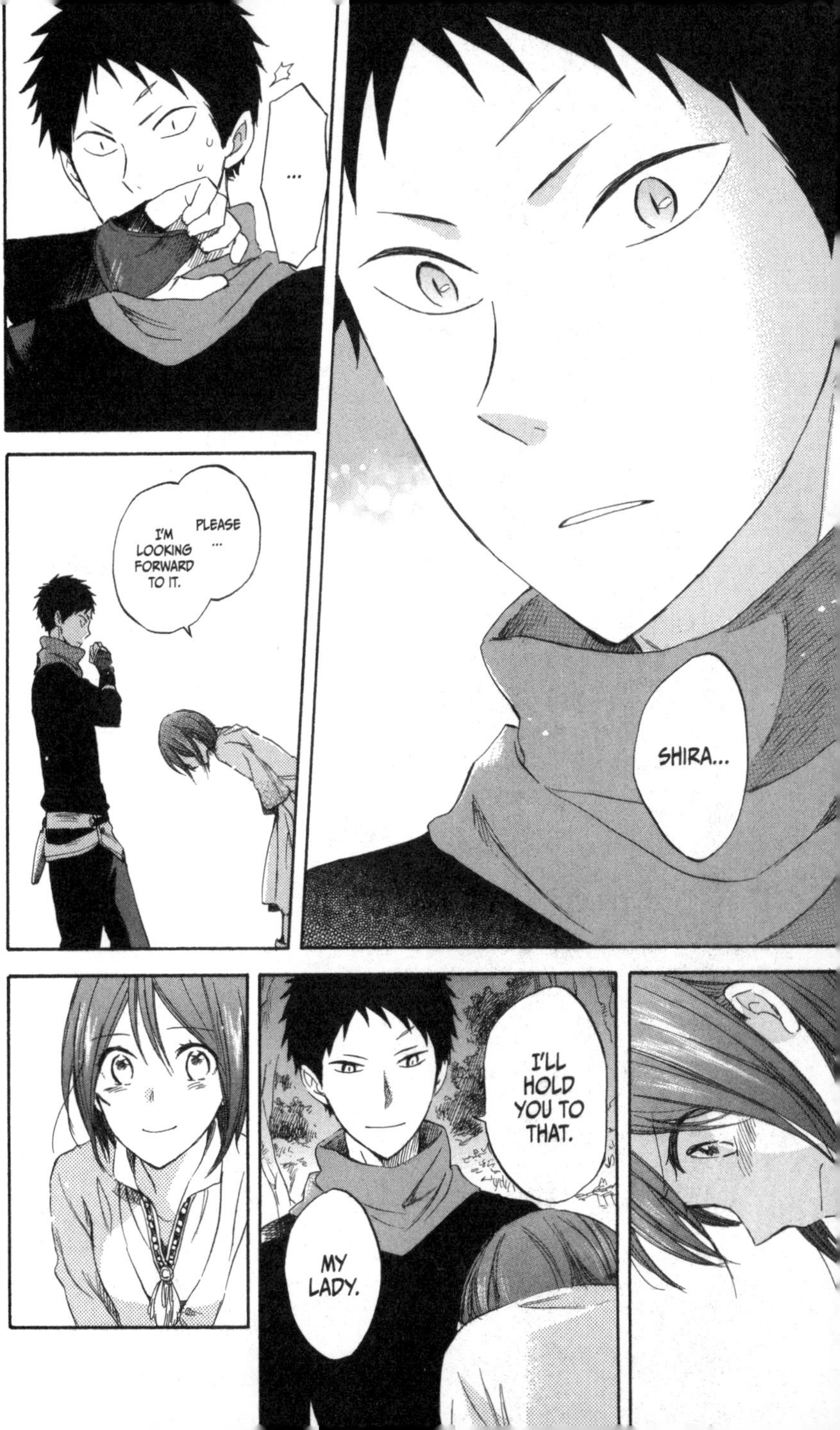
SHIRA...
...
PLEASE ...
I'M LOOKING FORWARD TO IT.
I'LL HOLD YOU TO THAT.
MY LADY.

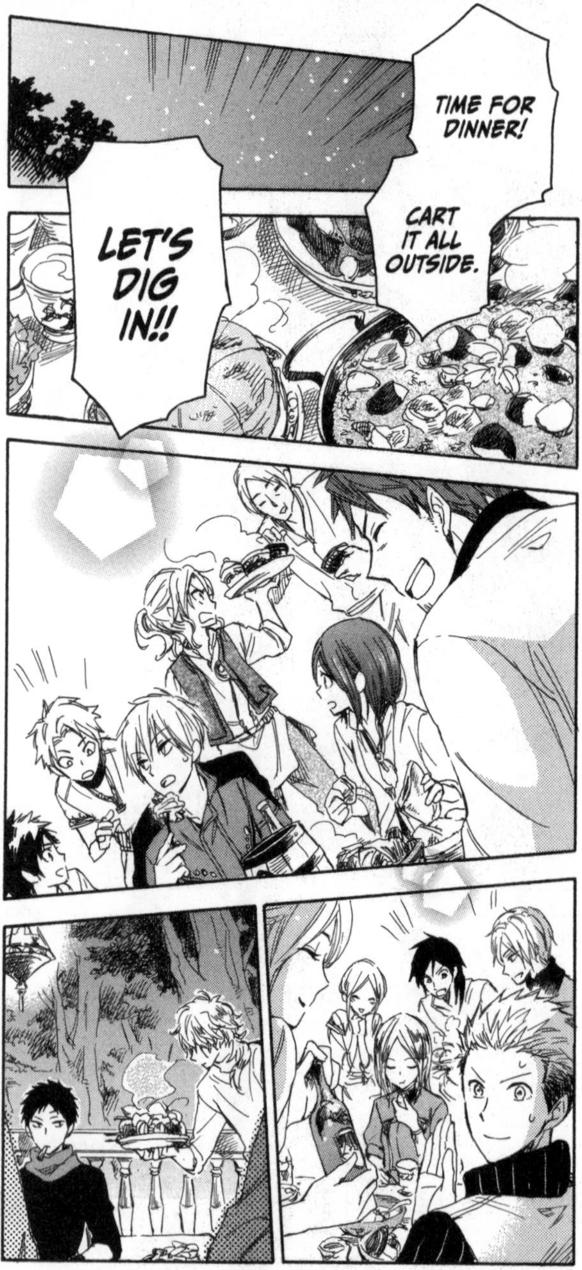
TIME FOR DINNER!
CART IT ALL OUTSIDE.
LET'S DIG IN!!

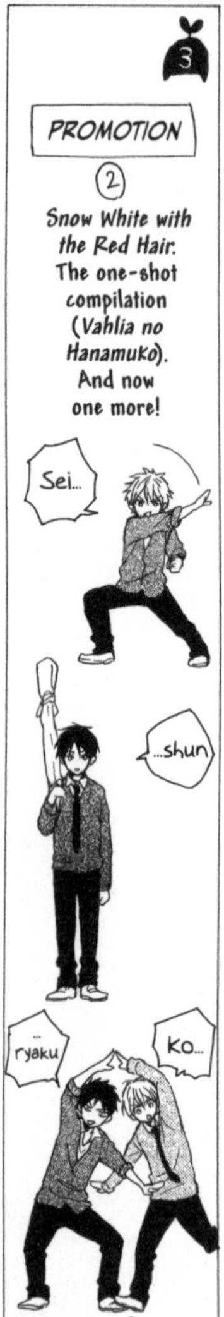
3
PROMOTION
2
Snow White with the Red Hair. The one-shot compilation (Vahlia no Hanamuko). And now one more!
Sei...
...shun
Ko...
...ryaku
TADAHHHH
Hon
Both volumes of Seishun Koryaku Hon are on sale now in Japan!

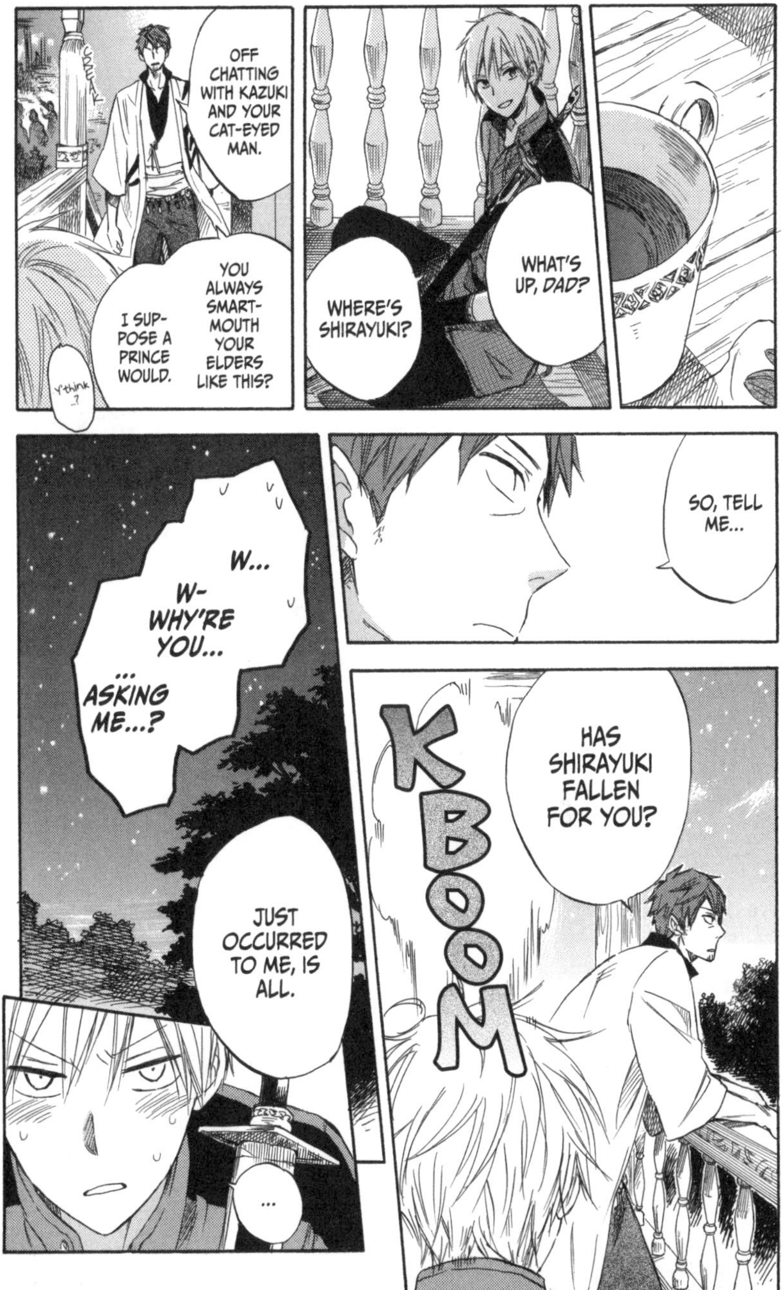
WHAT'S UP, DAD?
WHERE'S SHIRAYUKI?
OFF CHATTING WITH KAZUKI AND YOUR CAT-EYED MAN.
YOU ALWAYS SMART-MOUTH YOUR ELDERS LIKE THIS?
I SUP-POSE A PRINCE WOULD.
Y'think ...?
SO, TELL ME...
HAS SHIRAYUKI FALLEN FOR YOU?
KBOOM
W...
W-WHY'RE YOU...
... ASKING ME...?
JUST OCCURRED TO ME, IS ALL.
...

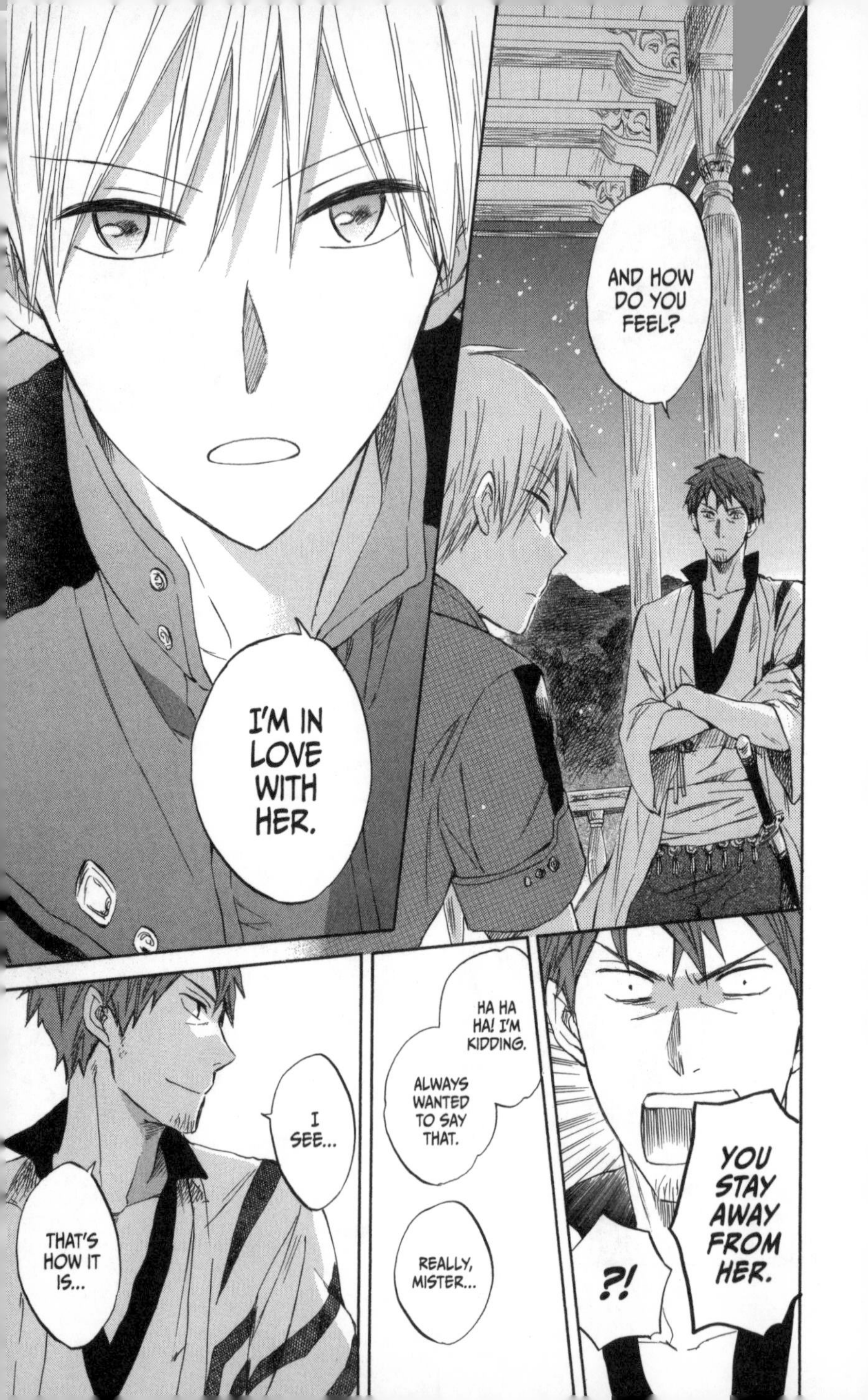
AND HOW DO YOU FEEL?
I'M IN LOVE WITH HER.
YOU STAY AWAY FROM HER.
?!
HA HA HA! I'M KIDDING.
ALWAYS WANTED TO SAY THAT.
REALLY, MISTER...
I SEE...
THAT'S HOW IT IS...

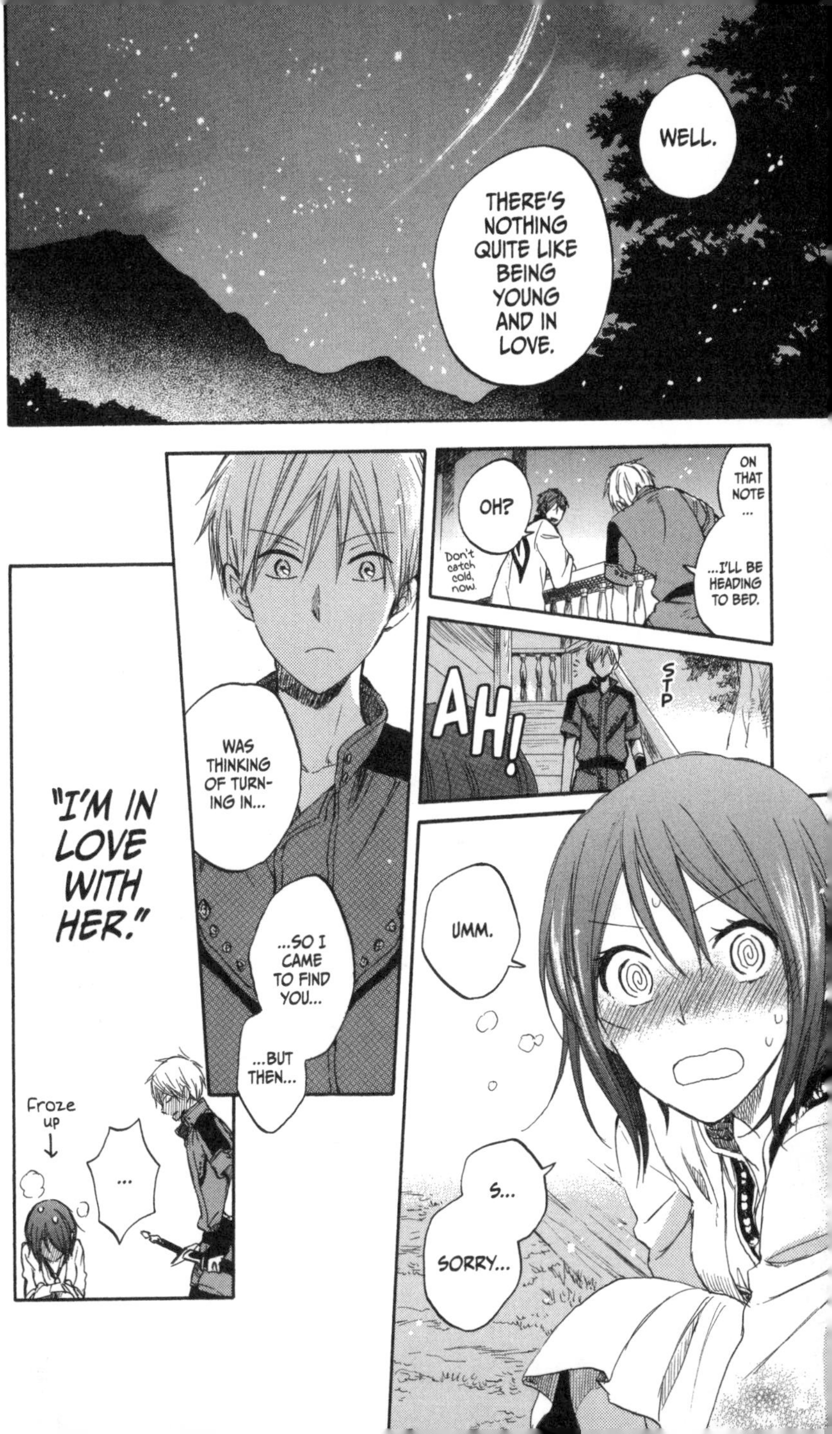
WELL.
THERE'S NOTHING QUITE LIKE BEING YOUNG AND IN LOVE.
ON THAT NOTE...
...I'LL BE HEADING TO BED.
OH?
Don't catch cold, now.
STP
AH!
WAS THINKING OF TURNING IN...
...SO I CAME TO FIND YOU...
...BUT THEN...
UMM.
S...
SORRY...
"I'M IN LOVE WITH HER."
Froze up ↓
...

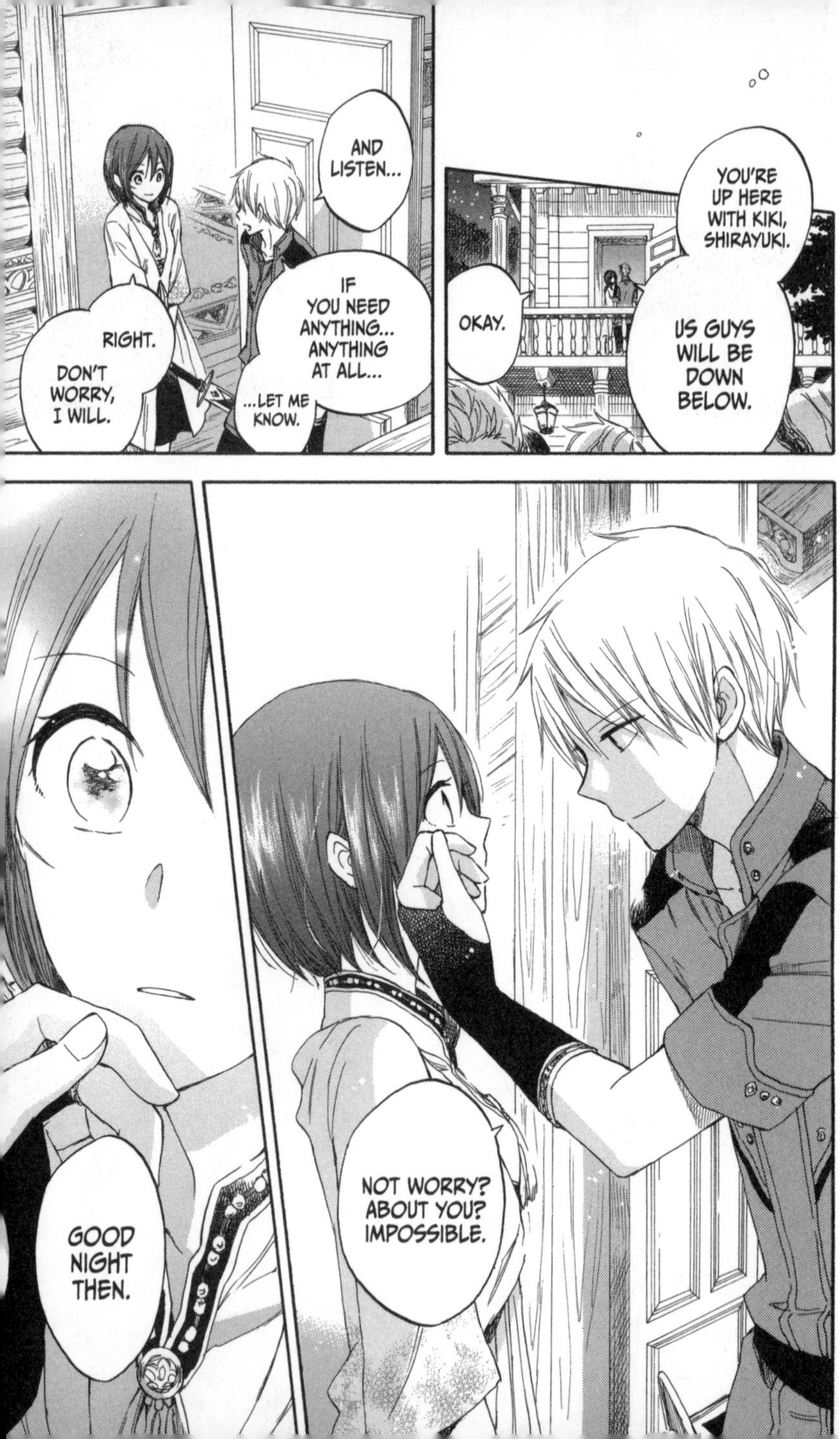
YOU'RE UP HERE WITH KIKI, SHIRAYUKI.
US GUYS WILL BE DOWN BELOW.
OKAY.
AND LISTEN...
IF YOU NEED ANYTHING... ANYTHING AT ALL...
...LET ME KNOW.
RIGHT.
DON'T WORRY, I WILL.
NOT WORRY? ABOUT YOU? IMPOSSIBLE.
GOOD NIGHT THEN.

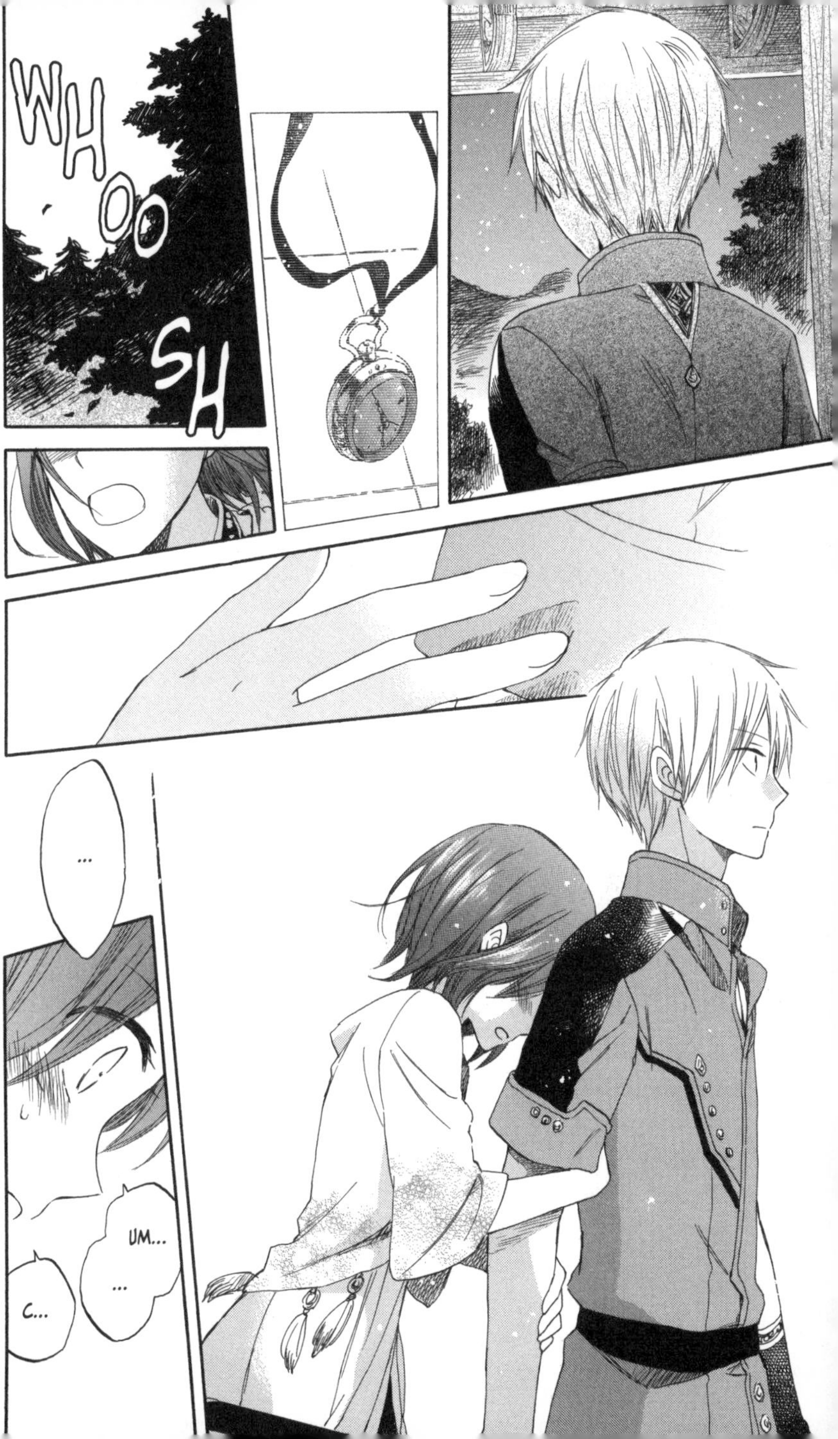

WHOOSH
...
UM...
...
C...

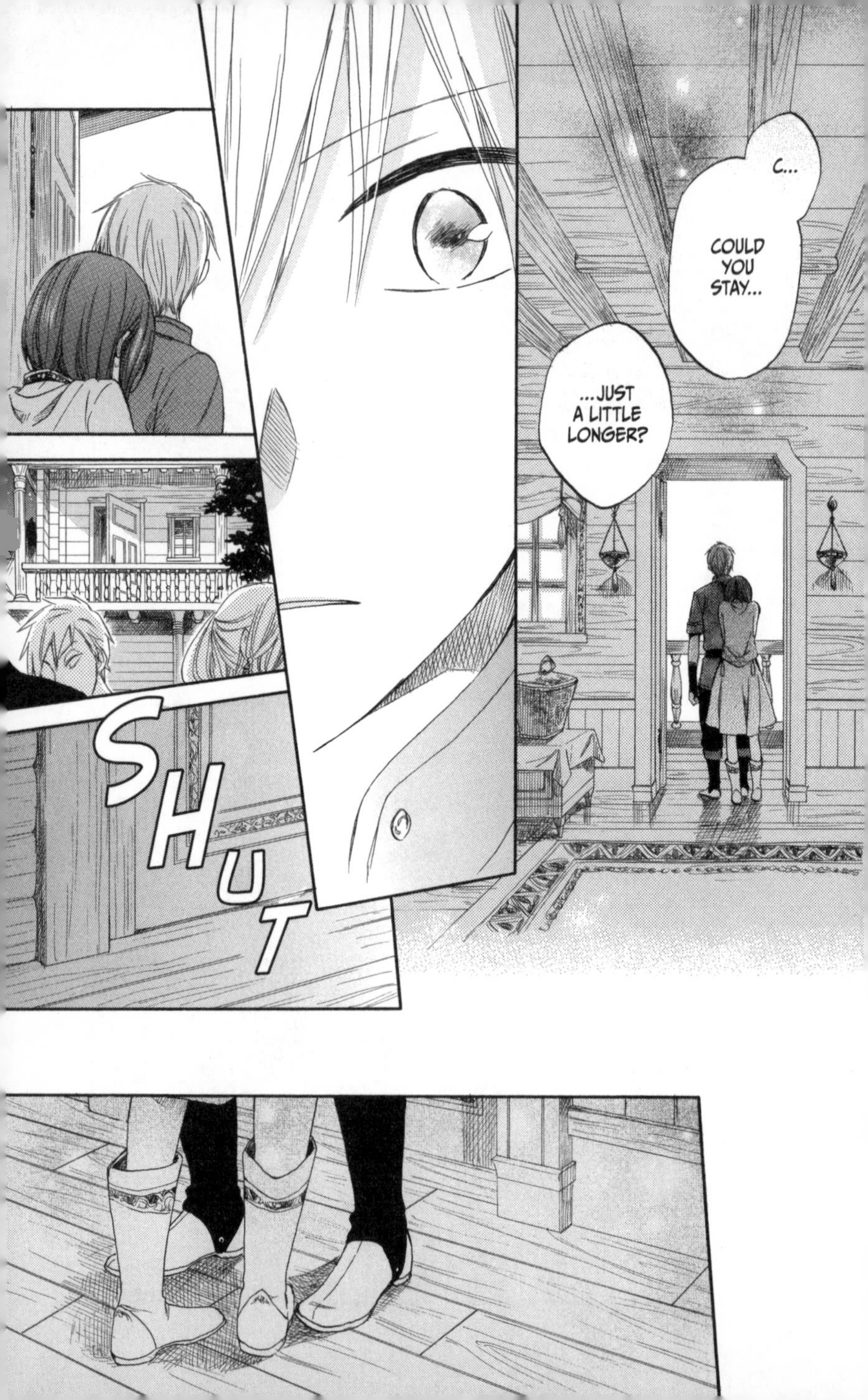
C...
COULD YOU STAY...
...JUST A LITTLE LONGER?
SHUT

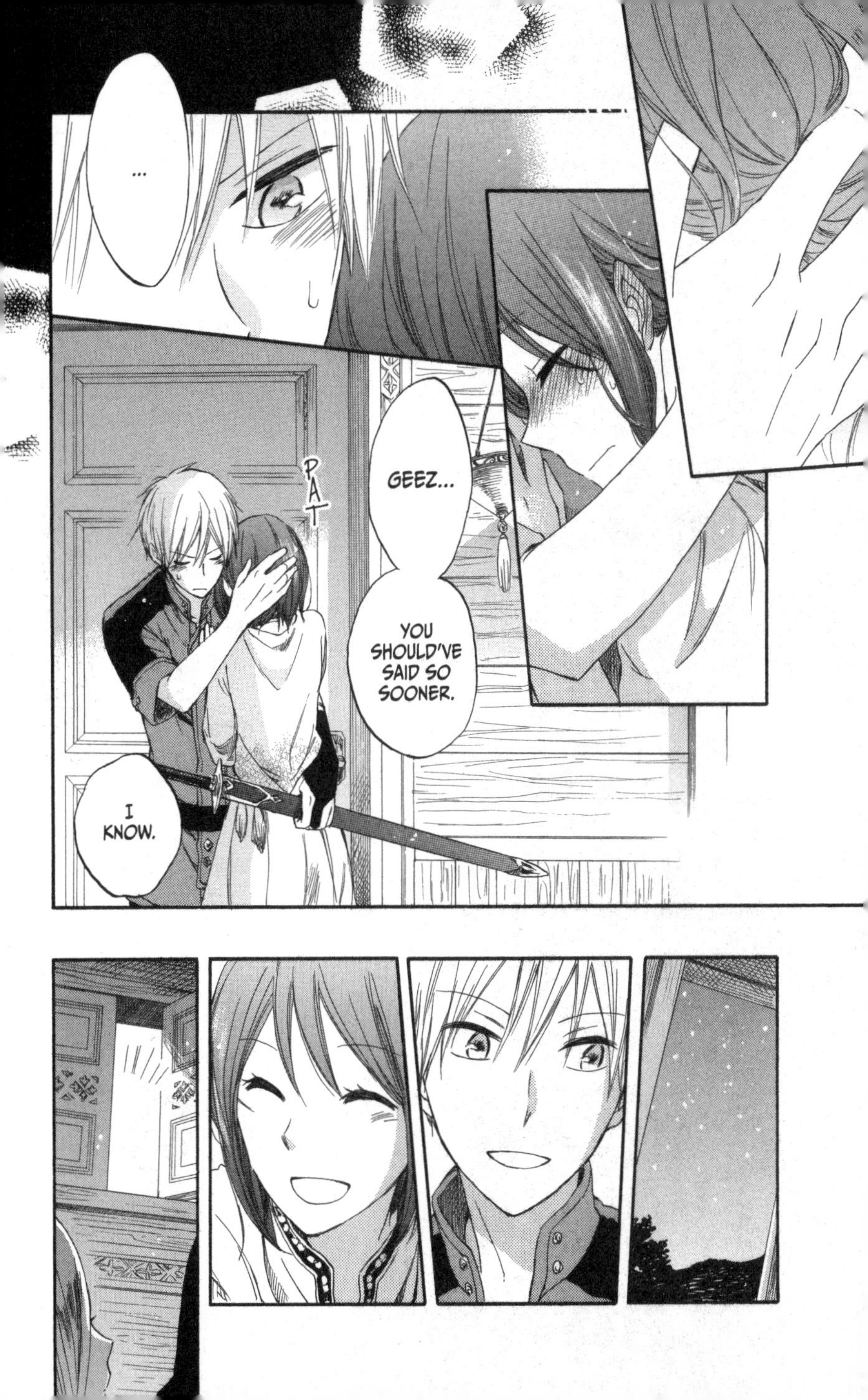
...
GEEZ...
YOU SHOULD'VE SAID SO SOONER.
PAT
I KNOW.

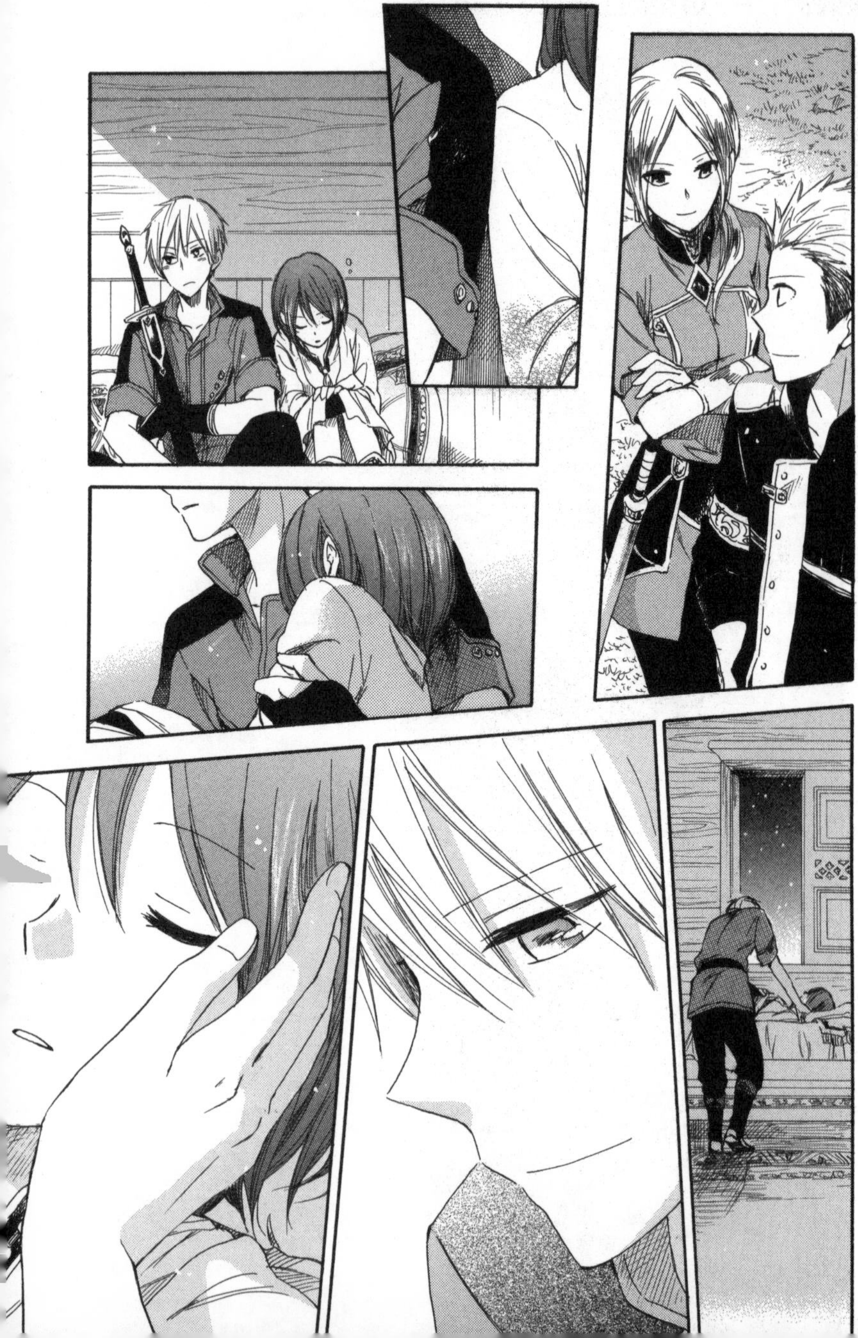

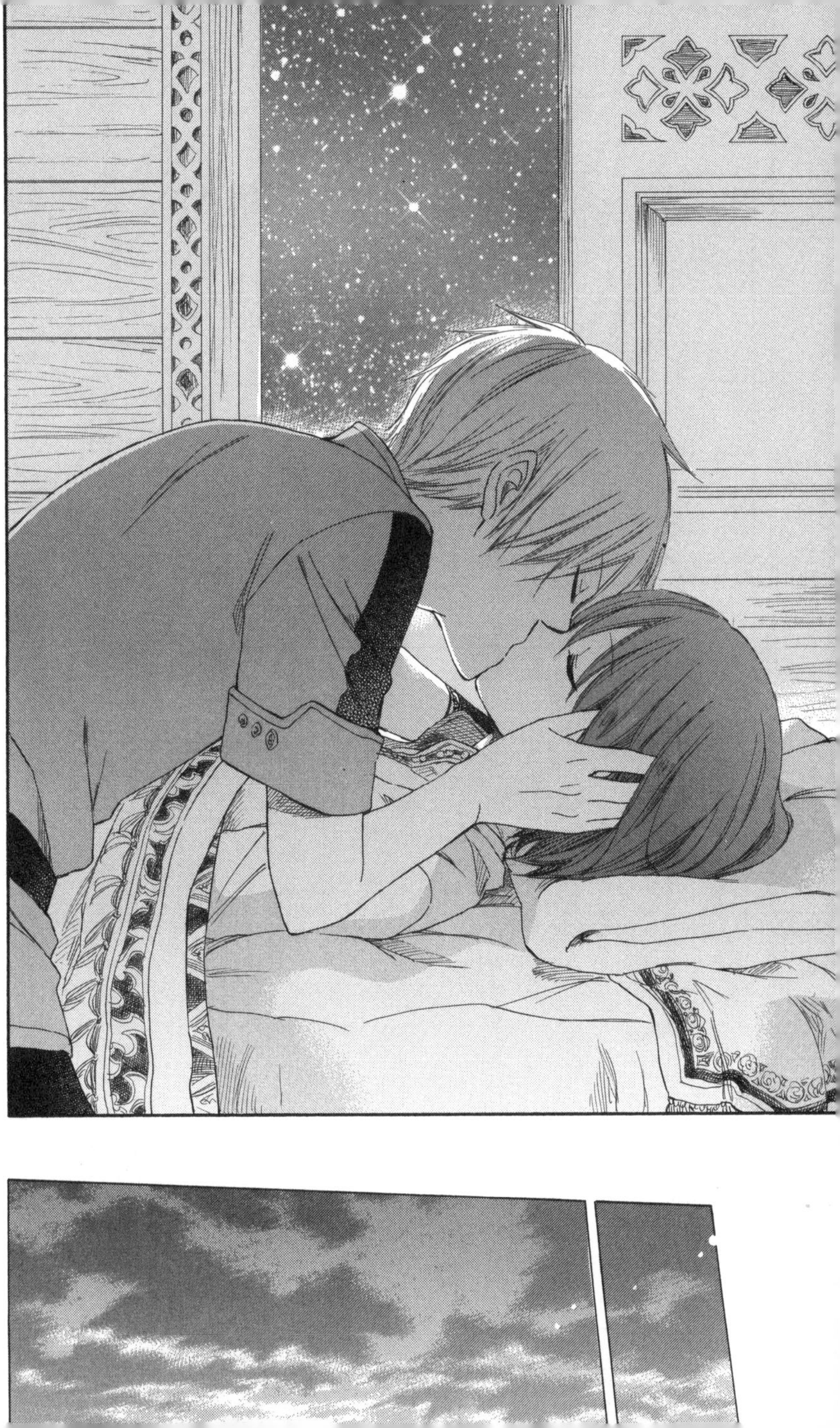

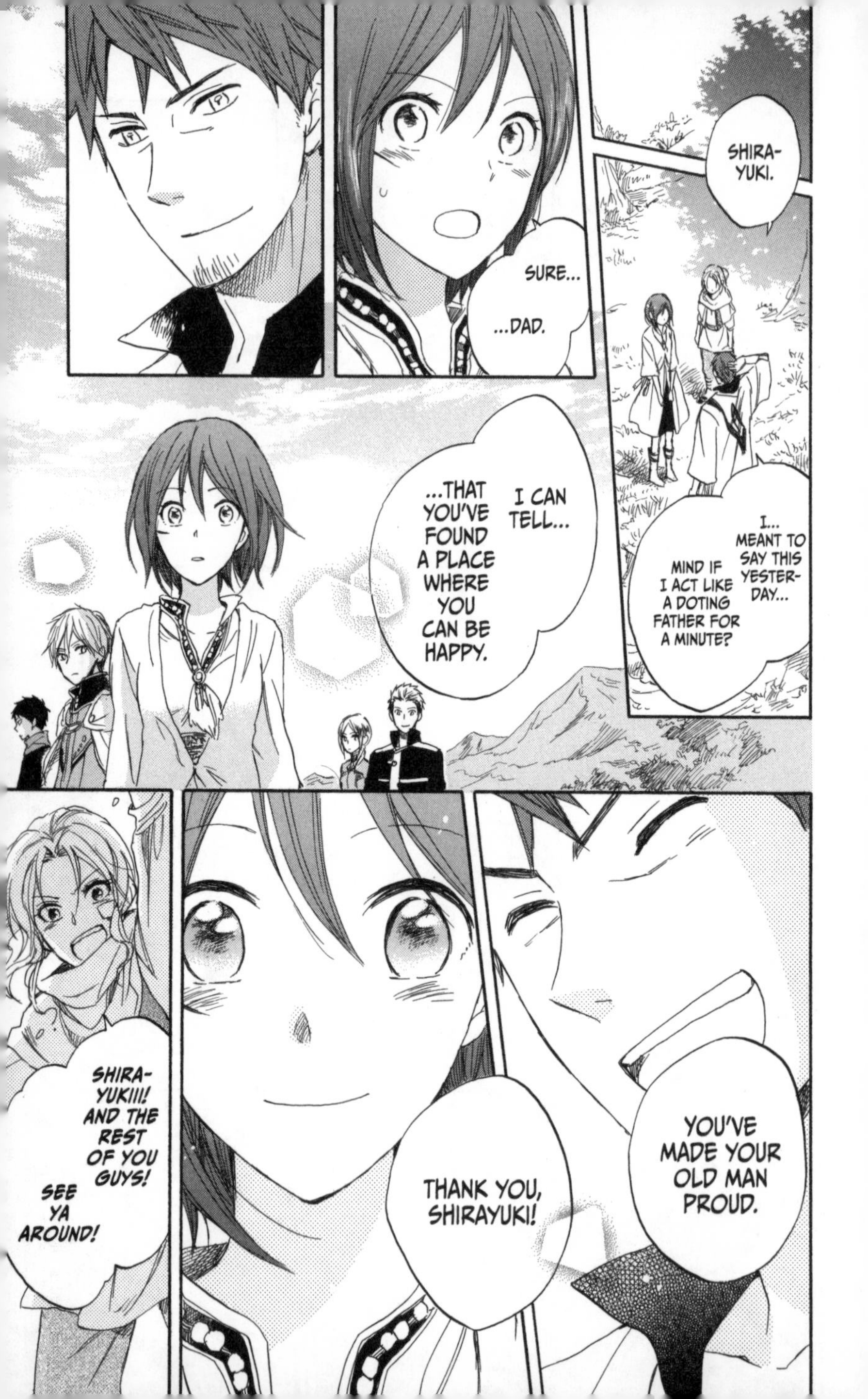
SHIRA-YUKI.
I... MEANT TO SAY THIS YESTER-DAY...
MIND IF I ACT LIKE A DOTING FATHER FOR A MINUTE?
SURE...
...DAD.
I CAN TELL...
...THAT YOU'VE FOUND A PLACE WHERE YOU CAN BE HAPPY.
YOU'VE MADE YOUR OLD MAN PROUD.
THANK YOU, SHIRAYUKI!
SHIRA-YUKIII! AND THE REST OF YOU GUYS!
SEE YA AROUND!

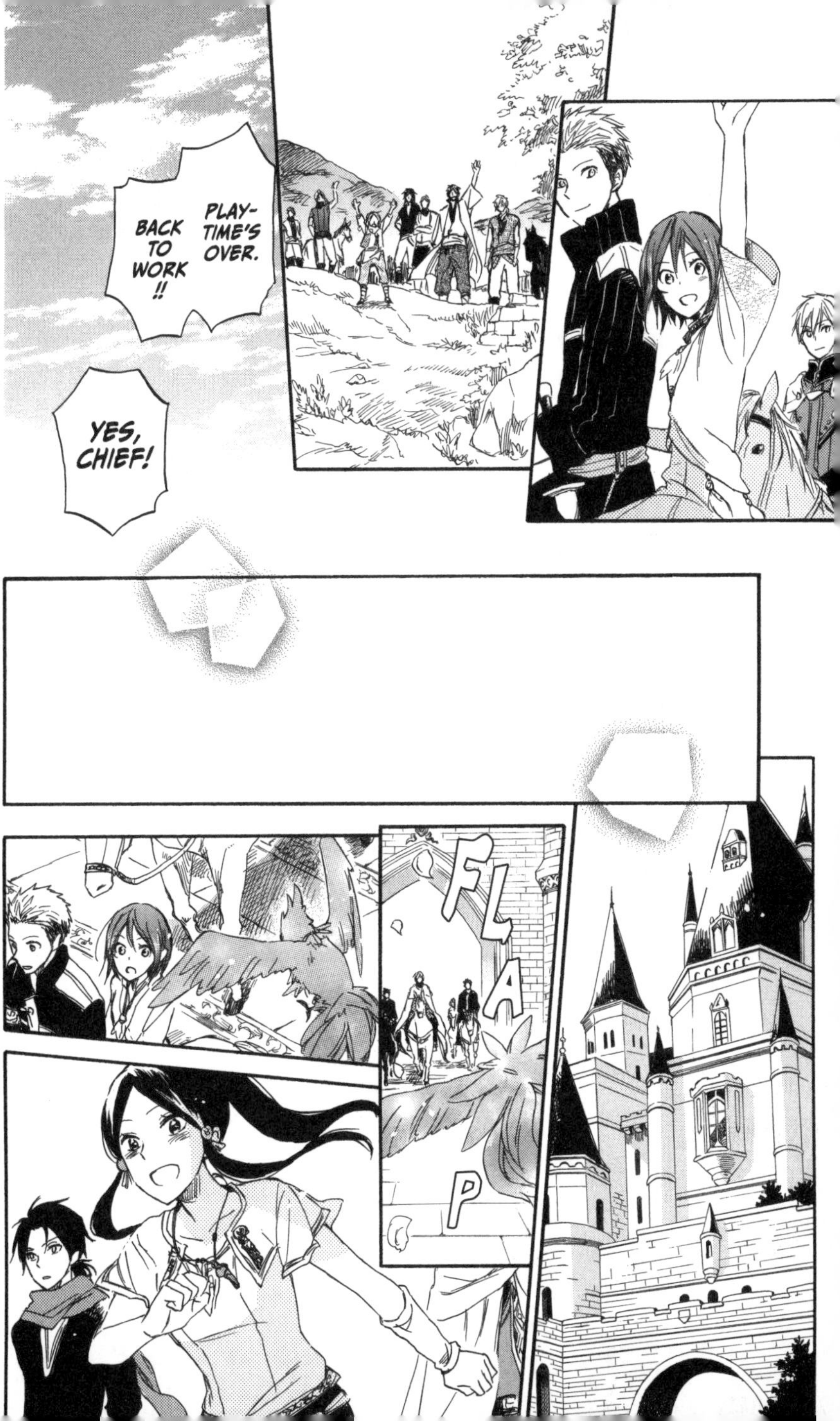
PLAY-TIME'S OVER.
BACK TO WORK!!
YES, CHIEF!
FLAP

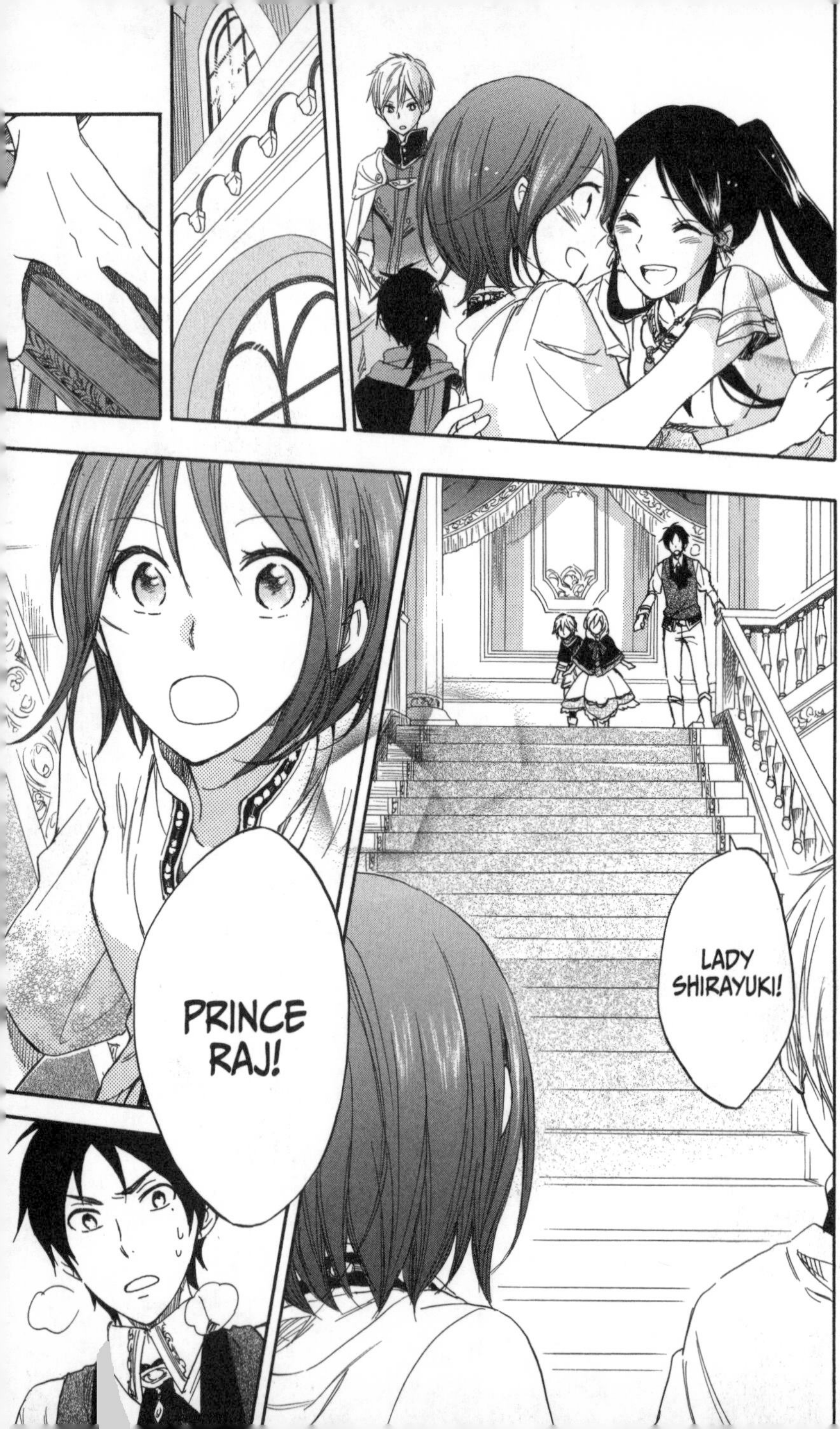
LADY SHIRAYUKI!
PRINCE RAJ!

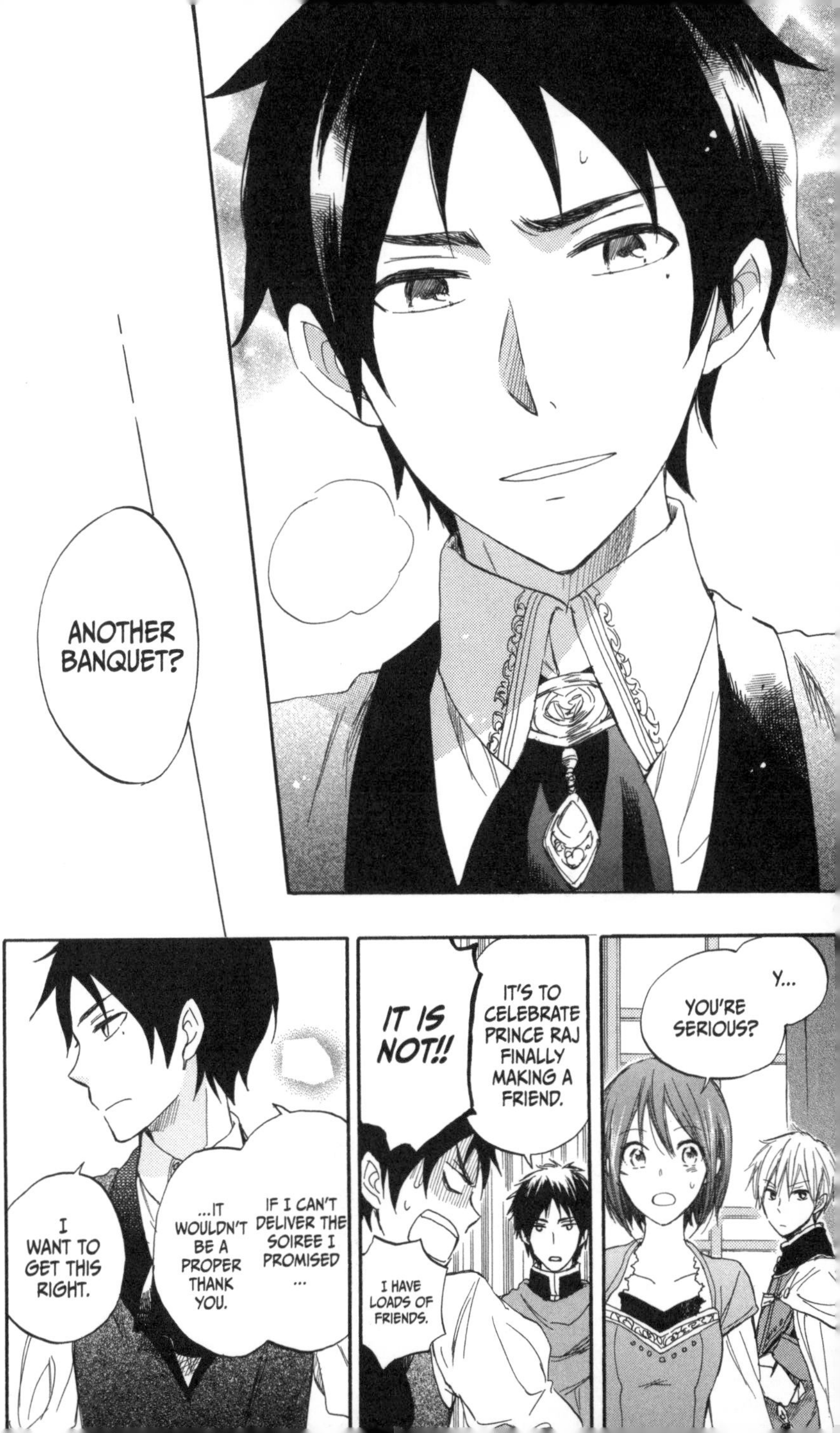
ANOTHER BANQUET?
Y... YOU'RE SERIOUS?
IT'S TO CELEBRATE PRINCE RAJ FINALLY MAKING A FRIEND.
IT IS NOT!!
I HAVE LOADS OF FRIENDS.
IF I CAN'T DELIVER THE SOIREE I PROMISED ...
...IT WOULDN'T BE A PROPER THANK YOU.
I WANT TO GET THIS RIGHT.

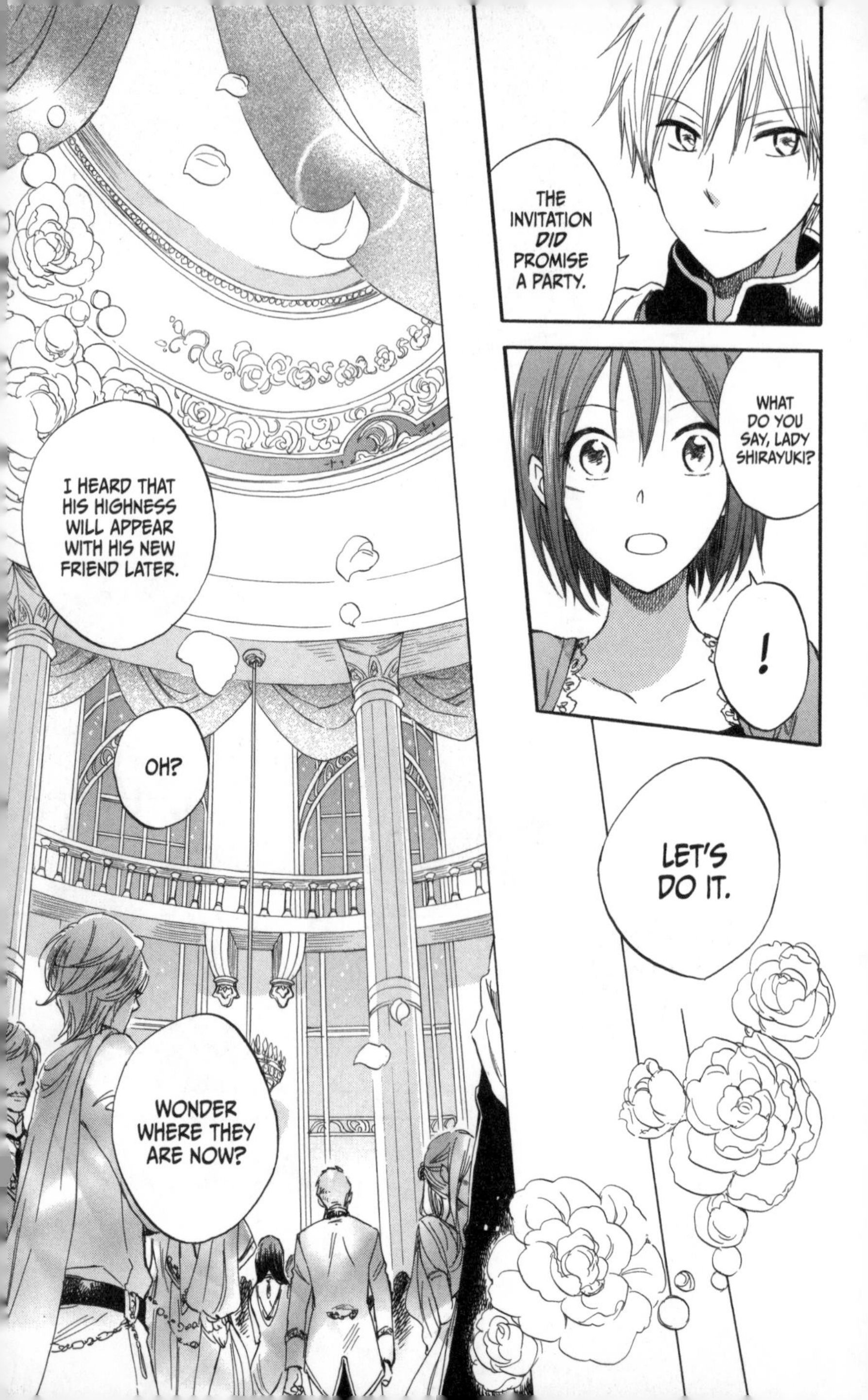
THE INVITATION DID PROMISE A PARTY.
WHAT DO YOU SAY, LADY SHIRAYUKI?
!
LET'S DO IT.
I HEARD THAT HIS HIGHNESS WILL APPEAR WITH HIS NEW FRIEND LATER.
OH?
WONDER WHERE THEY ARE NOW?

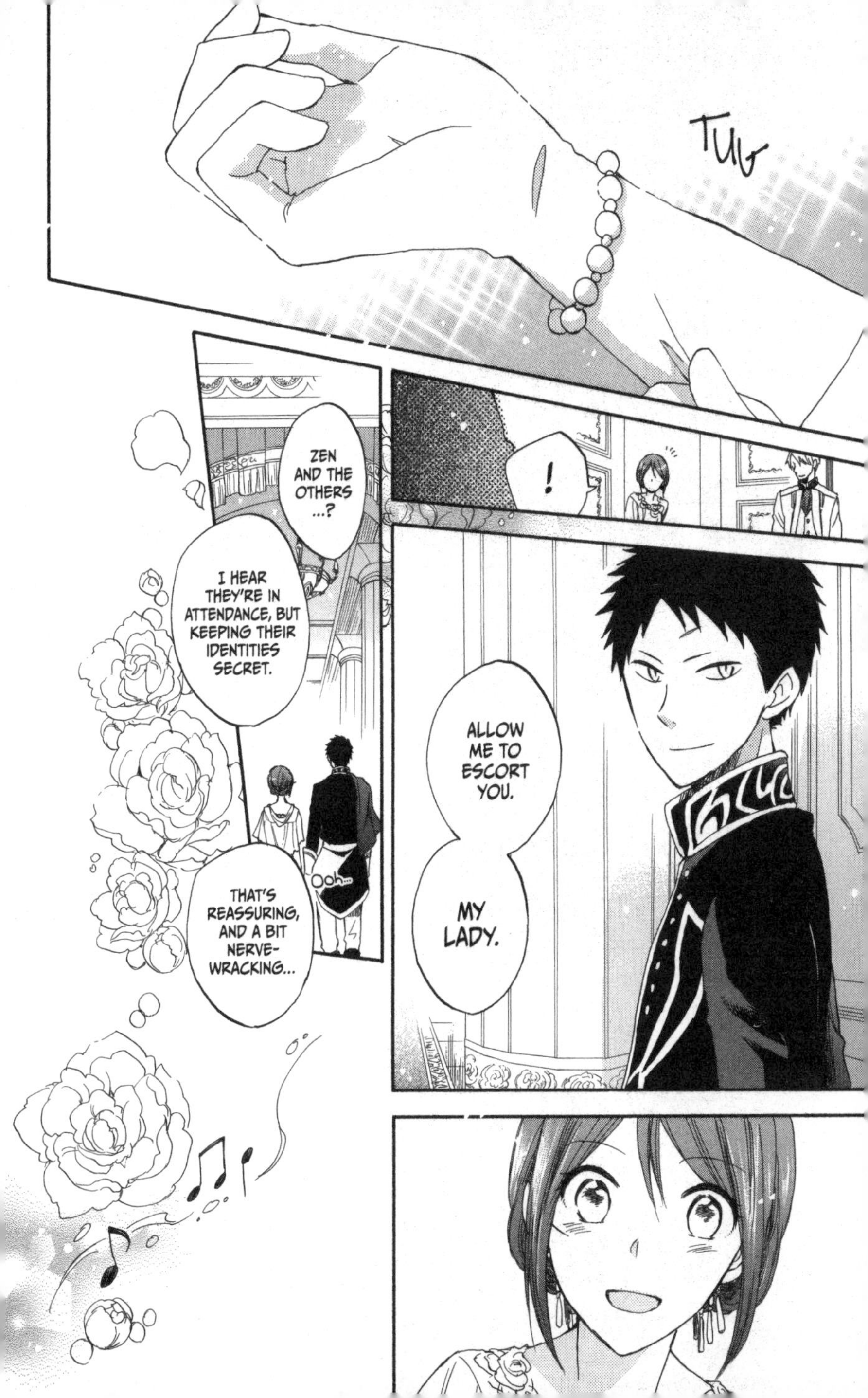
TUG
!
ALLOW ME TO ESCORT YOU.
MY LADY.
ZEN AND THE OTHERS ...?
I HEAR THEY'RE IN ATTENDANCE, BUT KEEPING THEIR IDENTITIES SECRET.
Ooh...
THAT'S REASSURING, AND A BIT NERVE-WRACKING...

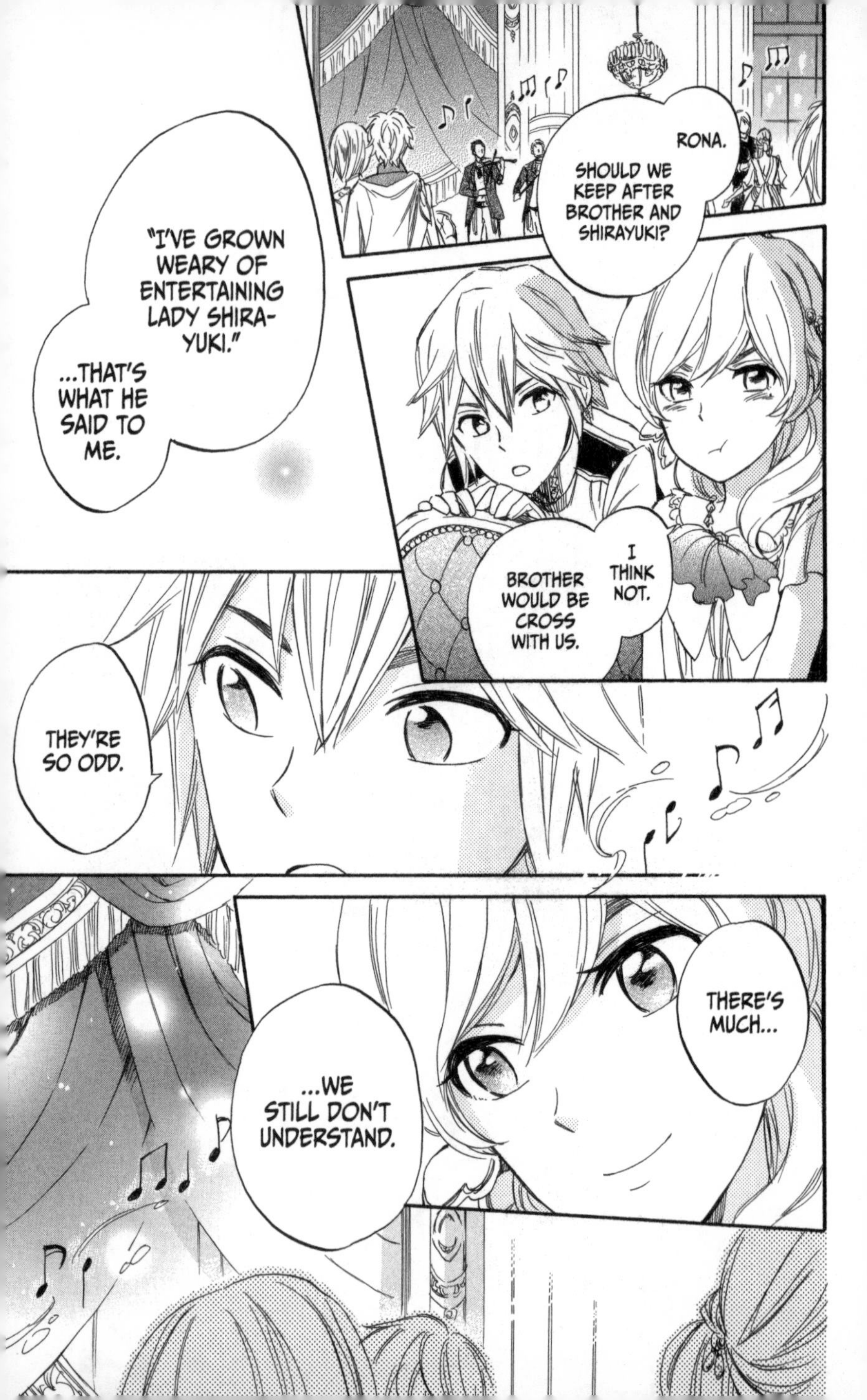
RONA.
SHOULD WE KEEP AFTER BROTHER AND SHIRAYUKI?
I THINK NOT.
BROTHER WOULD BE CROSS WITH US.
"I'VE GROWN WEARY OF ENTERTAINING LADY SHIRAYUKI."
...THAT'S WHAT HE SAID TO ME.
THEY'RE SO ODD.
THERE'S MUCH...
...WE STILL DON'T UNDERSTAND.

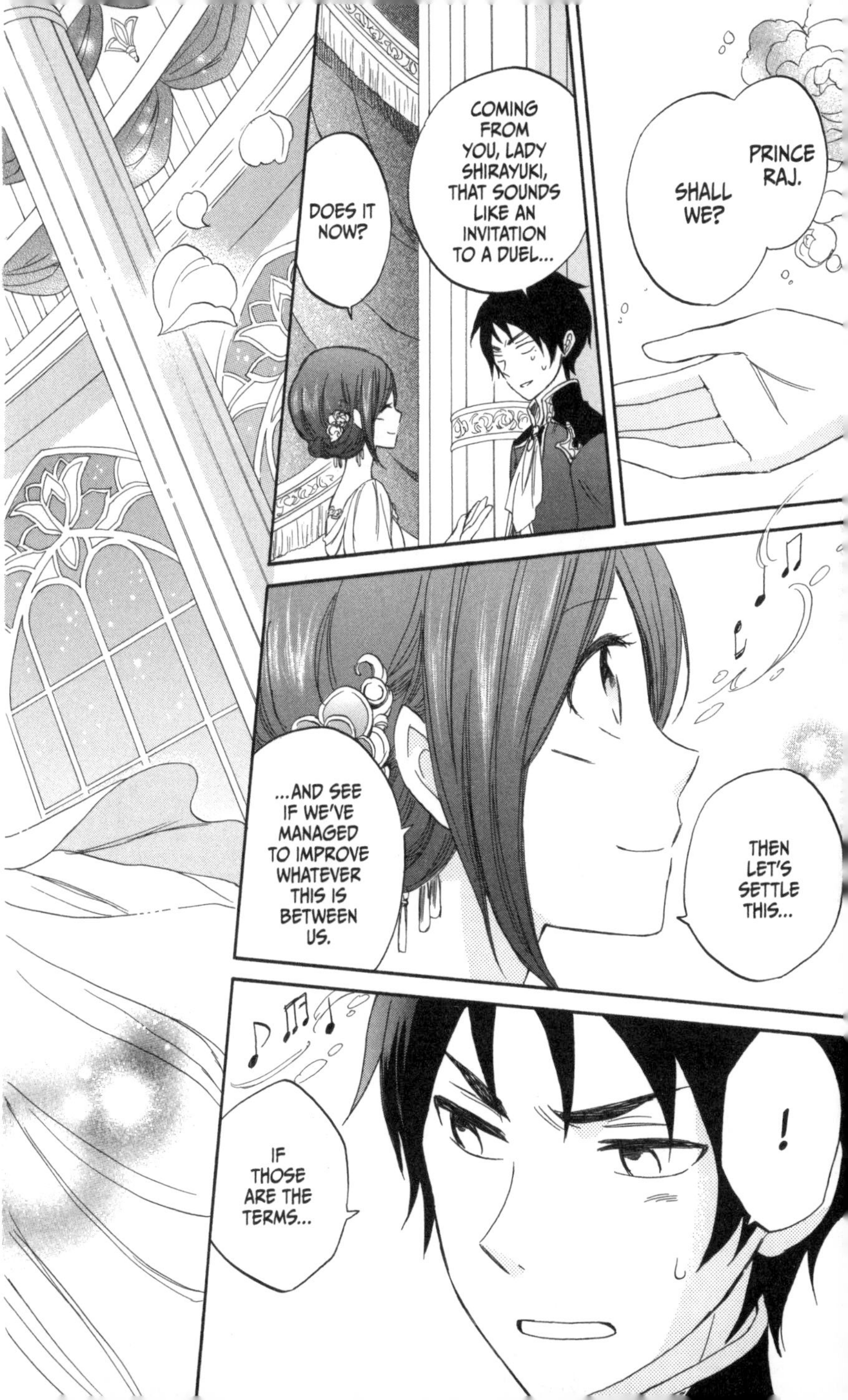
PRINCE RAJ.
SHALL WE?
COMING FROM YOU, LADY SHIRAYUKI, THAT SOUNDS LIKE AN INVITATION TO A DUEL...
DOES IT NOW?
THEN LET'S SETTLE THIS...
...AND SEE IF WE'VE MANAGED TO IMPROVE WHATEVER THIS IS BETWEEN US.
!
IF THOSE ARE THE TERMS...

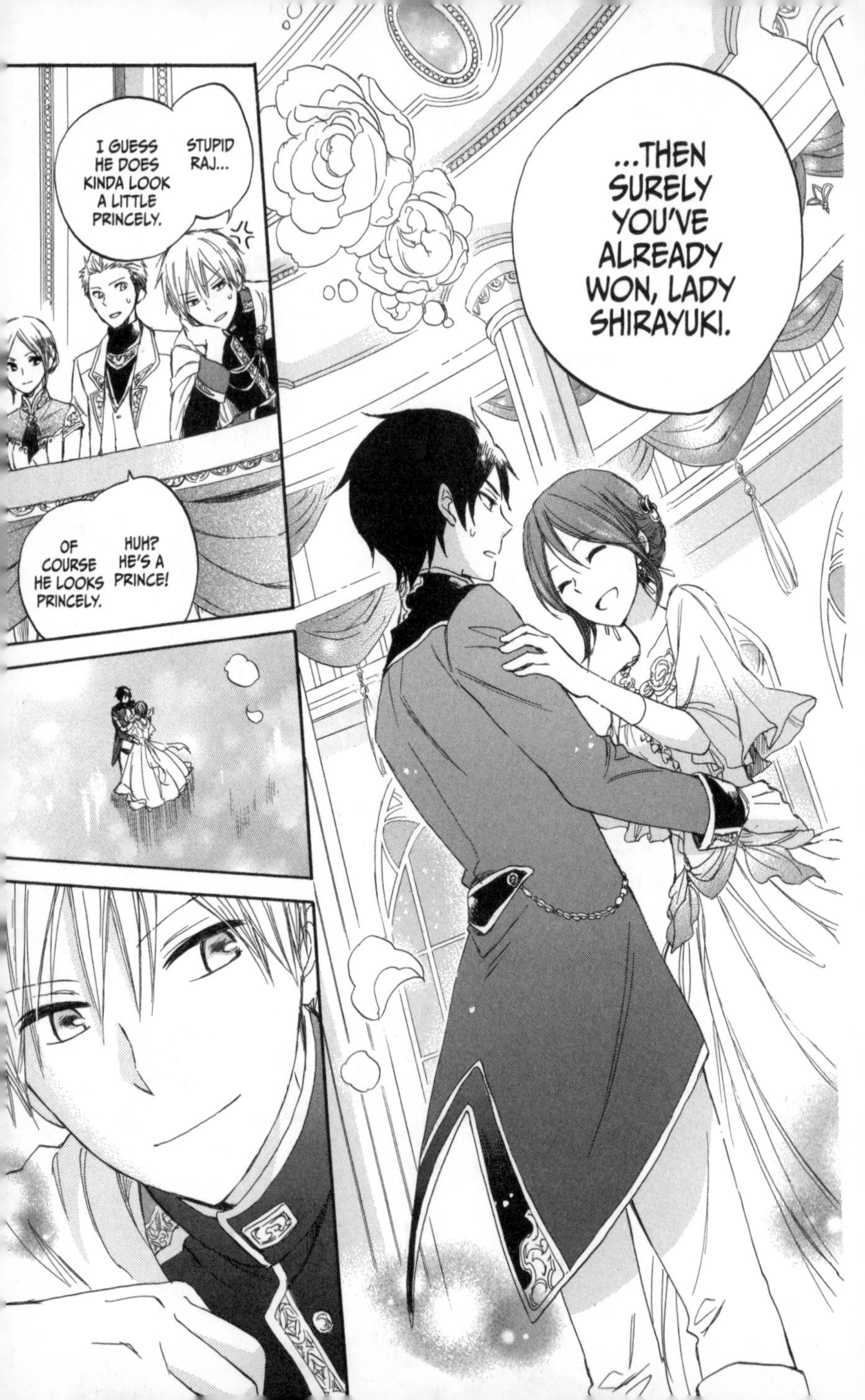
...THEN SURELY YOU'VE ALREADY WON, LADY SHIRAYUKI.
STUPID RAJ...
I GUESS HE DOES KINDA LOOK A LITTLE PRINCELY.
HUH? HE'S A PRINCE!
OF COURSE HE LOOKS PRINCELY.

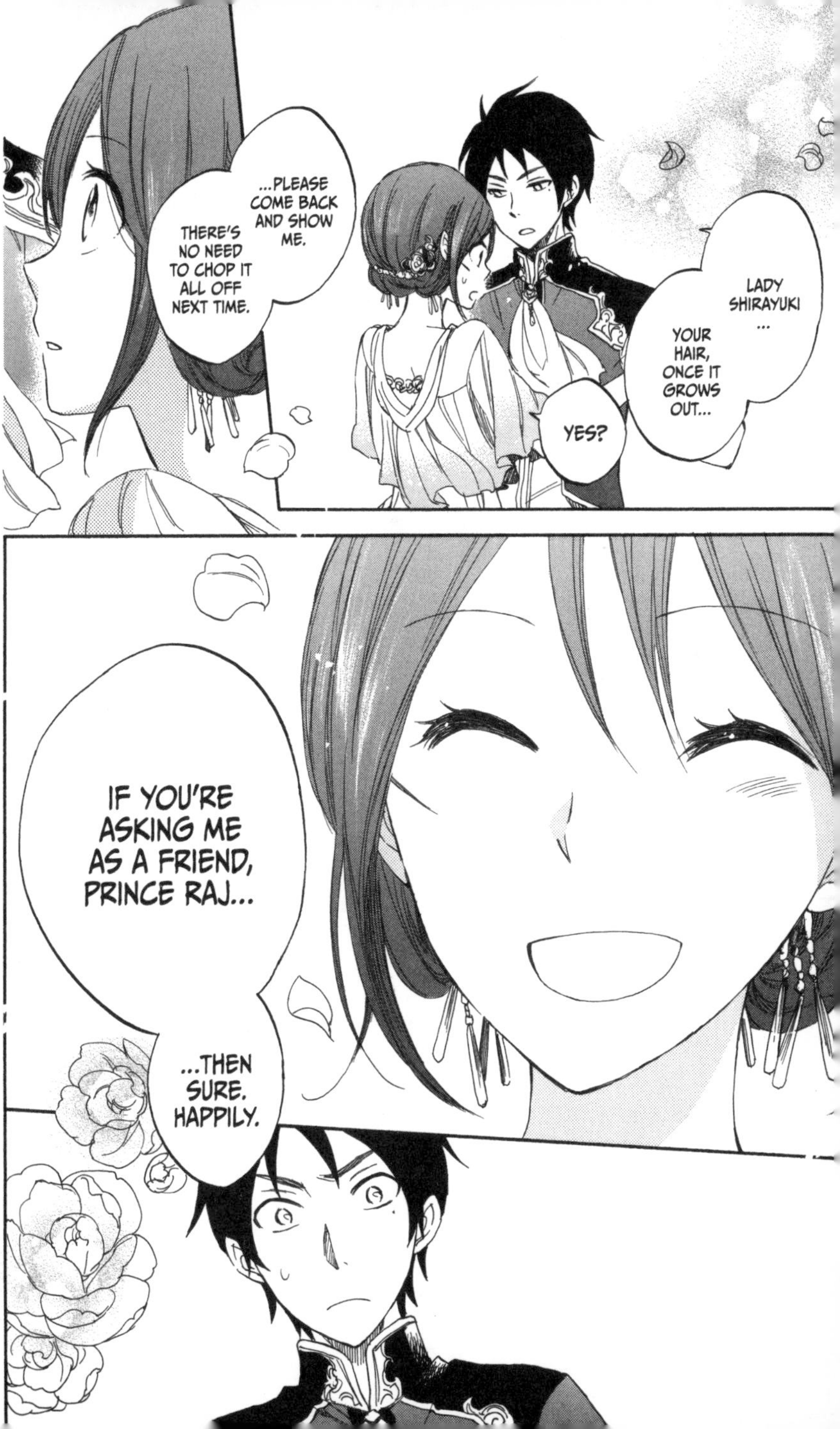
LADY SHIRAYUKI ...
YOUR HAIR, ONCE IT GROWS OUT...
YES?
...PLEASE COME BACK AND SHOW ME.
THERE'S NO NEED TO CHOP IT ALL OFF NEXT TIME.
IF YOU'RE ASKING ME AS A FRIEND, PRINCE RAJ...
...THEN SURE. HAPPILY.

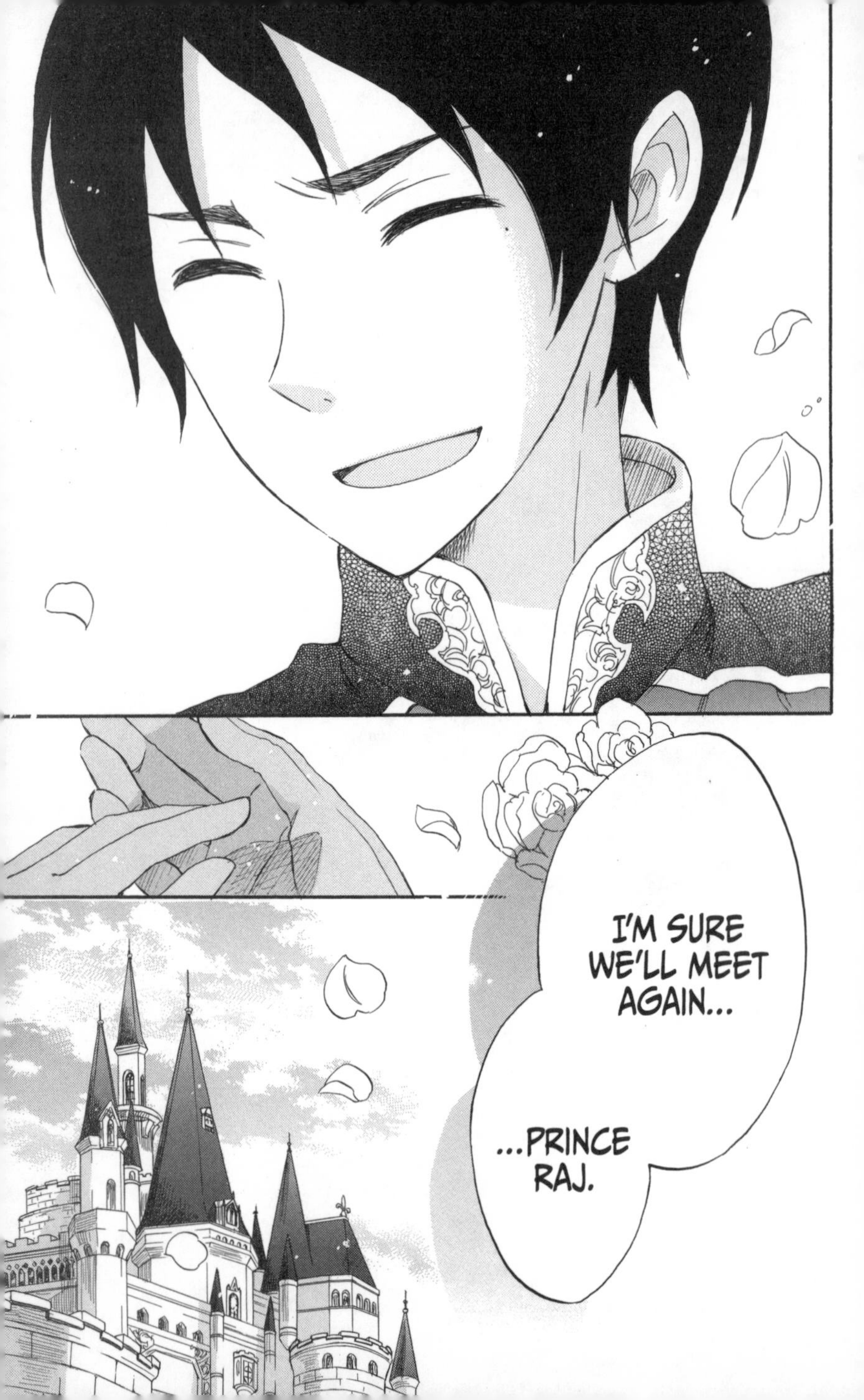
I'M SURE WE'LL MEET AGAIN...
...PRINCE RAJ.

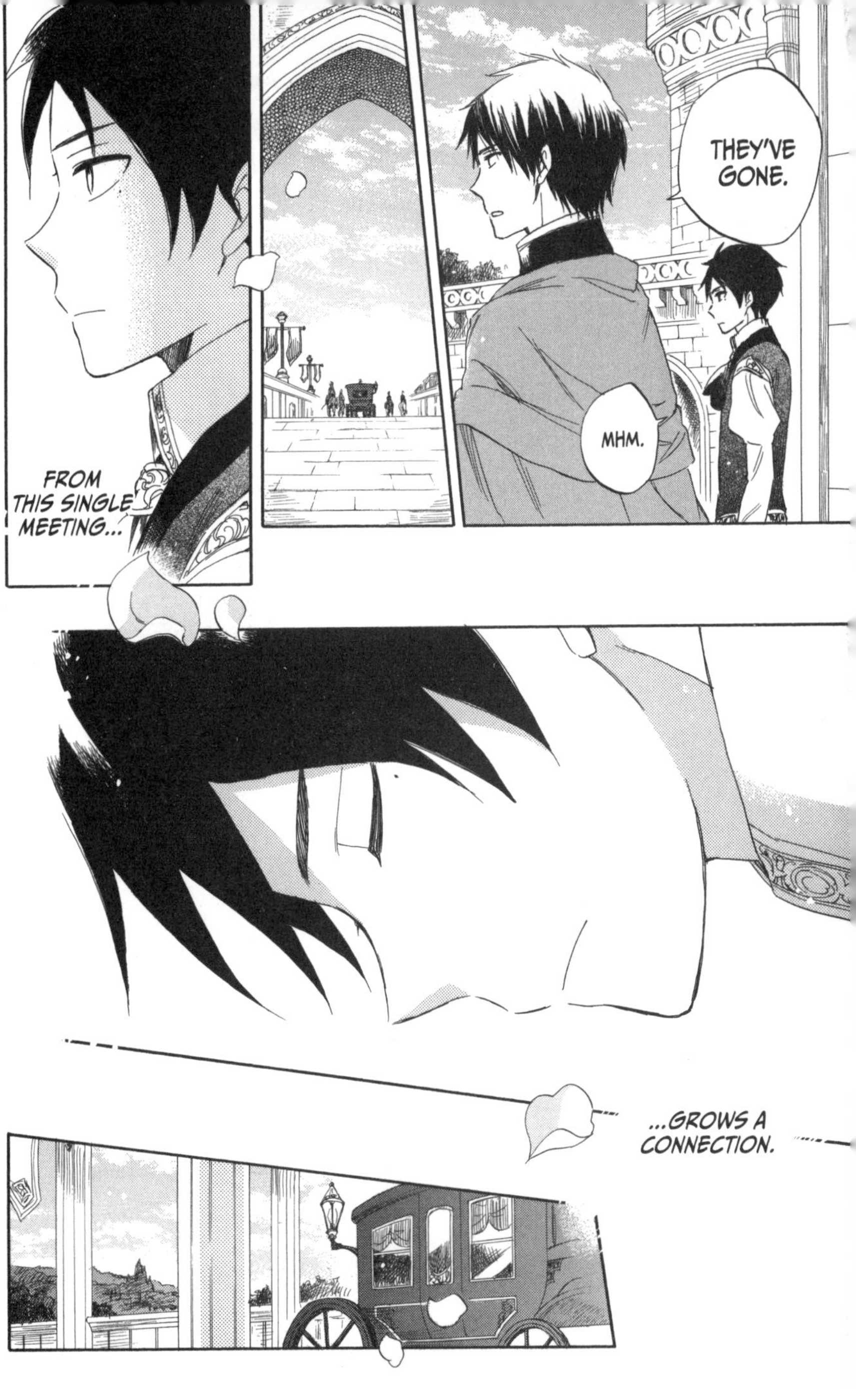
THEY'VE GONE.
MHM.
FROM THIS SINGLE MEETING...
...GROWS A CONNECTION.

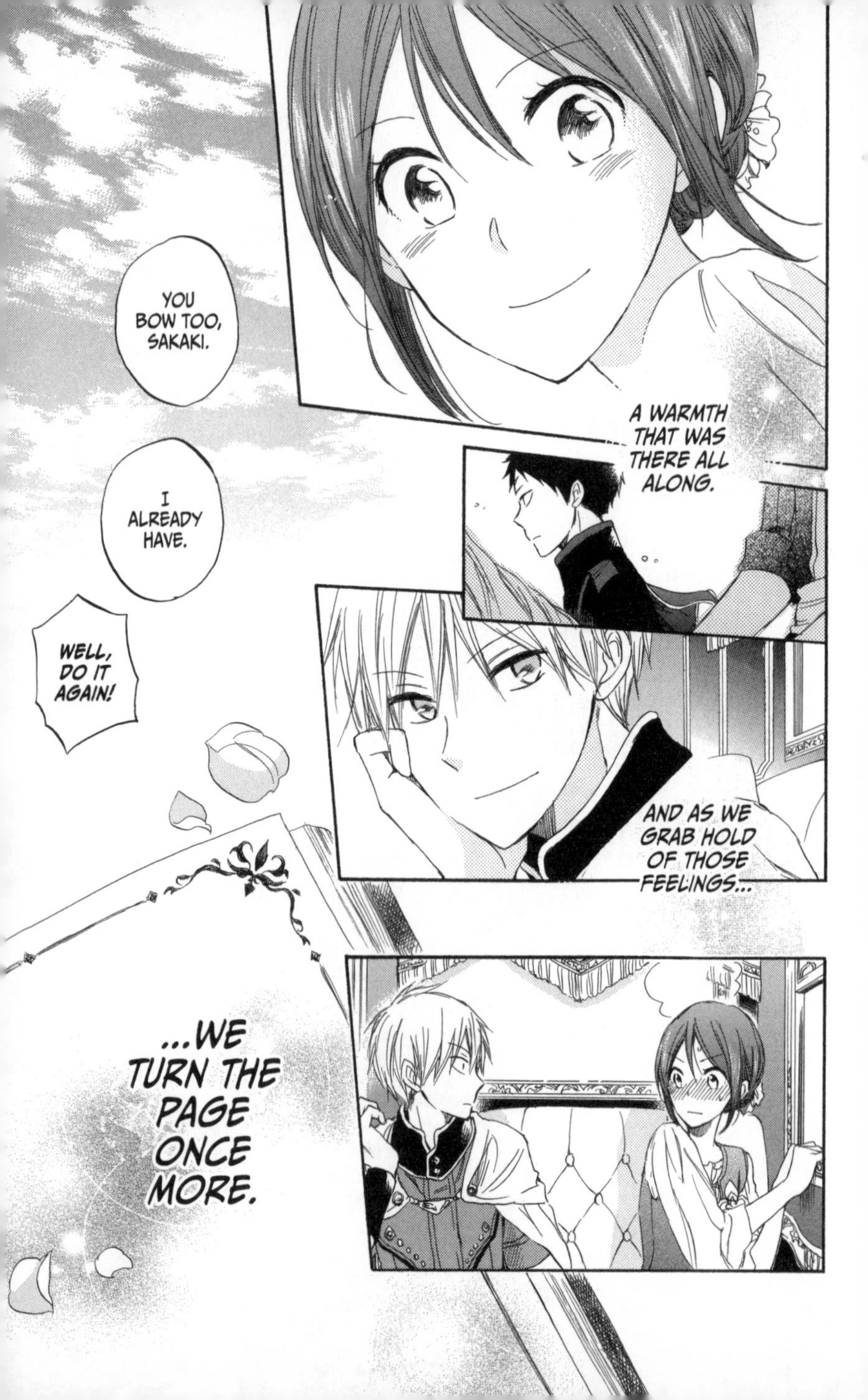
YOU BOW TOO, SAKAKI.
I ALREADY HAVE.
WELL, DO IT AGAIN!
A WARMTH THAT WAS THERE ALL ALONG.
AND AS WE GRAB HOLD OF THOSE FEELINGS...
...WE TURN THE PAGE ONCE MORE.

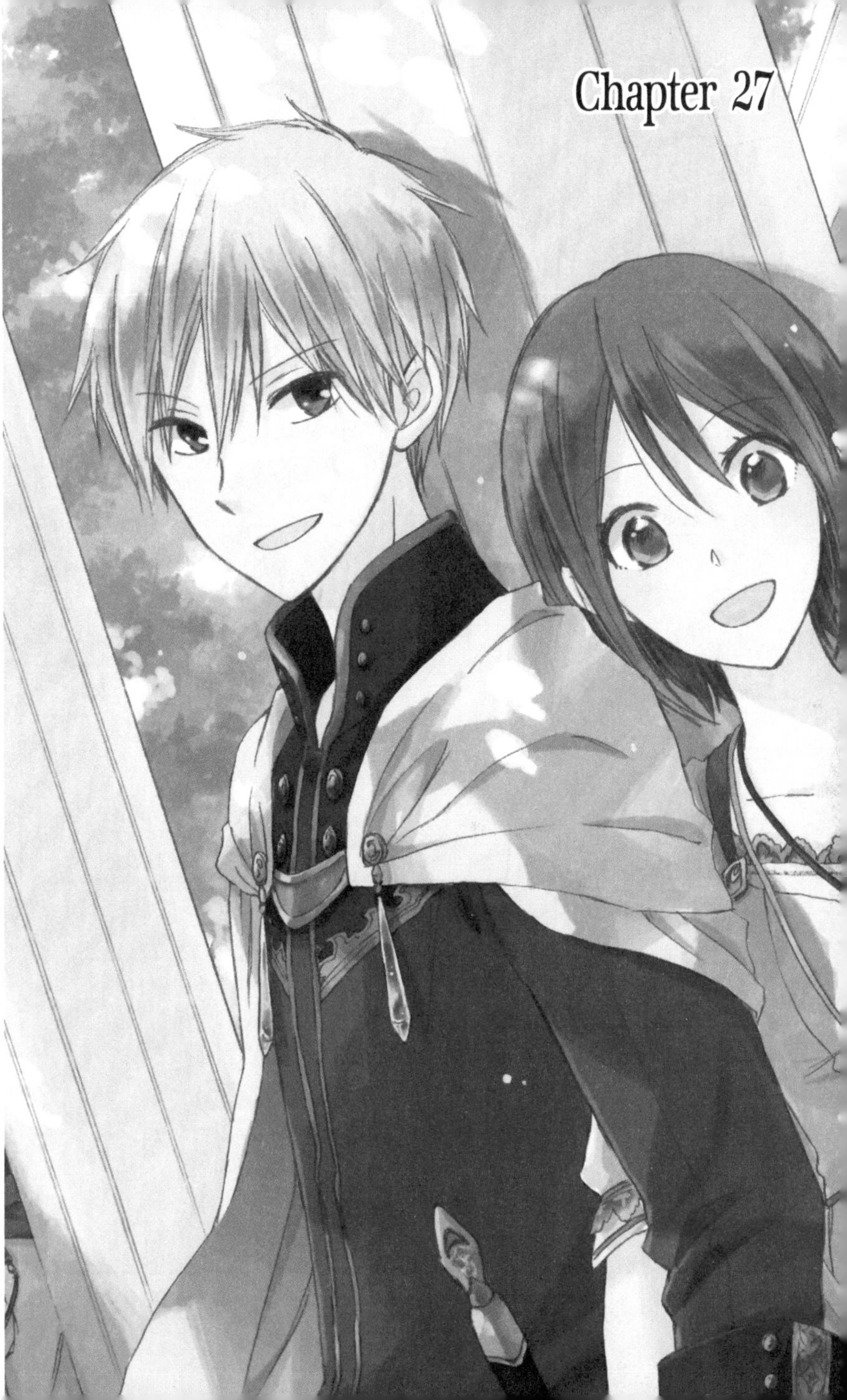
Chapter 27

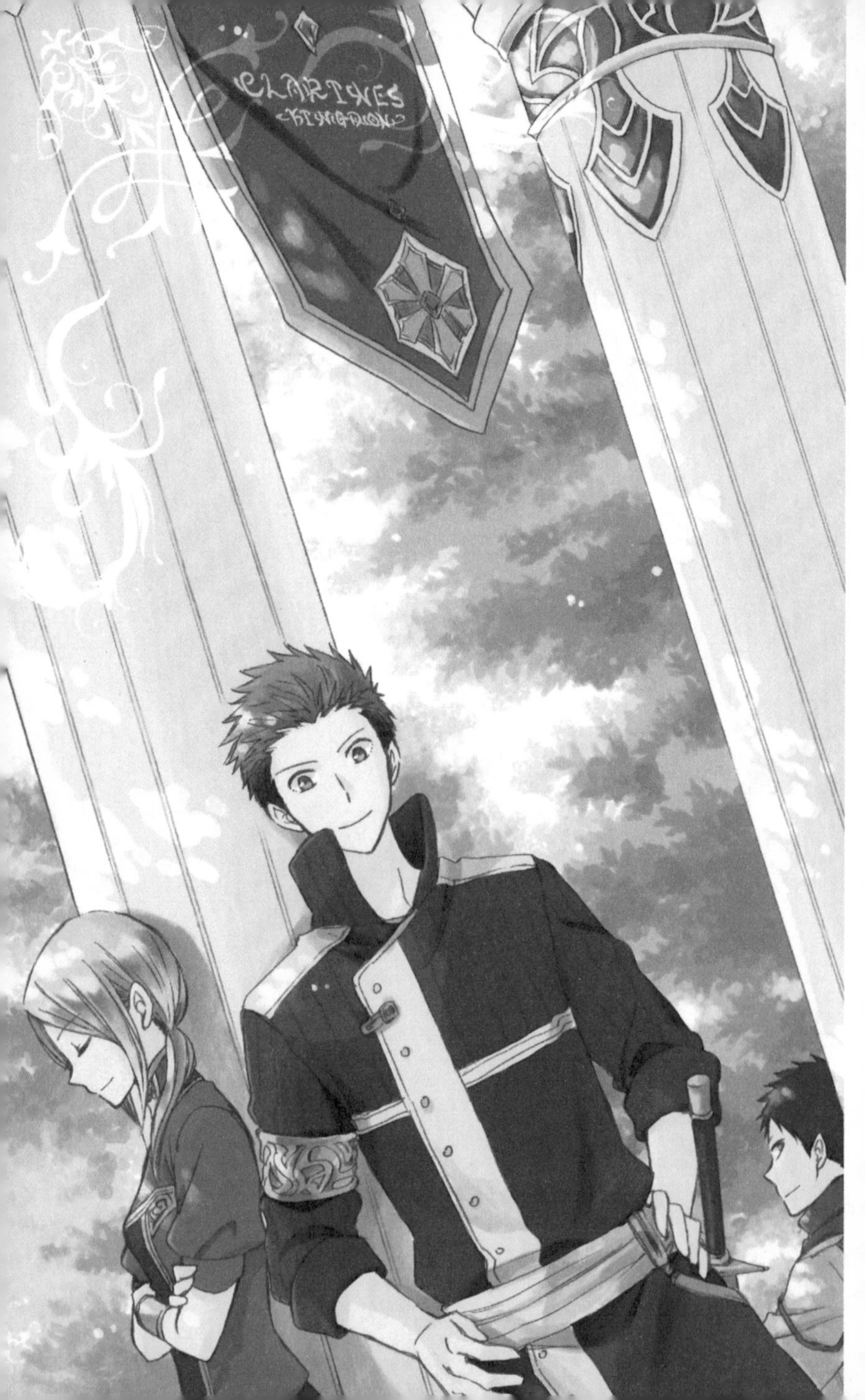
CLARINES
KINGDOM

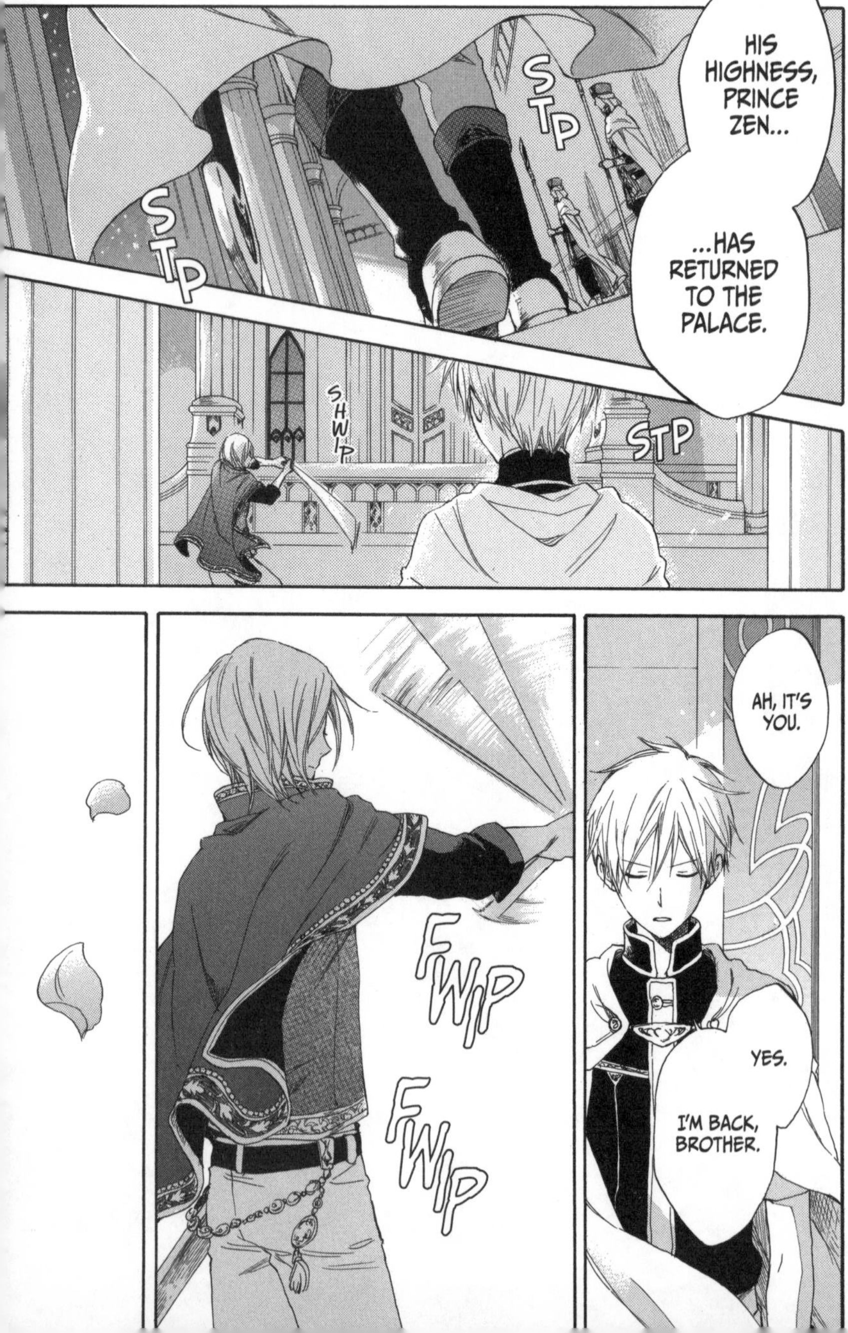
HIS HIGHNESS, PRINCE ZEN...
STP
STP
...HAS RETURNED TO THE PALACE.
STP
SHWIP
AH, IT'S YOU.
YES.
I'M BACK, BROTHER.
FWIP
FWIP

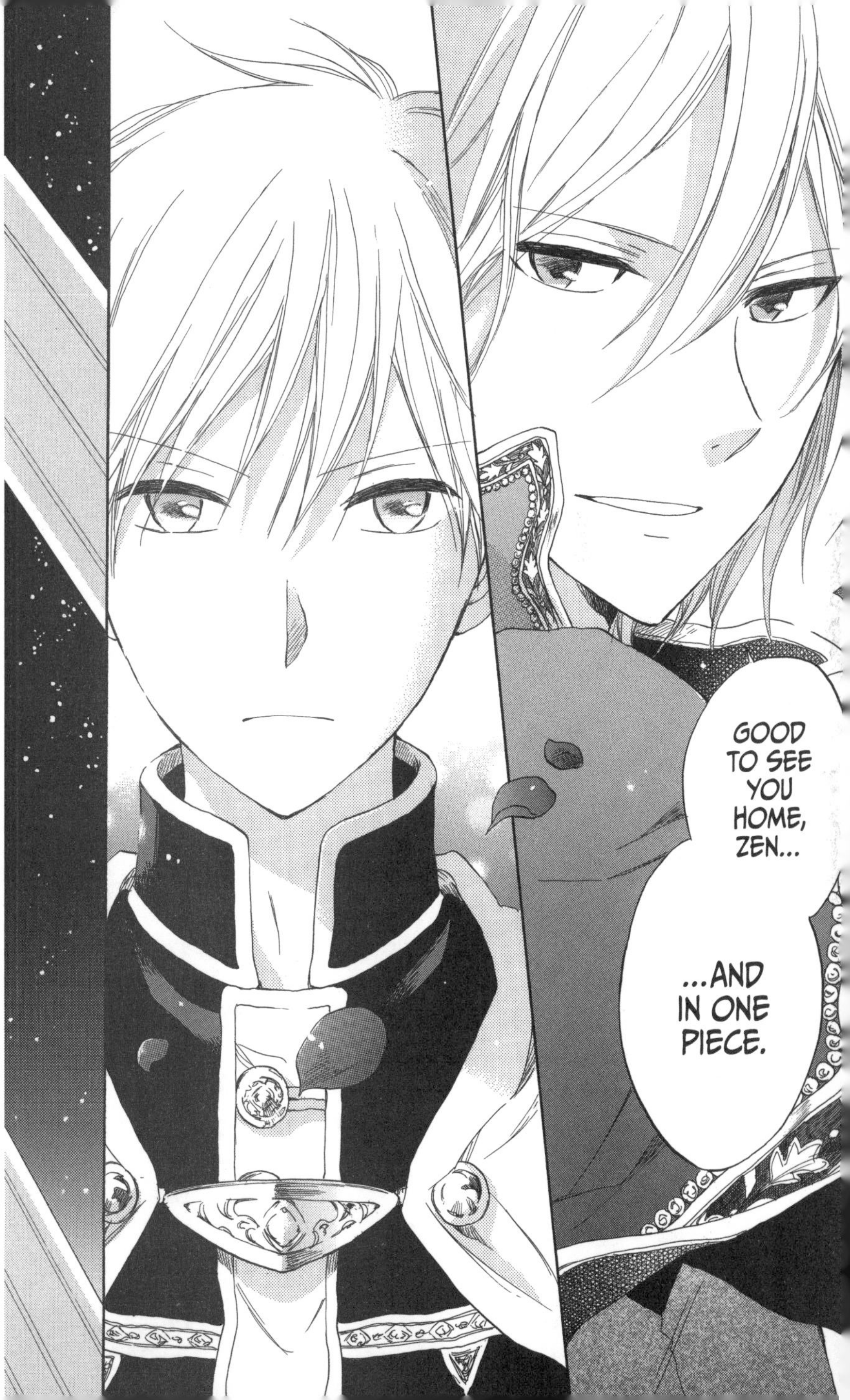
GOOD TO SEE YOU HOME, ZEN...
...AND IN ONE PIECE.

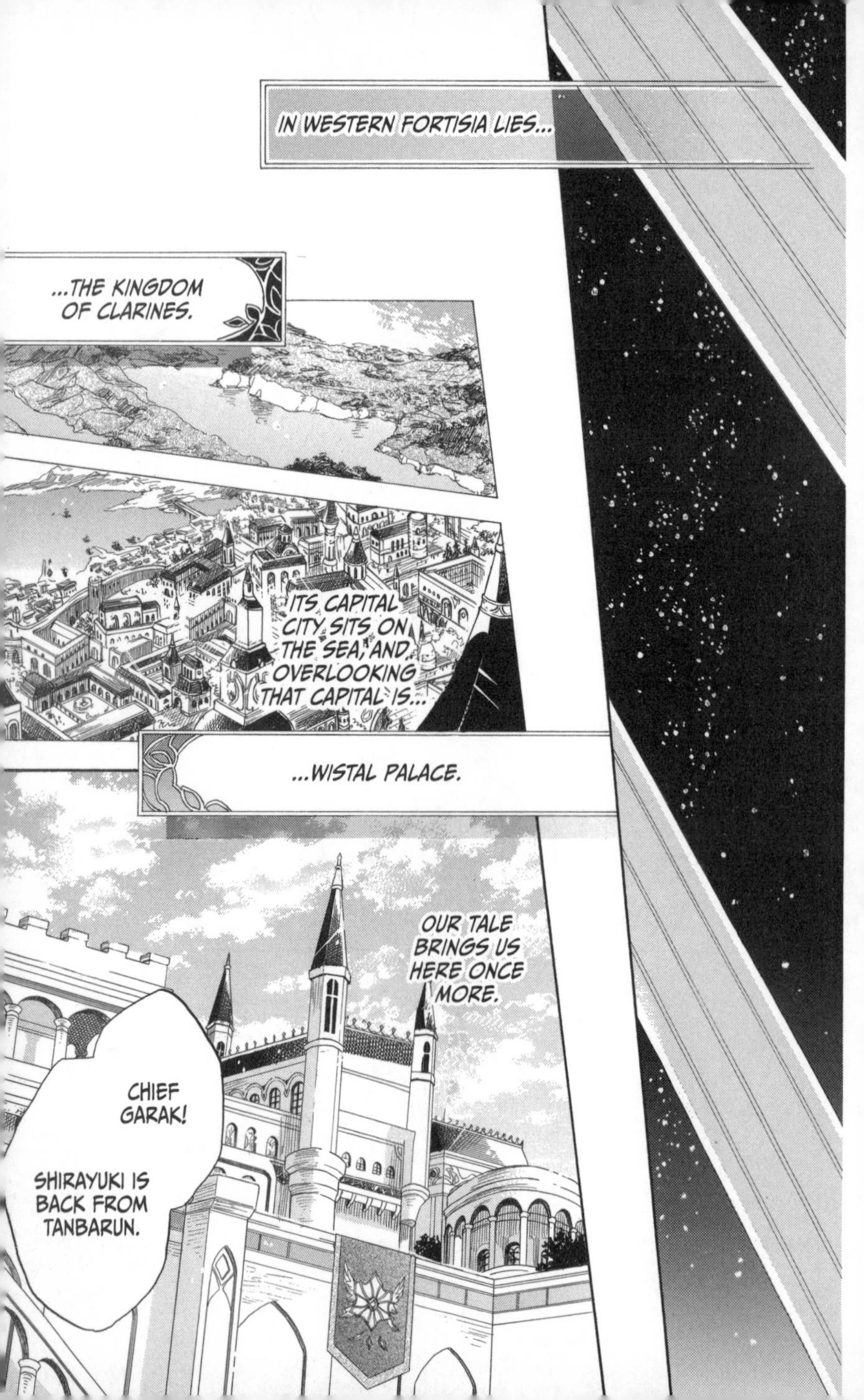
IN WESTERN FORTISIA LIES...
...THE KINGDOM OF CLARINES.
ITS CAPITAL CITY SITS ON THE SEA, AND, OVERLOOKING THAT CAPITAL IS...
...WISTAL PALACE.
OUR TALE BRINGS US HERE ONCE MORE.
CHIEF GARAK!
SHIRAYUKI IS BACK FROM TANBARUN.

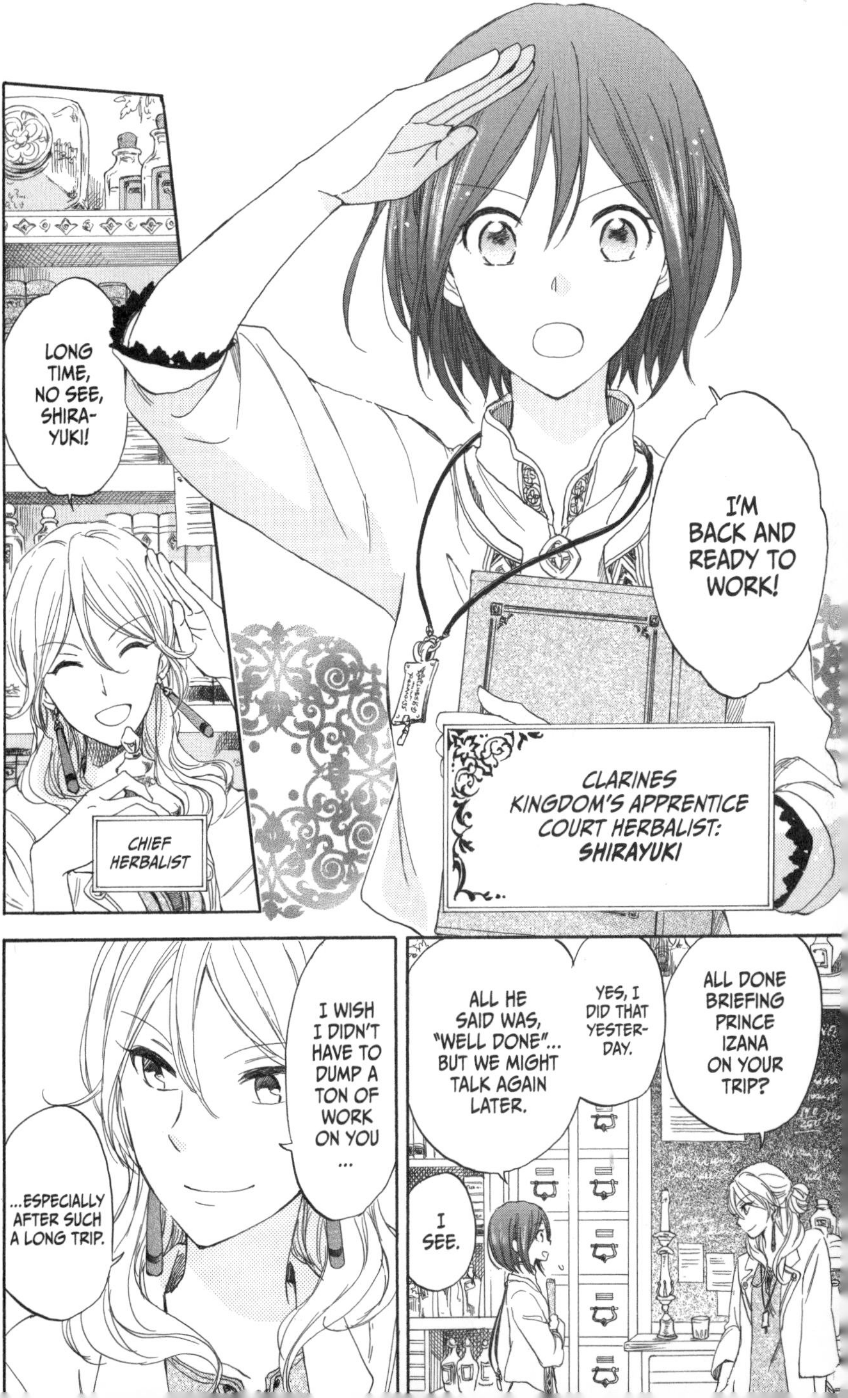
I'M BACK AND READY TO WORK!
CLARINES KINGDOM'S APPRENTICE COURT HERBALIST: SHIRAYUKI
LONG TIME, NO SEE, SHIRA-YUKI!
CHIEF HERBALIST
ALL DONE BRIEFING PRINCE IZANA ON YOUR TRIP?
YES, I DID THAT YESTER-DAY.
ALL HE SAID WAS, "WELL DONE"... BUT WE MIGHT TALK AGAIN LATER.
I SEE.
I WISH I DIDN'T HAVE TO DUMP A TON OF WORK ON YOU ...
...ESPECIALLY AFTER SUCH A LONG TRIP.

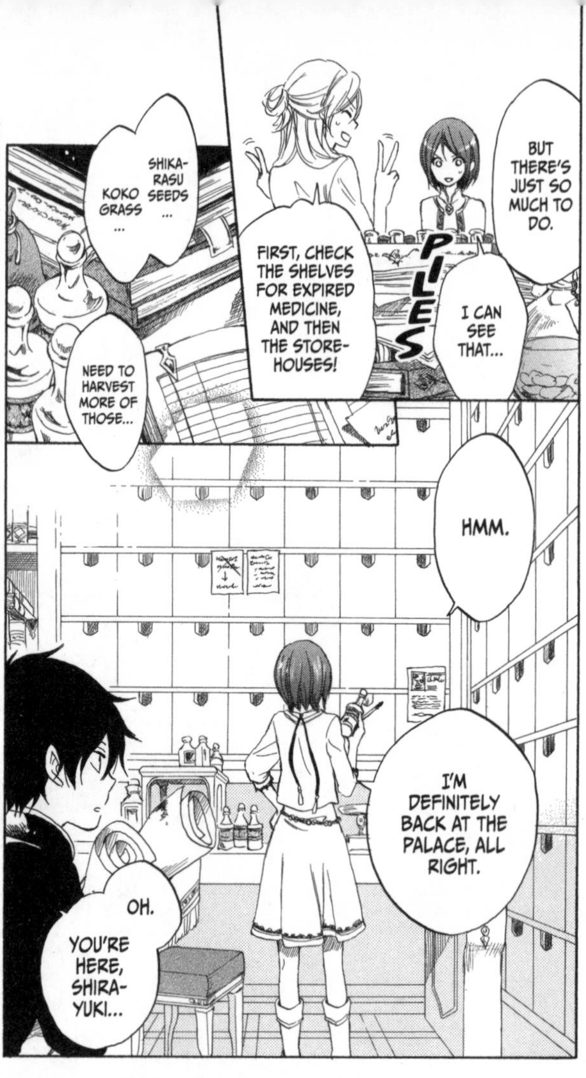
BUT THERE'S JUST SO MUCH TO DO.
FIRST, CHECK THE SHELVES FOR EXPIRED MEDICINE, AND THEN THE STORE-HOUSES!
PILES
I CAN SEE THAT...
SHIKA-RASU SEEDS...
KOKO GRASS...
NEED TO HARVEST MORE OF THOSE...
HMM.
I'M DEFINITELY BACK AT THE PALACE, ALL RIGHT.
OH.
YOU'RE HERE, SHIRA-YUKI...
PALACE EXHIBITION DAY?

4

Chapter 27 (this very one) was when the series switched magazines from *LaLa DX* to *LaLa* in Japan.

Because of the switch, I decided to do little reintroductions for the characters and setting in chapters 27 and 28.

I realize that might seem a little awkward here, in volume form, but I do hope you all enjoy the return to the hustle and bustle of Clarines and the palace.

Haven't seen you in a while, Ryu!

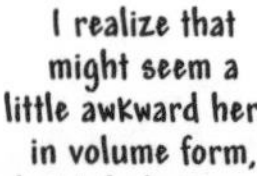
Uh-huh.

Ryu shows up a lot in these sidebars.

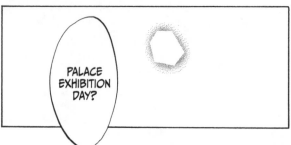

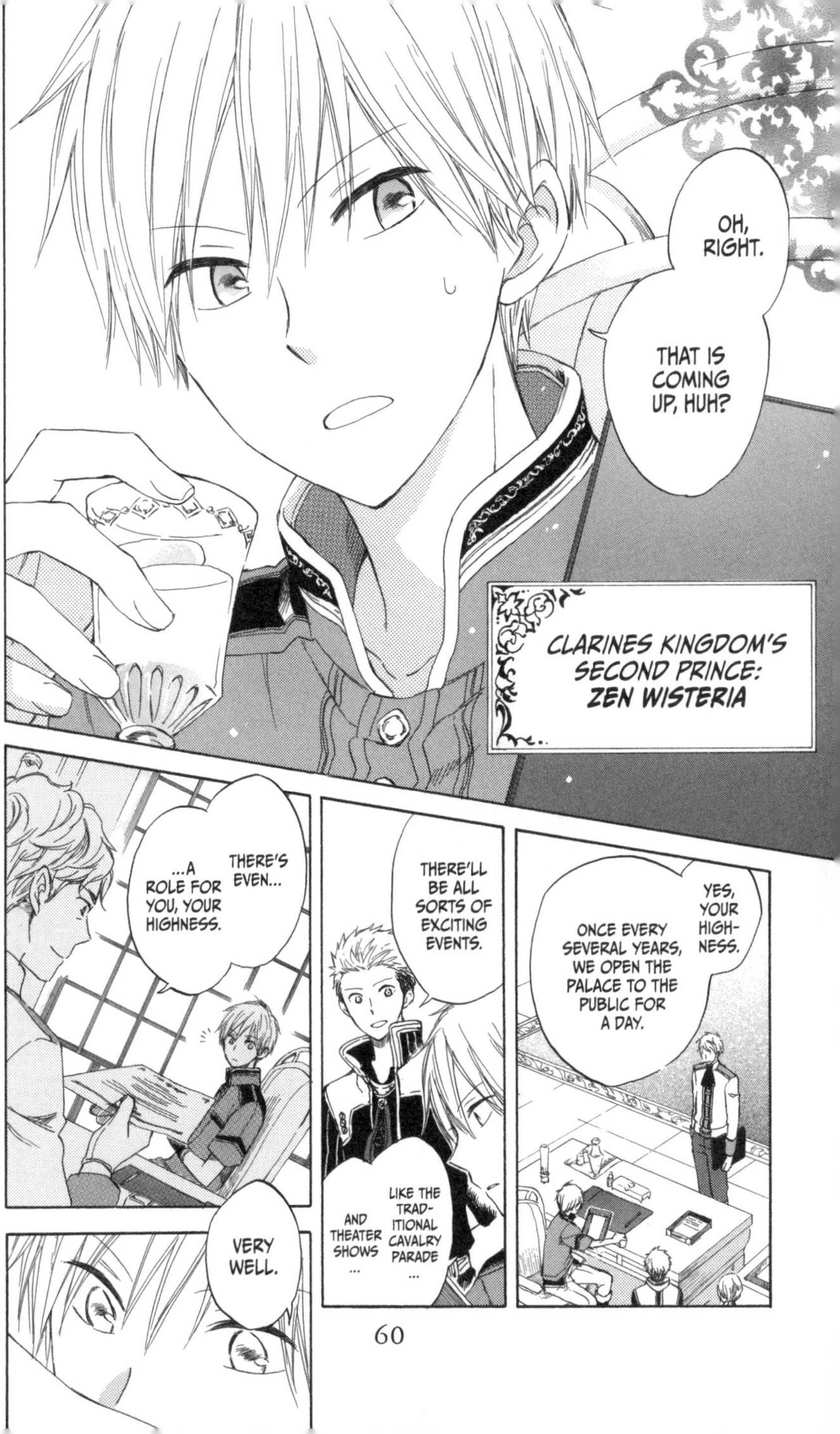
OH, RIGHT.
THAT IS COMING UP, HUH?
CLARINES KINGDOM'S SECOND PRINCE: ZEN WISTERIA
YES, YOUR HIGHNESS.
ONCE EVERY SEVERAL YEARS, WE OPEN THE PALACE TO THE PUBLIC FOR A DAY.
THERE'LL BE ALL SORTS OF EXCITING EVENTS.
LIKE THE TRADITIONAL CAVALRY PARADE...
AND THEATER SHOWS...
THERE'S EVEN...
...A ROLE FOR YOU, YOUR HIGHNESS.
VERY WELL.

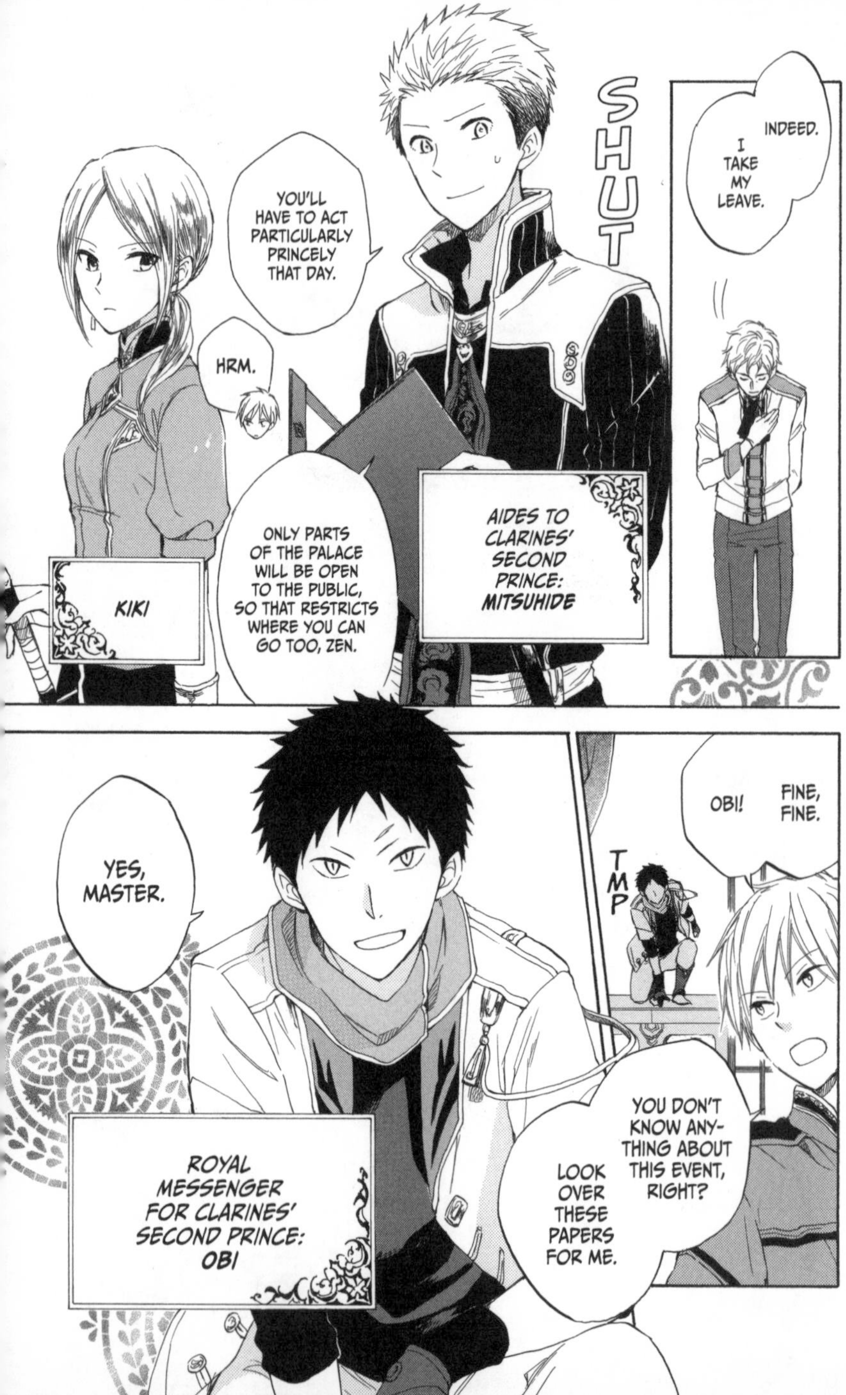
INDEED. I TAKE MY LEAVE.
SHUT
YOU'LL HAVE TO ACT PARTICULARLY PRINCELY THAT DAY.
HRM.
AIDES TO CLARINES' SECOND PRINCE: MITSUHIDE
ONLY PARTS OF THE PALACE WILL BE OPEN TO THE PUBLIC, SO THAT RESTRICTS WHERE YOU CAN GO TOO, ZEN.
KIKI
FINE, FINE.
OBI!
TMP
YOU DON'T KNOW ANY-THING ABOUT THIS EVENT, RIGHT?
LOOK OVER THESE PAPERS FOR ME.
YES, MASTER.
ROYAL MESSENGER FOR CLARINES' SECOND PRINCE: OBI

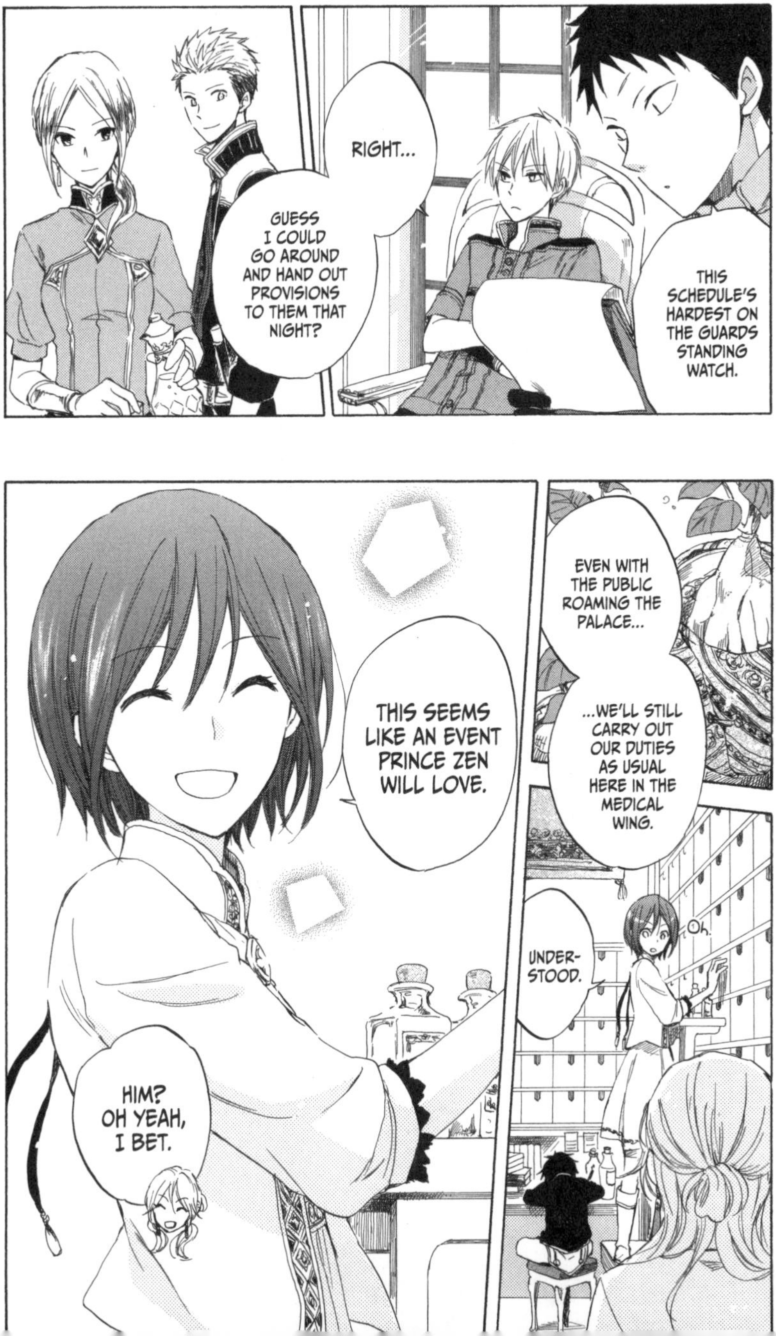
THIS SCHEDULE'S HARDEST ON THE GUARDS STANDING WATCH.
RIGHT...
GUESS I COULD GO AROUND AND HAND OUT PROVISIONS TO THEM THAT NIGHT?
EVEN WITH THE PUBLIC ROAMING THE PALACE...
...WE'LL STILL CARRY OUT OUR DUTIES AS USUAL HERE IN THE MEDICAL WING.
Oh.
UNDER-STOOD.
THIS SEEMS LIKE AN EVENT PRINCE ZEN WILL LOVE.
HIM? OH YEAH, I BET.

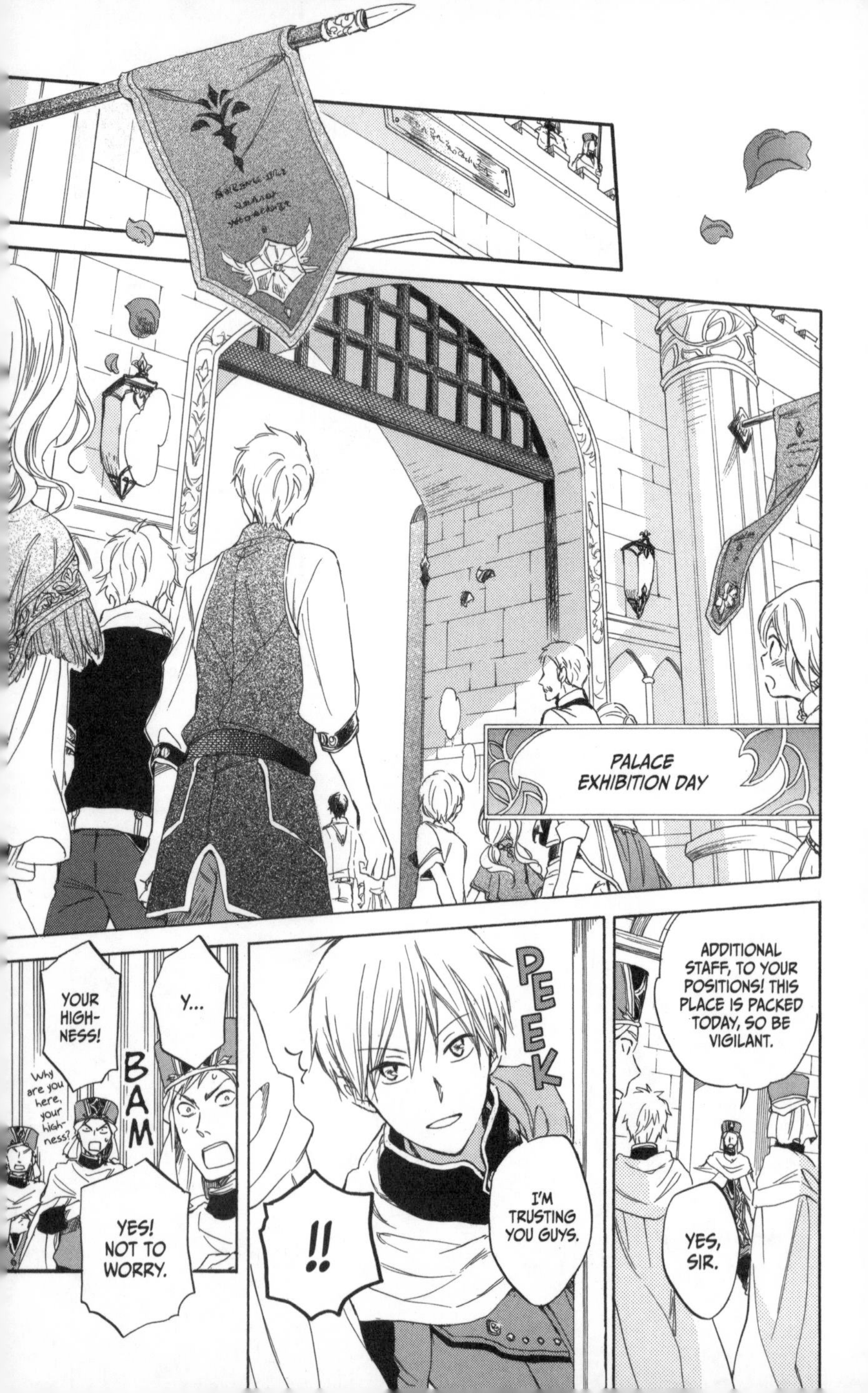
PALACE EXHIBITION DAY
ADDITIONAL STAFF, TO YOUR POSITIONS! THIS PLACE IS PACKED TODAY, SO BE VIGILANT.
YES, SIR.
PEEK
I'M TRUSTING YOU GUYS.
!!
Y...
YOUR HIGH-NESS!
BAM
Why are you here, your high-ness?
YES! NOT TO WORRY.

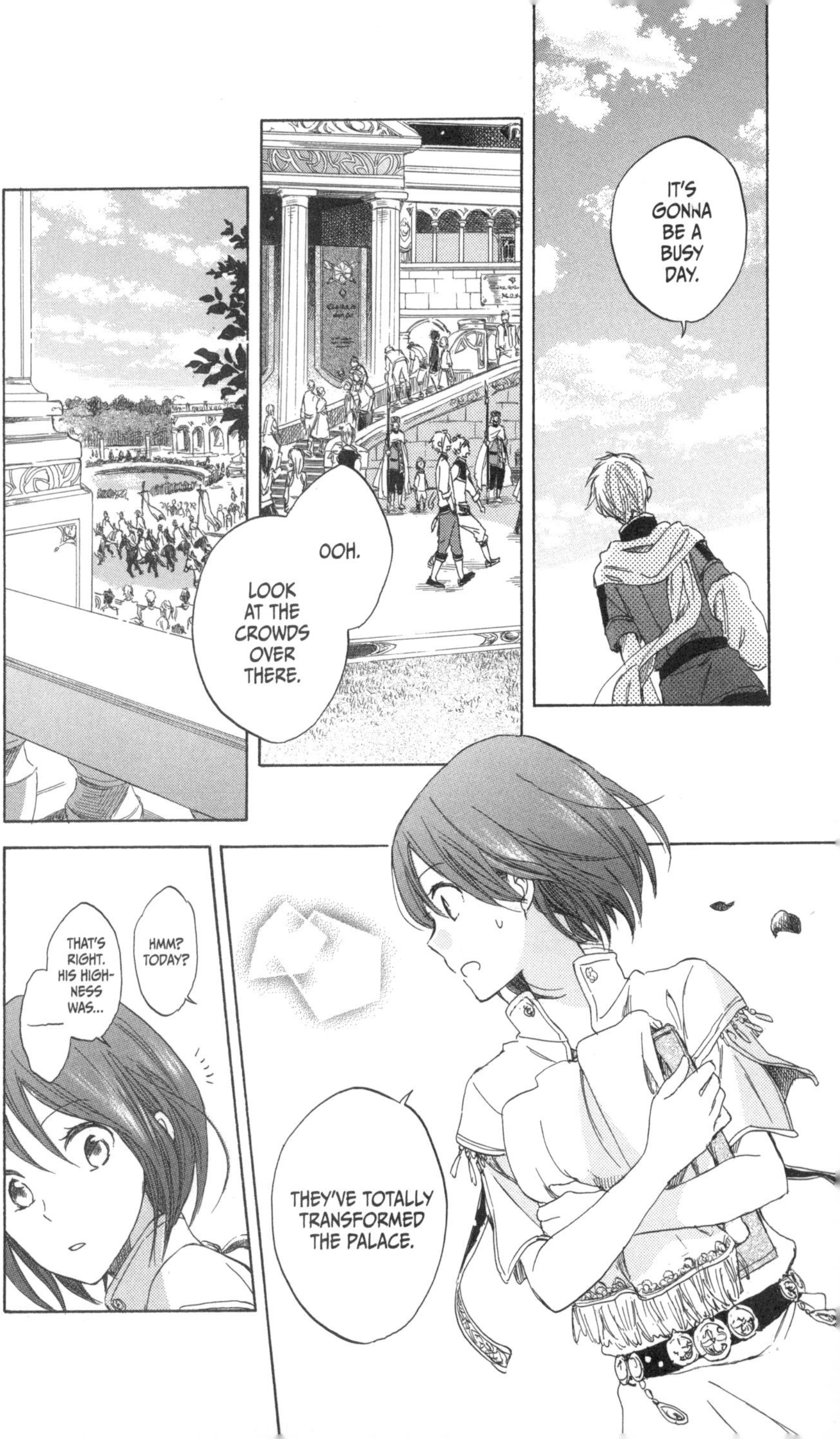
IT'S GONNA BE A BUSY DAY.
OOH.
LOOK AT THE CROWDS OVER THERE.
THEY'VE TOTALLY TRANSFORMED THE PALACE.
HMM? TODAY?
THAT'S RIGHT. HIS HIGH-NESS WAS...

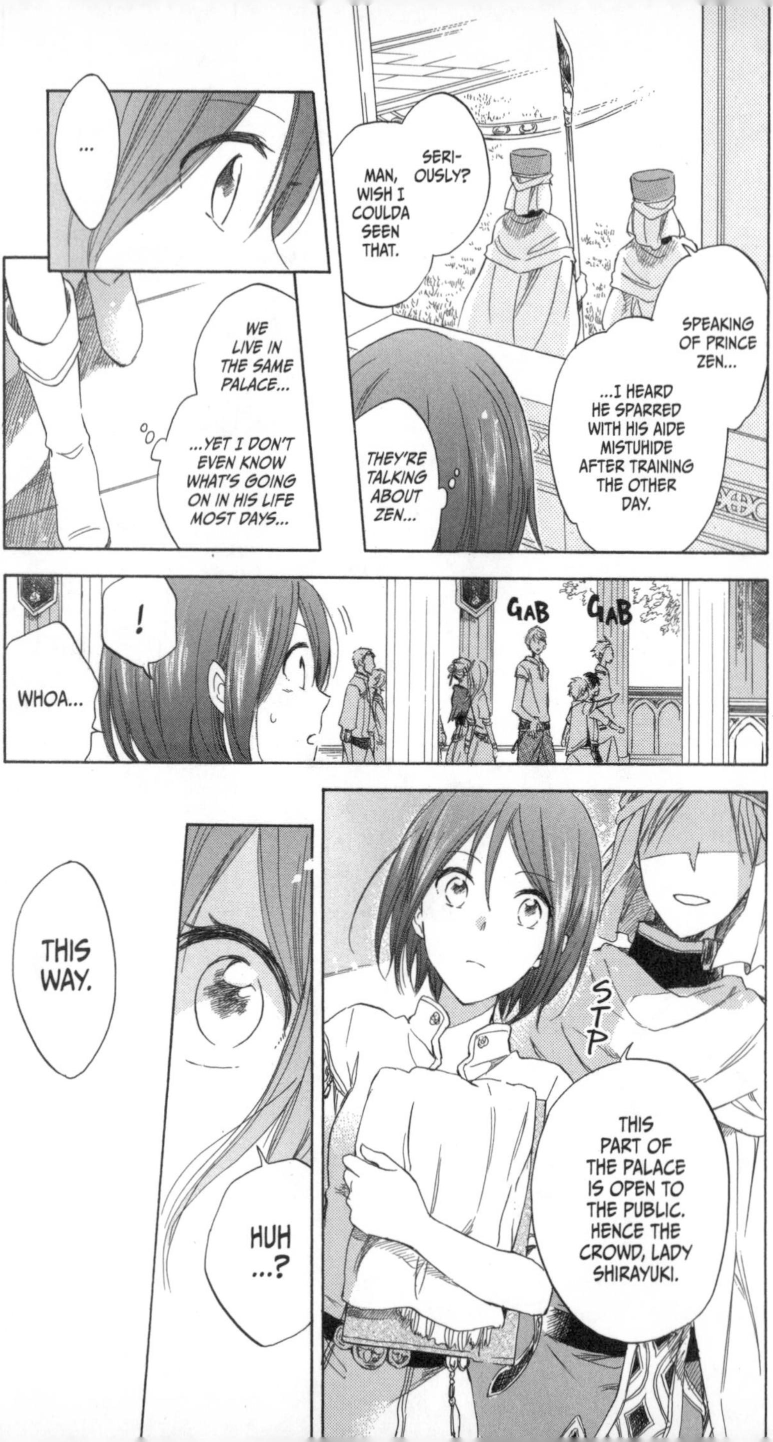
SPEAKING OF PRINCE ZEN...
...I HEARD HE SPARRED WITH HIS AIDE MISTUHIDE AFTER TRAINING THE OTHER DAY.
SERI-OUSLY?
MAN, WISH I COULDA SEEN THAT.
THEY'RE TALKING ABOUT ZEN...
...
WE LIVE IN THE SAME PALACE...
...YET I DON'T EVEN KNOW WHAT'S GOING ON IN HIS LIFE MOST DAYS...
GAB
GAB
!
WHOA...
STP
THIS PART OF THE PALACE IS OPEN TO THE PUBLIC. HENCE THE CROWD, LADY SHIRAYUKI.
THIS WAY.
HUH ...?

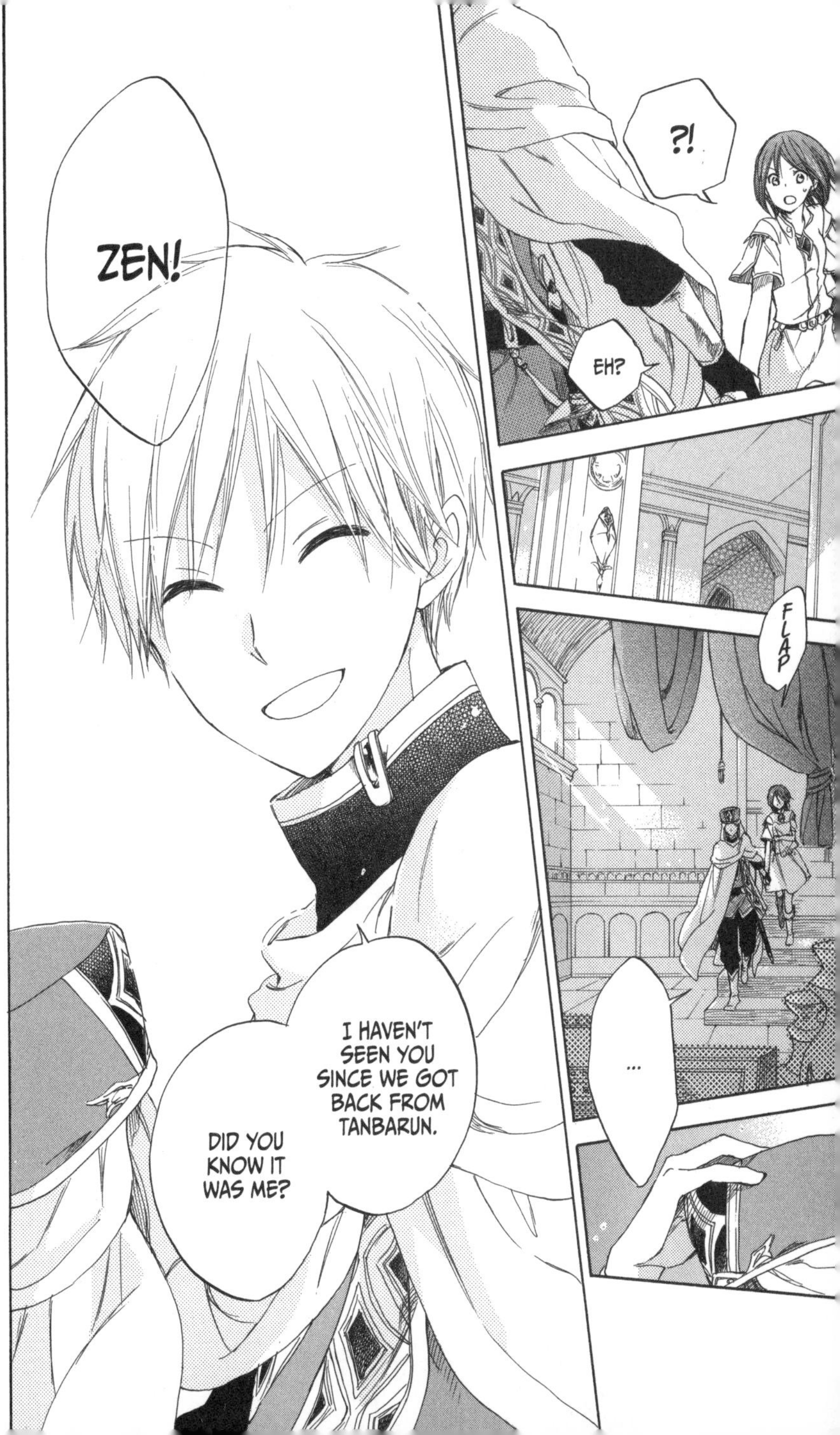
?!
EH?
FLAP
...
ZEN!
I HAVEN'T SEEN YOU SINCE WE GOT BACK FROM TANBARUN.
DID YOU KNOW IT WAS ME?

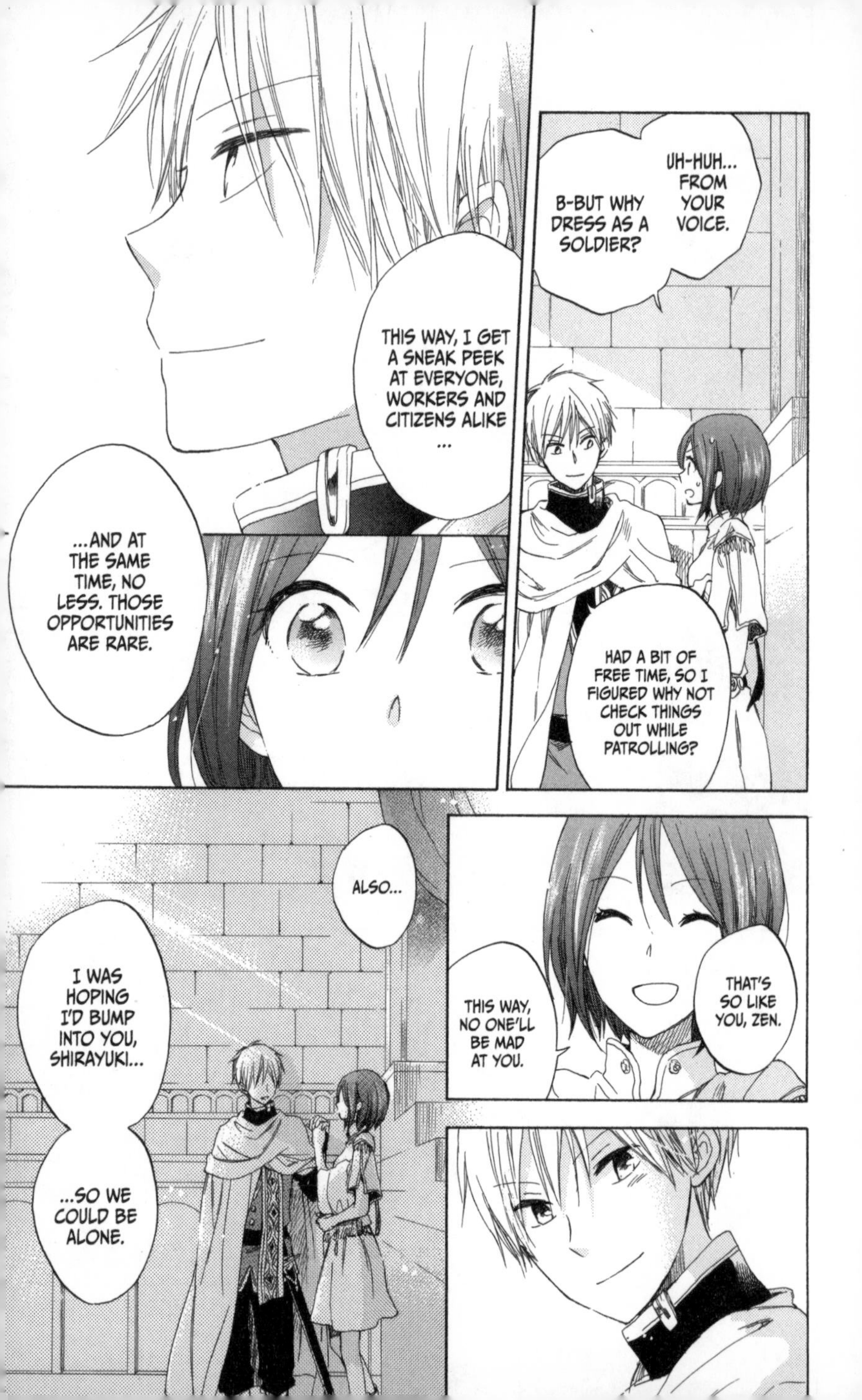
UH-HUH... FROM YOUR VOICE.
B-BUT WHY DRESS AS A SOLDIER?
HAD A BIT OF FREE TIME, SO I FIGURED WHY NOT CHECK THINGS OUT WHILE PATROLLING?
THIS WAY, I GET A SNEAK PEEK AT EVERYONE, WORKERS AND CITIZENS ALIKE ...
...AND AT THE SAME TIME, NO LESS. THOSE OPPORTUNITIES ARE RARE.
THAT'S SO LIKE YOU, ZEN.
THIS WAY, NO ONE'LL BE MAD AT YOU.
ALSO...
I WAS HOPING I'D BUMP INTO YOU, SHIRAYUKI...
...SO WE COULD BE ALONE.

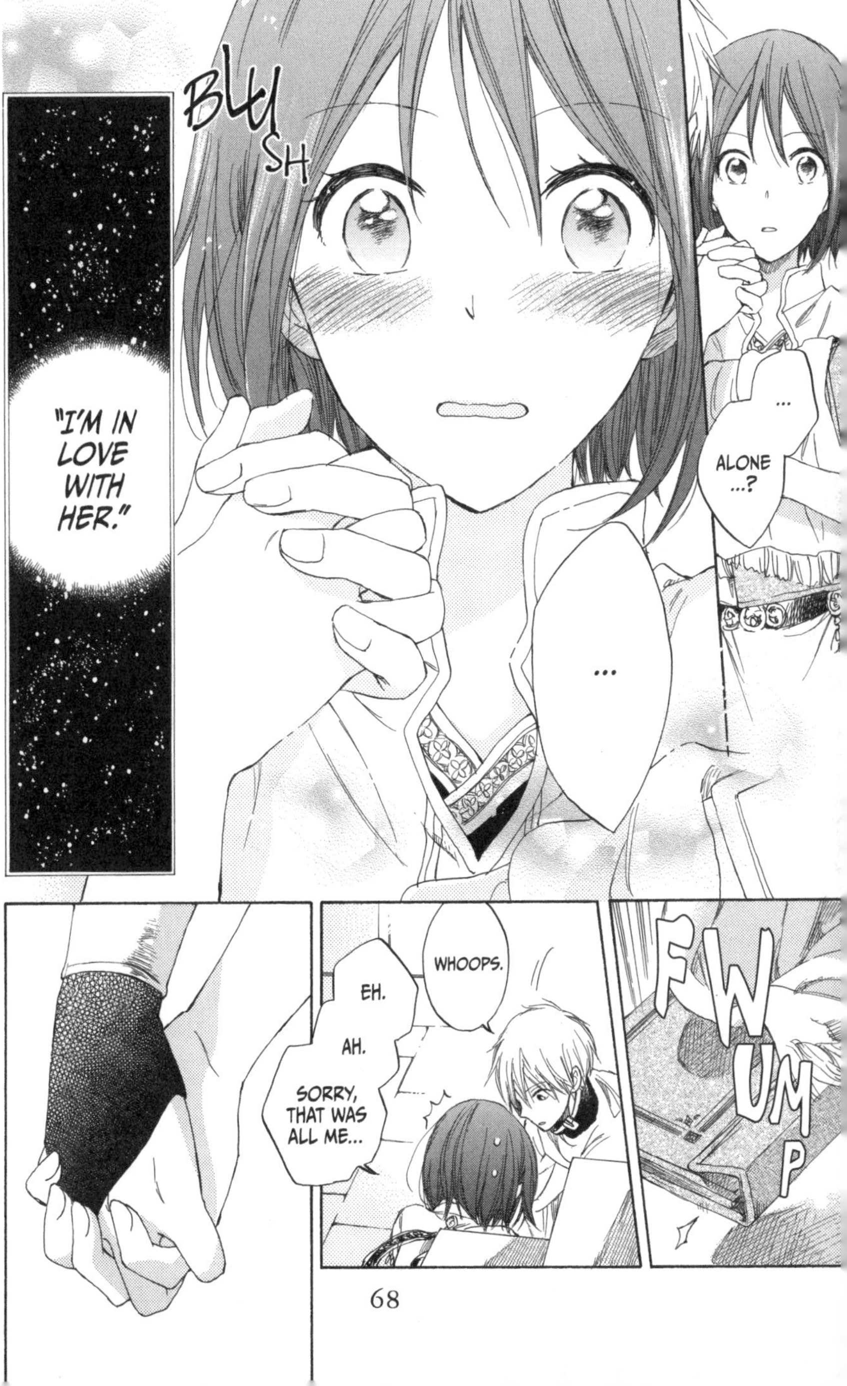
...
ALONE ...?
BLUSH
...
"I'M IN LOVE WITH HER."
FWUMP
WHOOPS.
EH.
AH.
SORRY, THAT WAS ALL ME...

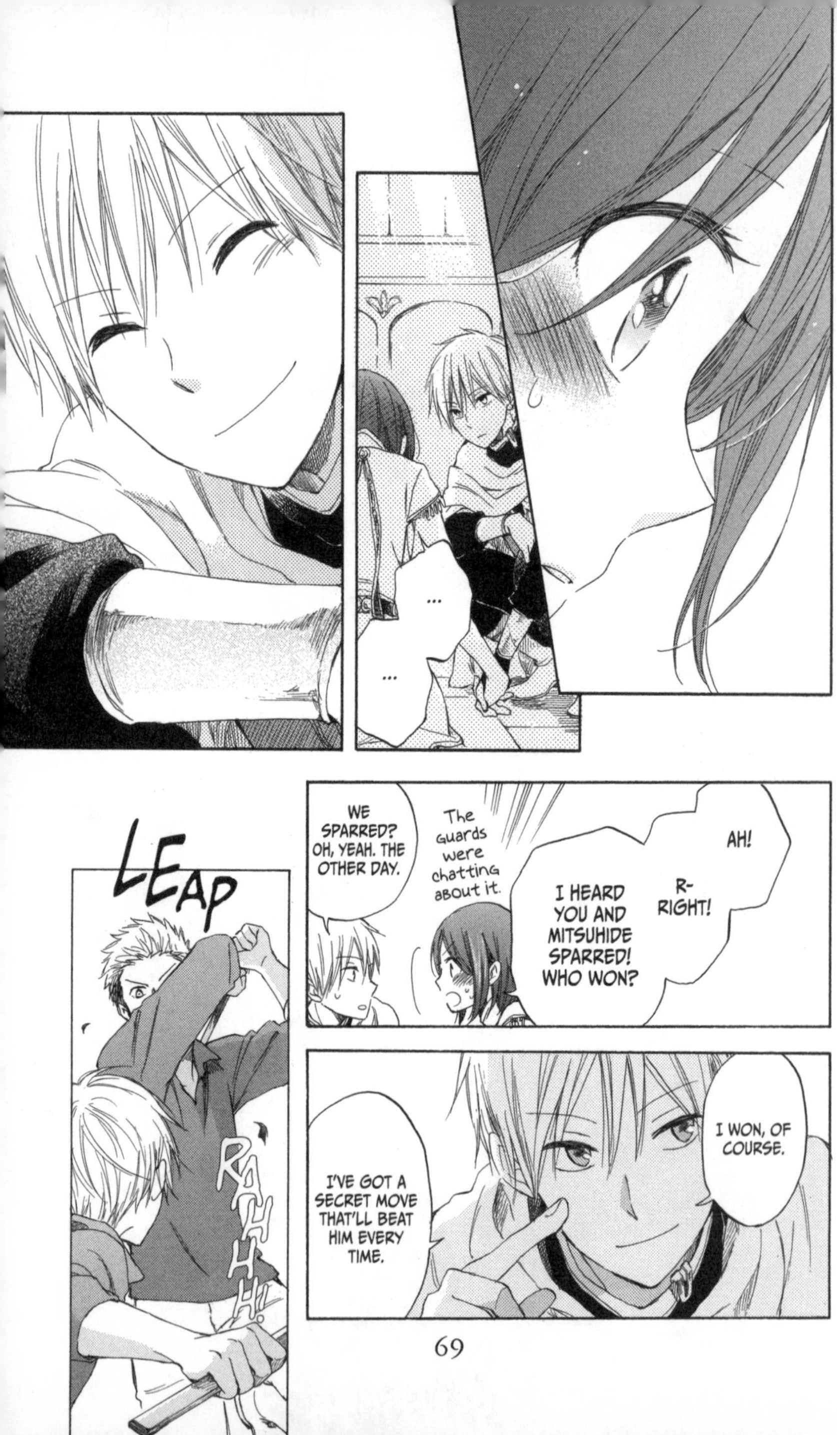
...
...
AH!
R- RIGHT!
I HEARD YOU AND MITSUHIDE SPARRED! WHO WON?
The Guards were chatting about it.
WE SPARRED? OH, YEAH. THE OTHER DAY.
I WON, OF COURSE.
I'VE GOT A SECRET MOVE THAT'LL BEAT HIM EVERY TIME.
LEAP
RAHHH!

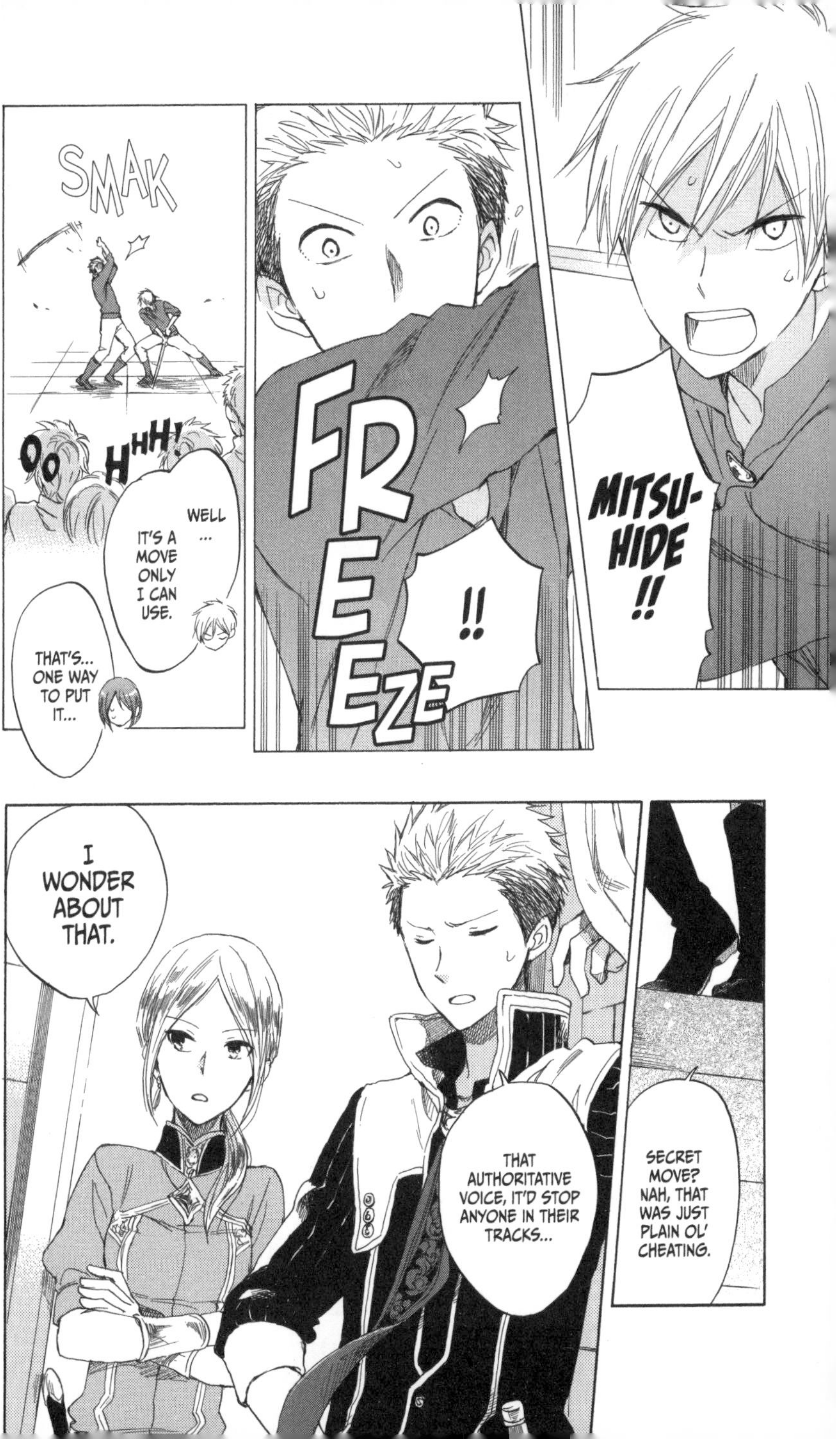
MITSU-HIDE!!
FREEZE
!!
SMAK
OOHHH!
WELL...
IT'S A MOVE ONLY I CAN USE.
THAT'S... ONE WAY TO PUT IT...
SECRET MOVE? NAH, THAT WAS JUST PLAIN OL' CHEATING.
THAT AUTHORITATIVE VOICE, IT'D STOP ANYONE IN THEIR TRACKS...
I WONDER ABOUT THAT.

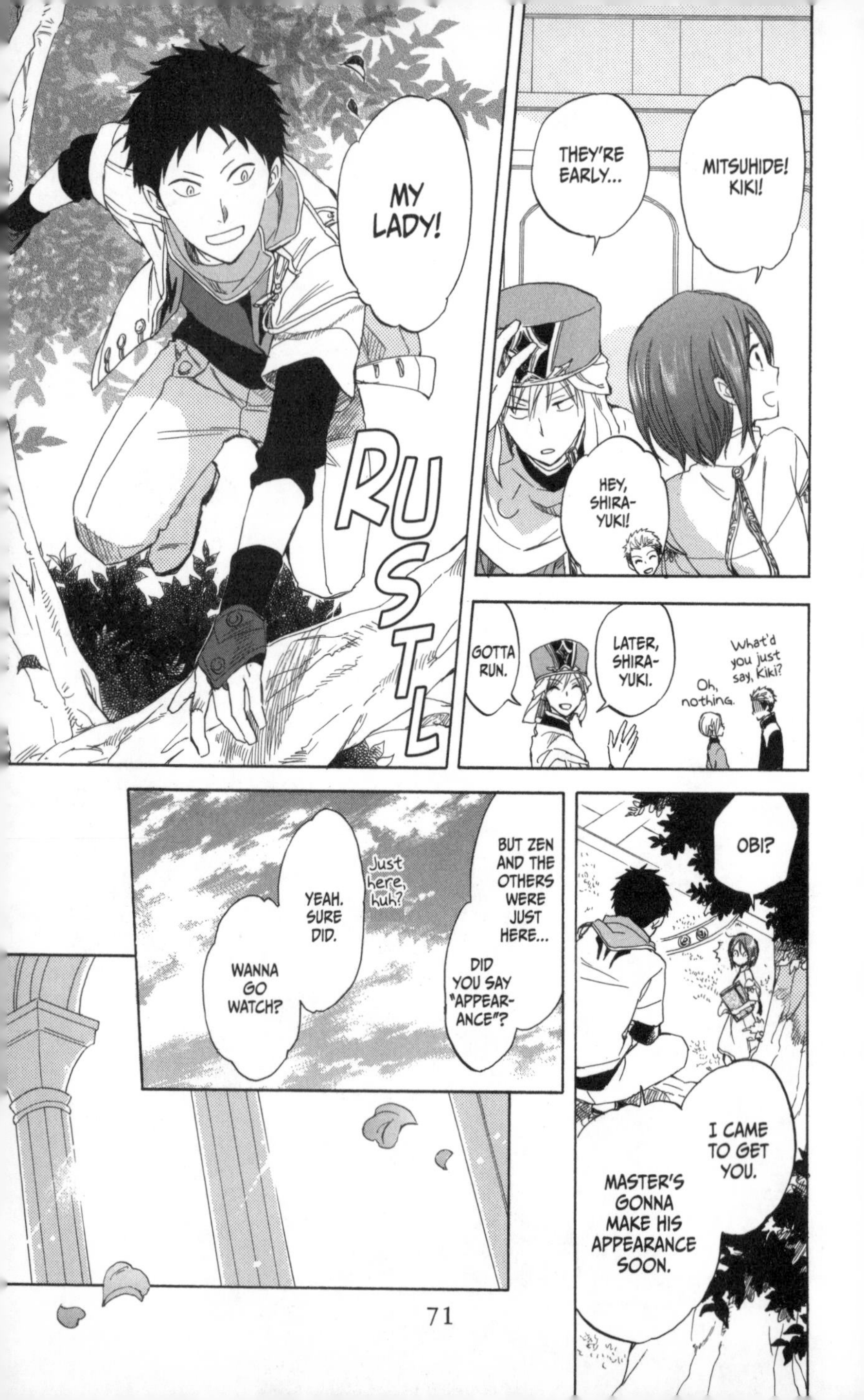
MITSUHIDE! KIKI!
THEY'RE EARLY...
HEY, SHIRA-YUKI!
LATER, SHIRA-YUKI.
GOTTA RUN.
What'd you just say, Kiki?
Oh, nothing.
MY LADY!
RUSTL
OBI?
I CAME TO GET YOU.
MASTER'S GONNA MAKE HIS APPEARANCE SOON.
BUT ZEN AND THE OTHERS WERE JUST HERE...
DID YOU SAY "APPEARANCE"?
Just here, huh?
YEAH. SURE DID.
WANNA GO WATCH?

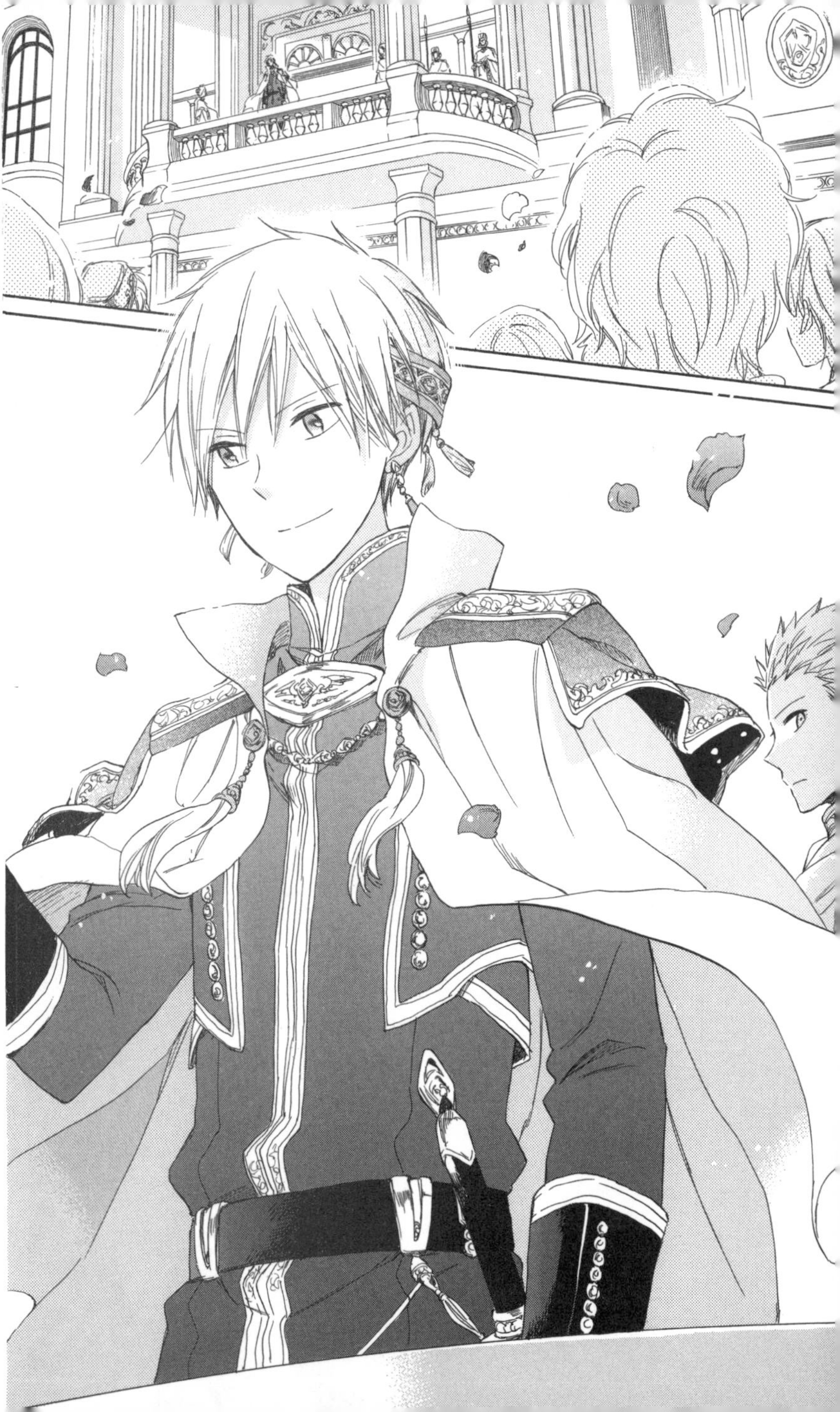

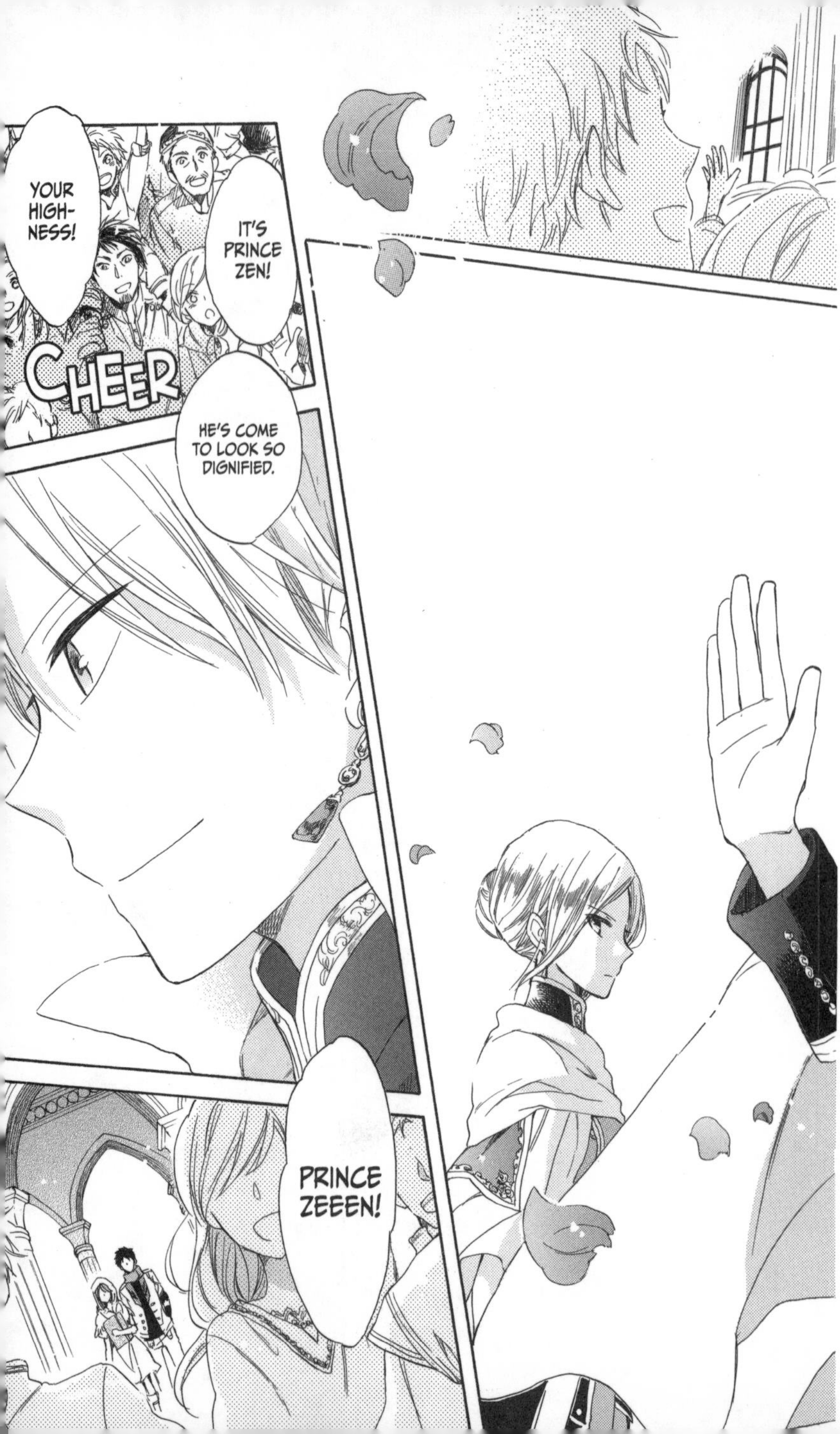
IT'S PRINCE ZEN!
YOUR HIGHNESS!
CHEER
HE'S COME TO LOOK SO DIGNIFIED.
PRINCE ZEEEN!

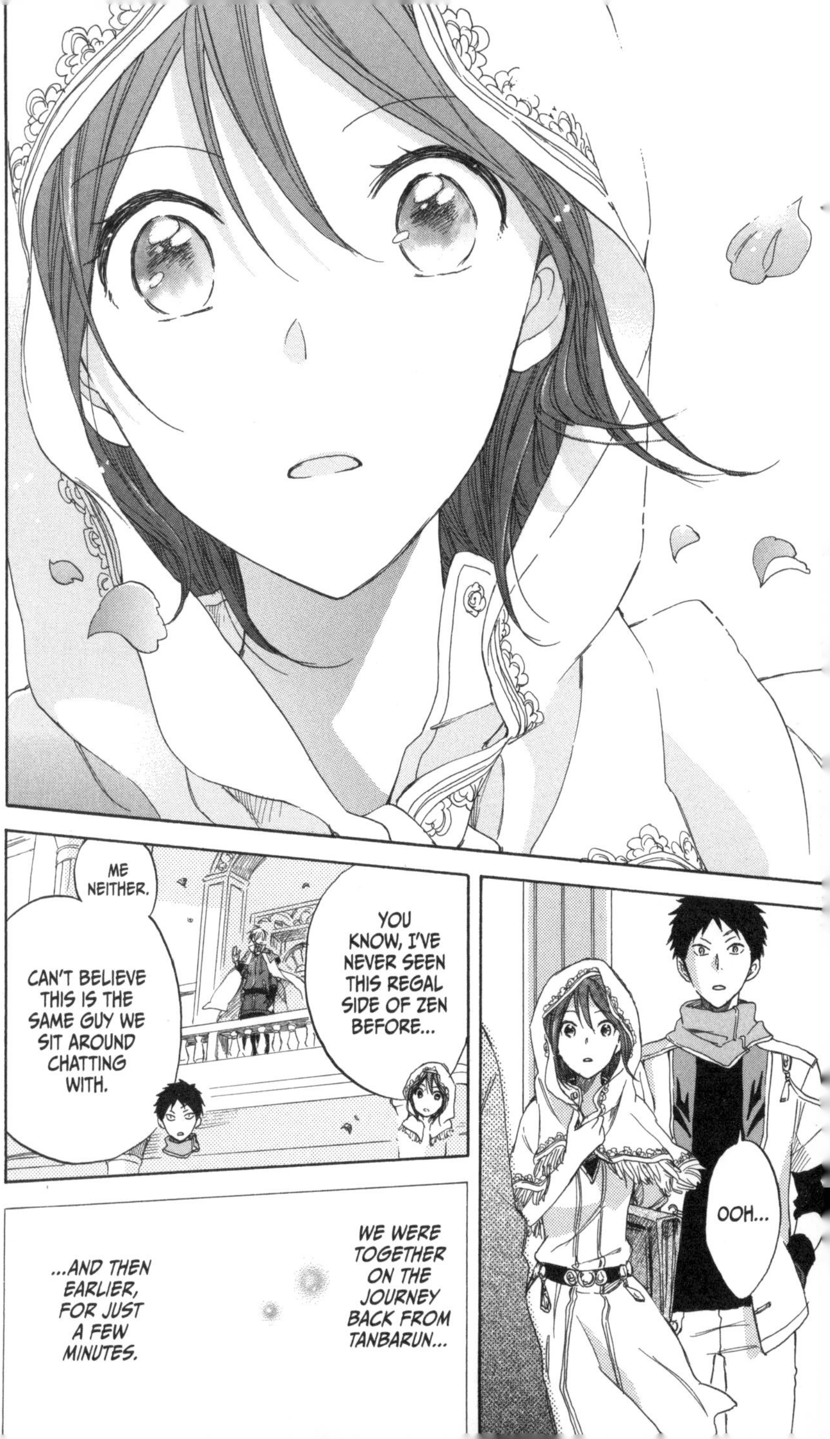
OOH...
YOU KNOW, I'VE NEVER SEEN THIS REGAL SIDE OF ZEN BEFORE...
ME NEITHER.
CAN'T BELIEVE THIS IS THE SAME GUY WE SIT AROUND CHATTING WITH.
WE WERE TOGETHER ON THE JOURNEY BACK FROM TANBARUN...
...AND THEN EARLIER, FOR JUST A FEW MINUTES.

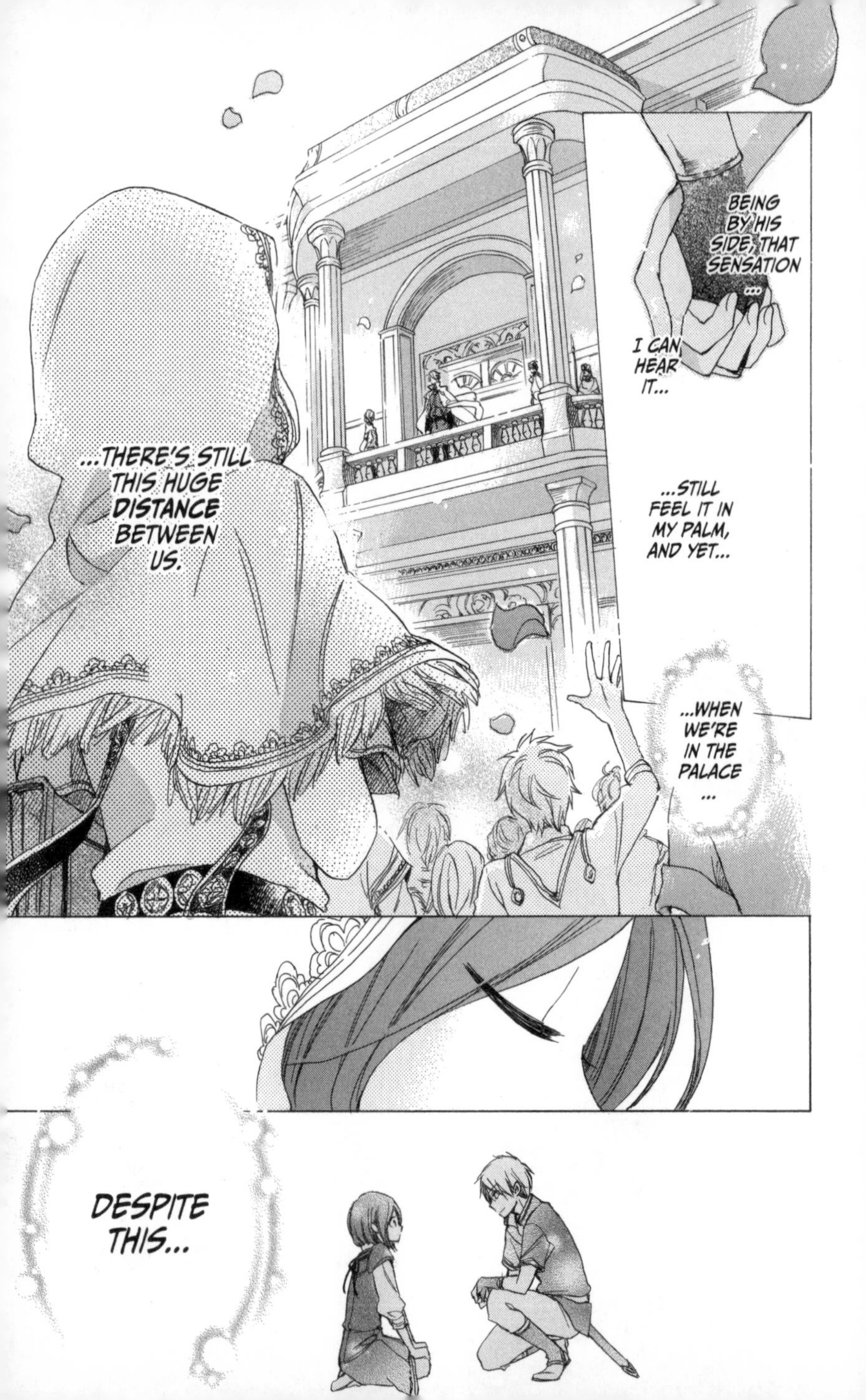
BEING BY HIS SIDE, THAT SENSATION ...
I CAN HEAR IT...
...STILL FEEL IT IN MY PALM, AND YET...
...WHEN WE'RE IN THE PALACE ...
...THERE'S STILL THIS HUGE DISTANCE BETWEEN US.
DESPITE THIS...

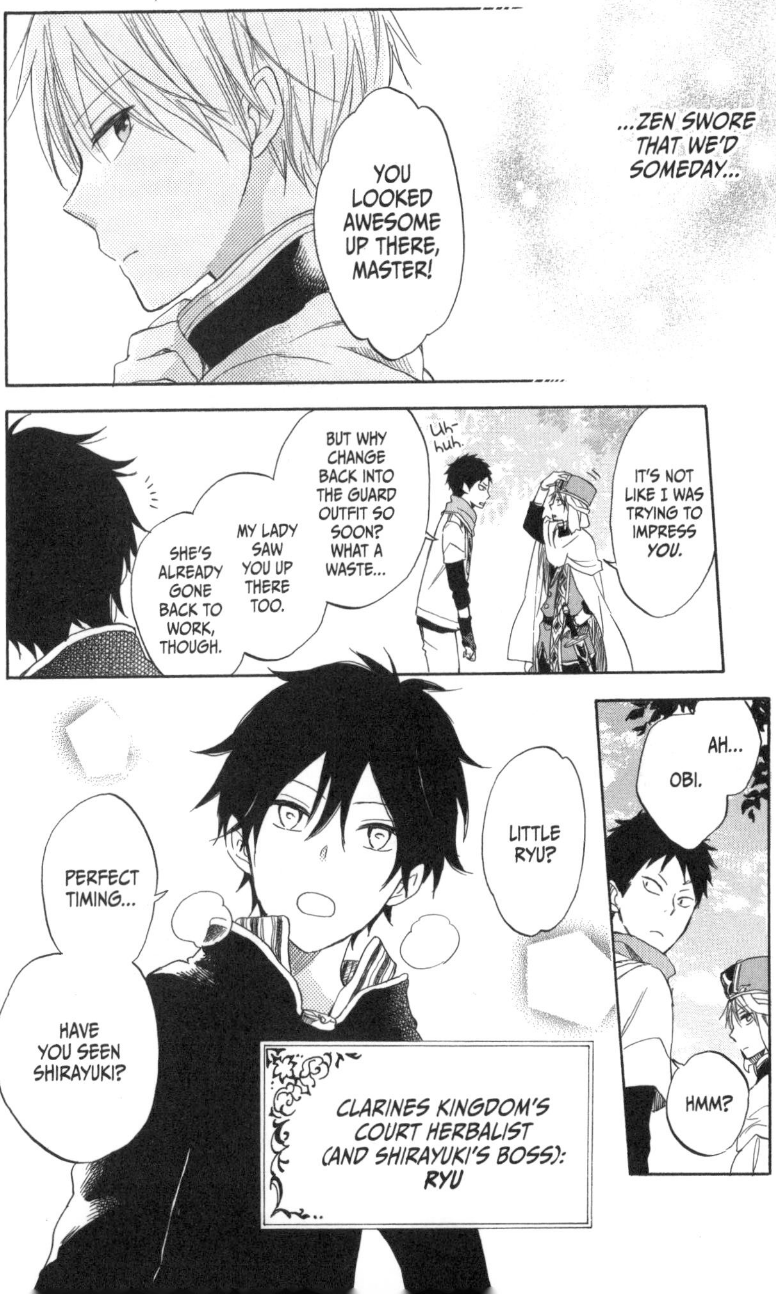
...ZEN SWORE THAT WE'D SOMEDAY...
YOU LOOKED AWESOME UP THERE, MASTER!
IT'S NOT LIKE I WAS TRYING TO IMPRESS *YOU.*
Uh-huh.
BUT WHY CHANGE BACK INTO THE GUARD OUTFIT SO SOON? WHAT A WASTE...
MY LADY SAW YOU UP THERE TOO.
SHE'S ALREADY GONE BACK TO WORK, THOUGH.
AH... OBI.
HMM?
LITTLE RYU?
PERFECT TIMING...
HAVE YOU SEEN SHIRAYUKI?
CLARINES KINGDOM'S COURT HERBALIST (AND SHIRAYUKI'S BOSS): RYU

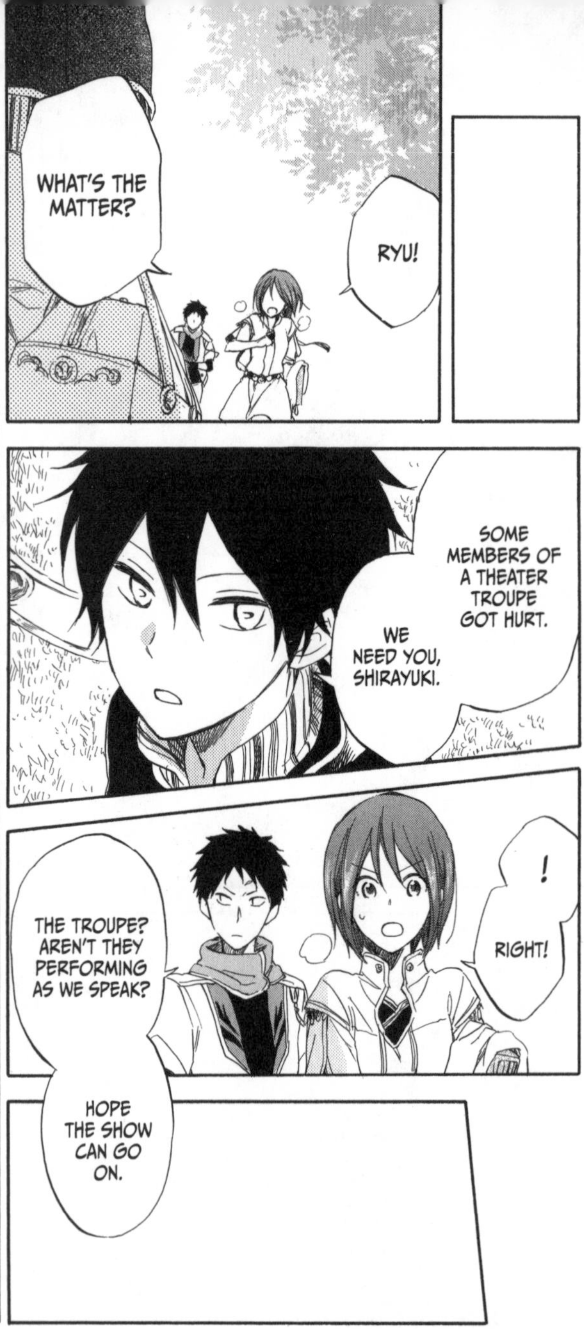
RYU!
WHAT'S THE MATTER?
SOME MEMBERS OF A THEATER TROUPE GOT HURT.
WE NEED YOU, SHIRAYUKI.
!
RIGHT!
THE TROUPE? AREN'T THEY PERFORMING AS WE SPEAK?
HOPE THE SHOW CAN GO ON.

5

With spoilers? Maybe?

CHAPTER 26

The resolution to the Tanbarun arc.

I wanted to fit the whole arc in a single volume, but alas... Even the pirates weren't ready for that!

While I was drawing the second banquet scene, my mother and older sister saw Kiki standing there without a fancy dress and said...

"WHAT THE HECK?!"

...at the same time (it was scary), so I gave Kiki a costume change.

Looking back, her dress isn't too different from her normal clothes...

I wonder if I'll ever really dress her up. Would you even want to wear fancy clothes, Kiki...?

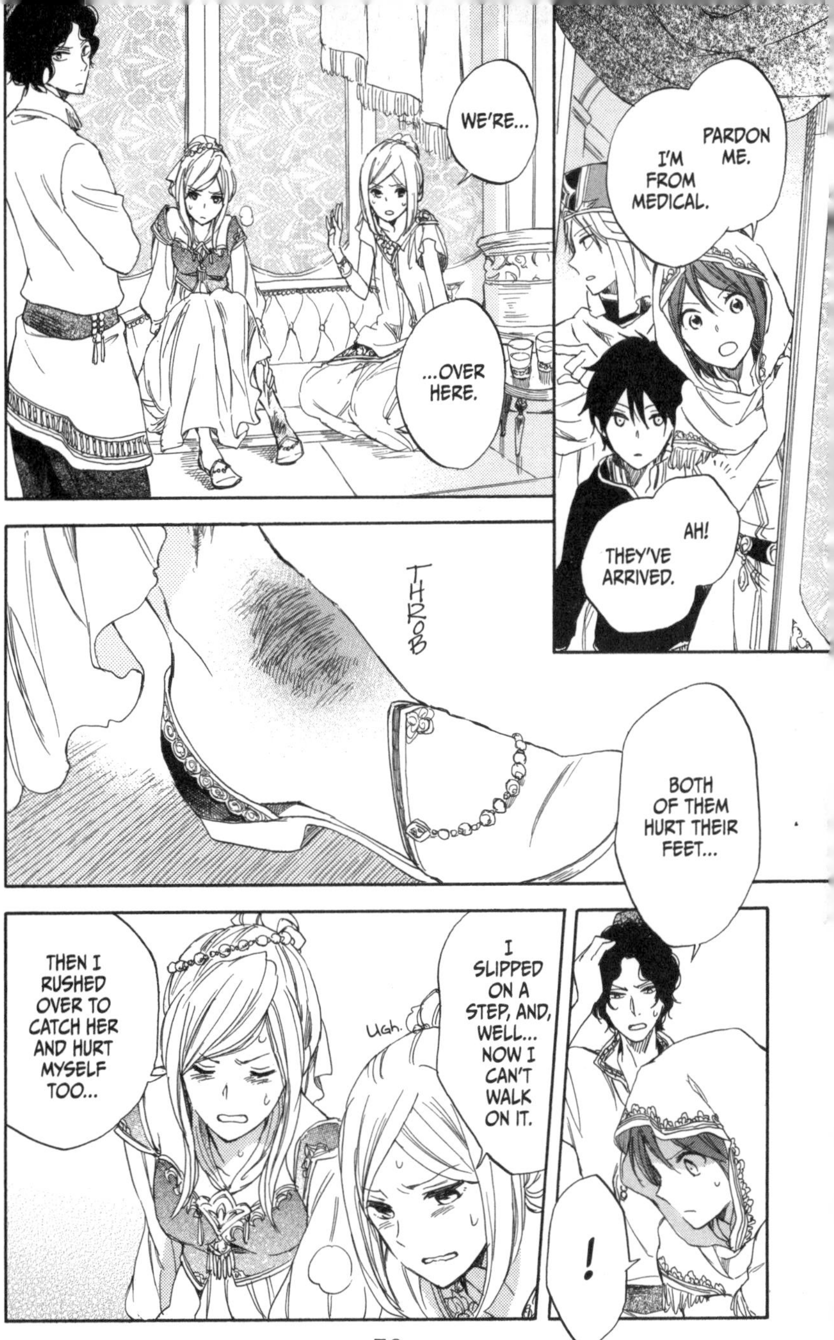
PARDON ME.
I'M FROM MEDICAL.
AH! THEY'VE ARRIVED.
WE'RE...
...OVER HERE.
THROB
BOTH OF THEM HURT THEIR FEET...
!
I SLIPPED ON A STEP, AND, WELL... NOW I CAN'T WALK ON IT.
Ugh.
THEN I RUSHED OVER TO CATCH HER AND HURT MYSELF TOO...

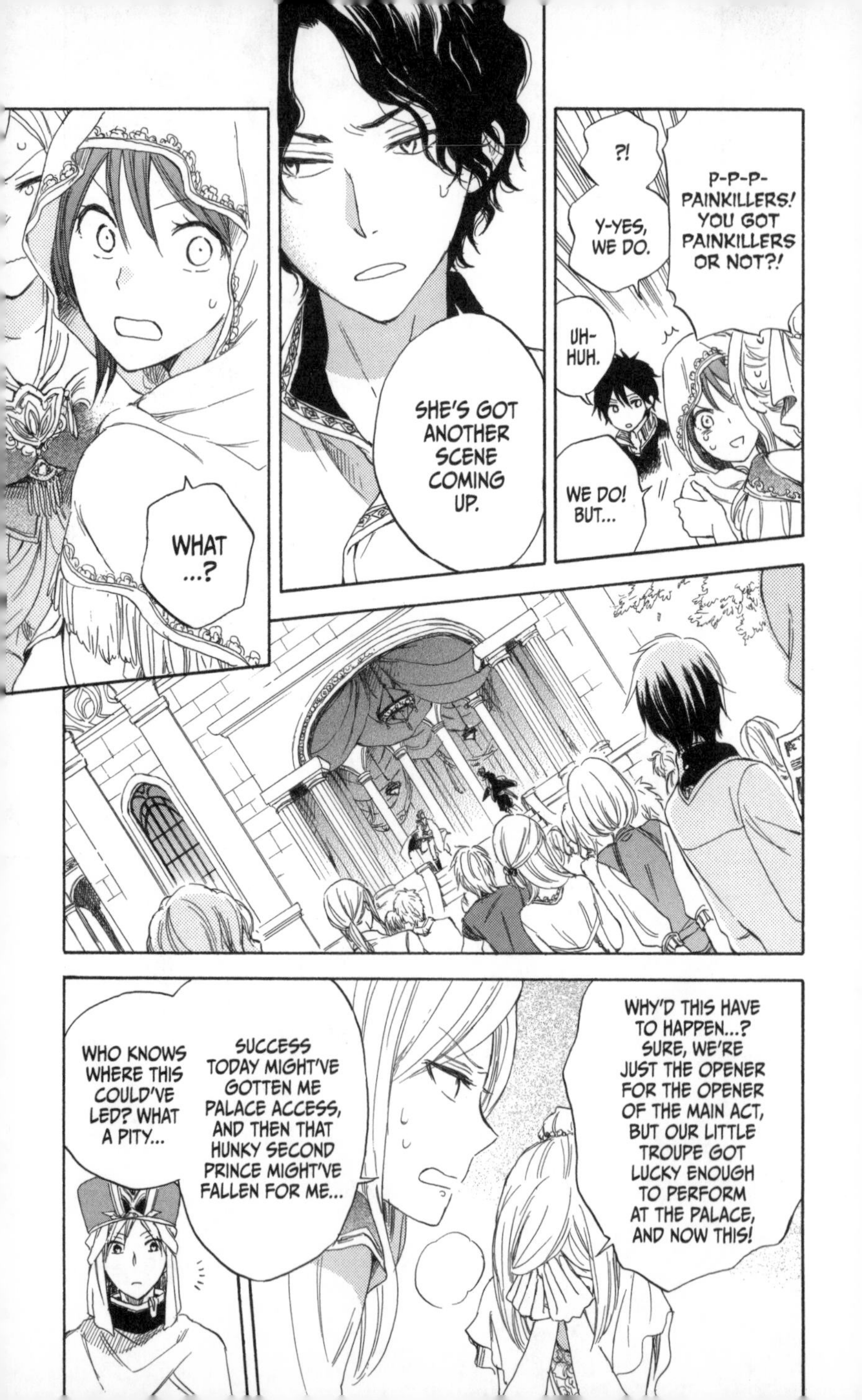
P-P-P-PAINKILLERS! YOU GOT PAINKILLERS OR NOT?!
?!
Y-YES, WE DO.
UH-HUH.
WE DO! BUT...
SHE'S GOT ANOTHER SCENE COMING UP.
WHAT ...?
WHY'D THIS HAVE TO HAPPEN...? SURE, WE'RE JUST THE OPENER FOR THE OPENER OF THE MAIN ACT, BUT OUR LITTLE TROUPE GOT LUCKY ENOUGH TO PERFORM AT THE PALACE, AND NOW THIS!
SUCCESS TODAY MIGHT'VE GOTTEN ME PALACE ACCESS, AND THEN THAT HUNKY SECOND PRINCE MIGHT'VE FALLEN FOR ME...
WHO KNOWS WHERE THIS COULD'VE LED? WHAT A PITY...

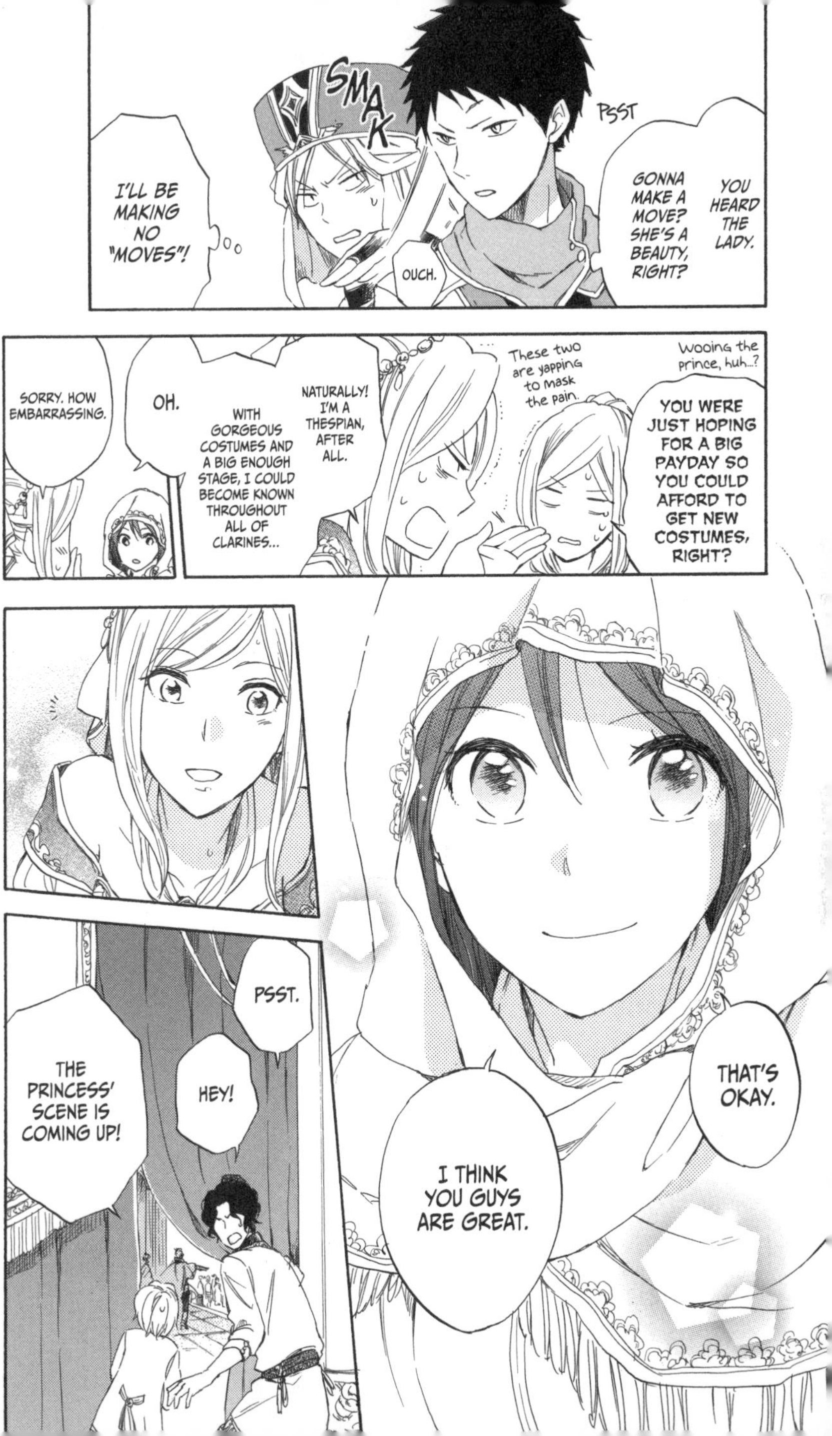
PSST
YOU HEARD THE LADY.
GONNA MAKE A MOVE? SHE'S A BEAUTY, RIGHT?
SMAK
OUCH.
I'LL BE MAKING NO "MOVES"!
Wooing the prince, huh...?
YOU WERE JUST HOPING FOR A BIG PAYDAY SO YOU COULD AFFORD TO GET NEW COSTUMES, RIGHT?
These two are yapping to mask the pain.
NATURALLY! I'M A THESPIAN, AFTER ALL.
WITH GORGEOUS COSTUMES AND A BIG ENOUGH STAGE, I COULD BECOME KNOWN THROUGHOUT ALL OF CLARINES...
OH.
SORRY. HOW EMBARRASSING.
THAT'S OKAY.
I THINK YOU GUYS ARE GREAT.
PSST.
HEY!
THE PRINCESS' SCENE IS COMING UP!

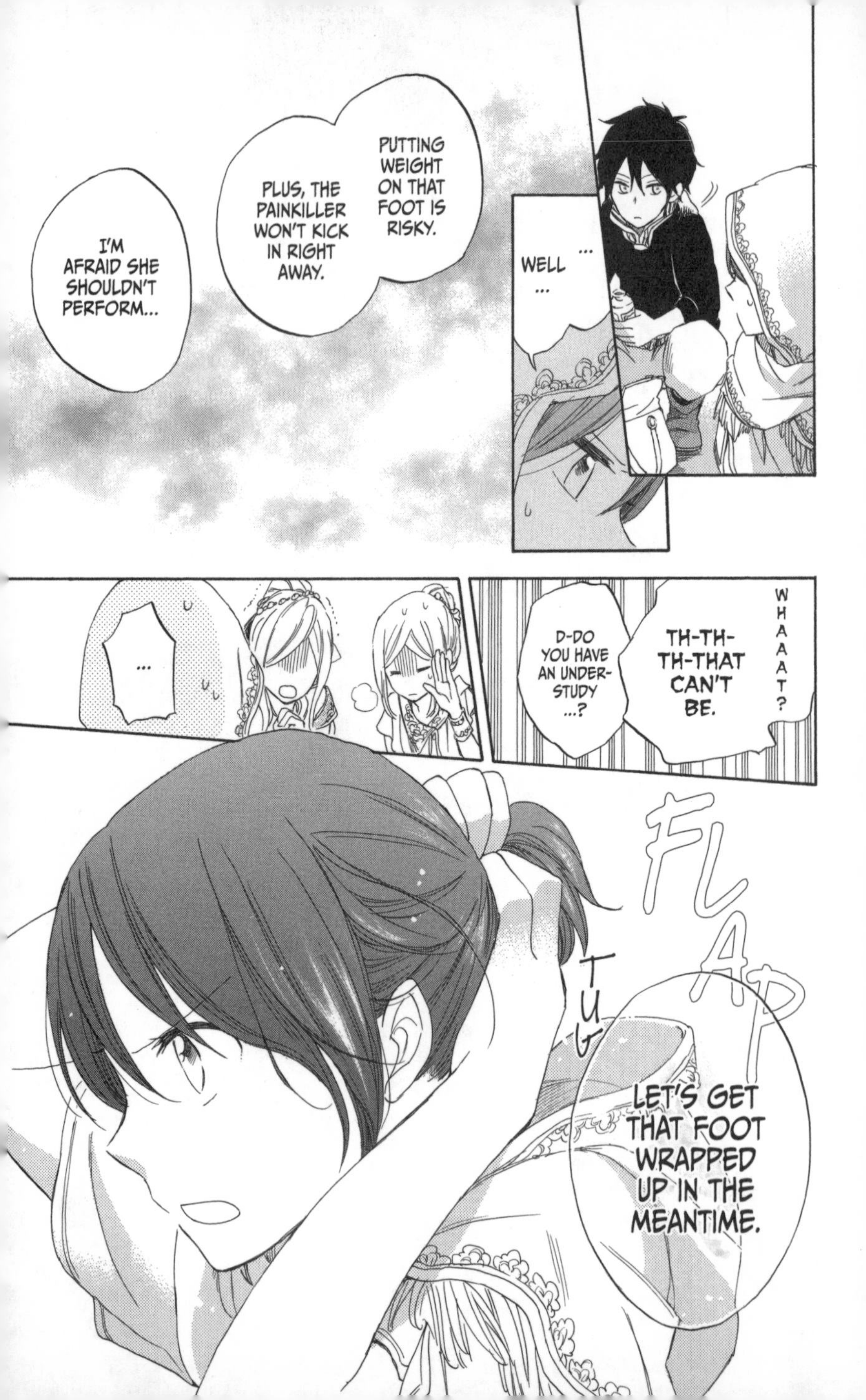
...WELL...
PUTTING WEIGHT ON THAT FOOT IS RISKY.
PLUS, THE PAINKILLER WON'T KICK IN RIGHT AWAY.
I'M AFRAID SHE SHOULDN'T PERFORM...
WHAAAT?
TH-TH-TH-THAT CAN'T BE.
D-DO YOU HAVE AN UNDER-STUDY ...?
...
FLAP
TUG
LET'S GET THAT FOOT WRAPPED UP IN THE MEANTIME.

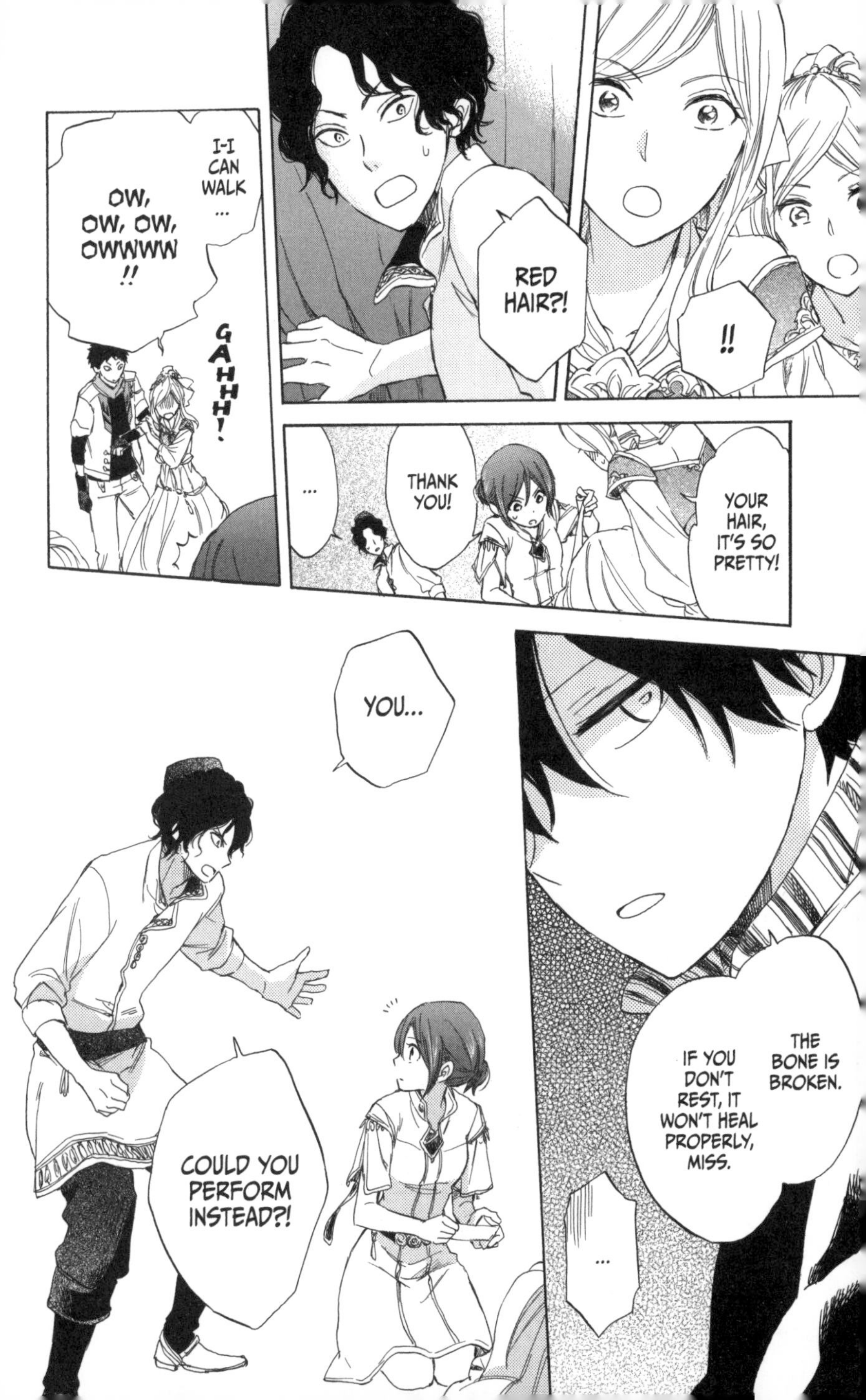
!!
RED HAIR?!
YOUR HAIR, IT'S SO PRETTY!
THANK YOU!
...
I-I CAN WALK ...
OW, OW, OW, OWWWW!!
GAHHH!
THE BONE IS BROKEN.
IF YOU DON'T REST, IT WON'T HEAL PROPERLY, MISS.
...
YOU...
COULD YOU PERFORM INSTEAD?!

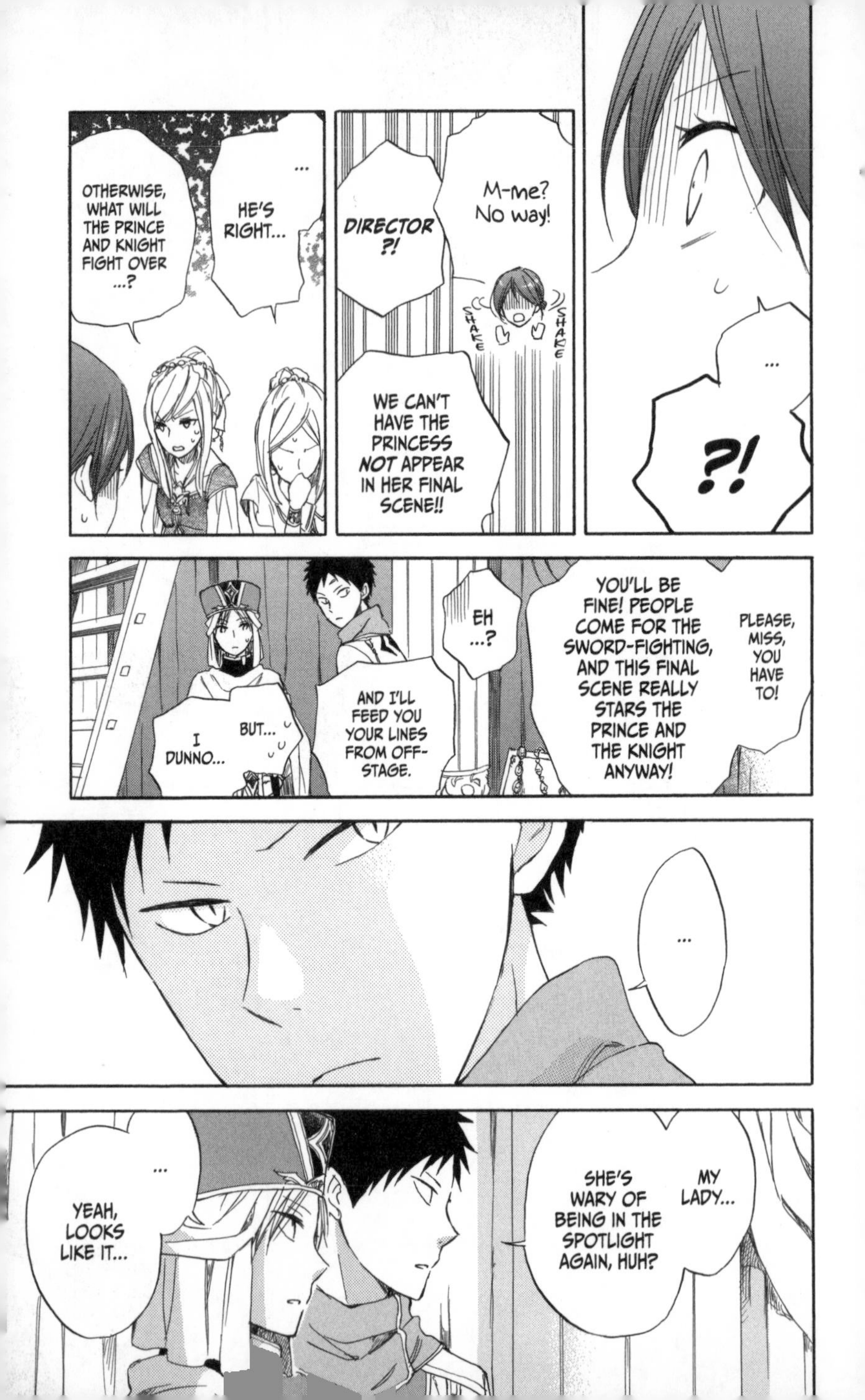
...
?!
M-me? No way!
DIRECTOR?!
SHAKE
SHAKE
WE CAN'T HAVE THE PRINCESS NOT APPEAR IN HER FINAL SCENE!!
...
HE'S RIGHT...
OTHERWISE, WHAT WILL THE PRINCE AND KNIGHT FIGHT OVER...?
PLEASE, MISS, YOU HAVE TO!
YOU'LL BE FINE! PEOPLE COME FOR THE SWORD-FIGHTING, AND THIS FINAL SCENE REALLY STARS THE PRINCE AND THE KNIGHT ANYWAY!
EH...?
AND I'LL FEED YOU YOUR LINES FROM OFF-STAGE.
BUT...
I DUNNO...
...
MY LADY...
SHE'S WARY OF BEING IN THE SPOTLIGHT AGAIN, HUH?
...
YEAH, LOOKS LIKE IT...

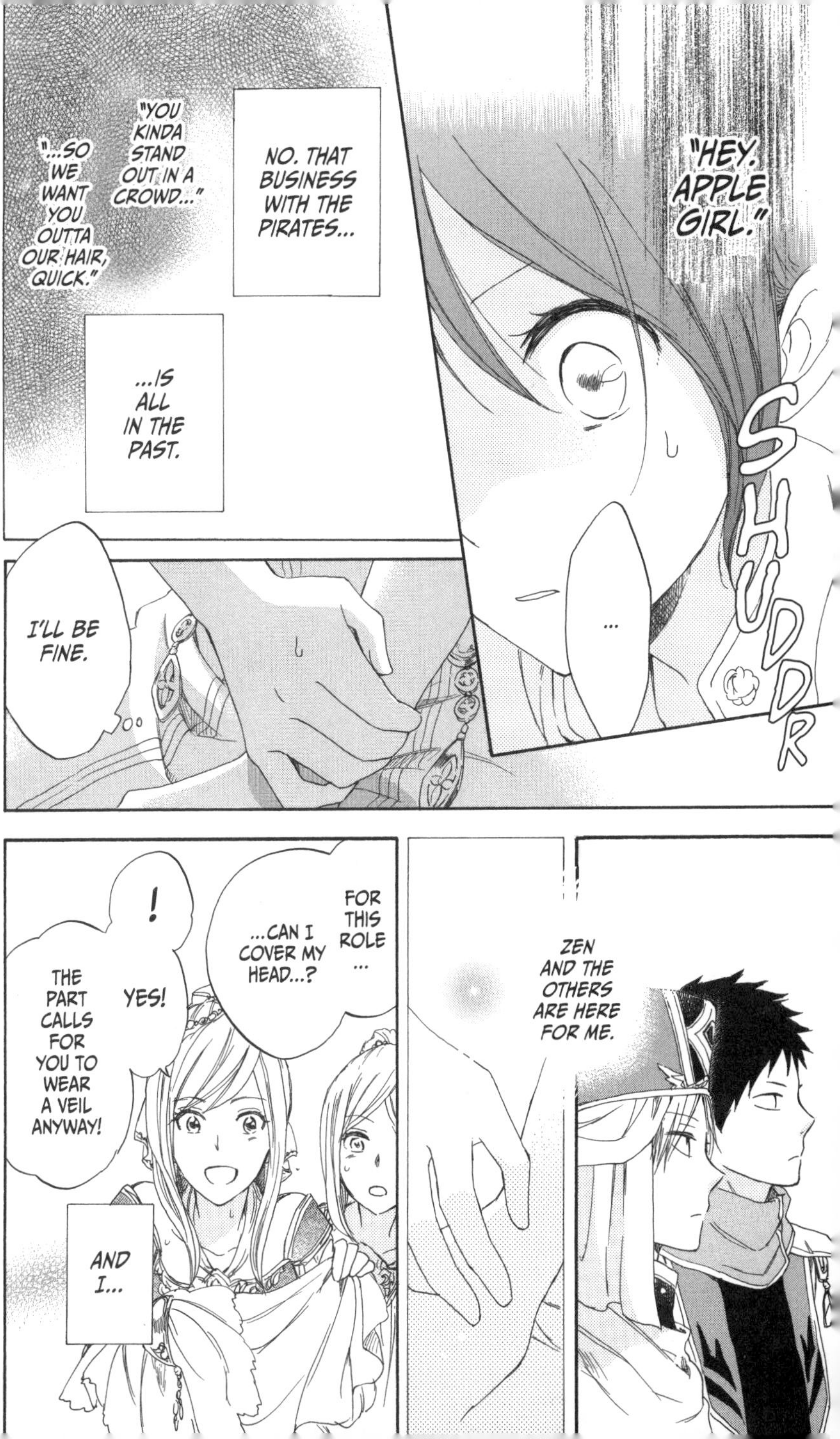
"HEY. APPLE GIRL."
SHUDDR
...
NO. THAT BUSINESS WITH THE PIRATES...
"YOU KINDA STAND OUT IN A CROWD..."
"...SO WE WANT YOU OUTTA OUR HAIR, QUICK."
...IS ALL IN THE PAST.
I'LL BE FINE.
ZEN AND THE OTHERS ARE HERE FOR ME.
FOR THIS ROLE...
...CAN I COVER MY HEAD...?
!
YES!
THE PART CALLS FOR YOU TO WEAR A VEIL ANYWAY!
AND I...

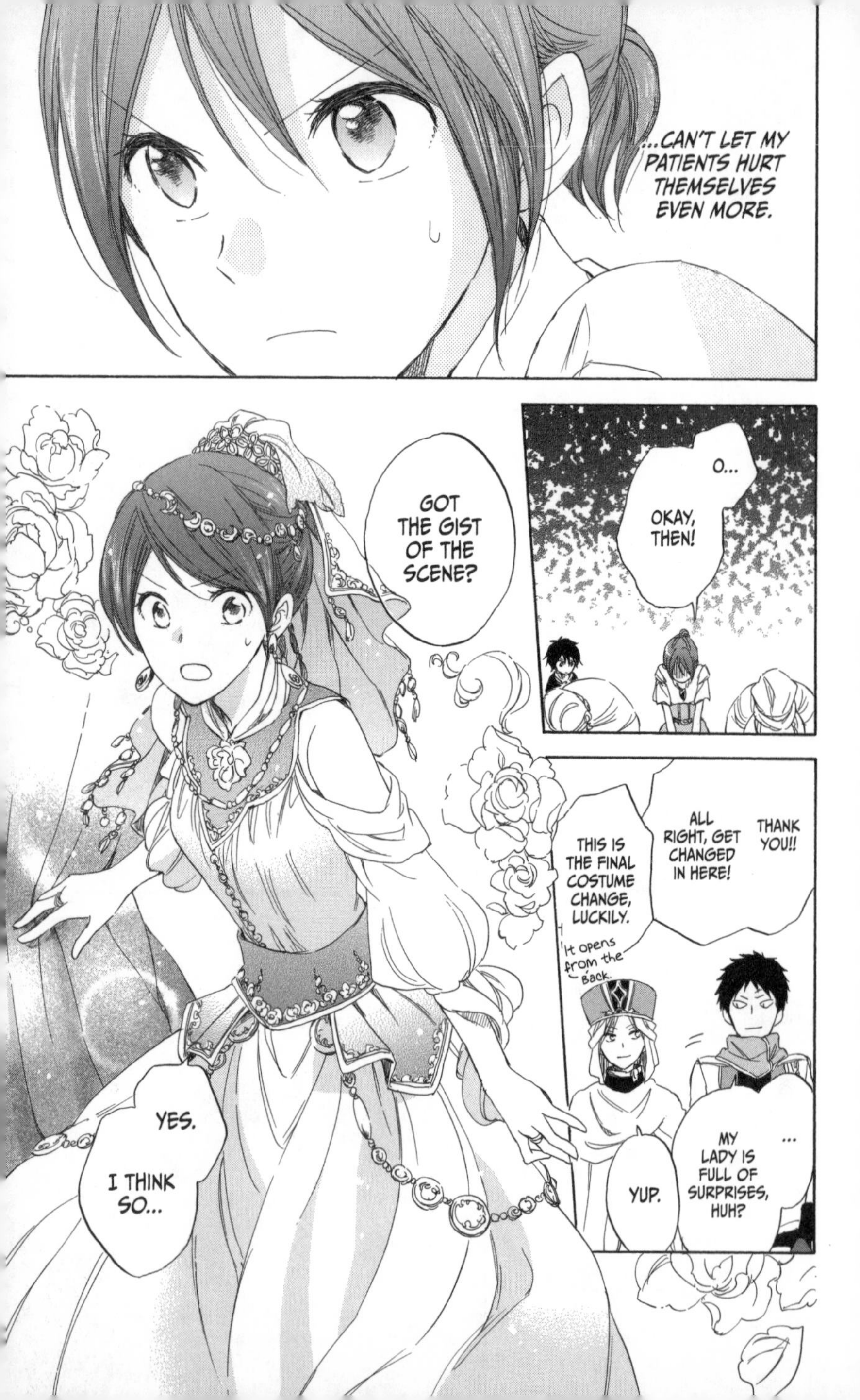
...CAN'T LET MY PATIENTS HURT THEMSELVES EVEN MORE.
O...
OKAY, THEN!
THANK YOU!!
ALL RIGHT, GET CHANGED IN HERE!
THIS IS THE FINAL COSTUME CHANGE, LUCKILY.
It opens from the back.
...
MY LADY IS FULL OF SURPRISES, HUH?
YUP.
GOT THE GIST OF THE SCENE?
YES.
I THINK SO...

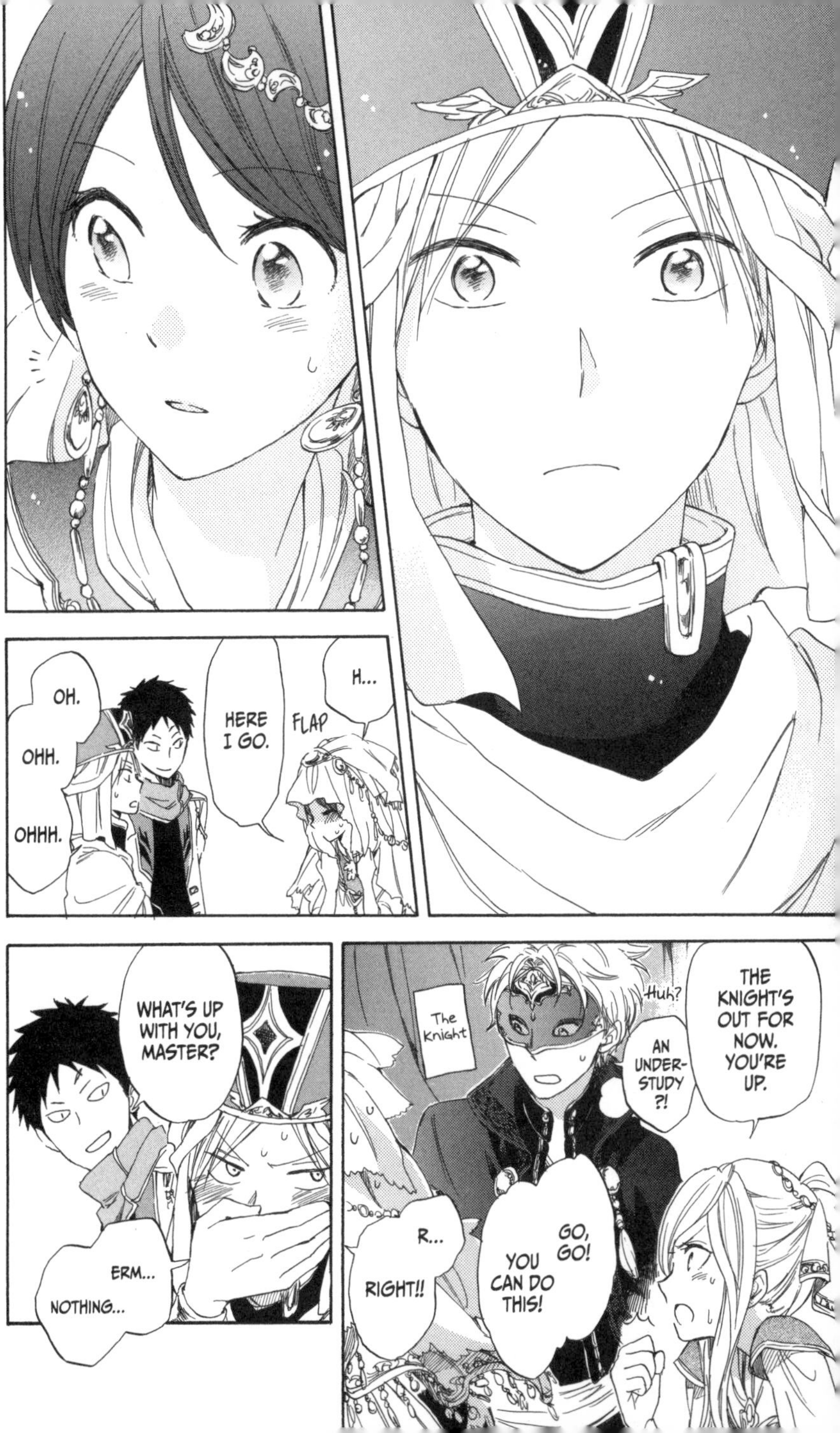
H...
FLAP
HERE I GO.
OH.
OHH.
OHHH.
THE KNIGHT'S OUT FOR NOW. YOU'RE UP.
Huh?
AN UNDER-STUDY?!
The Knight
GO, GO!
YOU CAN DO THIS!
R...
RIGHT!!
WHAT'S UP WITH YOU, MASTER?
ERM...
NOTHING...

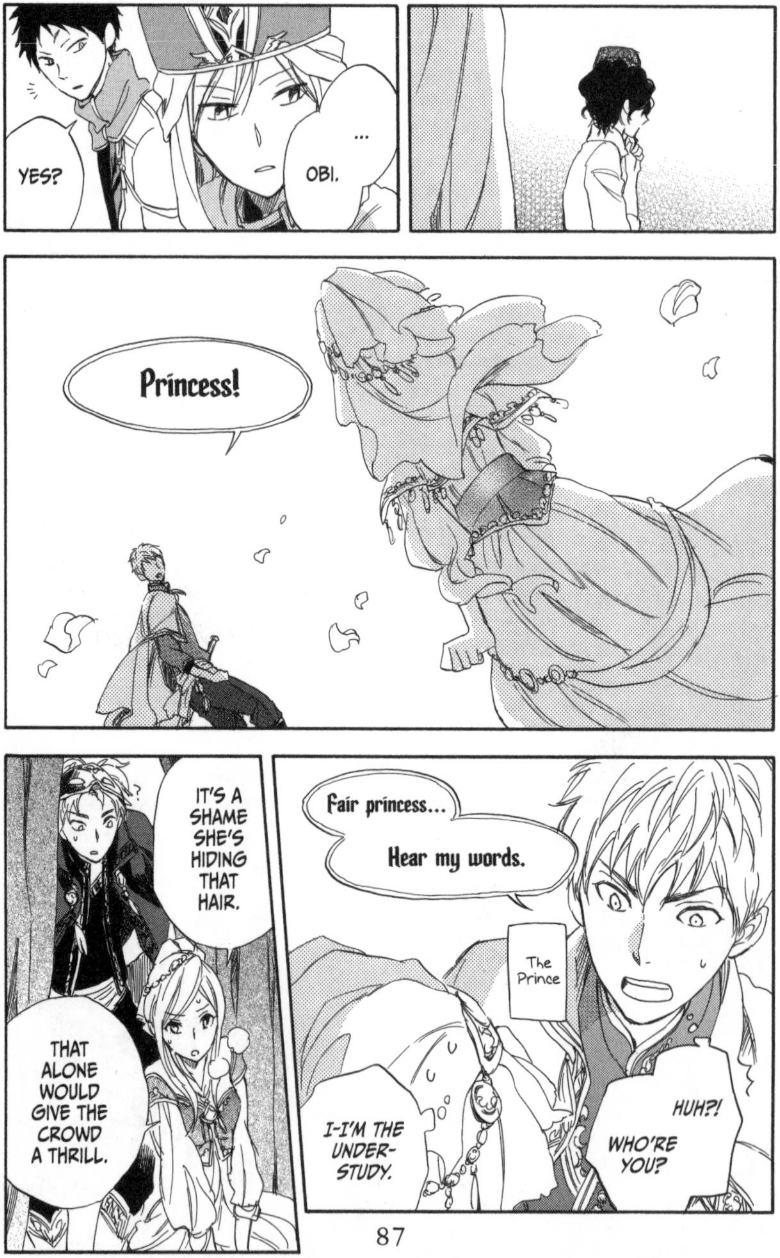
...
OBI.
YES?
Princess!
Fair princess...
Hear my words.
The Prince
HUH?!
WHO'RE YOU?
I-I'M THE UNDER-STUDY.
IT'S A SHAME SHE'S HIDING THAT HAIR.
THAT ALONE WOULD GIVE THE CROWD A THRILL.

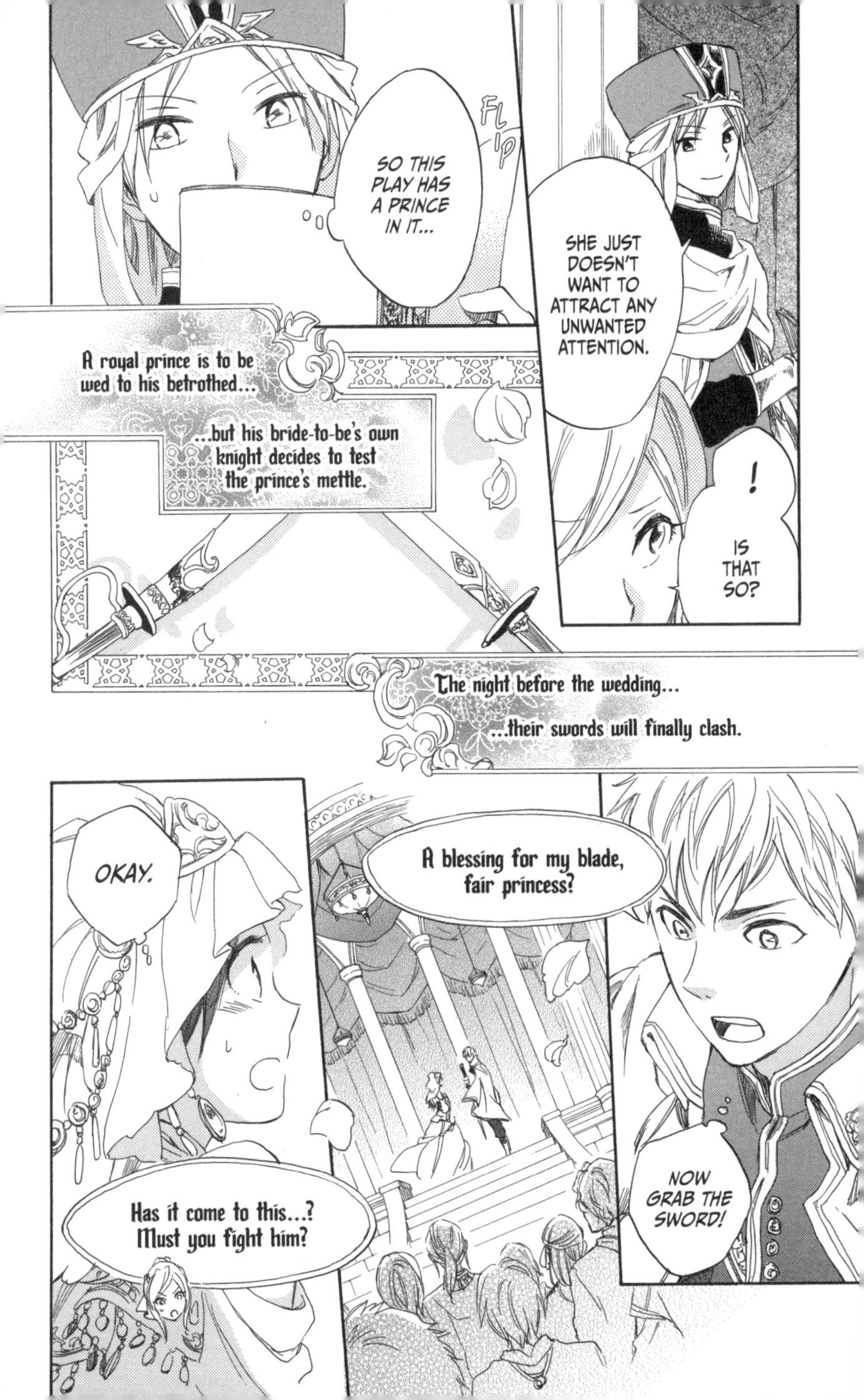
SHE JUST DOESN'T WANT TO ATTRACT ANY UNWANTED ATTENTION.
!
IS THAT SO?
FLIP
SO THIS PLAY HAS A PRINCE IN IT...
A royal prince is to be wed to his betrothed...
...but his bride-to-be's own knight decides to test the prince's mettle.
The night before the wedding...
...their swords will finally clash.
NOW GRAB THE SWORD!
A blessing for my blade, fair princess?
OKAY.
Has it come to this...? Must you fight him?

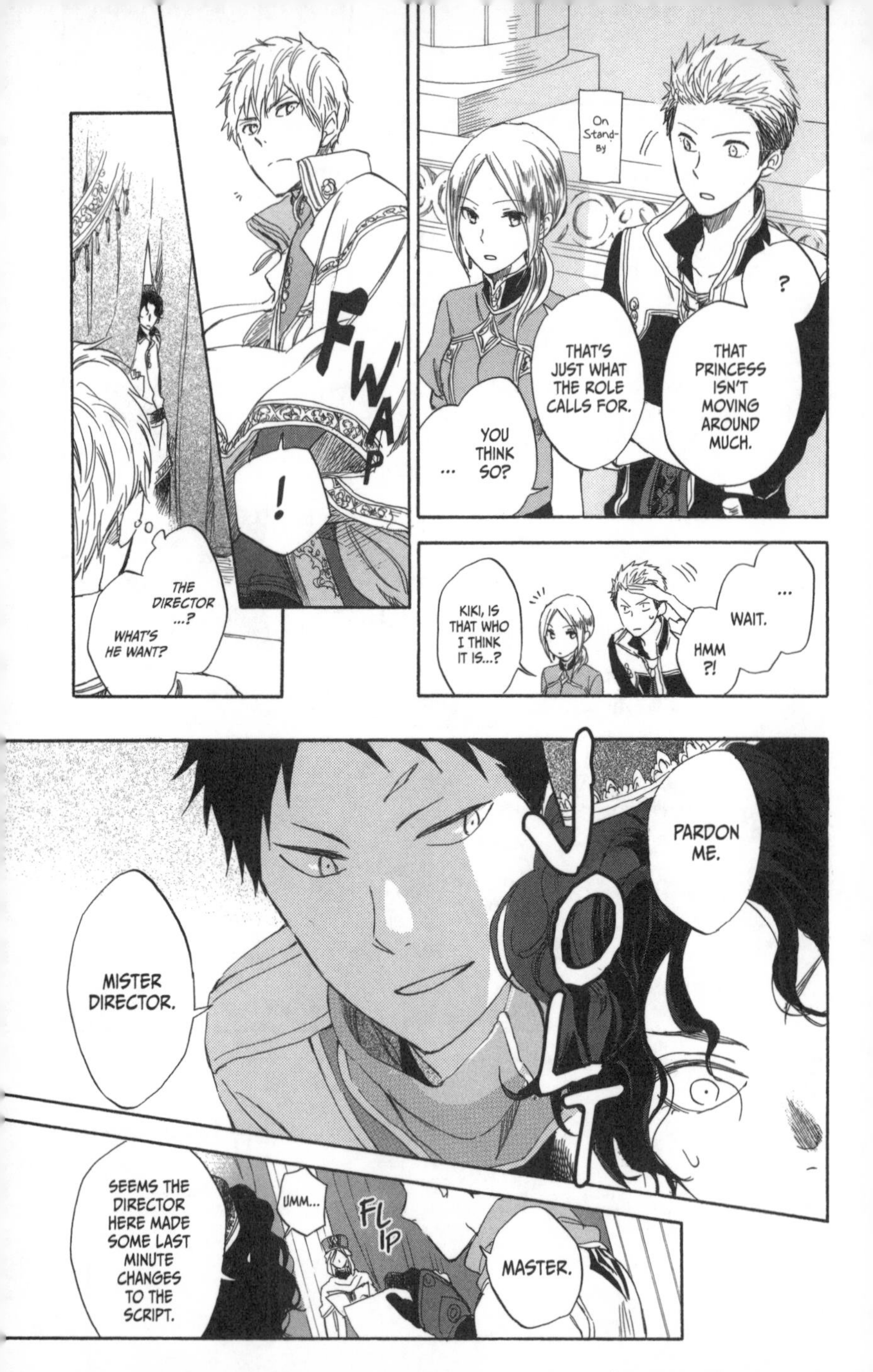

On Stand-By
?
THAT PRINCESS ISN'T MOVING AROUND MUCH.
THAT'S JUST WHAT THE ROLE CALLS FOR.
... YOU THINK SO?
... WAIT.
HMM ?!
KIKI, IS THAT WHO I THINK IT IS...?
FWAP
!
THE DIRECTOR ...? WHAT'S HE WANT?
PARDON ME.
VOLT
MISTER DIRECTOR.
MASTER.
FLIP
UMM...
SEEMS THE DIRECTOR HERE MADE SOME LAST MINUTE CHANGES TO THE SCRIPT.

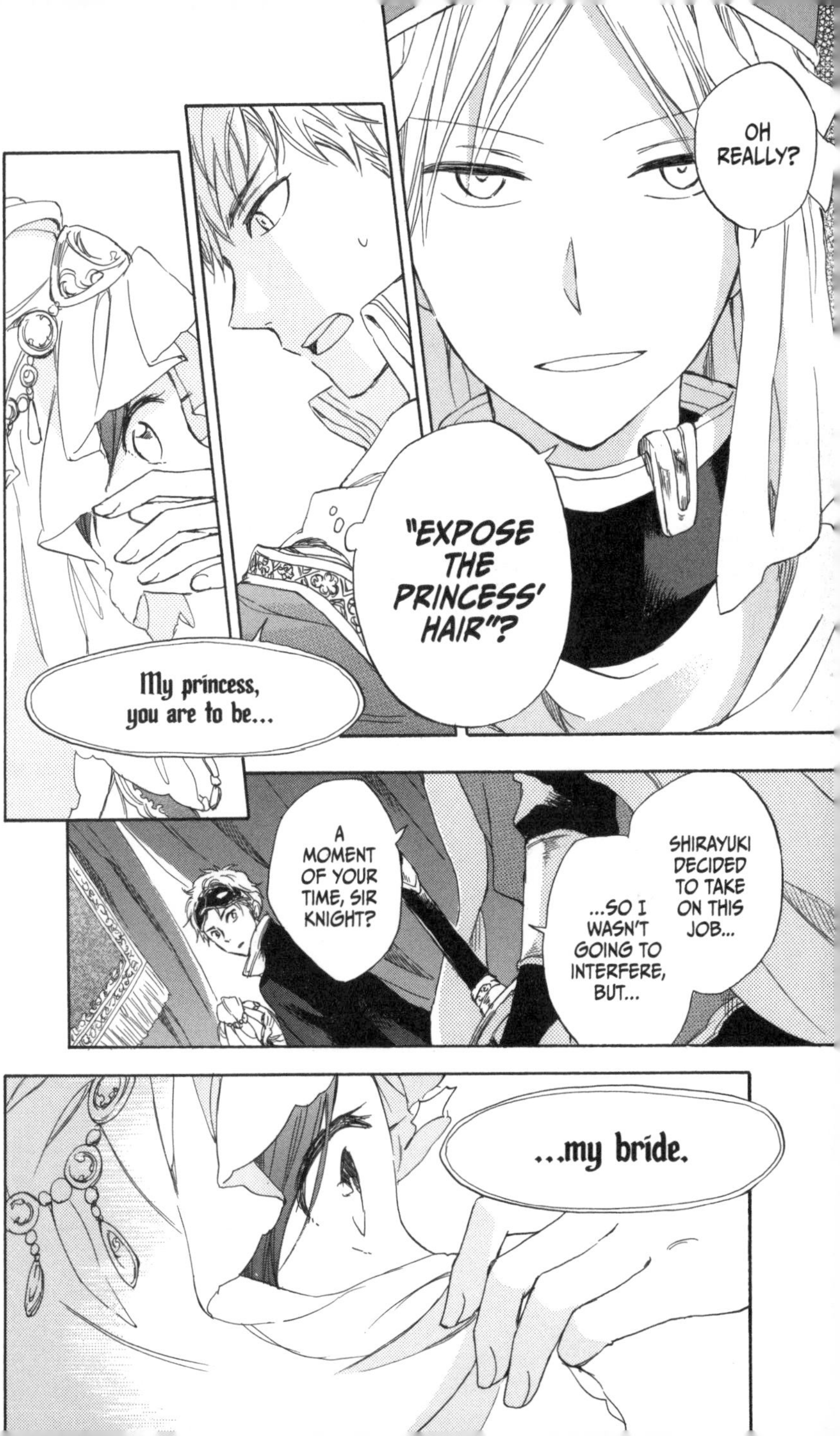
OH REALLY?
"EXPOSE THE PRINCESS' HAIR"?
My princess, you are to be...
SHIRAYUKI DECIDED TO TAKE ON THIS JOB...
...SO I WASN'T GOING TO INTERFERE, BUT...
A MOMENT OF YOUR TIME, SIR KNIGHT?
...my bride.

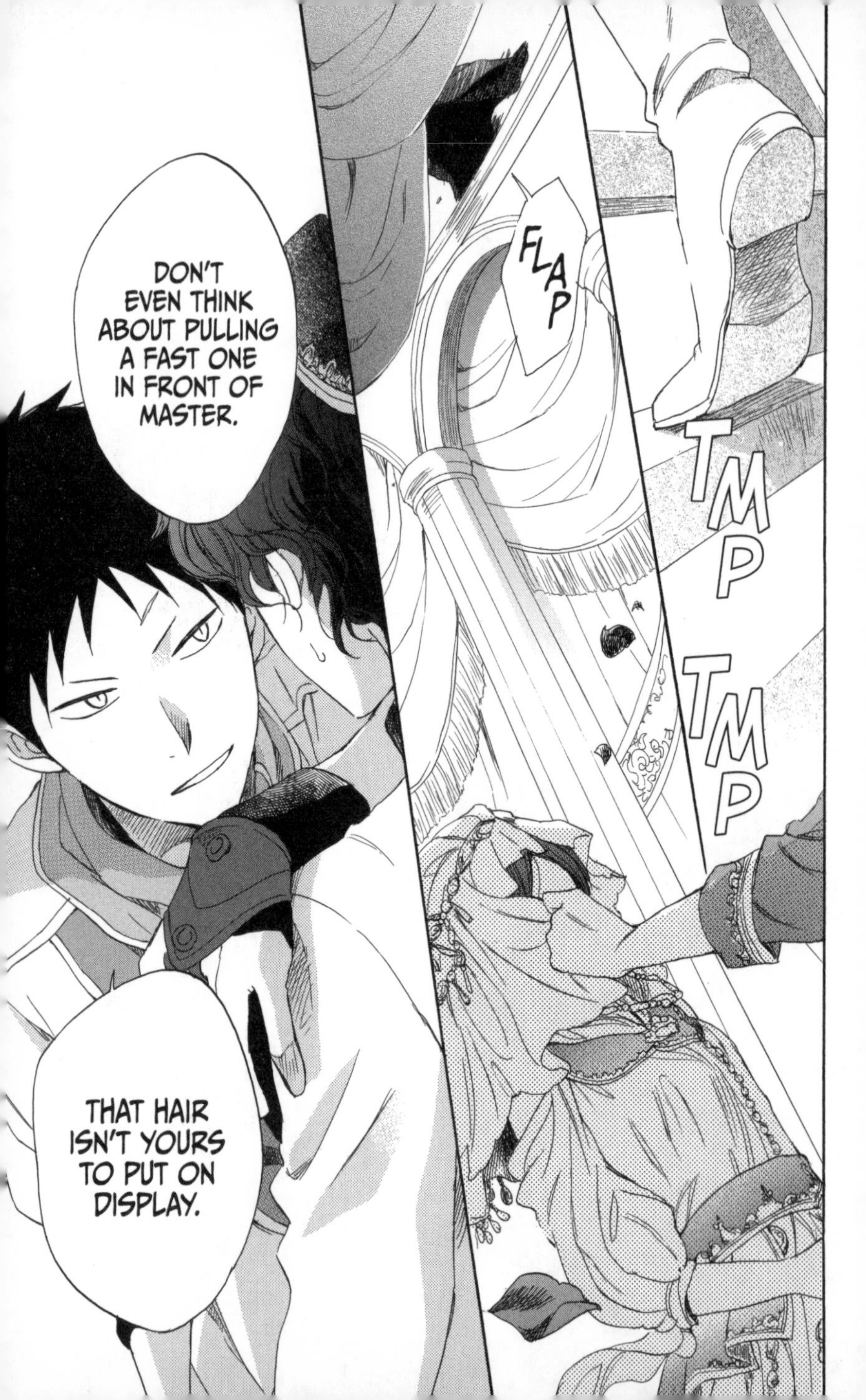
TMP
TMP
FLAP
DON'T EVEN THINK ABOUT PULLING A FAST ONE IN FRONT OF MASTER.
THAT HAIR ISN'T YOURS TO PUT ON DISPLAY.

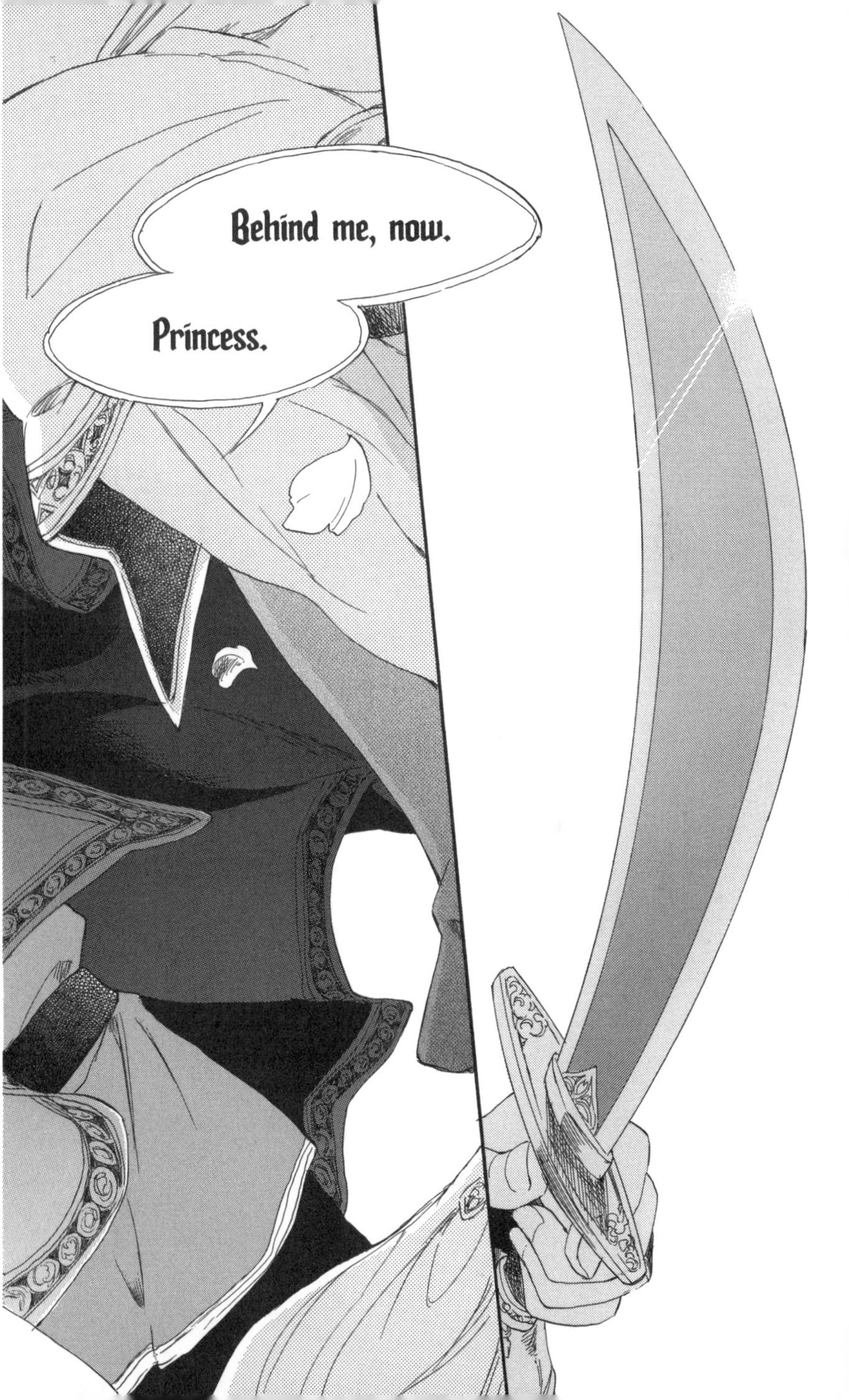
Behind me, now.
Princess.

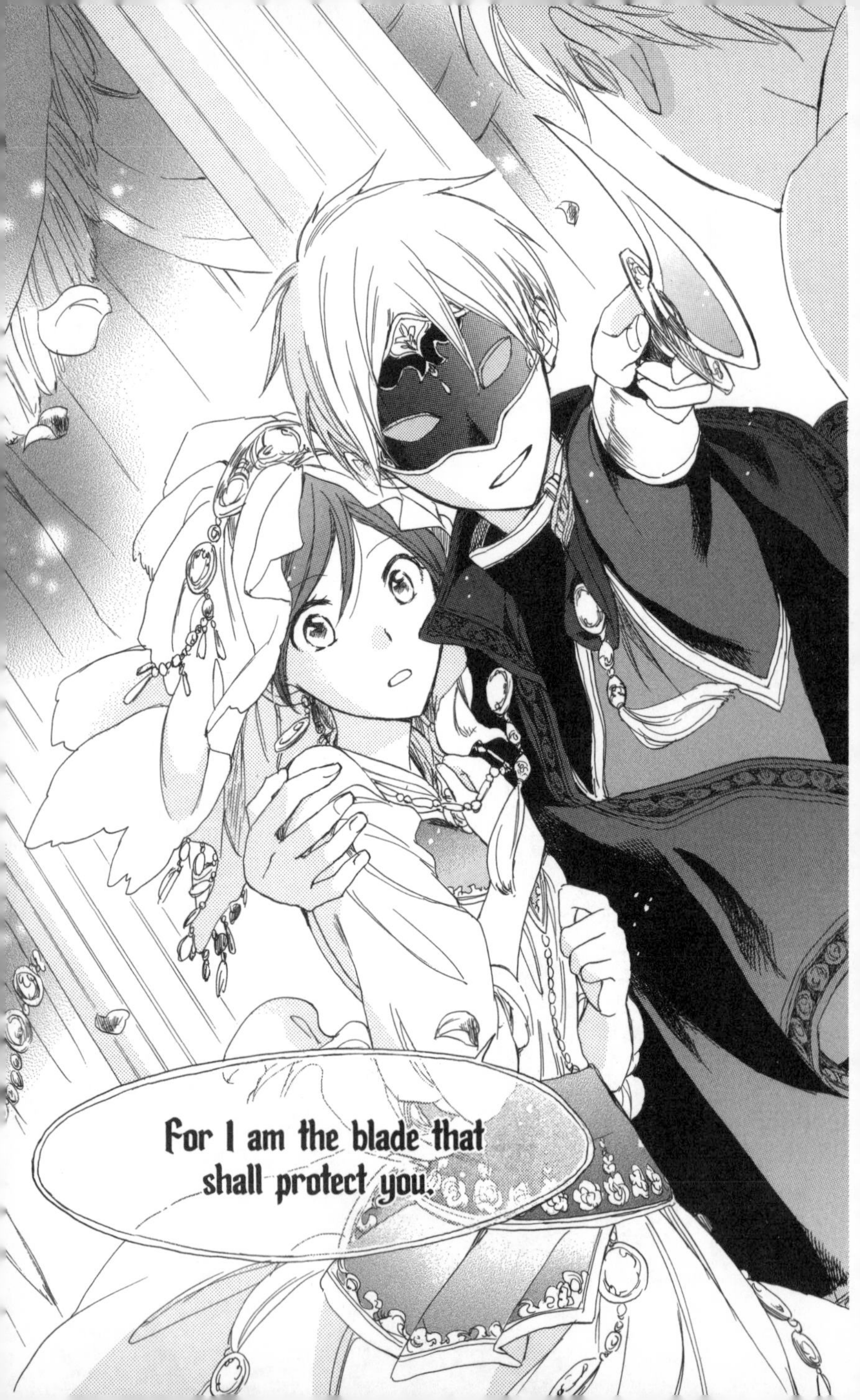
For I am the blade that shall protect you.

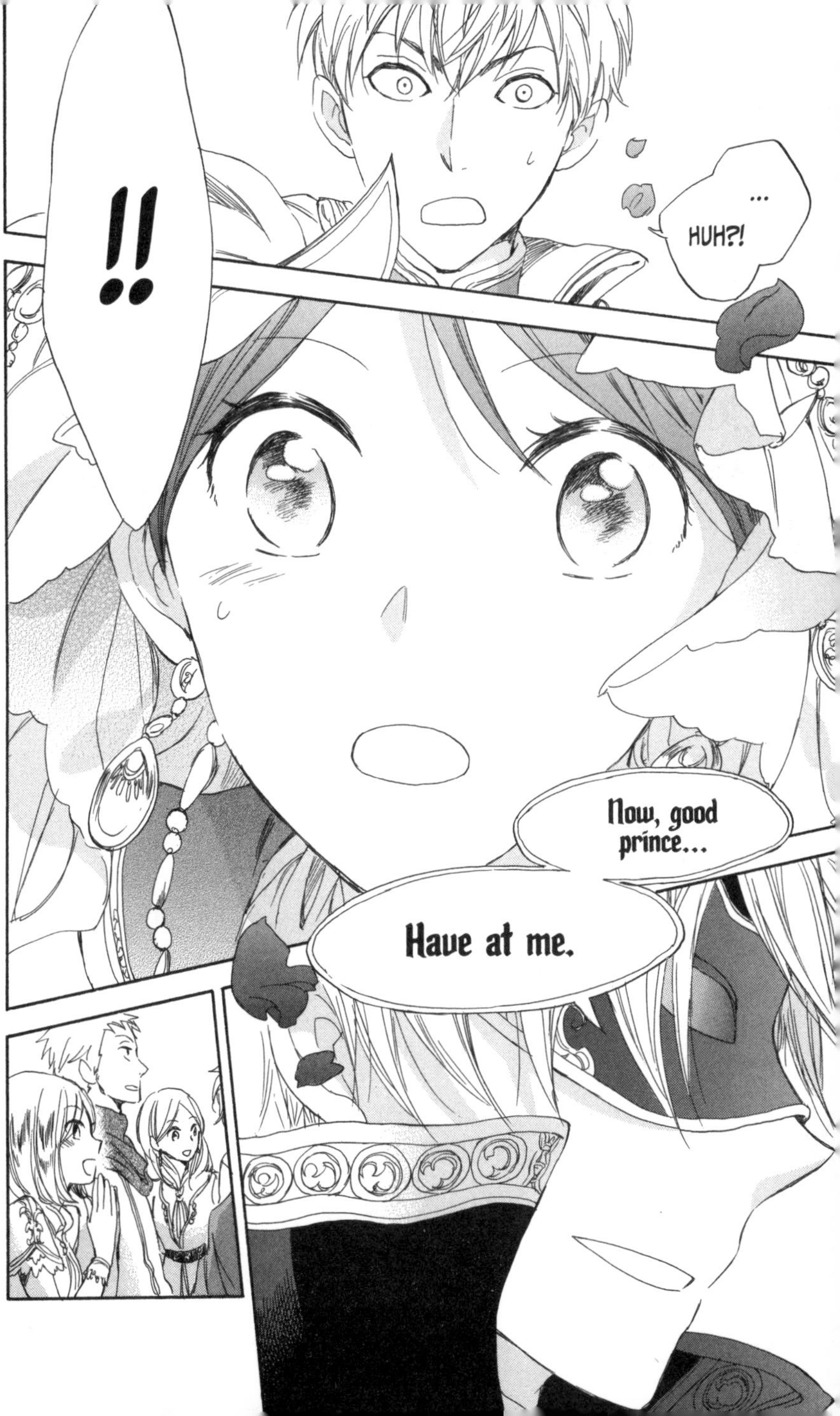
... HUH?!
!!
Now, good prince...
Have at me.

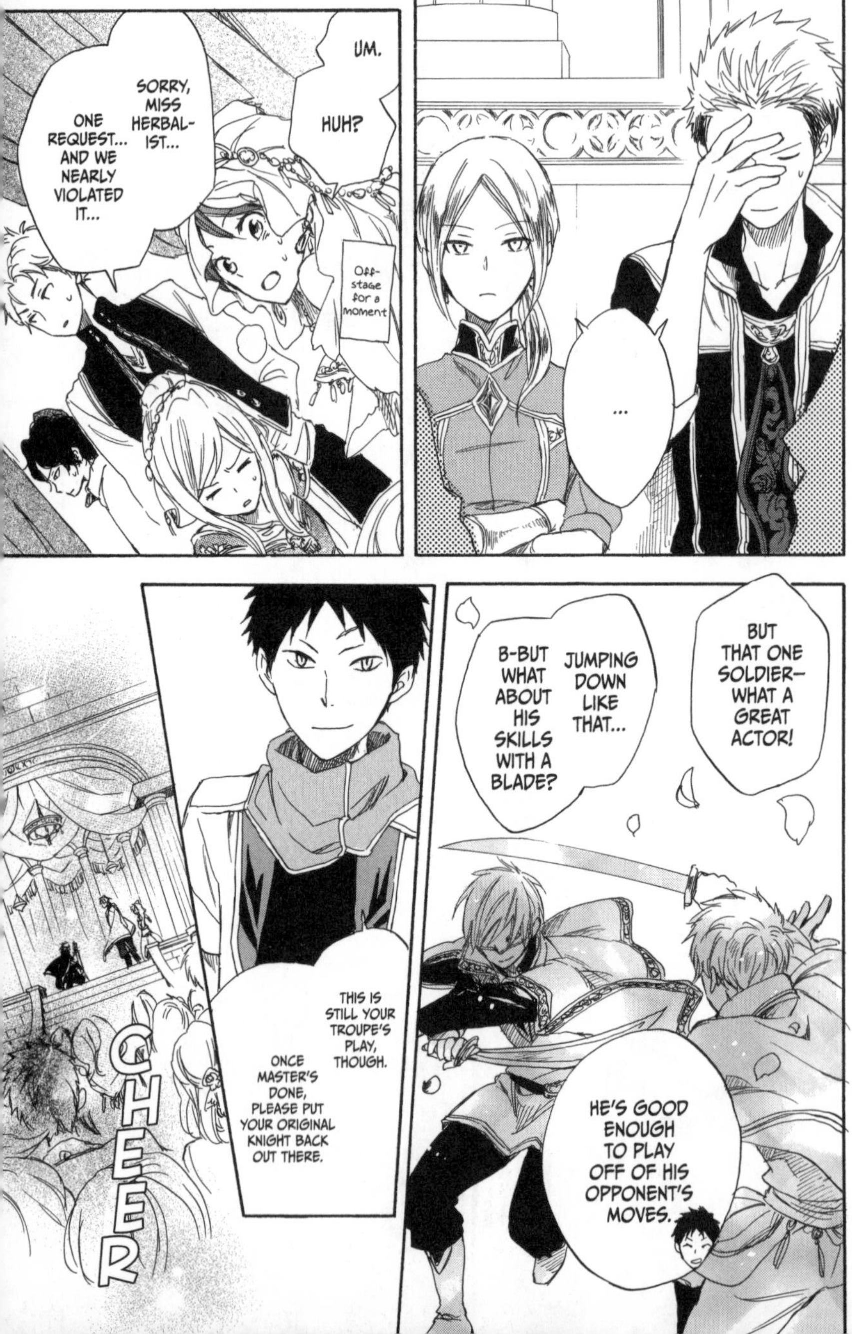
...
UM.
HUH?
SORRY, MISS HERBAL-IST...
ONE REQUEST... AND WE NEARLY VIOLATED IT...
Off-stage for a moment
BUT THAT ONE SOLDIER—WHAT A GREAT ACTOR!
JUMPING DOWN LIKE THAT...
B-BUT WHAT ABOUT HIS SKILLS WITH A BLADE?
HE'S GOOD ENOUGH TO PLAY OFF OF HIS OPPONENT'S MOVES.
THIS IS STILL YOUR TROUPE'S PLAY, THOUGH.
ONCE MASTER'S DONE, PLEASE PUT YOUR ORIGINAL KNIGHT BACK OUT THERE.
CHEER

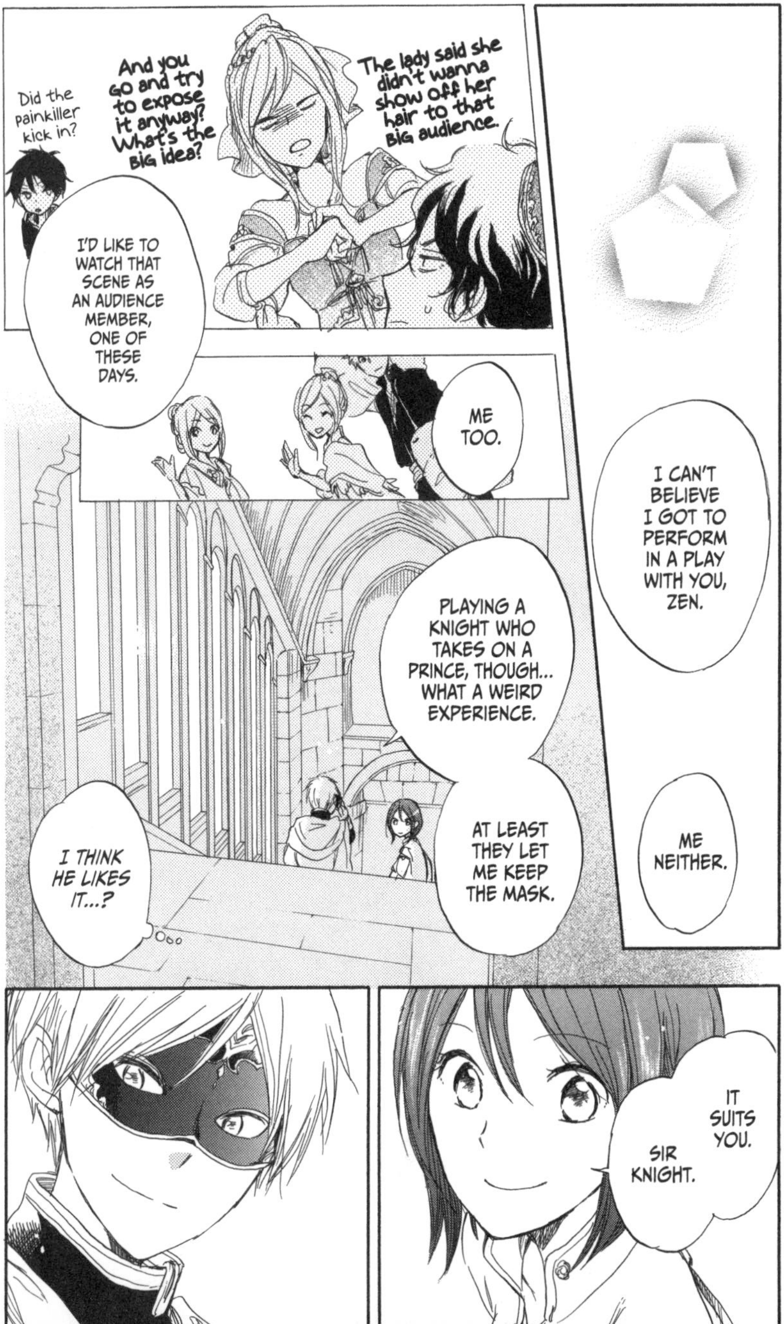
I CAN'T BELIEVE I GOT TO PERFORM IN A PLAY WITH YOU, ZEN.
ME NEITHER.
The lady said she didn't wanna show off her hair to that big audience.
And you go and try to expose it anyway? What's the big idea?
Did the painkiller kick in?
I'D LIKE TO WATCH THAT SCENE AS AN AUDIENCE MEMBER, ONE OF THESE DAYS.
ME TOO.
PLAYING A KNIGHT WHO TAKES ON A PRINCE, THOUGH... WHAT A WEIRD EXPERIENCE.
AT LEAST THEY LET ME KEEP THE MASK.
I THINK HE LIKES IT...?
IT SUITS YOU.
SIR KNIGHT.

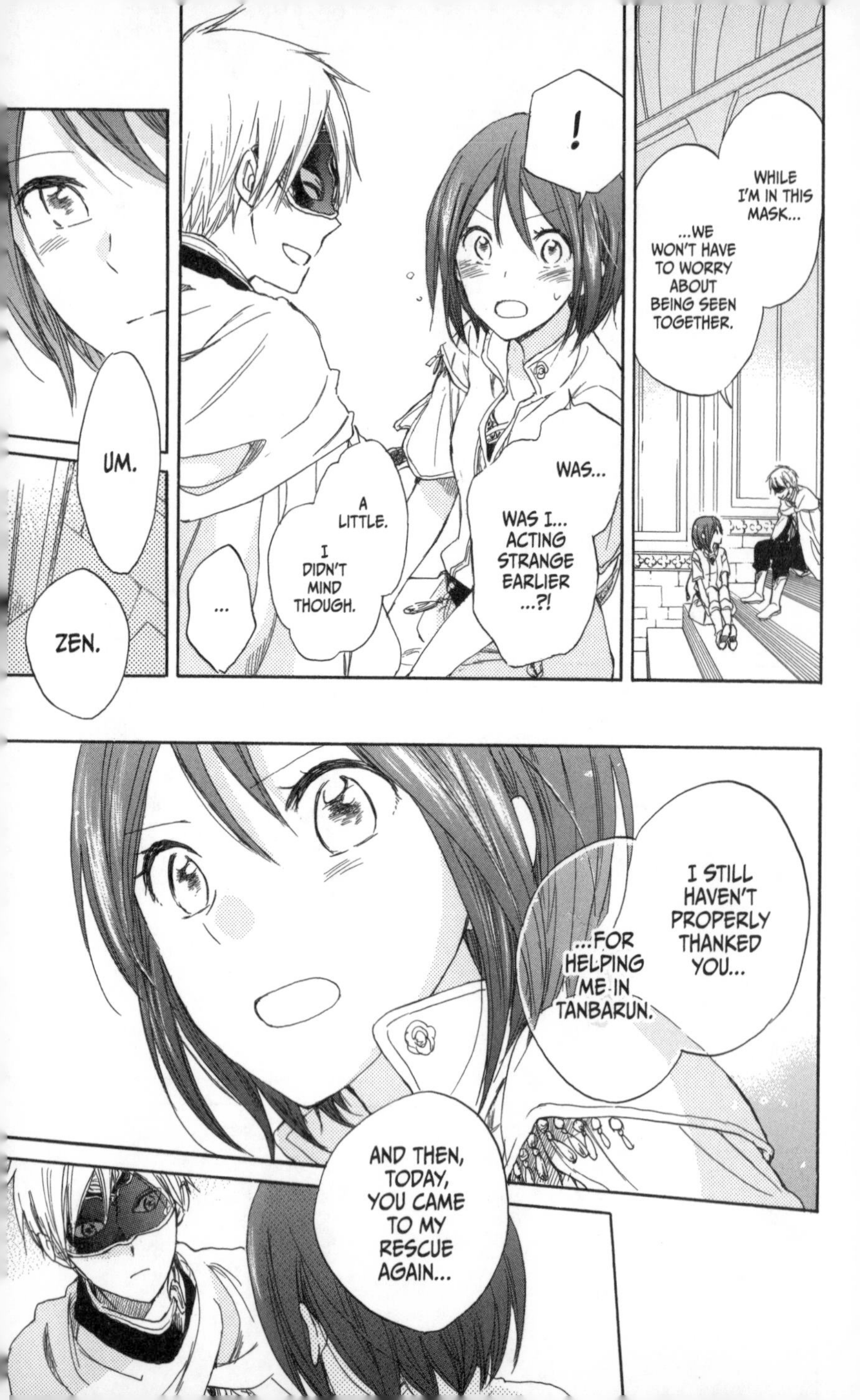
WHILE I'M IN THIS MASK...
...WE WON'T HAVE TO WORRY ABOUT BEING SEEN TOGETHER.
!
WAS...
WAS I... ACTING STRANGE EARLIER ...?!
A LITTLE.
I DIDN'T MIND THOUGH.
...
UM.
ZEN.
I STILL HAVEN'T PROPERLY THANKED YOU...
...FOR HELPING ME IN TANBARUN.
AND THEN, TODAY, YOU CAME TO MY RESCUE AGAIN...

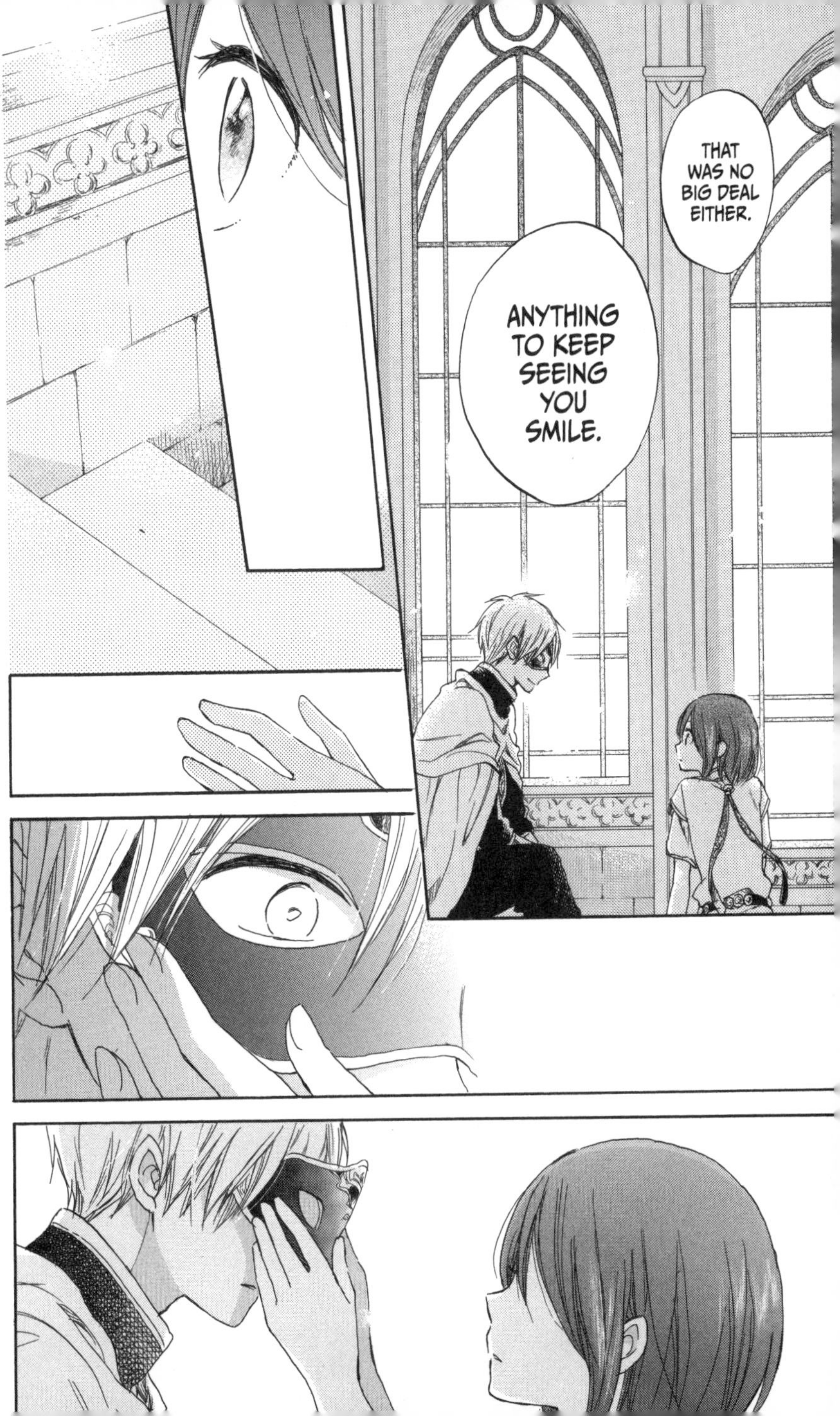
THAT WAS NO BIG DEAL EITHER.
ANYTHING TO KEEP SEEING YOU SMILE.

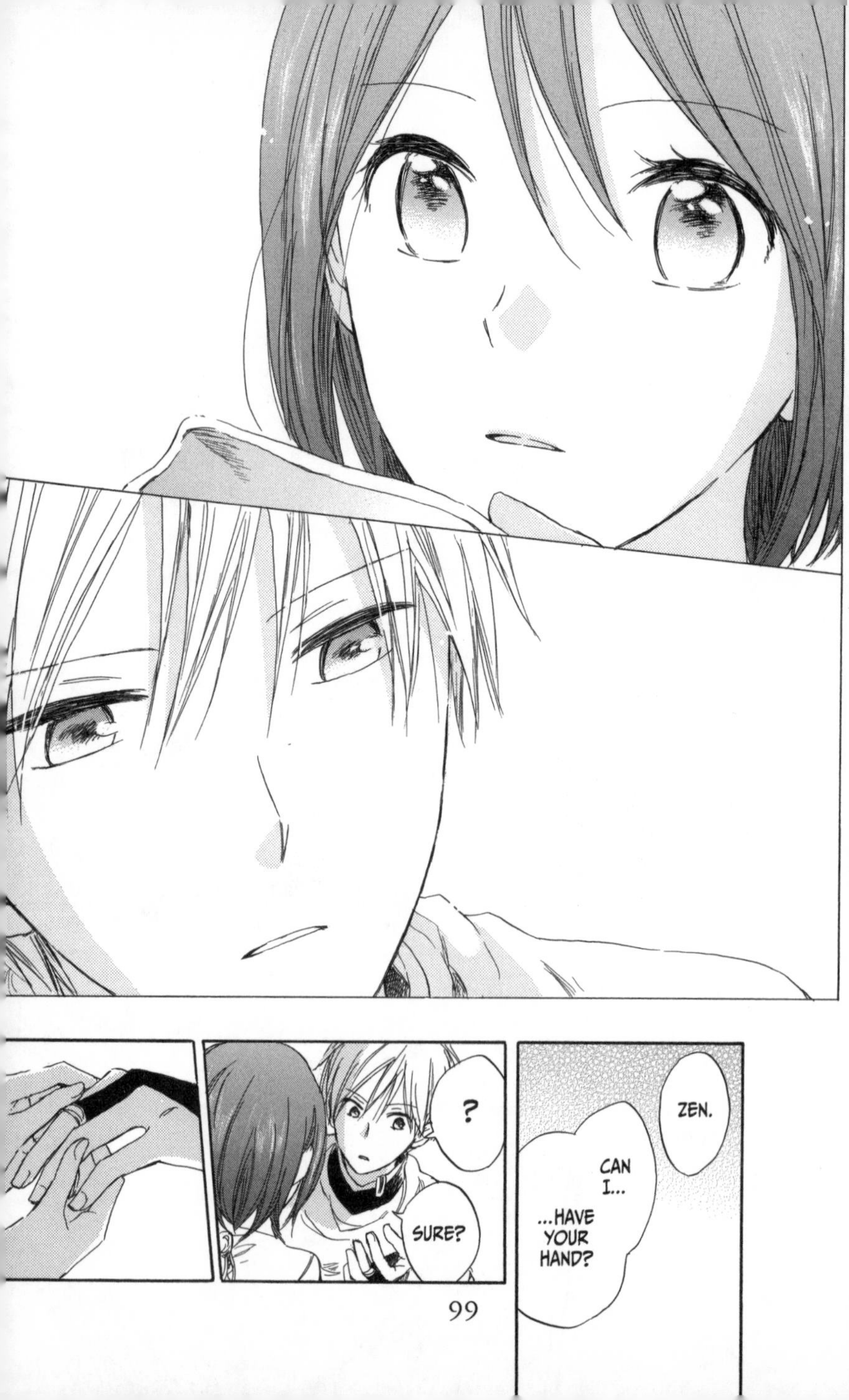
ZEN.
CAN I...
...HAVE YOUR HAND?
?
SURE?

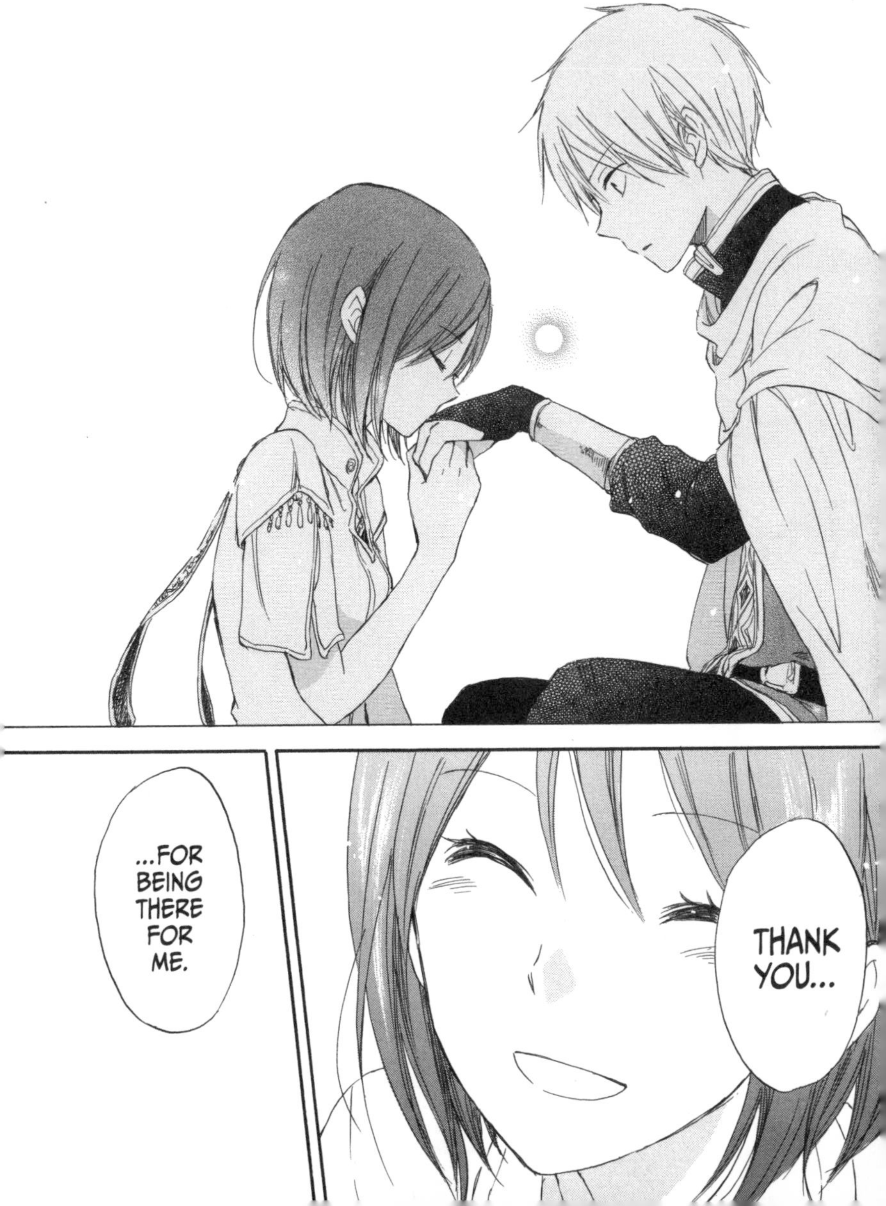
THANK YOU...
...FOR BEING THERE FOR ME.

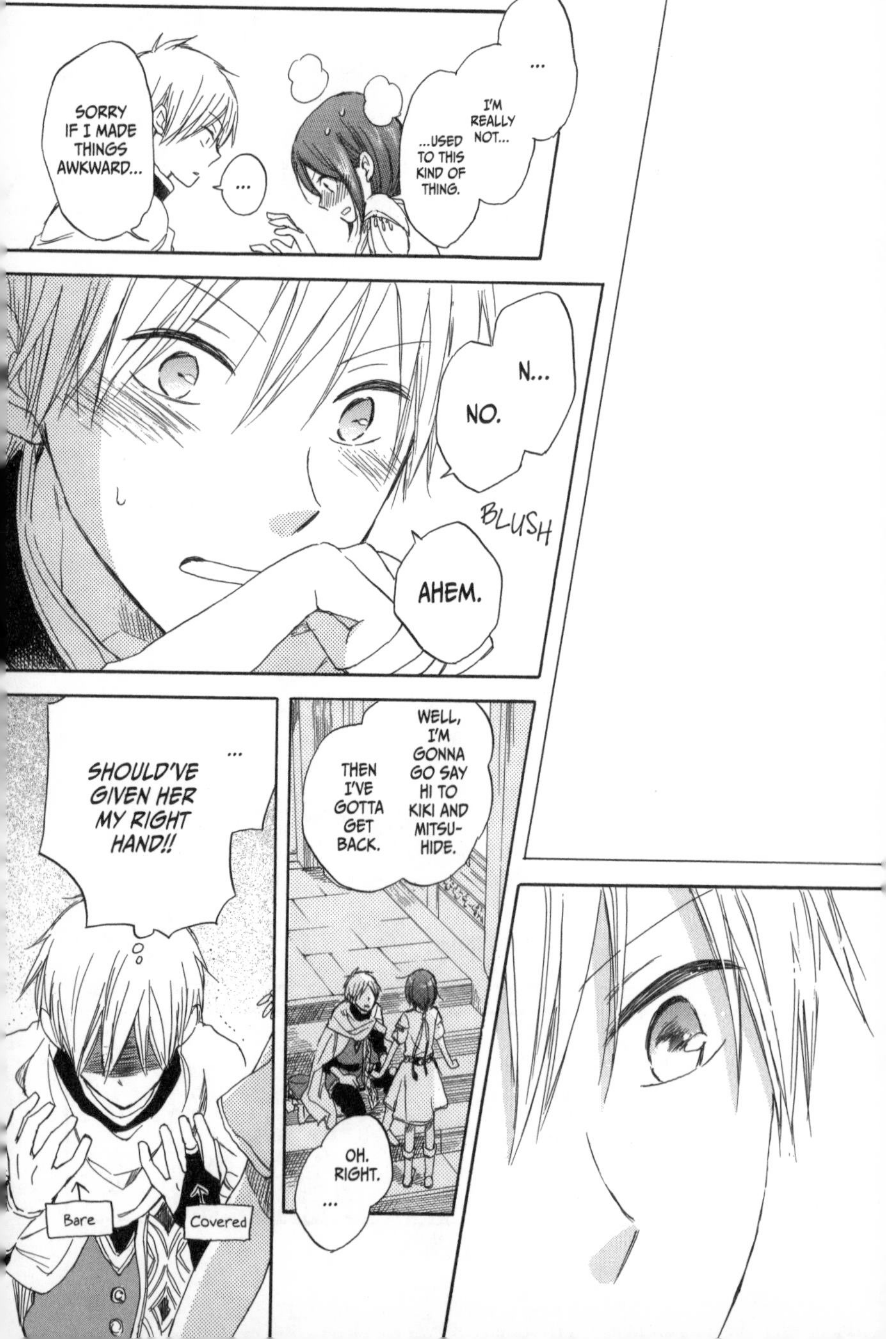
...
I'M REALLY NOT...
...USED TO THIS KIND OF THING.
...
SORRY IF I MADE THINGS AWKWARD...
N... NO.
BLUSH
AHEM.
WELL, I'M GONNA GO SAY HI TO KIKI AND MITSUHIDE.
THEN I'VE GOTTA GET BACK.
OH. RIGHT.
...
...
SHOULD'VE GIVEN HER MY RIGHT HAND!!
Bare
Covered

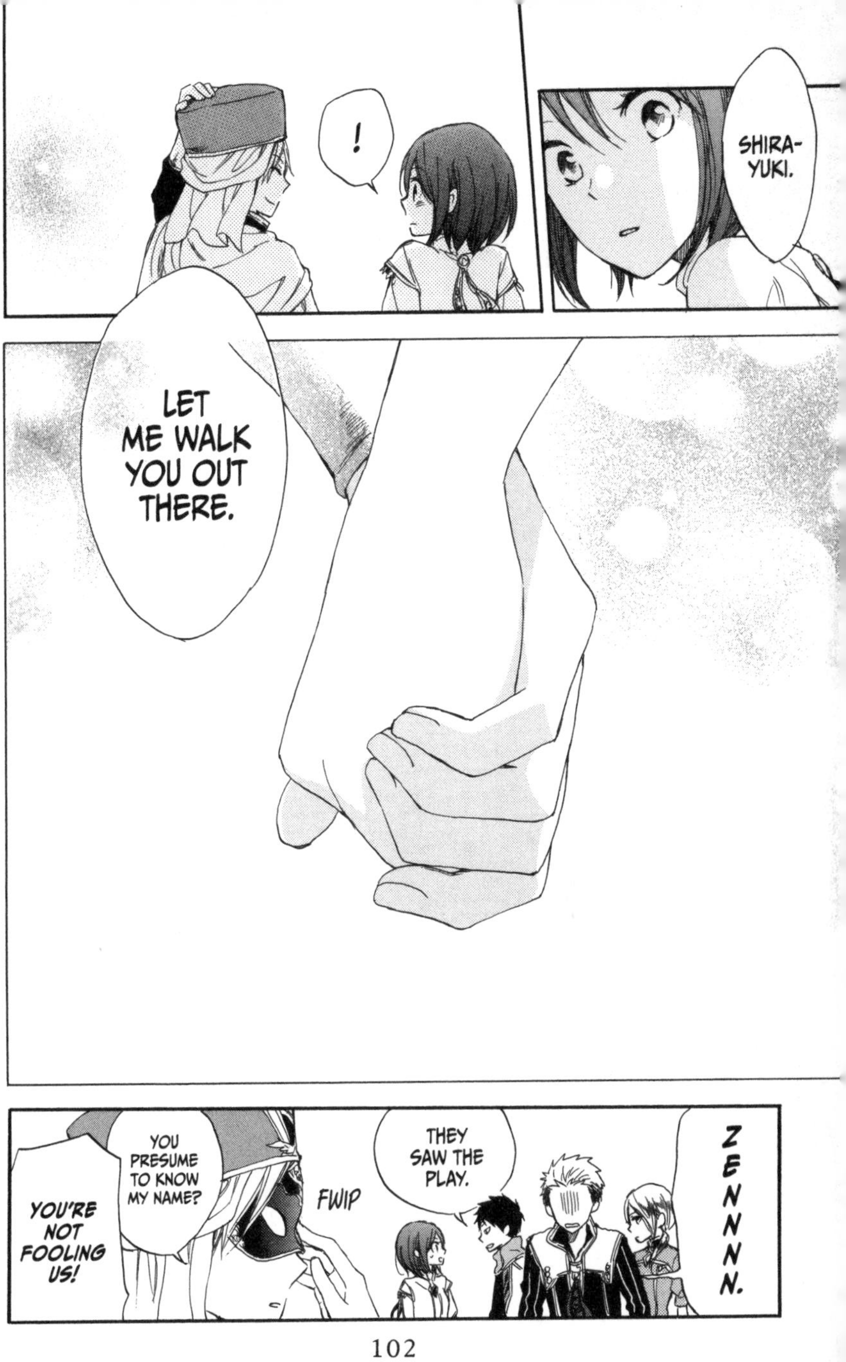
SHIRA-YUKI.
!
LET ME WALK YOU OUT THERE.
ZENNNN.
THEY SAW THE PLAY.
FWIP
YOU PRESUME TO KNOW MY NAME?
YOU'RE NOT FOOLING US!

Chapter 28

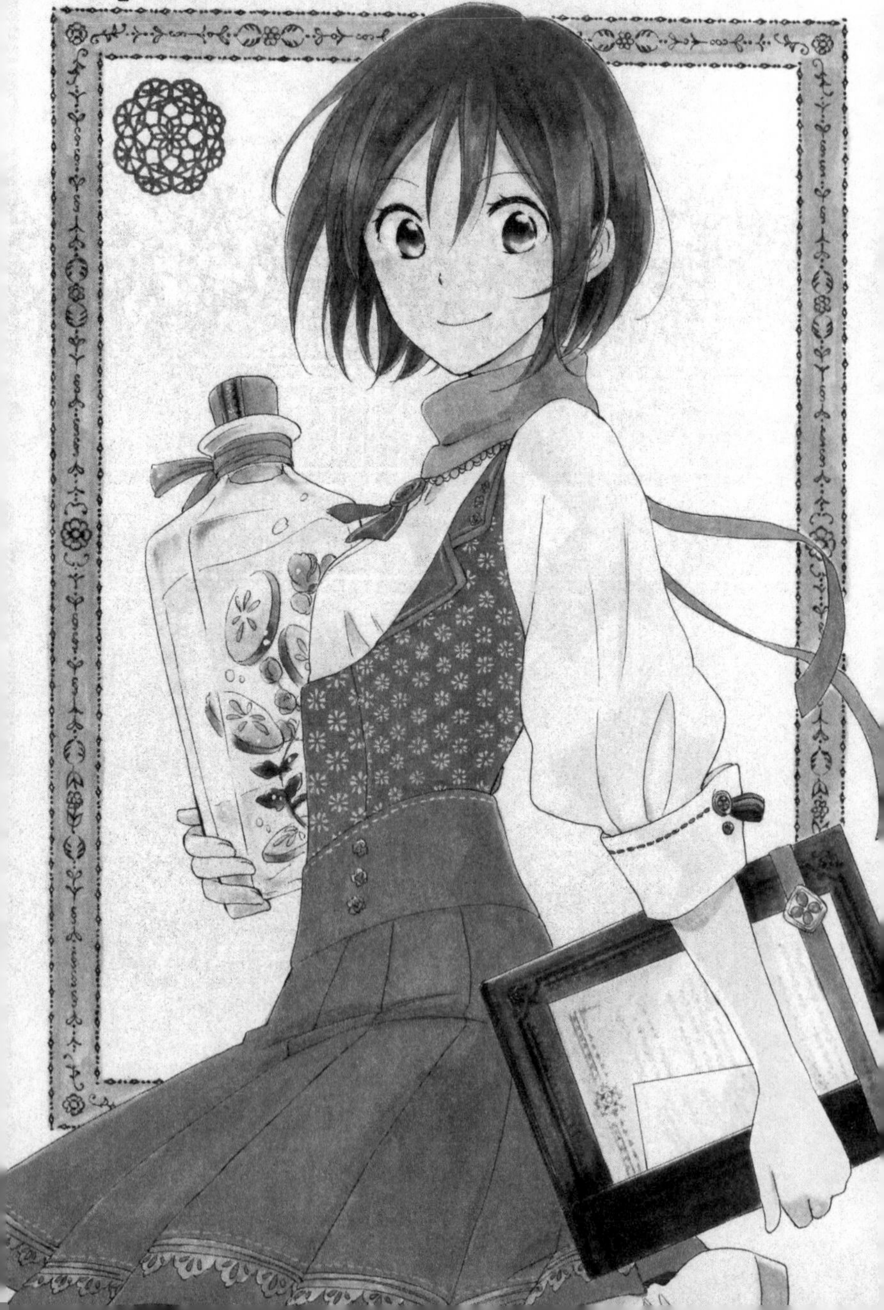

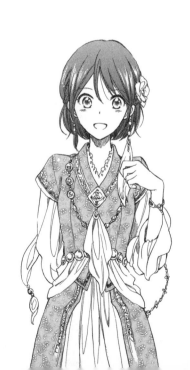

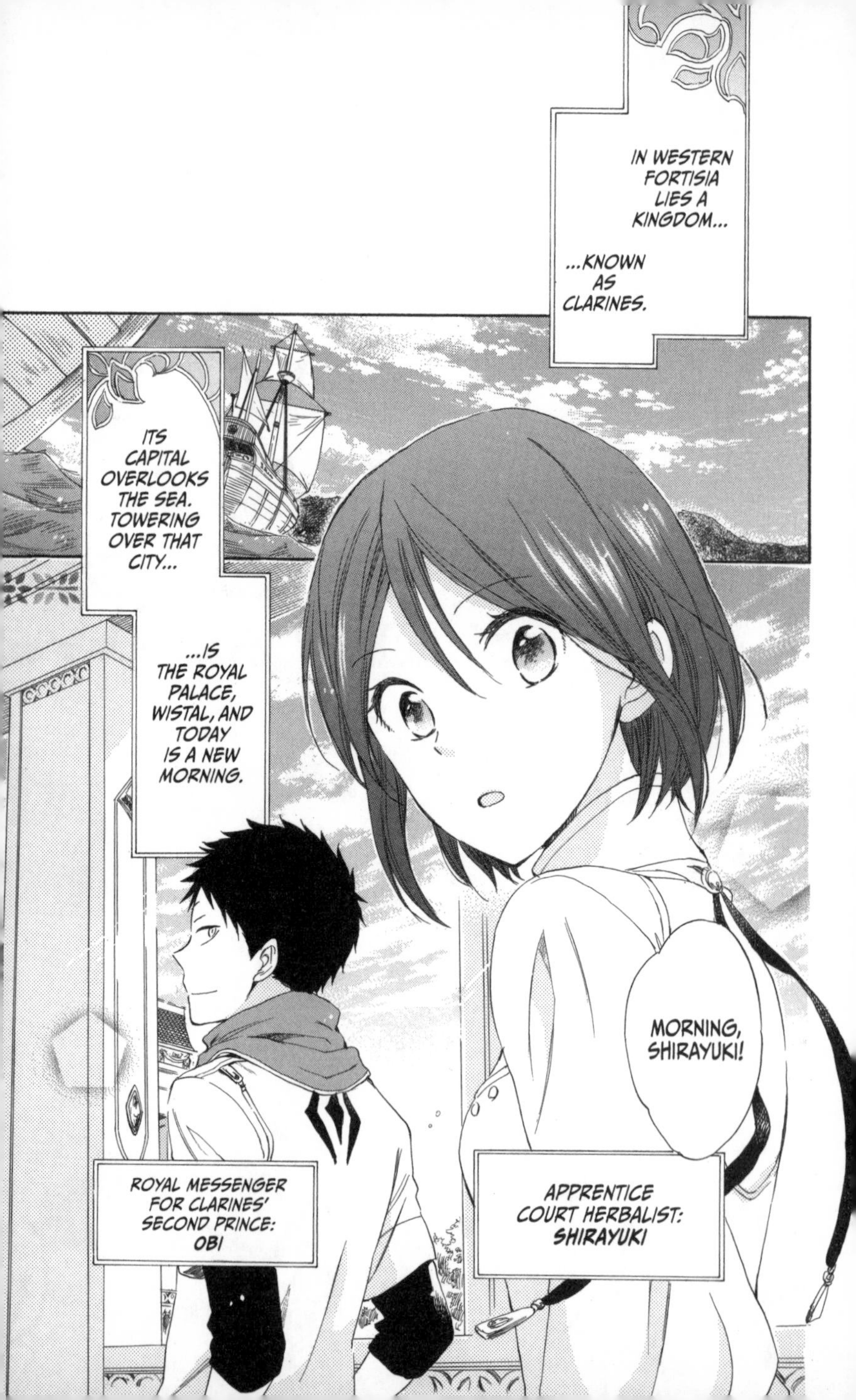
IN WESTERN FORTISIA LIES A KINGDOM...
...KNOWN AS CLARINES.
ITS CAPITAL OVERLOOKS THE SEA. TOWERING OVER THAT CITY...
...IS THE ROYAL PALACE, WISTAL, AND TODAY IS A NEW MORNING.
MORNING, SHIRAYUKI!
APPRENTICE COURT HERBALIST: SHIRAYUKI
ROYAL MESSENGER FOR CLARINES' SECOND PRINCE: OBI

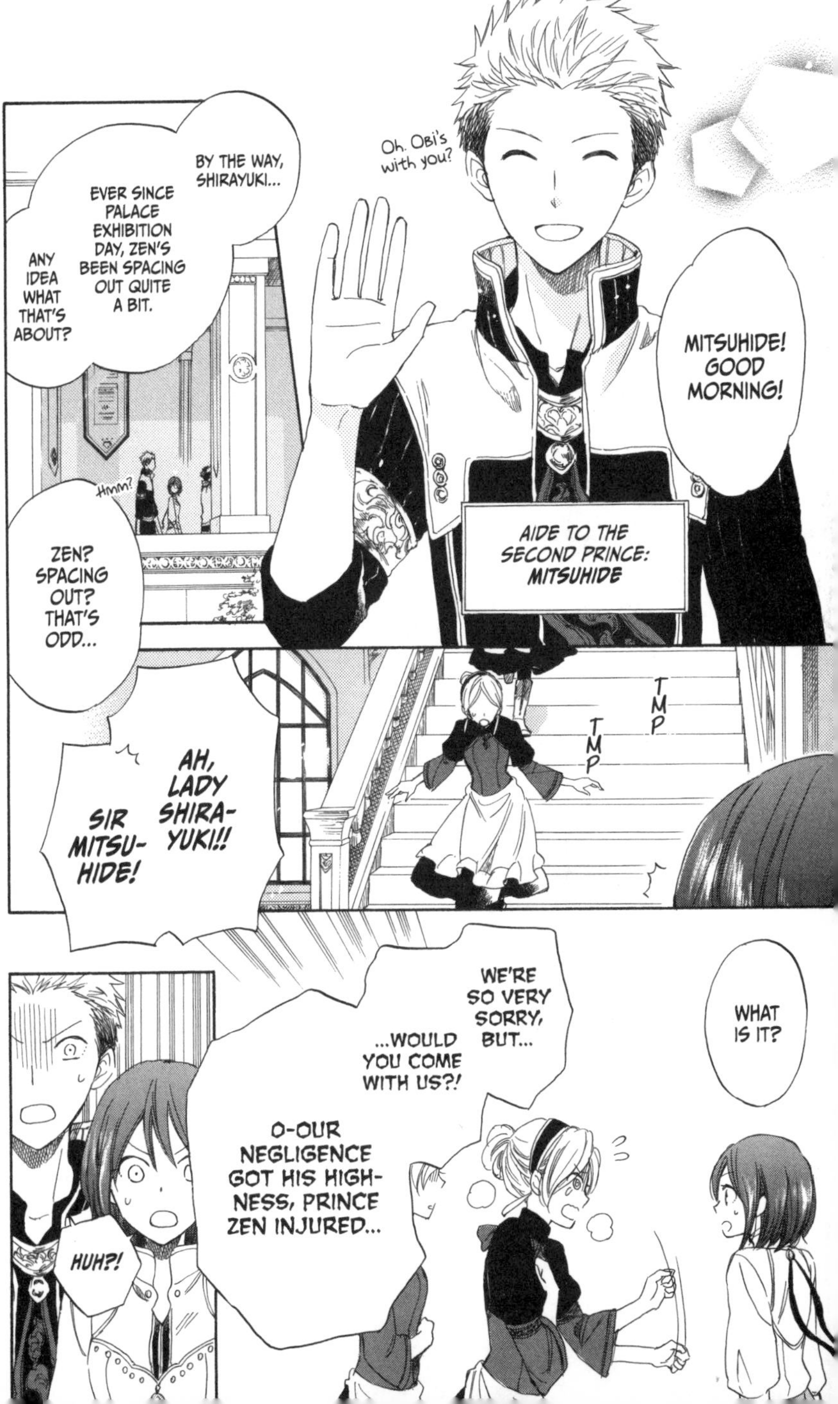
MITSUHIDE! GOOD MORNING!
Oh. Obi's with you?
AIDE TO THE SECOND PRINCE: MITSUHIDE
BY THE WAY, SHIRAYUKI...
EVER SINCE PALACE EXHIBITION DAY, ZEN'S BEEN SPACING OUT QUITE A BIT.
ANY IDEA WHAT THAT'S ABOUT?
Hmm?
ZEN? SPACING OUT? THAT'S ODD...
TMP
TMP
AH, LADY SHIRAYUKI!!
SIR MITSUHIDE!
WHAT IS IT?
WE'RE SO VERY SORRY, BUT...
...WOULD YOU COME WITH US?!
O-OUR NEGLIGENCE GOT HIS HIGHNESS, PRINCE ZEN INJURED...
HUH?!

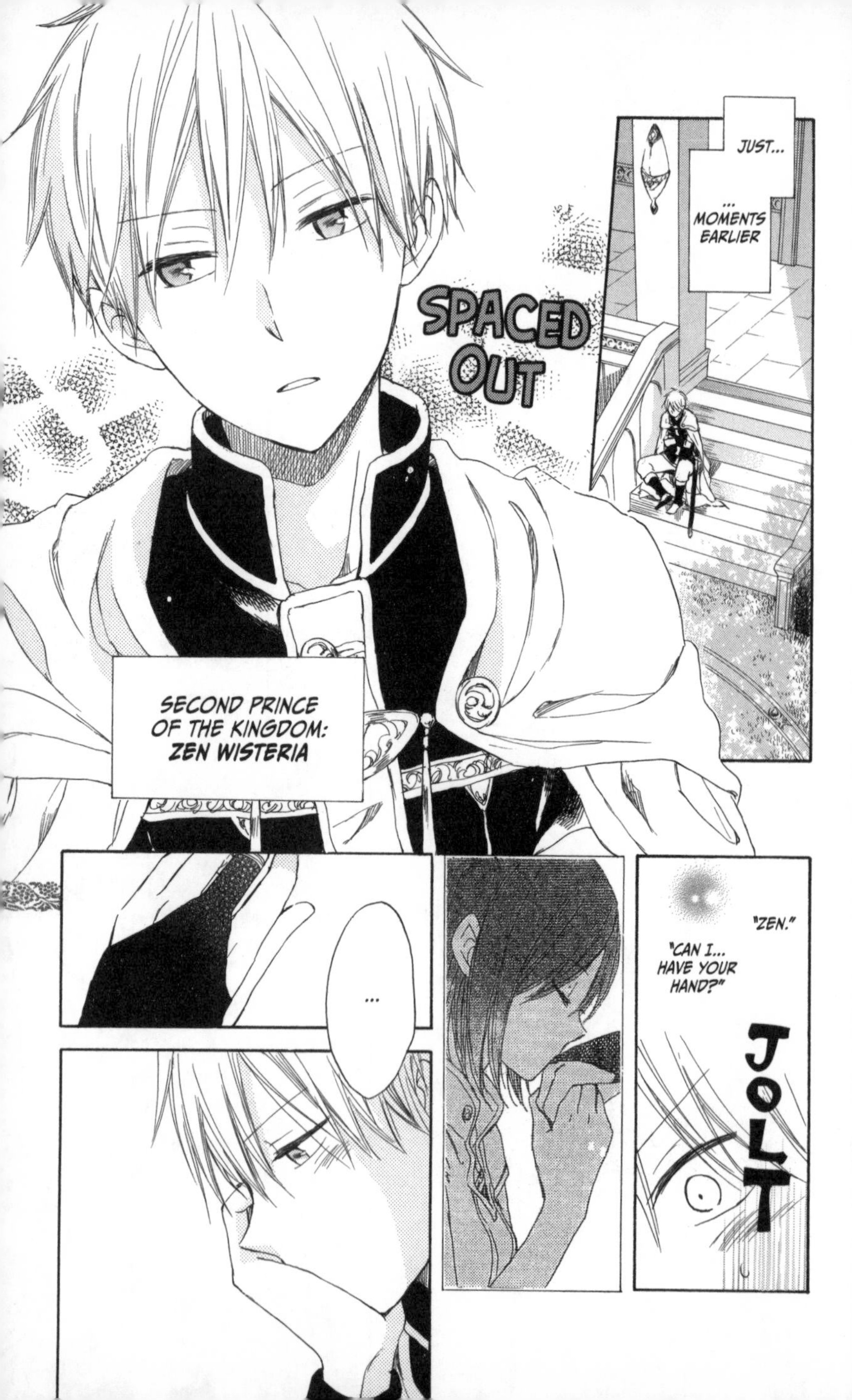
JUST...
... MOMENTS EARLIER
SPACED OUT
SECOND PRINCE OF THE KINGDOM: ZEN WISTERIA
"ZEN."
"CAN I... HAVE YOUR HAND?"
JOLT
...

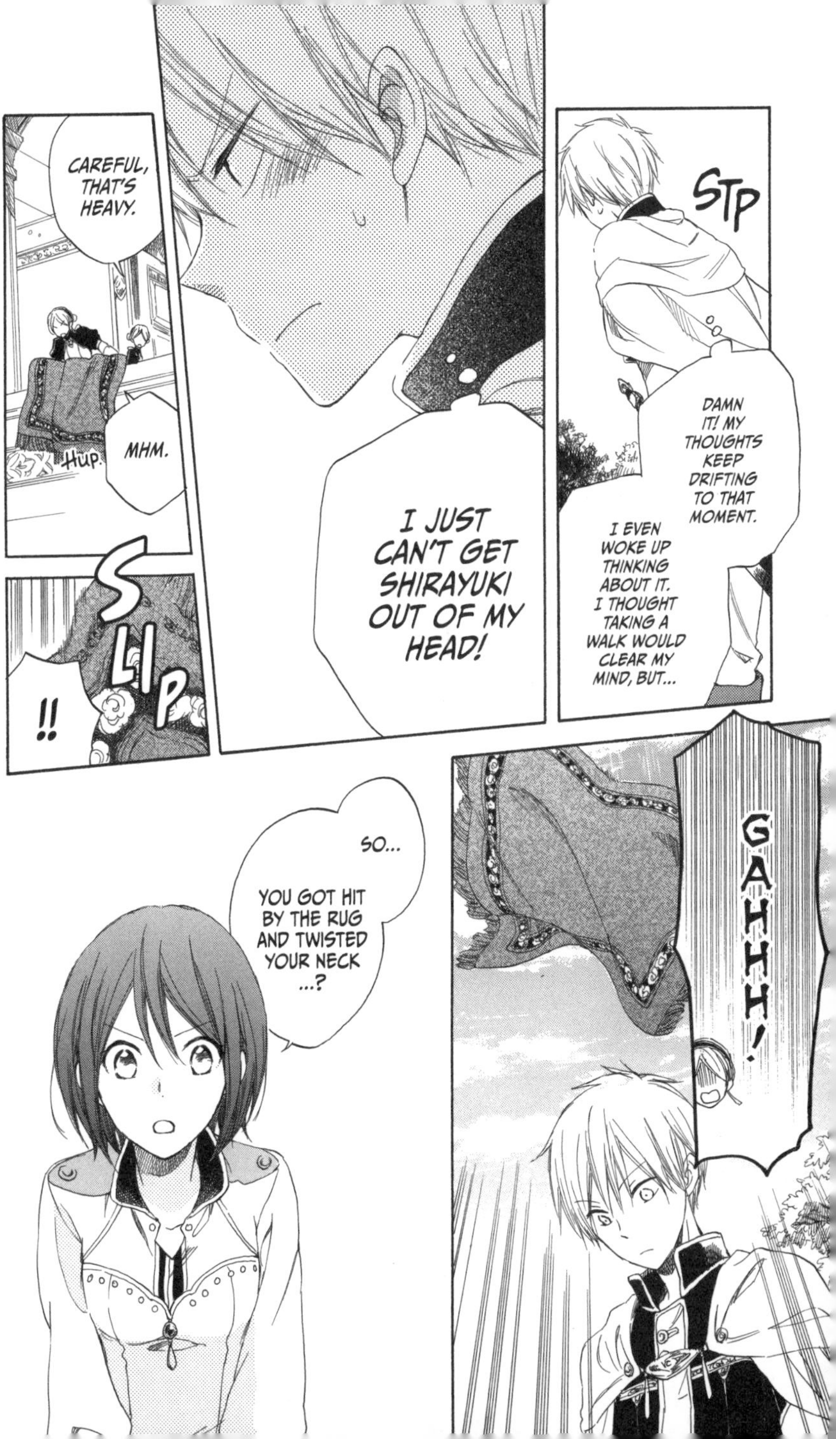
STP
DAMN IT! MY THOUGHTS KEEP DRIFTING TO THAT MOMENT.
I EVEN WOKE UP THINKING ABOUT IT. I THOUGHT TAKING A WALK WOULD CLEAR MY MIND, BUT...
I JUST CAN'T GET SHIRAYUKI OUT OF MY HEAD!
CAREFUL, THAT'S HEAVY.
Hup.
MHM.
SLIP
!!
GAHHH!
SO...
YOU GOT HIT BY THE RUG AND TWISTED YOUR NECK ...?

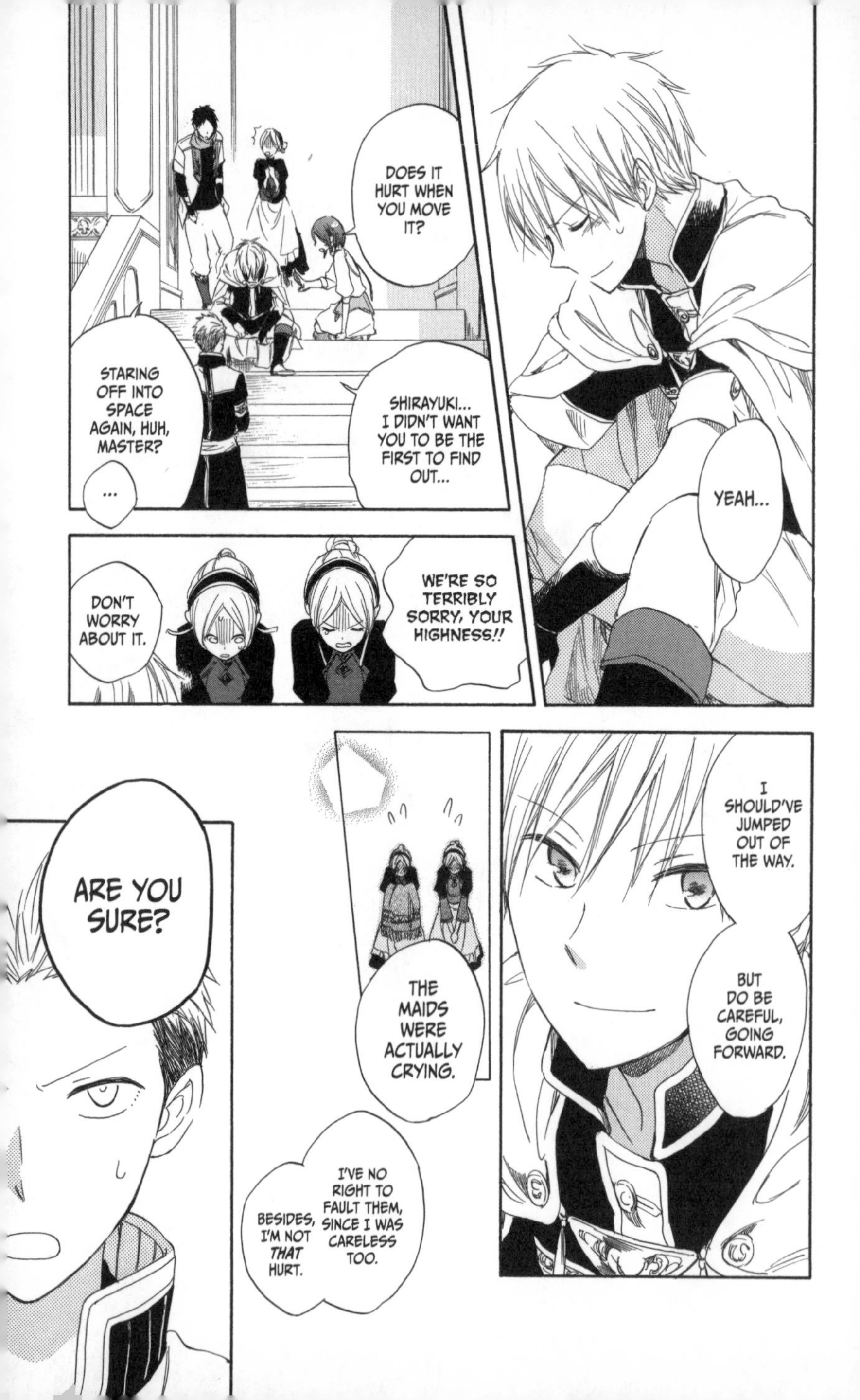
YEAH...
DOES IT HURT WHEN YOU MOVE IT?
SHIRAYUKI... I DIDN'T WANT YOU TO BE THE FIRST TO FIND OUT...
STARING OFF INTO SPACE AGAIN, HUH, MASTER?
...
WE'RE SO TERRIBLY SORRY, YOUR HIGHNESS!!
DON'T WORRY ABOUT IT.
I SHOULD'VE JUMPED OUT OF THE WAY.
BUT DO BE CAREFUL, GOING FORWARD.
THE MAIDS WERE ACTUALLY CRYING.
I'VE NO RIGHT TO FAULT THEM, SINCE I WAS CARELESS TOO.
BESIDES, I'M NOT *THAT* HURT.
ARE YOU SURE?

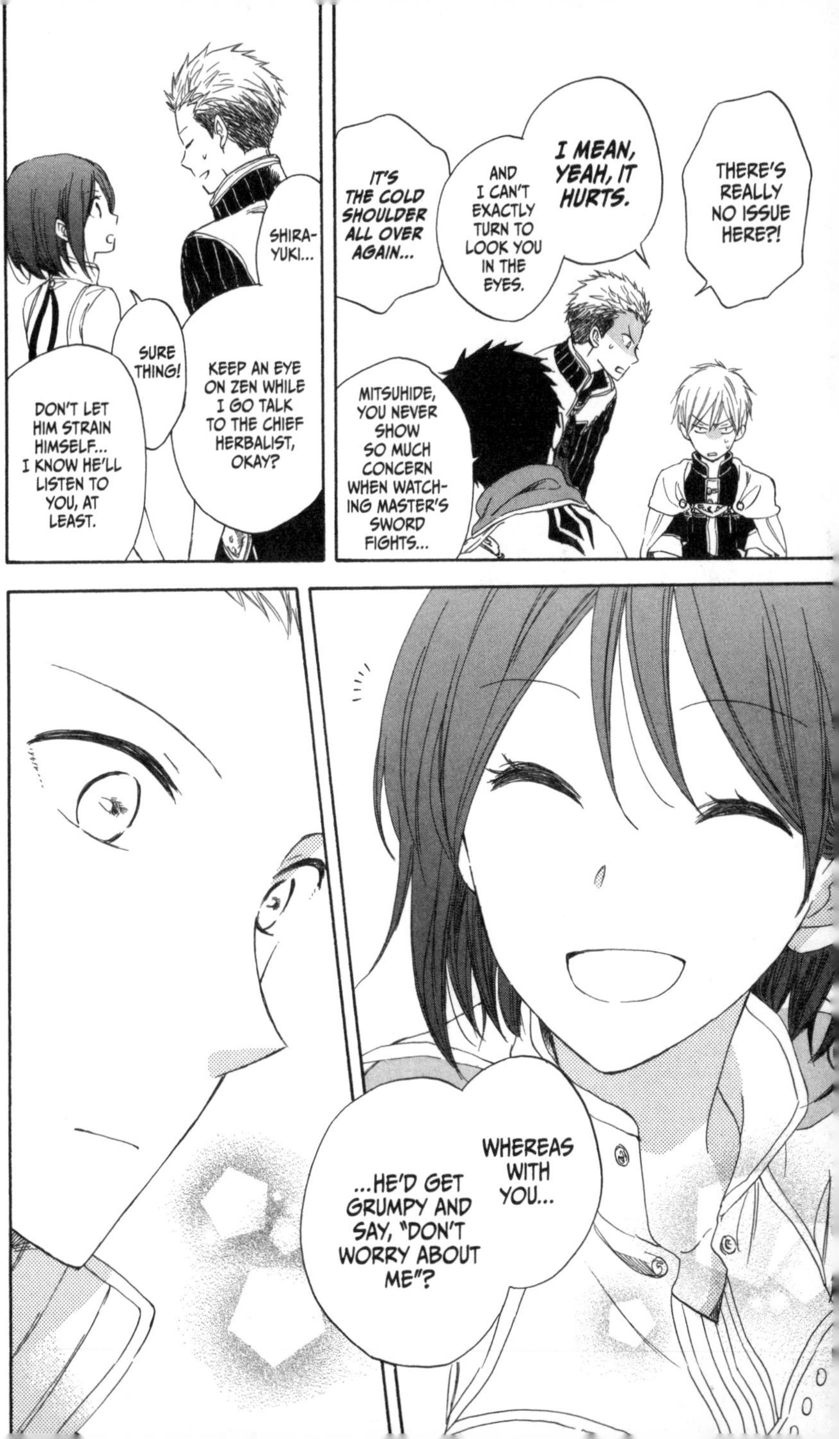
THERE'S REALLY NO ISSUE HERE?!
I MEAN, YEAH, IT HURTS.
AND I CAN'T EXACTLY TURN TO LOOK YOU IN THE EYES.
IT'S THE COLD SHOULDER ALL OVER AGAIN...
MITSUHIDE, YOU NEVER SHOW SO MUCH CONCERN WHEN WATCHING MASTER'S SWORD FIGHTS...
SHIRA-YUKI...
KEEP AN EYE ON ZEN WHILE I GO TALK TO THE CHIEF HERBALIST, OKAY?
SURE THING!
DON'T LET HIM STRAIN HIMSELF... I KNOW HE'LL LISTEN TO YOU, AT LEAST.
WHEREAS WITH YOU...
...HE'D GET GRUMPY AND SAY, "DON'T WORRY ABOUT ME"?

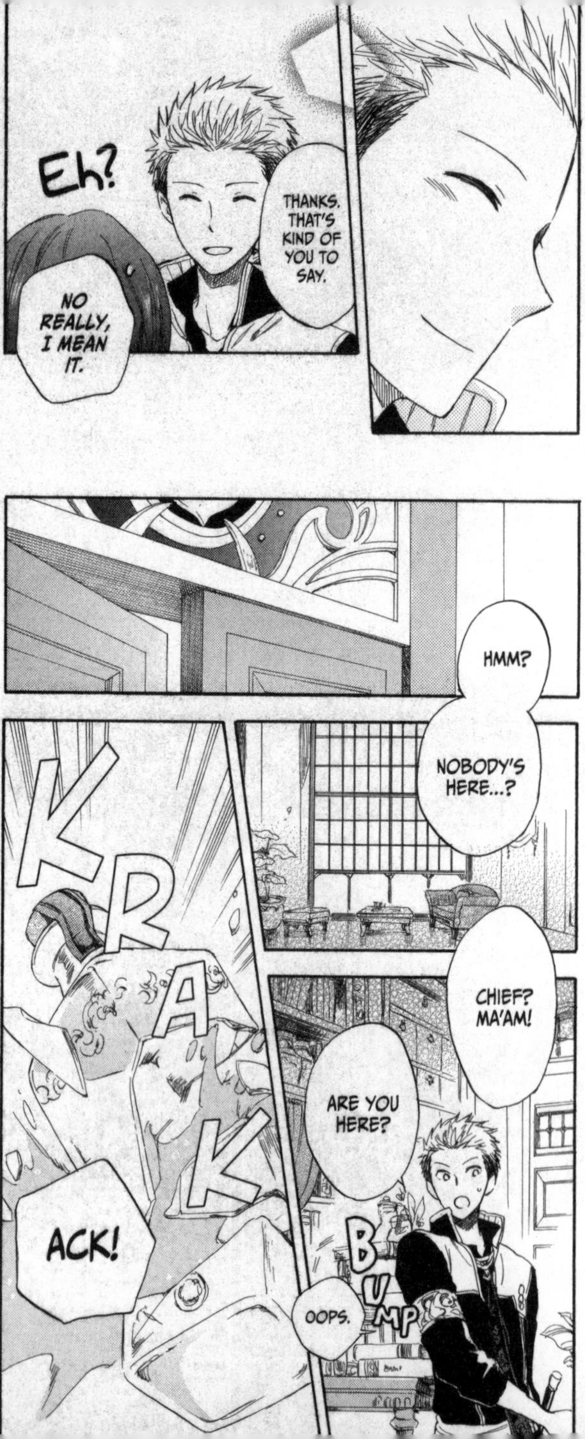
THANKS. THAT'S KIND OF YOU TO SAY.
Eh?
NO REALLY, I MEAN IT.
HMM?
NOBODY'S HERE...?
CHIEF? MA'AM!
ARE YOU HERE?
BUMP
OOPS.
KRAK
ACK!

Beware: Spoilers

CHAPTER 27

Did Zen end up looking like some nameless background character while in soldier garb?

Please don't say yes. I really hope not.

Zen read through the play's script to make sure that Shirayuki, as the understudy, didn't have any romantic scenes coming up.

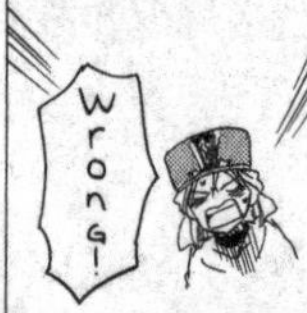
Wrong!

Oh no! That nameless background character is mad at me for some reason.

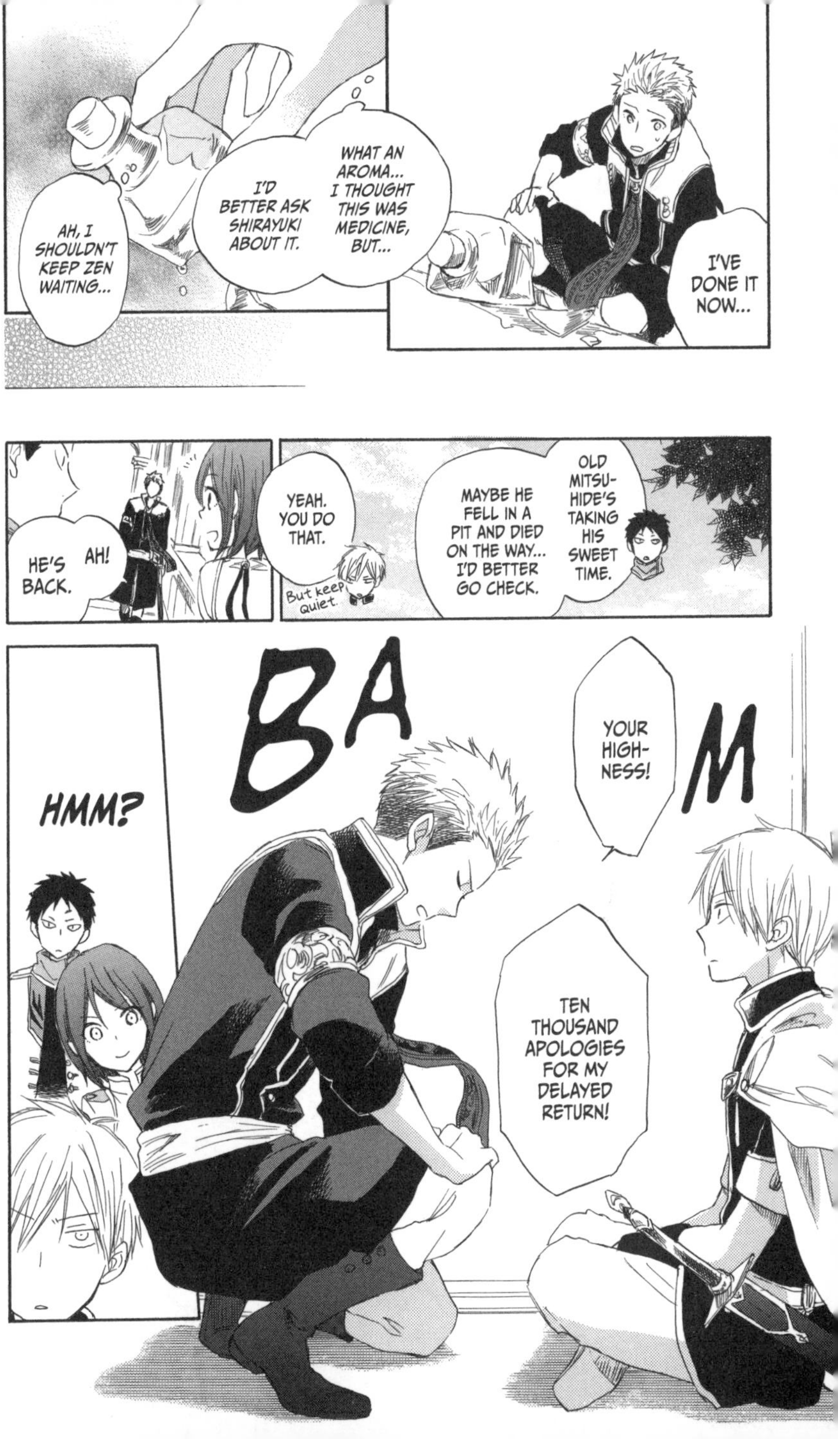
I'VE DONE IT NOW...
WHAT AN AROMA... I THOUGHT THIS WAS MEDICINE, BUT...
I'D BETTER ASK SHIRAYUKI ABOUT IT.
AH, I SHOULDN'T KEEP ZEN WAITING...
OLD MITSU-HIDE'S TAKING HIS SWEET TIME.
MAYBE HE FELL IN A PIT AND DIED ON THE WAY... I'D BETTER GO CHECK.
YEAH. YOU DO THAT.
But keep quiet.
AH!
HE'S BACK.
BAM
YOUR HIGH-NESS!
TEN THOUSAND APOLOGIES FOR MY DELAYED RETURN!
HMM?

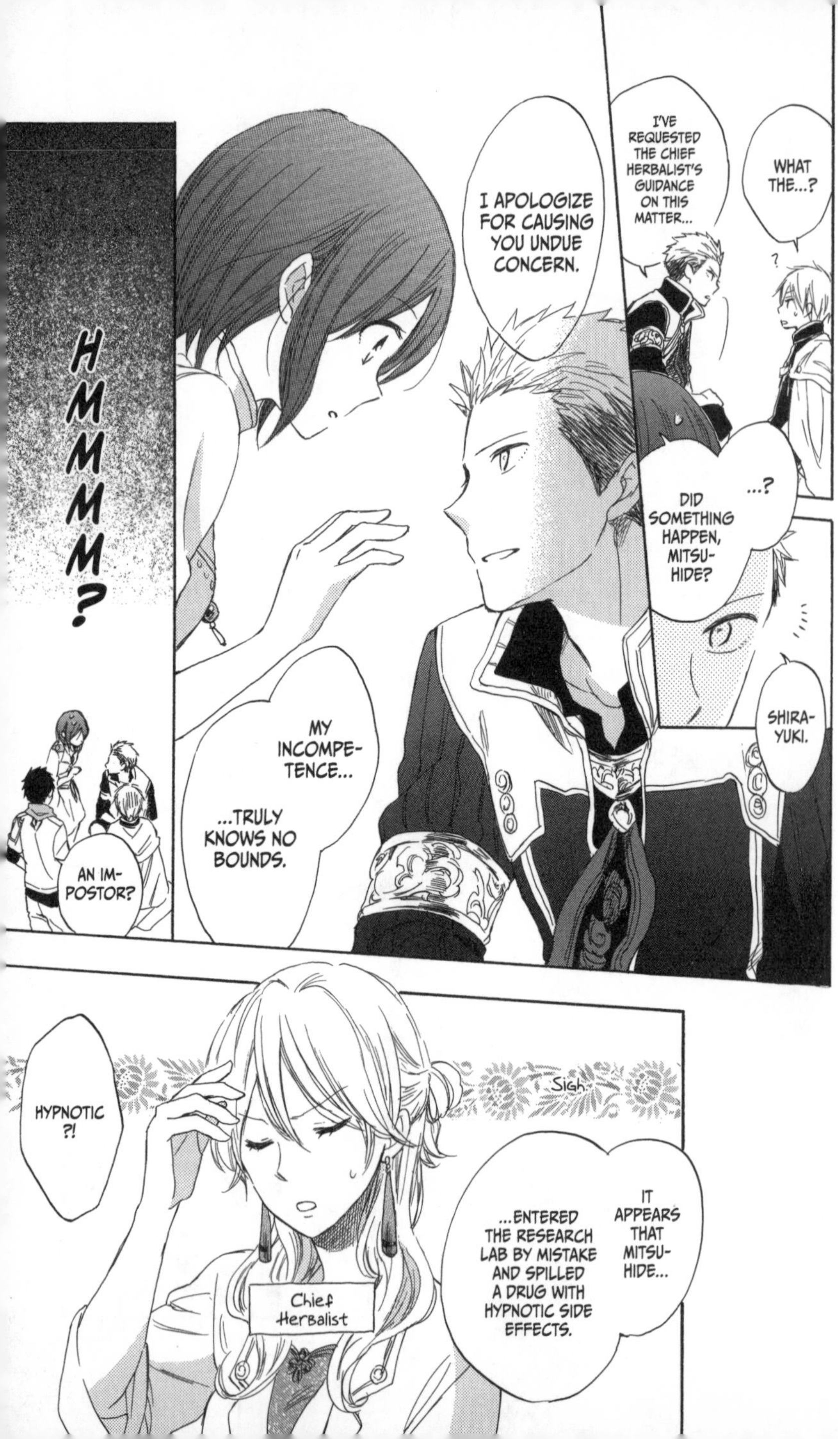
WHAT THE...?
I'VE REQUESTED THE CHIEF HERBALIST'S GUIDANCE ON THIS MATTER...
...?
DID SOMETHING HAPPEN, MITSU-HIDE?
SHIRA-YUKI.
I APOLOGIZE FOR CAUSING YOU UNDUE CONCERN.
MY INCOMPE-TENCE...
...TRULY KNOWS NO BOUNDS.
HMMMMM?
AN IM-POSTOR?
Sigh
IT APPEARS THAT MITSU-HIDE...
...ENTERED THE RESEARCH LAB BY MISTAKE AND SPILLED A DRUG WITH HYPNOTIC SIDE EFFECTS.
Chief Herbalist
HYPNOTIC ?!

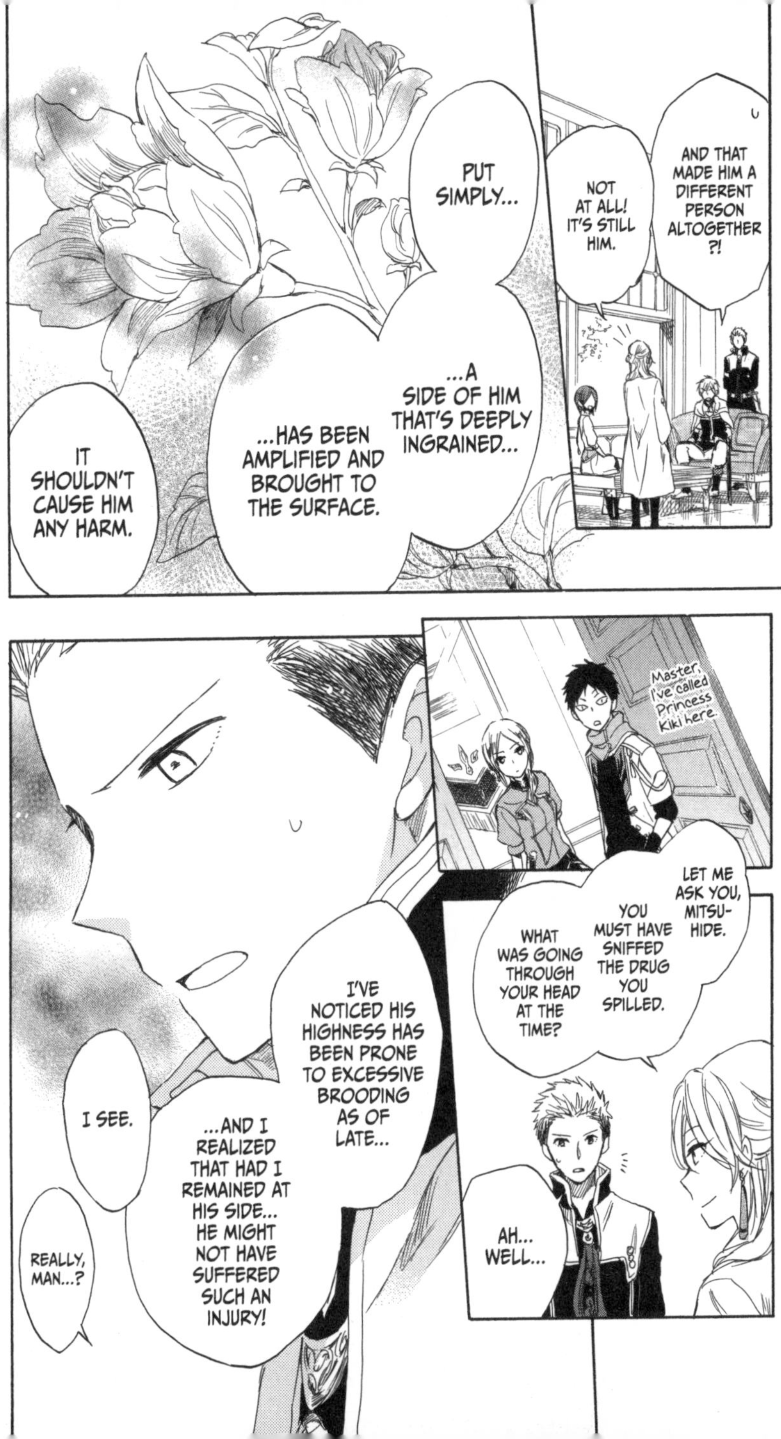
AND THAT MADE HIM A DIFFERENT PERSON ALTOGETHER?!
NOT AT ALL! IT'S STILL HIM.
PUT SIMPLY...
...A SIDE OF HIM THAT'S DEEPLY INGRAINED...
...HAS BEEN AMPLIFIED AND BROUGHT TO THE SURFACE.
IT SHOULDN'T CAUSE HIM ANY HARM.
Master, I've called Princess Kiki here.
LET ME ASK YOU, MITSU-HIDE.
YOU MUST HAVE SNIFFED THE DRUG YOU SPILLED.
WHAT WAS GOING THROUGH YOUR HEAD AT THE TIME?
AH... WELL...
I'VE NOTICED HIS HIGHNESS HAS BEEN PRONE TO EXCESSIVE BROODING AS OF LATE...
...AND I REALIZED THAT HAD I REMAINED AT HIS SIDE... HE MIGHT NOT HAVE SUFFERED SUCH AN INJURY!
I SEE.
REALLY, MAN...?

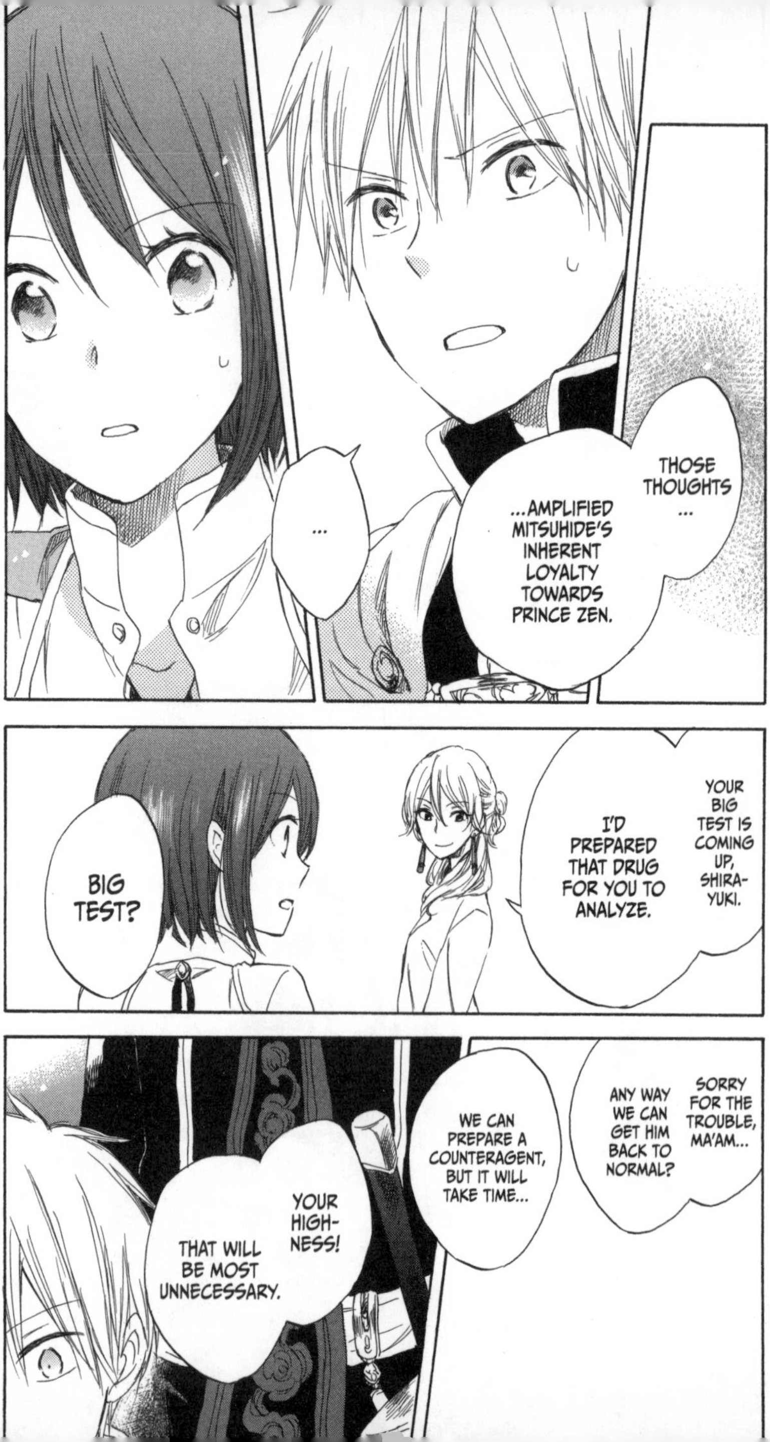
THOSE THOUGHTS ...
...AMPLIFIED MITSUHIDE'S INHERENT LOYALTY TOWARDS PRINCE ZEN.
...
YOUR BIG TEST IS COMING UP, SHIRA-YUKI.
I'D PREPARED THAT DRUG FOR YOU TO ANALYZE.
BIG TEST?
SORRY FOR THE TROUBLE, MA'AM...
ANY WAY WE CAN GET HIM BACK TO NORMAL?
WE CAN PREPARE A COUNTERAGENT, BUT IT WILL TAKE TIME...
YOUR HIGH-NESS!
THAT WILL BE MOST UNNECESSARY.

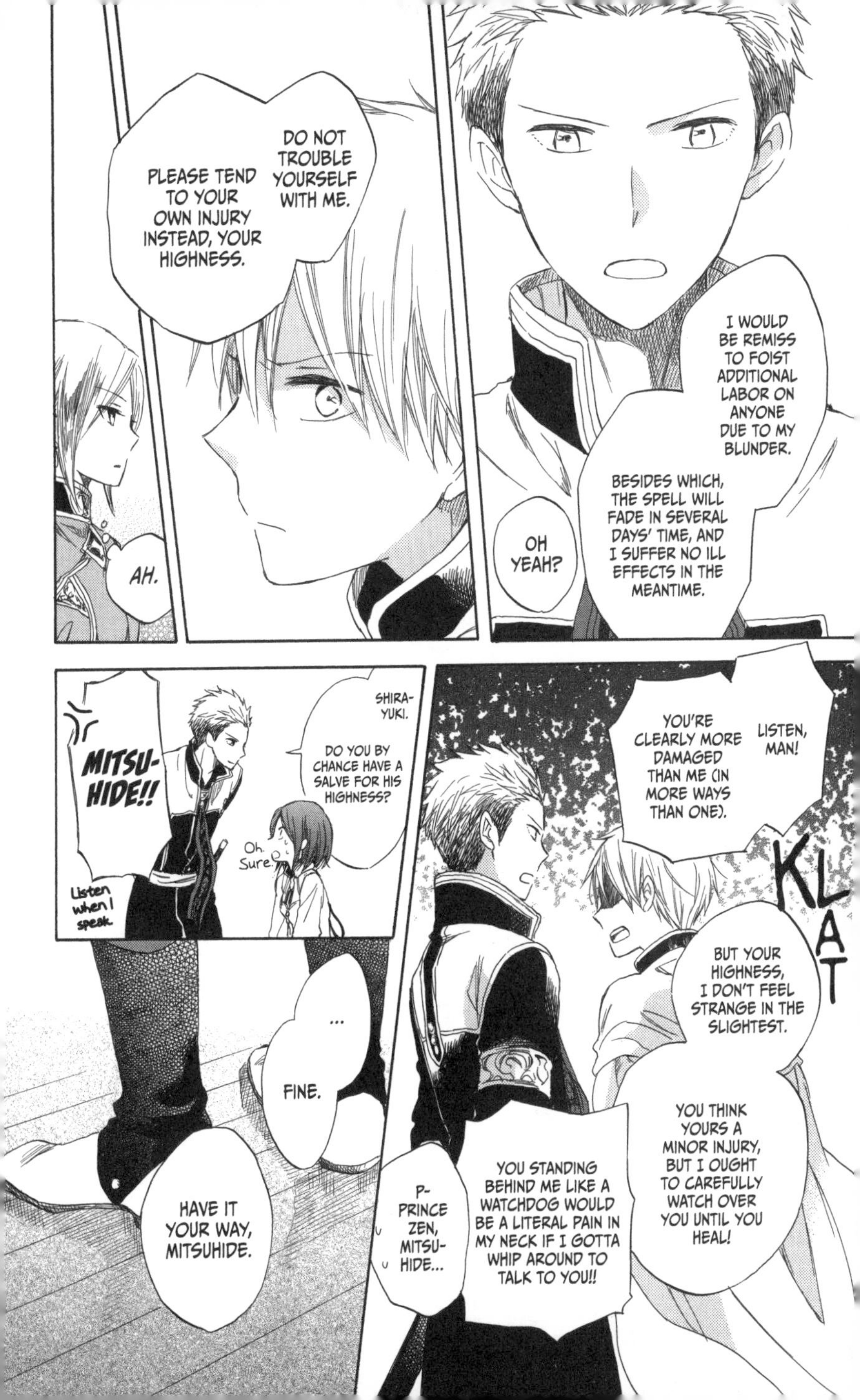
I WOULD BE REMISS TO FOIST ADDITIONAL LABOR ON ANYONE DUE TO MY BLUNDER.
BESIDES WHICH, THE SPELL WILL FADE IN SEVERAL DAYS' TIME, AND I SUFFER NO ILL EFFECTS IN THE MEANTIME.
OH YEAH?
DO NOT TROUBLE YOURSELF WITH ME.
PLEASE TEND TO YOUR OWN INJURY INSTEAD, YOUR HIGHNESS.
AH.
LISTEN, MAN!
YOU'RE CLEARLY MORE DAMAGED THAN ME (IN MORE WAYS THAN ONE).
KLAT
BUT YOUR HIGHNESS, I DON'T FEEL STRANGE IN THE SLIGHTEST.
YOU THINK YOURS A MINOR INJURY, BUT I OUGHT TO CAREFULLY WATCH OVER YOU UNTIL YOU HEAL!
YOU STANDING BEHIND ME LIKE A WATCHDOG WOULD BE A LITERAL PAIN IN MY NECK IF I GOTTA WHIP AROUND TO TALK TO YOU!!
P-PRINCE ZEN, MITSU-HIDE...
SHIRA-YUKI.
DO YOU BY CHANCE HAVE A SALVE FOR HIS HIGHNESS?
Oh. Sure.
MITSU-HIDE!!
Listen when I speak.
...
FINE.
HAVE IT YOUR WAY, MITSUHIDE.

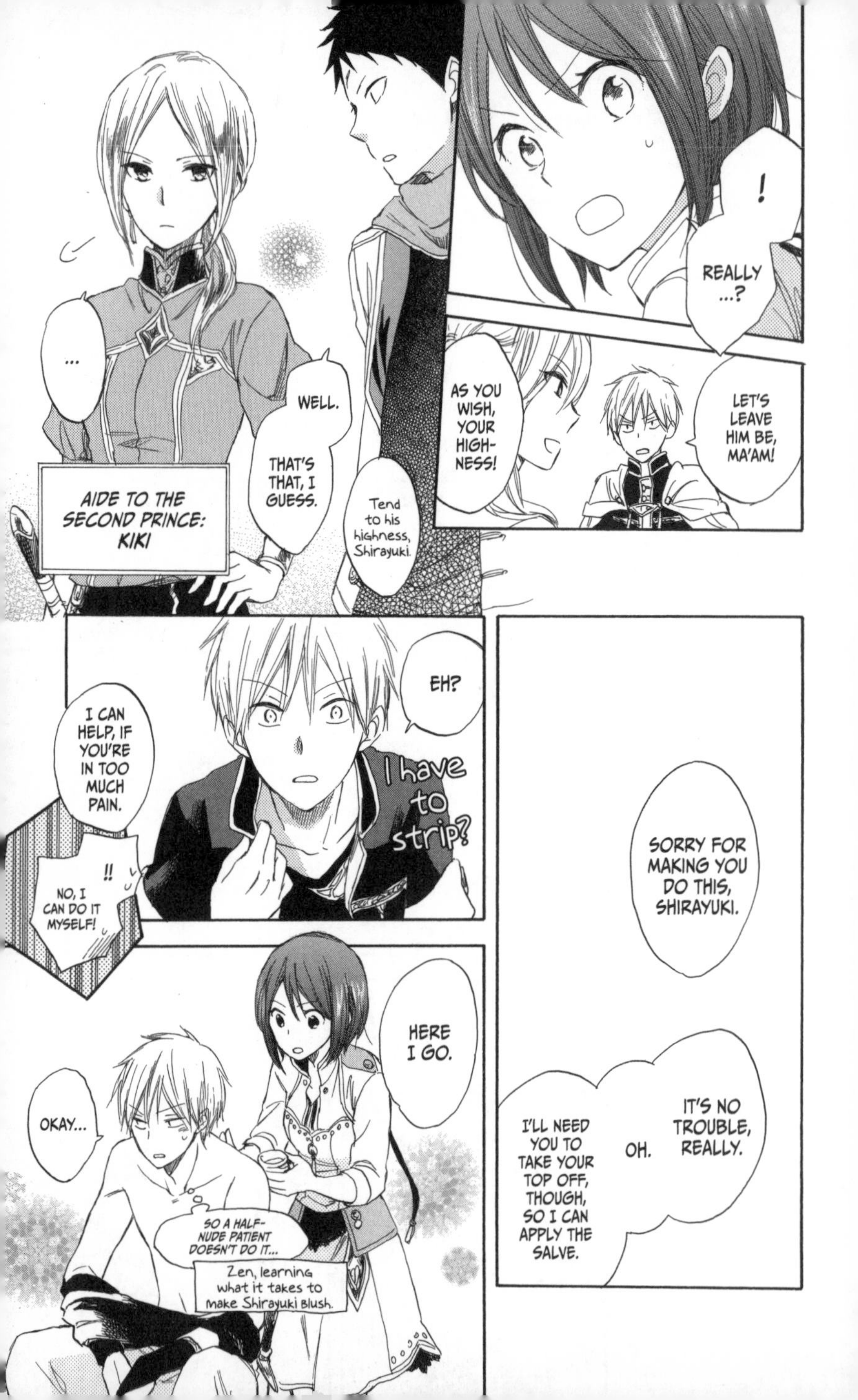
!
REALLY ...?
LET'S LEAVE HIM BE, MA'AM!
AS YOU WISH, YOUR HIGHNESS!
WELL.
THAT'S THAT, I GUESS.
Tend to his highness, Shirayuki.
...
AIDE TO THE SECOND PRINCE: KIKI
SORRY FOR MAKING YOU DO THIS, SHIRAYUKI.
IT'S NO TROUBLE, REALLY.
OH.
I'LL NEED YOU TO TAKE YOUR TOP OFF, THOUGH, SO I CAN APPLY THE SALVE.
EH?
I have to strip?
I CAN HELP, IF YOU'RE IN TOO MUCH PAIN.
!!
NO, I CAN DO IT MYSELF!
HERE I GO.
OKAY...
SO A HALF-NUDE PATIENT DOESN'T DO IT...
Zen, learning what it takes to make Shirayuki blush.

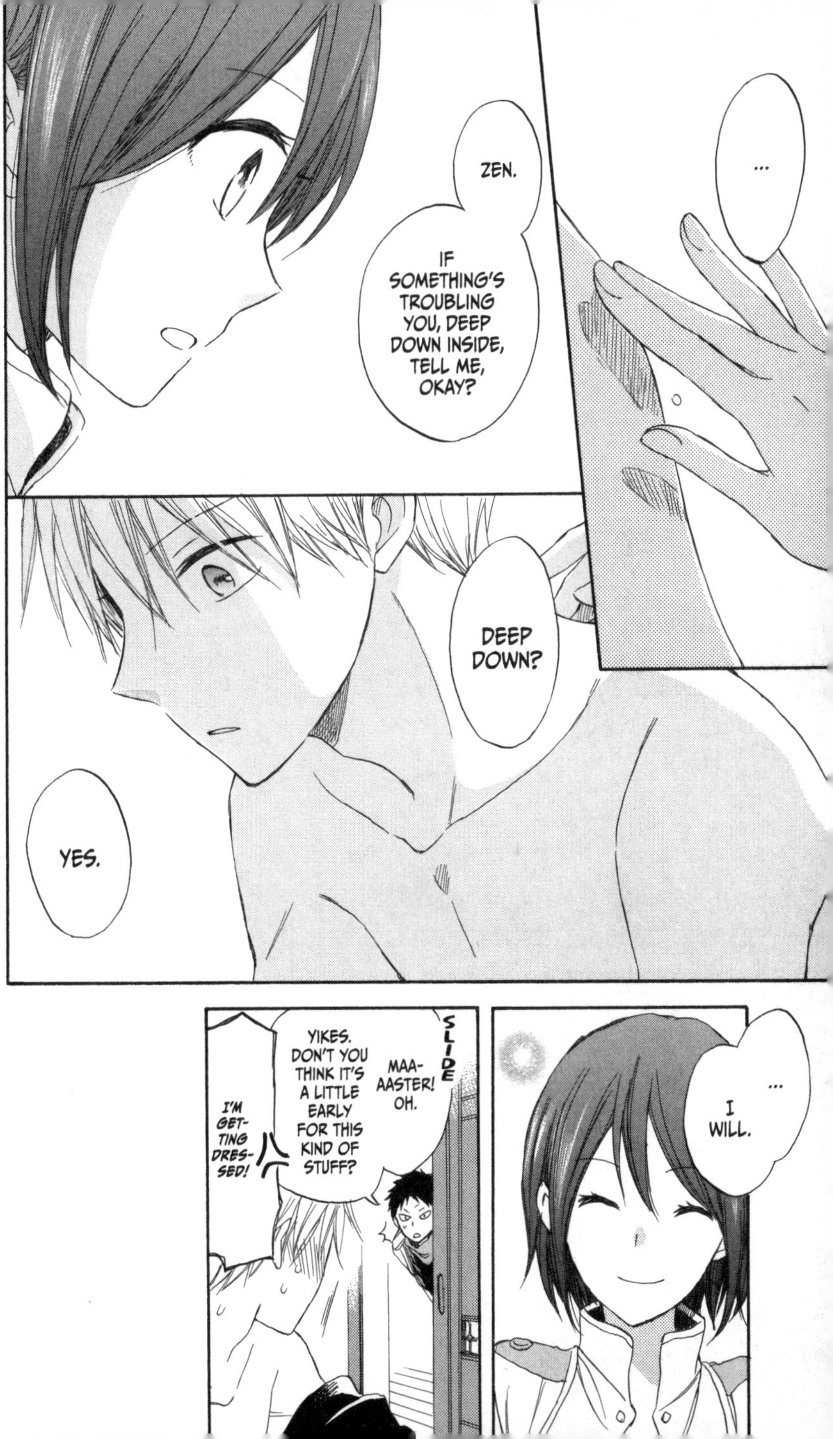
...
ZEN.
IF SOMETHING'S TROUBLING YOU, DEEP DOWN INSIDE, TELL ME, OKAY?
DEEP DOWN?
YES.
... I WILL.
SLIDE
MAA-AASTER! OH.
YIKES. DON'T YOU THINK IT'S A LITTLE EARLY FOR THIS KIND OF STUFF?
I'M GET-TING DRES-SED!

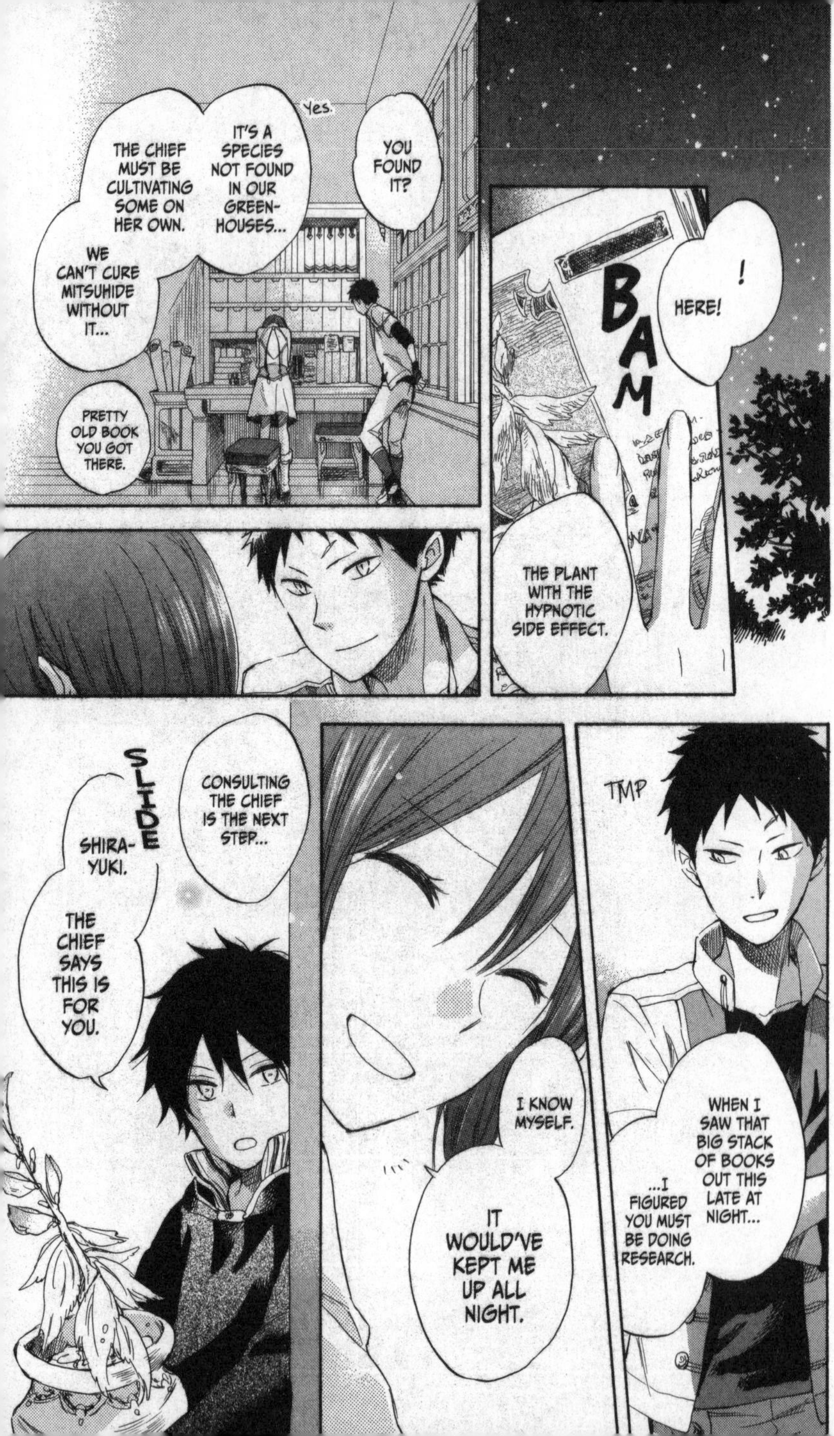
!
HERE!
BAM
THE PLANT WITH THE HYPNOTIC SIDE EFFECT.
YOU FOUND IT?
Yes.
IT'S A SPECIES NOT FOUND IN OUR GREEN-HOUSES...
THE CHIEF MUST BE CULTIVATING SOME ON HER OWN.
WE CAN'T CURE MITSUHIDE WITHOUT IT...
PRETTY OLD BOOK YOU GOT THERE.
TMP
WHEN I SAW THAT BIG STACK OF BOOKS OUT THIS LATE AT NIGHT...
...I FIGURED YOU MUST BE DOING RESEARCH.
I KNOW MYSELF.
IT WOULD'VE KEPT ME UP ALL NIGHT.
CONSULTING THE CHIEF IS THE NEXT STEP...
SLIDE
SHIRA-YUKI.
THE CHIEF SAYS THIS IS FOR YOU.

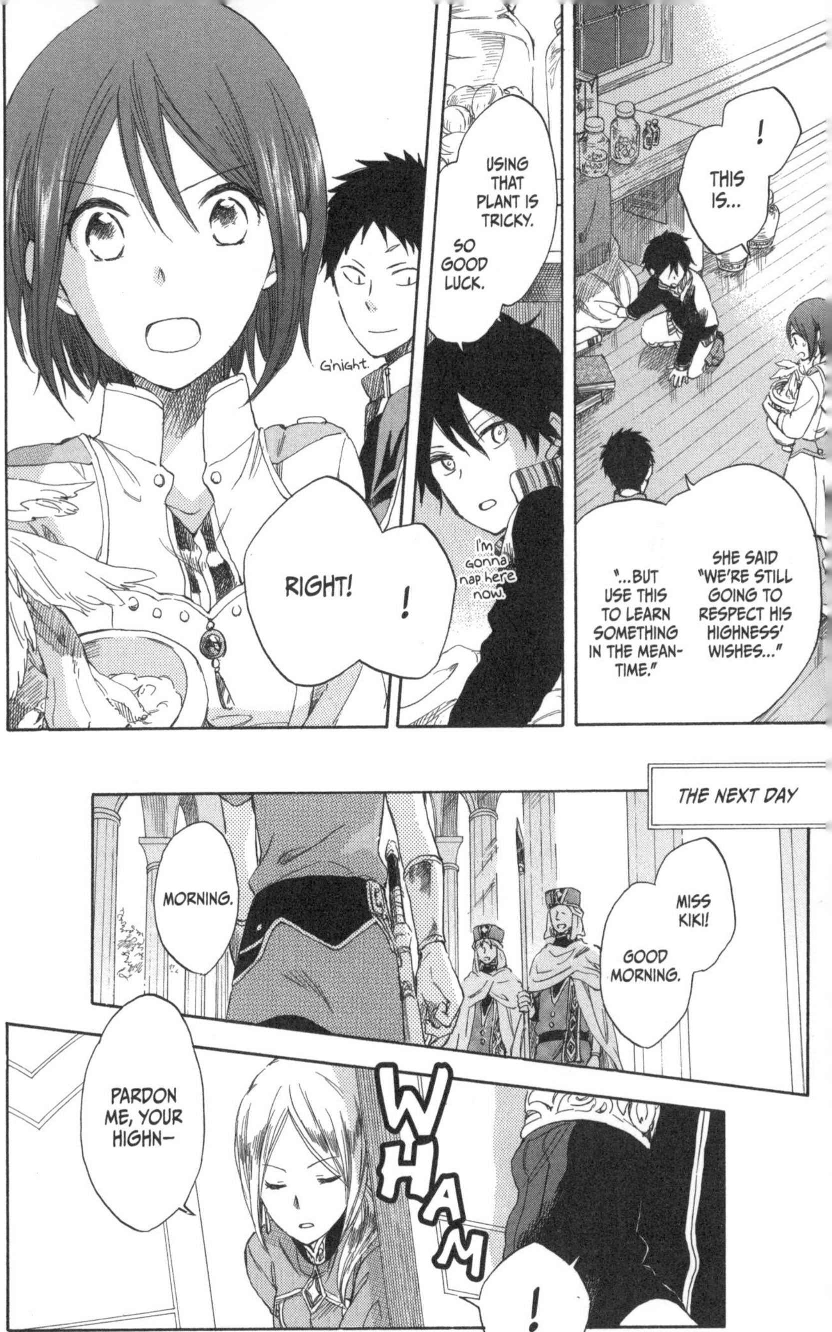
!
THIS IS...
SHE SAID "WE'RE STILL GOING TO RESPECT HIS HIGHNESS' WISHES..."
"...BUT USE THIS TO LEARN SOMETHING IN THE MEAN-TIME."
USING THAT PLANT IS TRICKY.
SO GOOD LUCK.
I'm gonna nap here now.
!
G'night.
RIGHT!
THE NEXT DAY
MISS KIKI!
GOOD MORNING.
MORNING.
WHAM
!
PARDON ME, YOUR HIGHN–

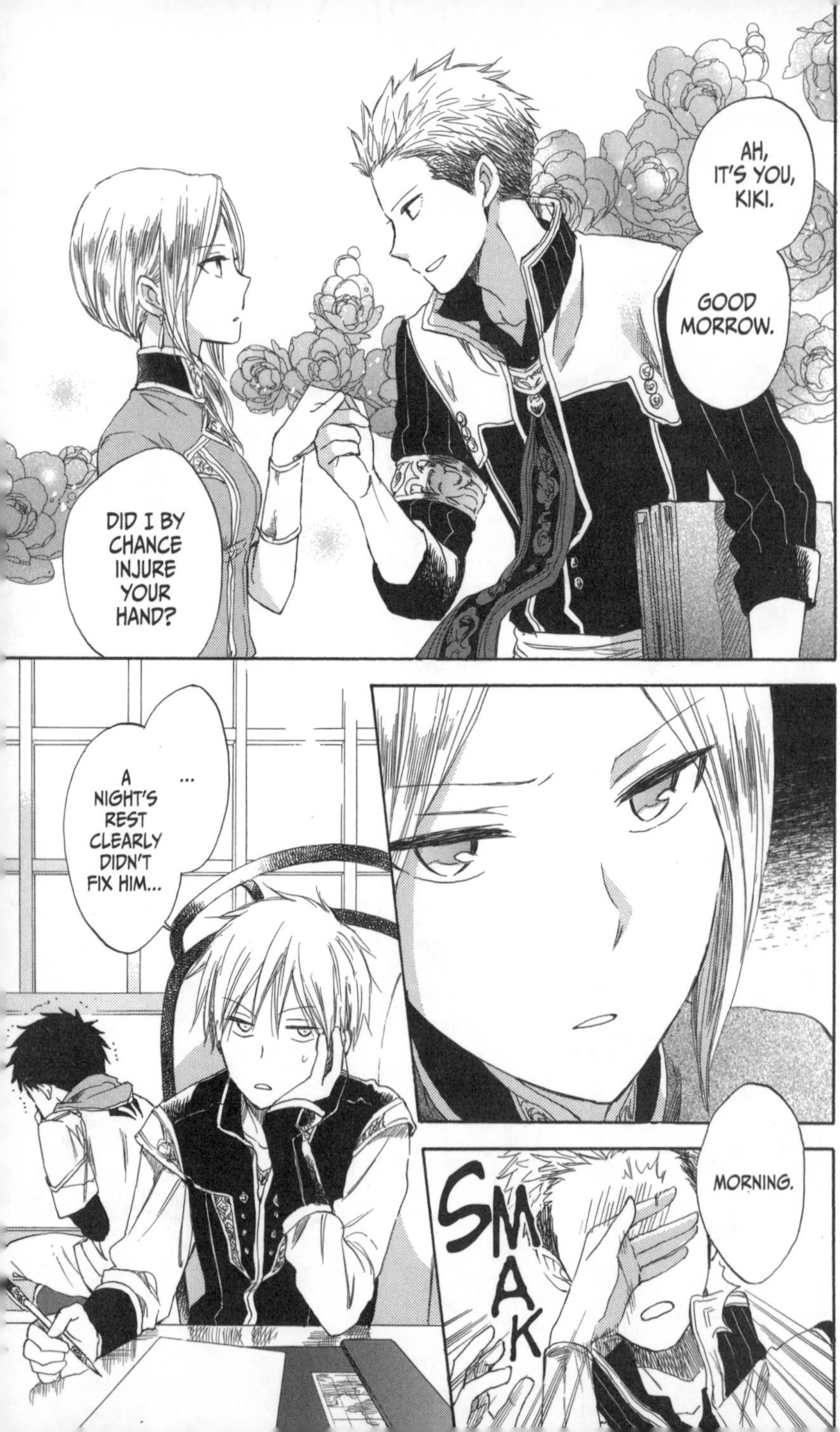
AH, IT'S YOU, KIKI.
GOOD MORROW.
DID I BY CHANCE INJURE YOUR HAND?
MORNING.
SMAK
...
A NIGHT'S REST CLEARLY DIDN'T FIX HIM...

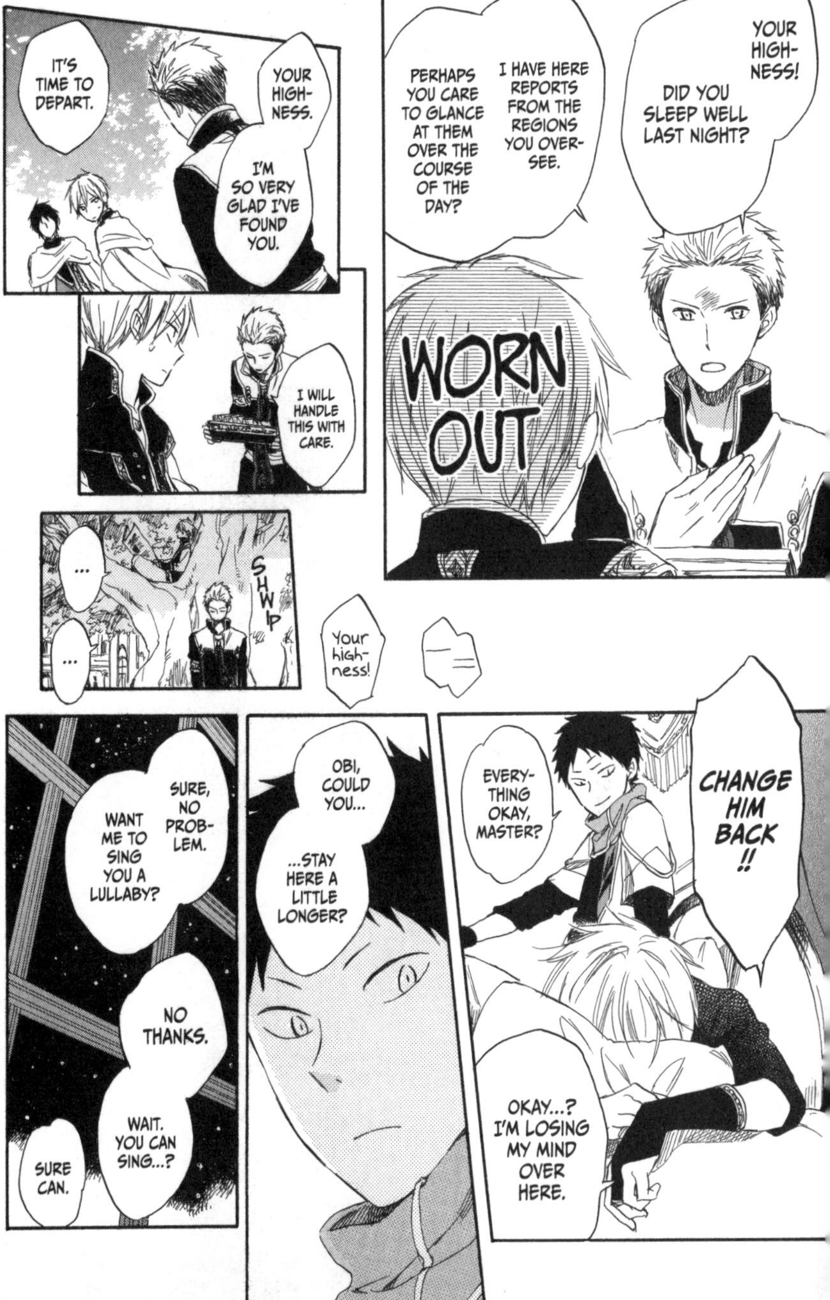
YOUR HIGHNESS!
DID YOU SLEEP WELL LAST NIGHT?
I HAVE HERE REPORTS FROM THE REGIONS YOU OVERSEE.
PERHAPS YOU CARE TO GLANCE AT THEM OVER THE COURSE OF THE DAY?
WORN OUT
YOUR HIGHNESS.
IT'S TIME TO DEPART.
I'M SO VERY GLAD I'VE FOUND YOU.
I WILL HANDLE THIS WITH CARE.
SHWIP
...
...
—
Your highness!
CHANGE HIM BACK!!
EVERYTHING OKAY, MASTER?
OKAY...? I'M LOSING MY MIND OVER HERE.
OBI, COULD YOU...
...STAY HERE A LITTLE LONGER?
SURE, NO PROBLEM.
WANT ME TO SING YOU A LULLABY?
NO THANKS.
WAIT. YOU CAN SING...?
SURE CAN.

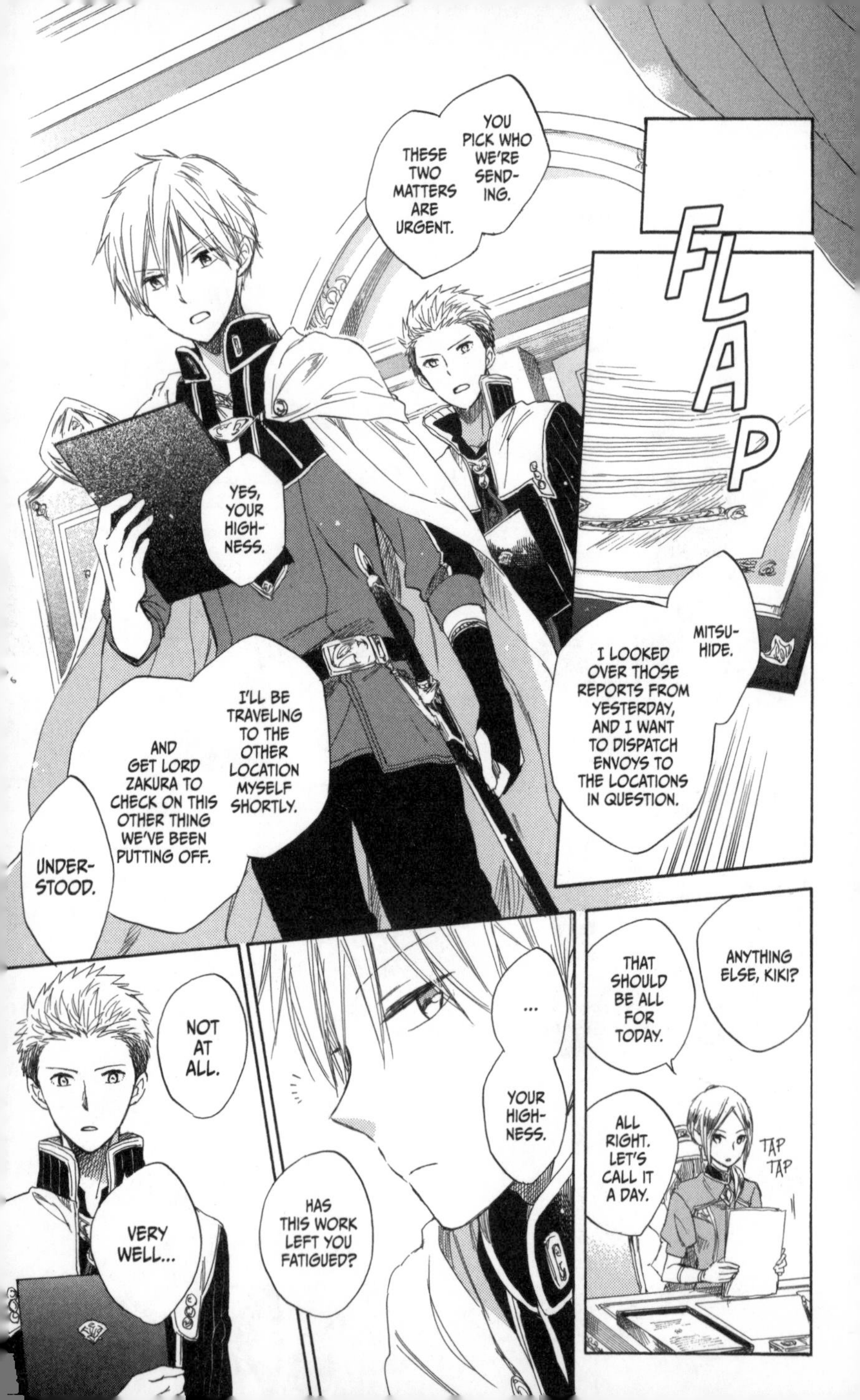
FLAP
MITSU-HIDE.
I LOOKED OVER THOSE REPORTS FROM YESTERDAY, AND I WANT TO DISPATCH ENVOYS TO THE LOCATIONS IN QUESTION.
THESE TWO MATTERS ARE URGENT. YOU PICK WHO WE'RE SEND-ING.
YES, YOUR HIGH-NESS.
I'LL BE TRAVELING TO THE OTHER LOCATION MYSELF SHORTLY.
AND GET LORD ZAKURA TO CHECK ON THIS OTHER THING WE'VE BEEN PUTTING OFF.
UNDER-STOOD.
ANYTHING ELSE, KIKI?
THAT SHOULD BE ALL FOR TODAY.
ALL RIGHT. LET'S CALL IT A DAY.
TAP TAP
...
YOUR HIGH-NESS.
HAS THIS WORK LEFT YOU FATIGUED?
NOT AT ALL.
VERY WELL...

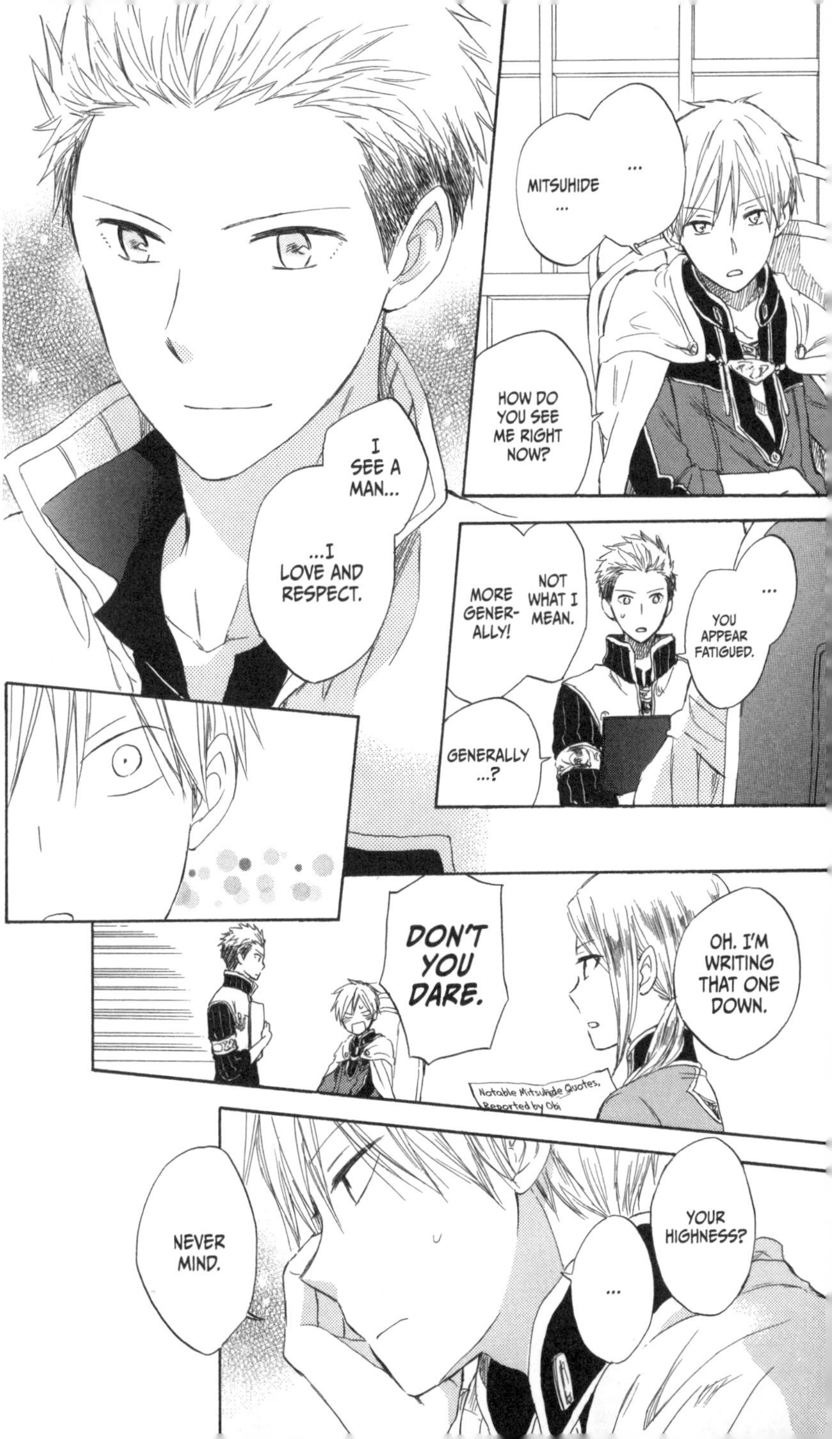
...
MITSUHIDE ...
HOW DO YOU SEE ME RIGHT NOW?
...
YOU APPEAR FATIGUED.
NOT WHAT I MEAN.
MORE GENERALLY!
GENERALLY ...?
I SEE A MAN...
...I LOVE AND RESPECT.
OH. I'M WRITING THAT ONE DOWN.
DON'T YOU DARE.
Notable Mitsuhide Quotes, Reported by Obi
YOUR HIGHNESS?
...
NEVER MIND.

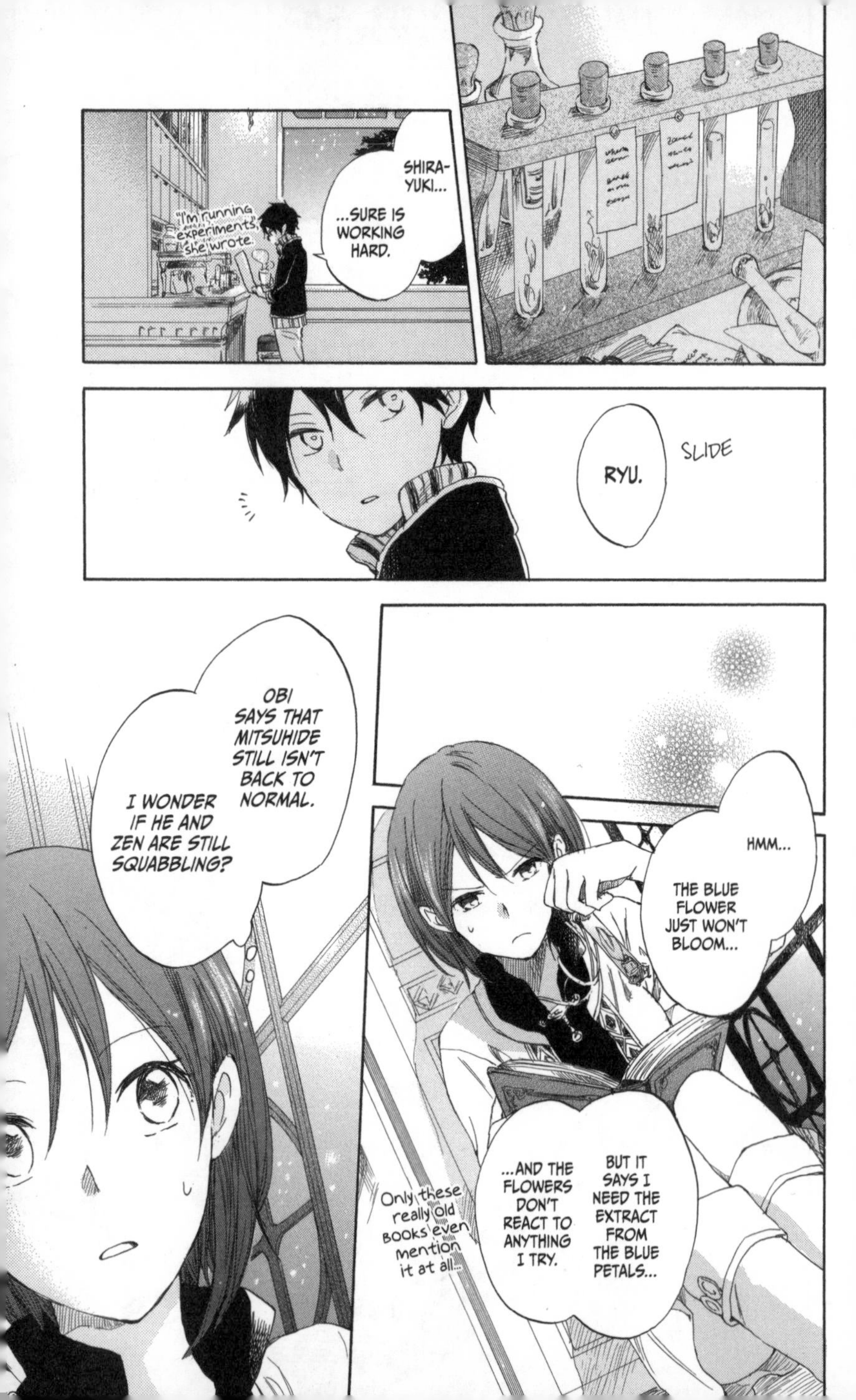
SHIRA-YUKI...
...SURE IS WORKING HARD.
"I'm running experiments," she wrote.
SLIDE
RYU.
HMM...
THE BLUE FLOWER JUST WON'T BLOOM...
BUT IT SAYS I NEED THE EXTRACT FROM THE BLUE PETALS...
...AND THE FLOWERS DON'T REACT TO ANYTHING I TRY.
Only these really old books even mention it at all...
OBI SAYS THAT MITSUHIDE STILL ISN'T BACK TO NORMAL.
I WONDER IF HE AND ZEN ARE STILL SQUABBLING?

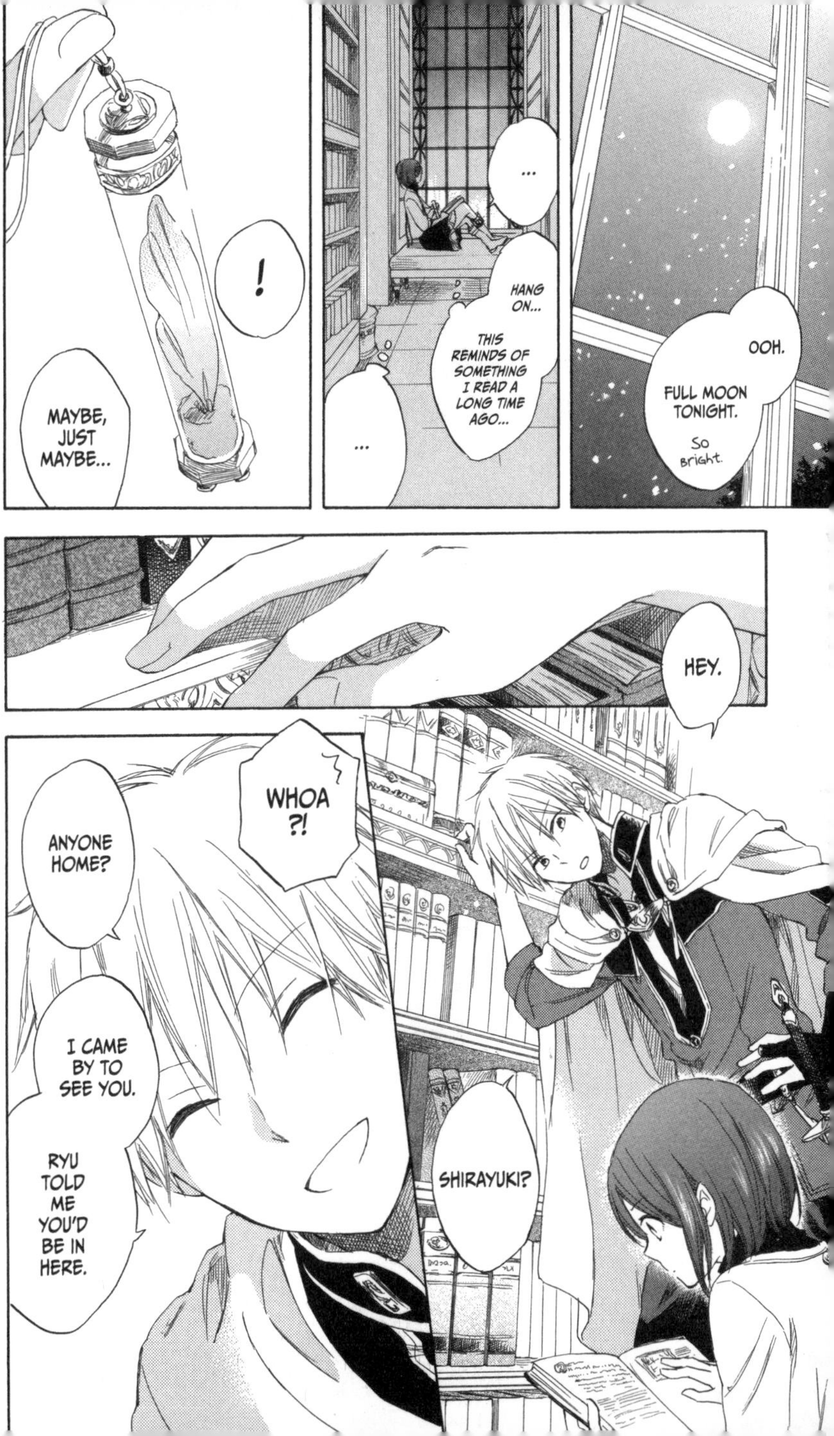
OOH.
FULL MOON TONIGHT.
So bright.
...
HANG ON...
THIS REMINDS OF SOMETHING I READ A LONG TIME AGO...
...
!
MAYBE, JUST MAYBE...
HEY.
SHIRAYUKI?
WHOA ?!
ANYONE HOME?
I CAME BY TO SEE YOU.
RYU TOLD ME YOU'D BE IN HERE.

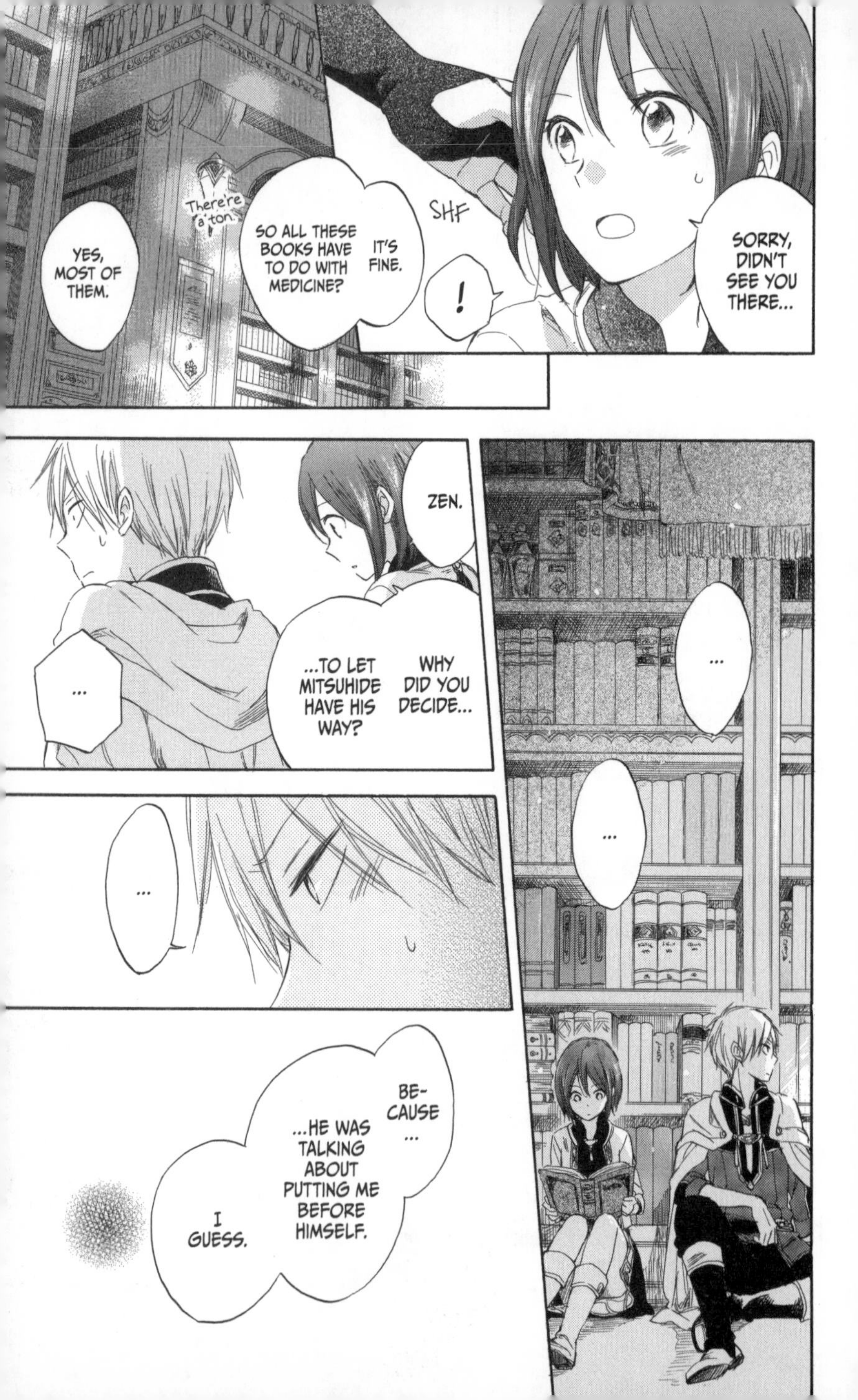
SORRY, DIDN'T SEE YOU THERE...
!
SHF
IT'S FINE.
SO ALL THESE BOOKS HAVE TO DO WITH MEDICINE?
There're a ton.
YES, MOST OF THEM.
...
...
ZEN.
WHY DID YOU DECIDE...
...TO LET MITSUHIDE HAVE HIS WAY?
...
...
BE-CAUSE...
...HE WAS TALKING ABOUT PUTTING ME BEFORE HIMSELF.
I GUESS.

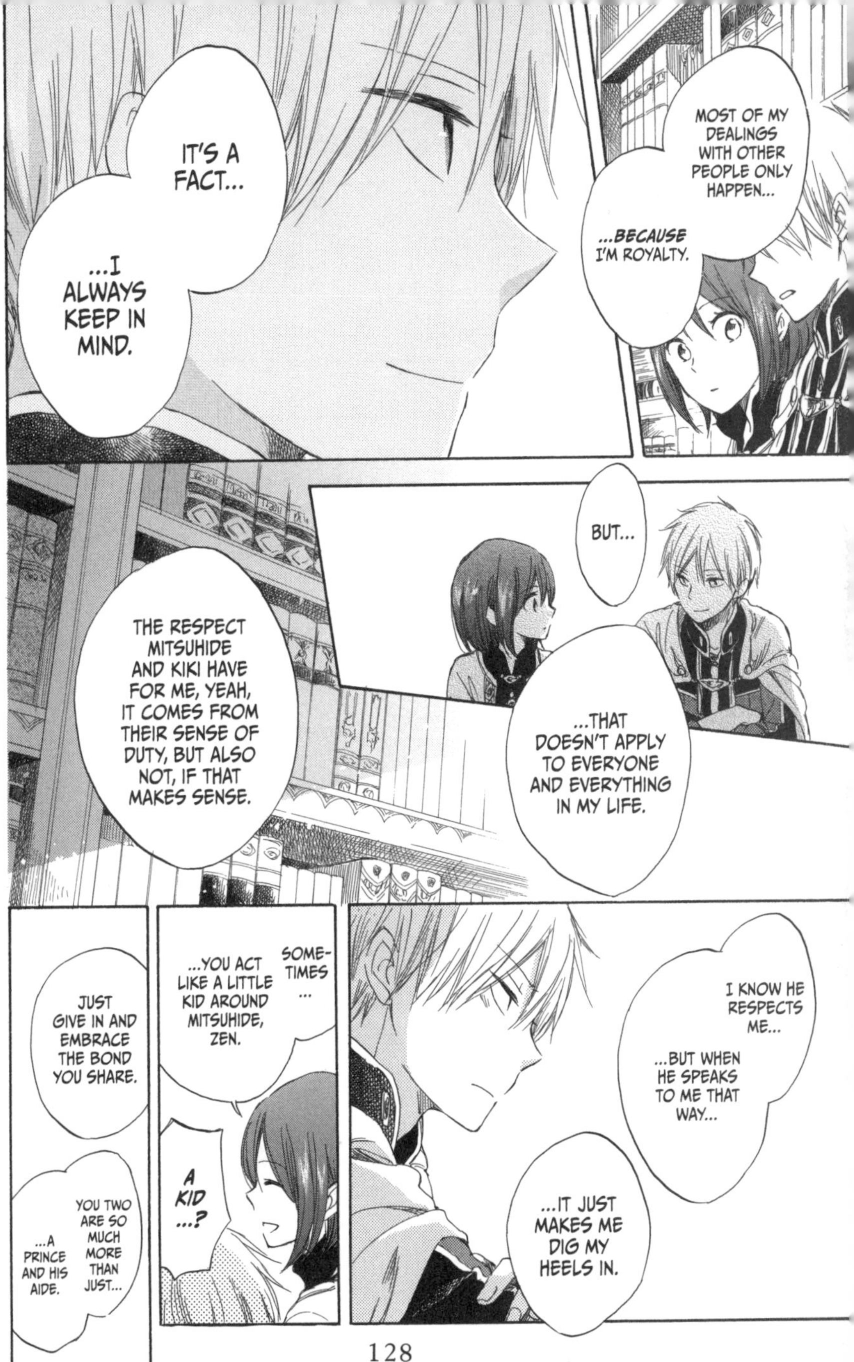
MOST OF MY DEALINGS WITH OTHER PEOPLE ONLY HAPPEN...
...*BECAUSE* I'M ROYALTY.
IT'S A FACT...
...I ALWAYS KEEP IN MIND.
BUT...
...THAT DOESN'T APPLY TO EVERYONE AND EVERYTHING IN MY LIFE.
THE RESPECT MITSUHIDE AND KIKI HAVE FOR ME, YEAH, IT COMES FROM THEIR SENSE OF DUTY, BUT ALSO NOT, IF THAT MAKES SENSE.
I KNOW HE RESPECTS ME...
...BUT WHEN HE SPEAKS TO ME THAT WAY...
...IT JUST MAKES ME DIG MY HEELS IN.
SOME-TIMES...
...YOU ACT LIKE A LITTLE KID AROUND MITSUHIDE, ZEN.
A KID...?
JUST GIVE IN AND EMBRACE THE BOND YOU SHARE.
YOU TWO ARE SO MUCH MORE THAN JUST...
...A PRINCE AND HIS AIDE.

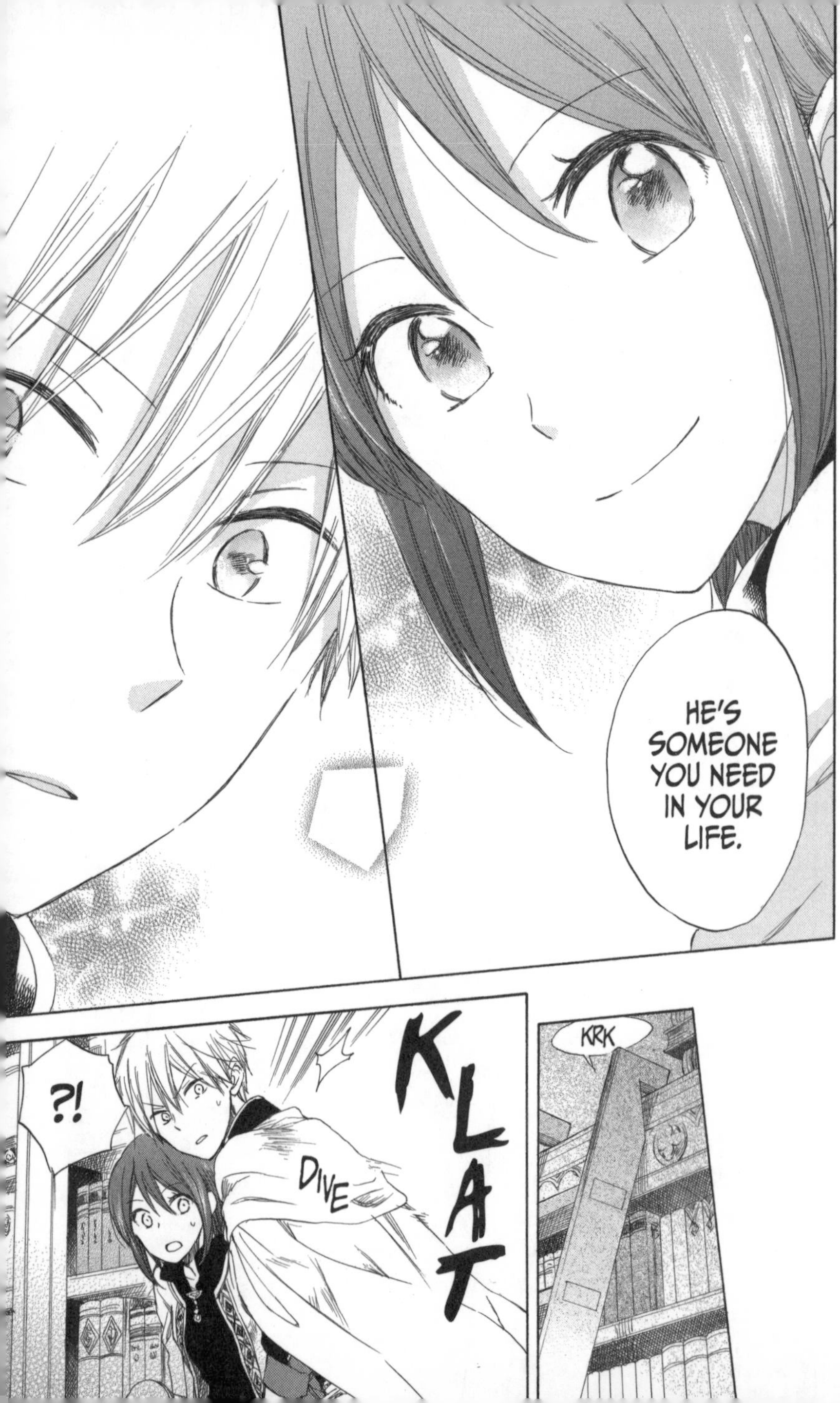
HE'S SOMEONE YOU NEED IN YOUR LIFE.
KRK
KLAT
?!
DIVE

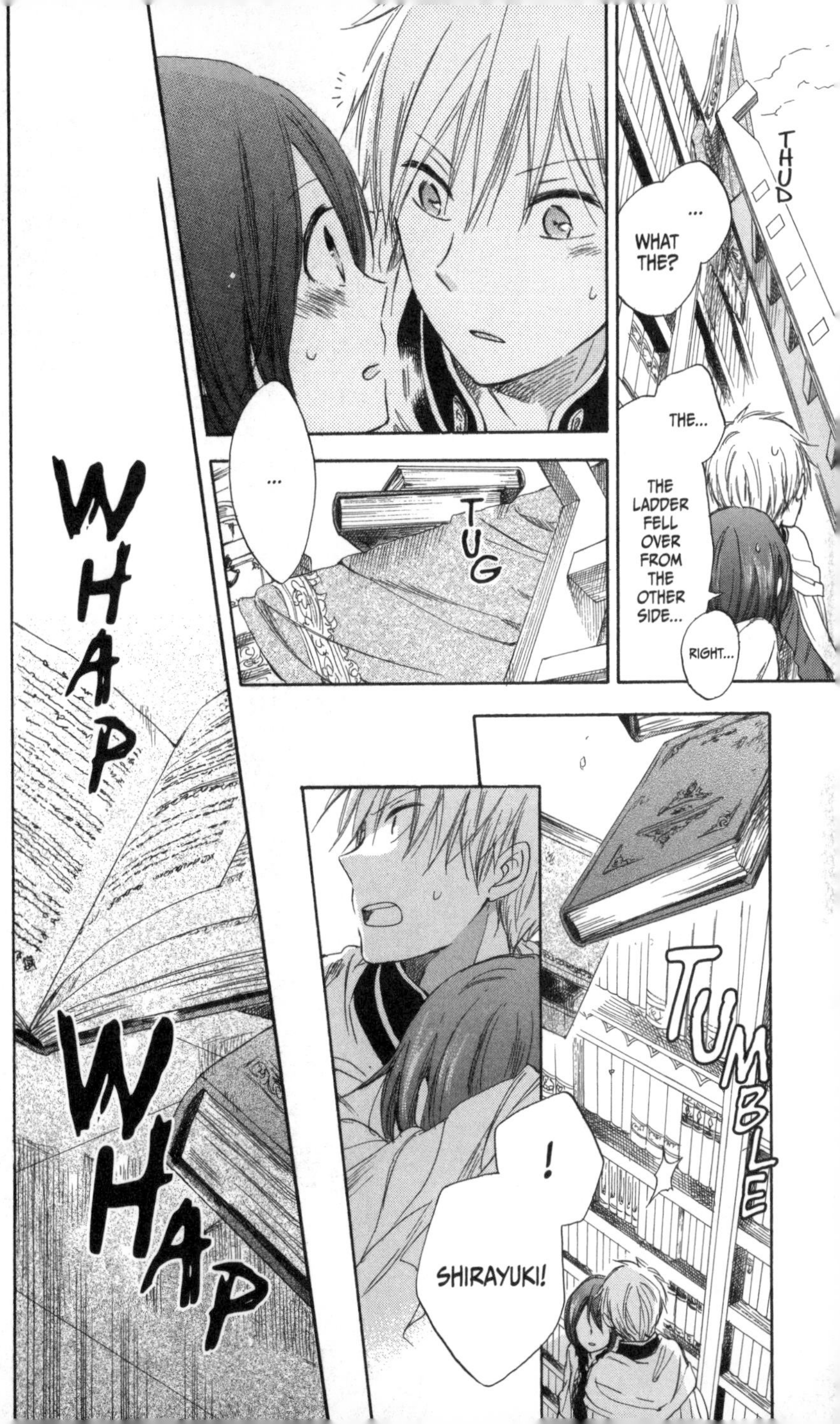

THUD
... WHAT THE?
THE...
THE LADDER FELL OVER FROM THE OTHER SIDE...
RIGHT...
...
TUG
TUMBLE
!
SHIRAYUKI!
WHAP
WHAP

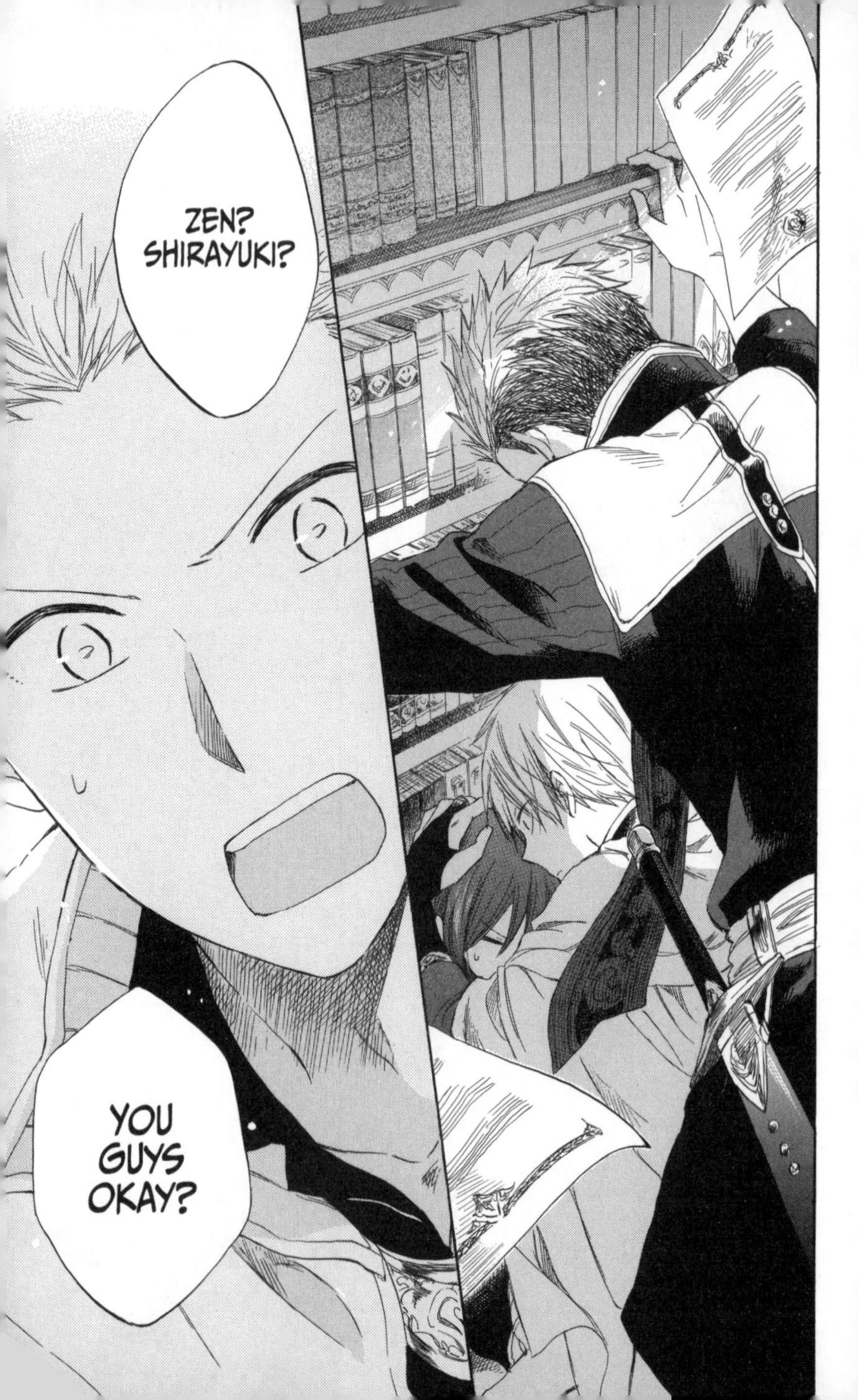
ZEN? SHIRAYUKI?
YOU GUYS OKAY?

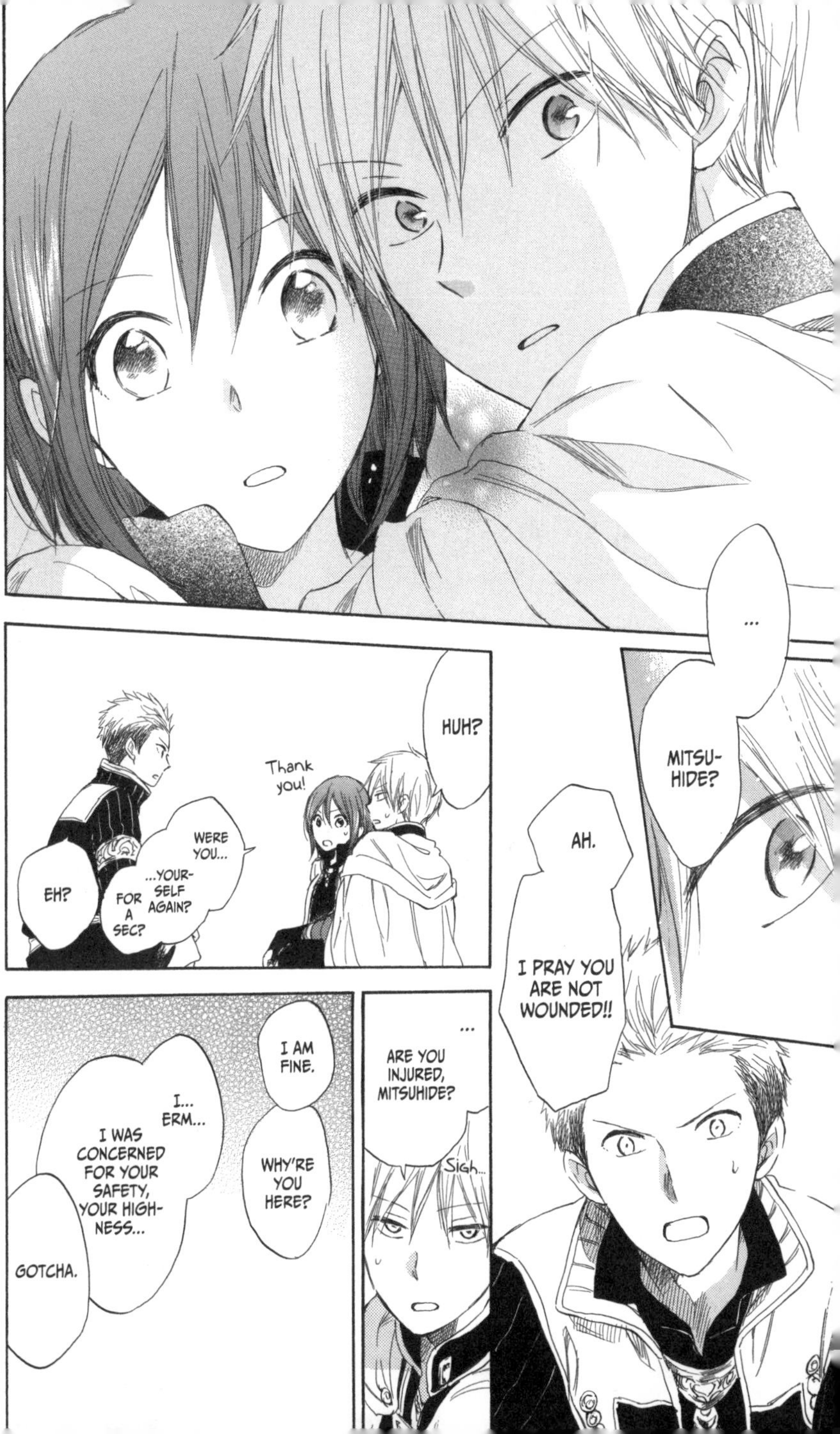
...
MITSU-HIDE?
HUH?
Thank you!
WERE YOU...
...YOUR-SELF AGAIN?
FOR A SEC?
EH?
AH.
I PRAY YOU ARE NOT WOUNDED!!
...
ARE YOU INJURED, MITSUHIDE?
Sigh...
I AM FINE.
WHY'RE YOU HERE?
I... ERM...
I WAS CONCERNED FOR YOUR SAFETY, YOUR HIGHNESS...
GOTCHA.

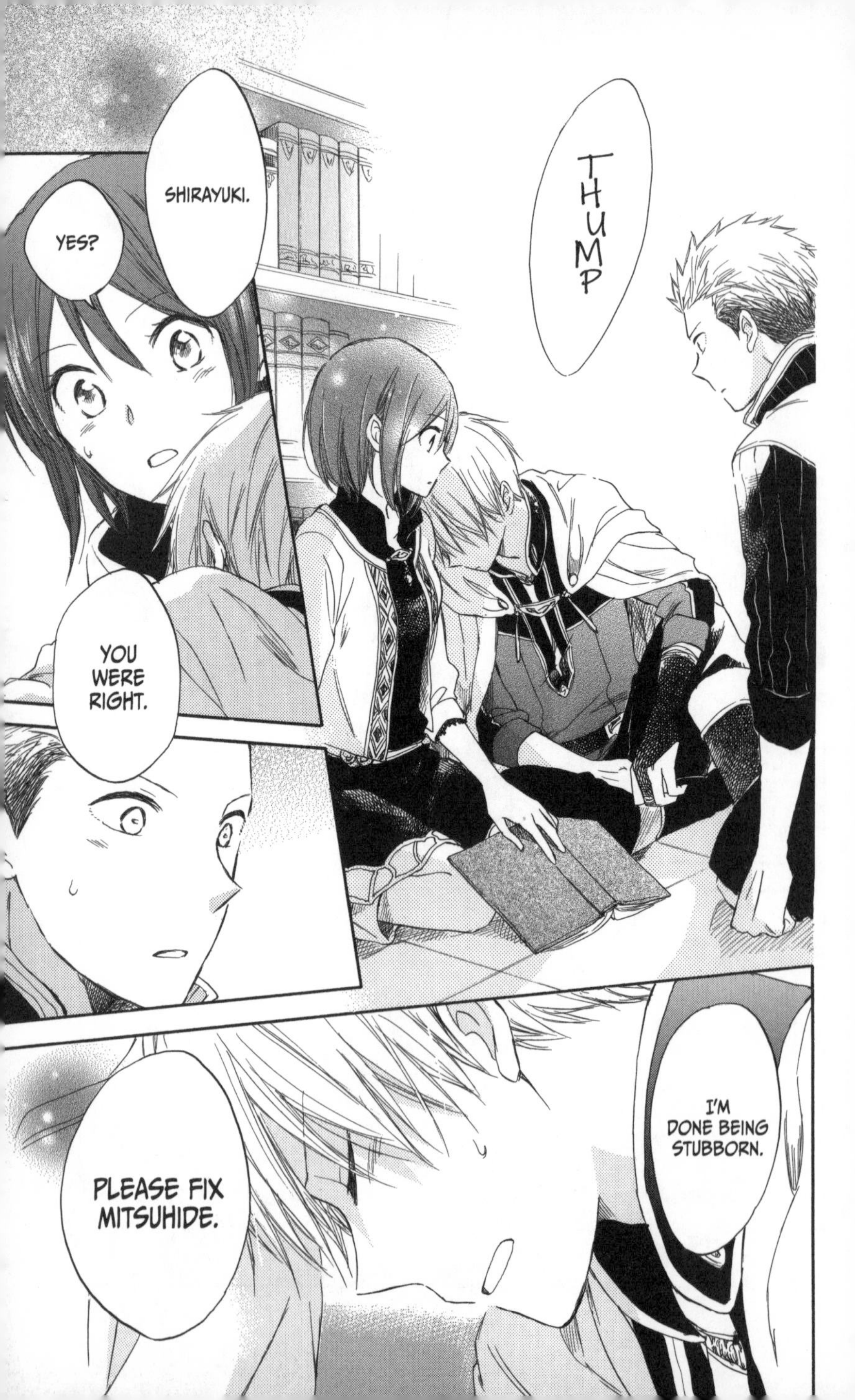
THUMP
SHIRAYUKI.
YES?
YOU WERE RIGHT.
I'M DONE BEING STUBBORN.
PLEASE FIX MITSUHIDE.

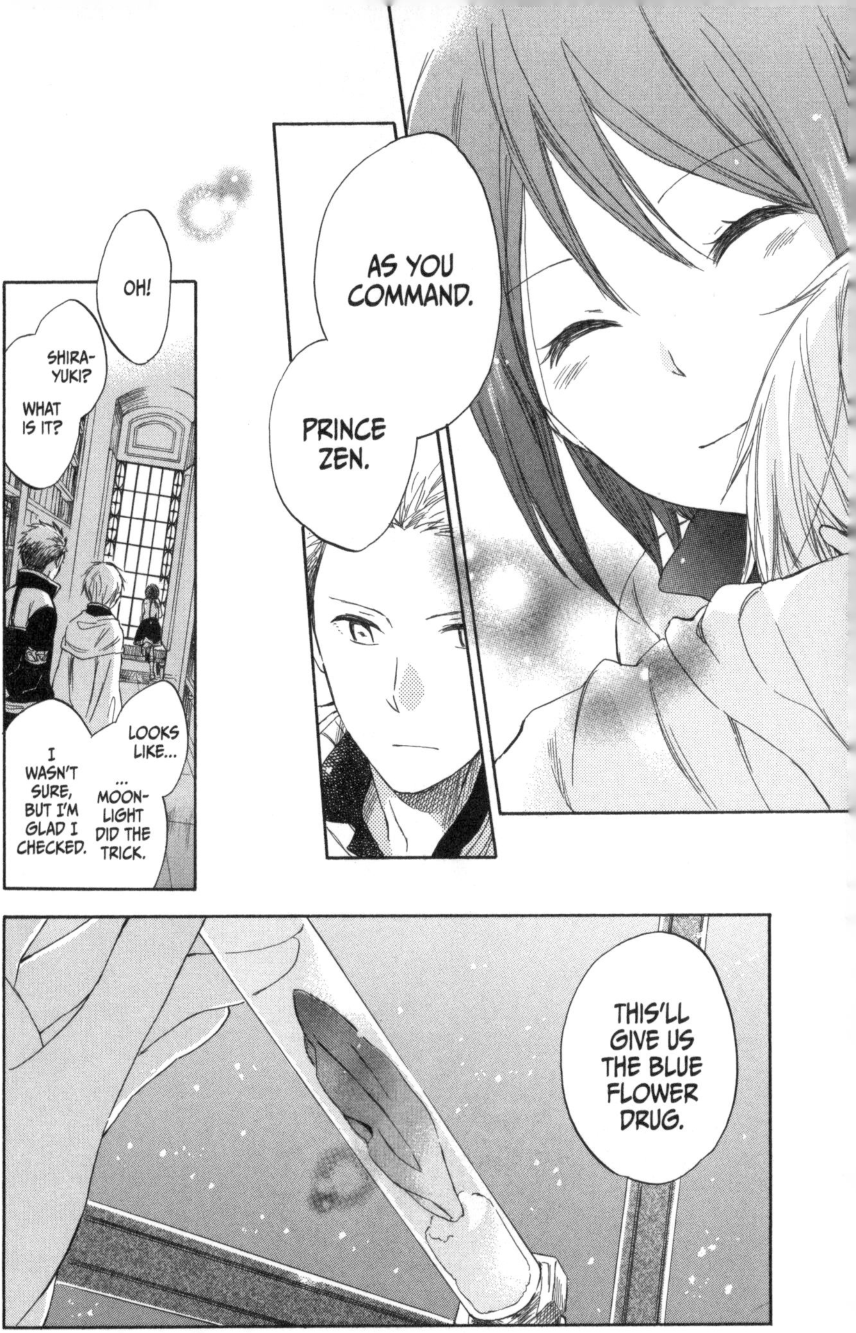
AS YOU COMMAND.
PRINCE ZEN.
OH!
SHIRA-YUKI?
WHAT IS IT?
LOOKS LIKE...
... MOON-LIGHT DID THE TRICK.
I WASN'T SURE, BUT I'M GLAD I CHECKED.
THIS'LL GIVE US THE BLUE FLOWER DRUG.

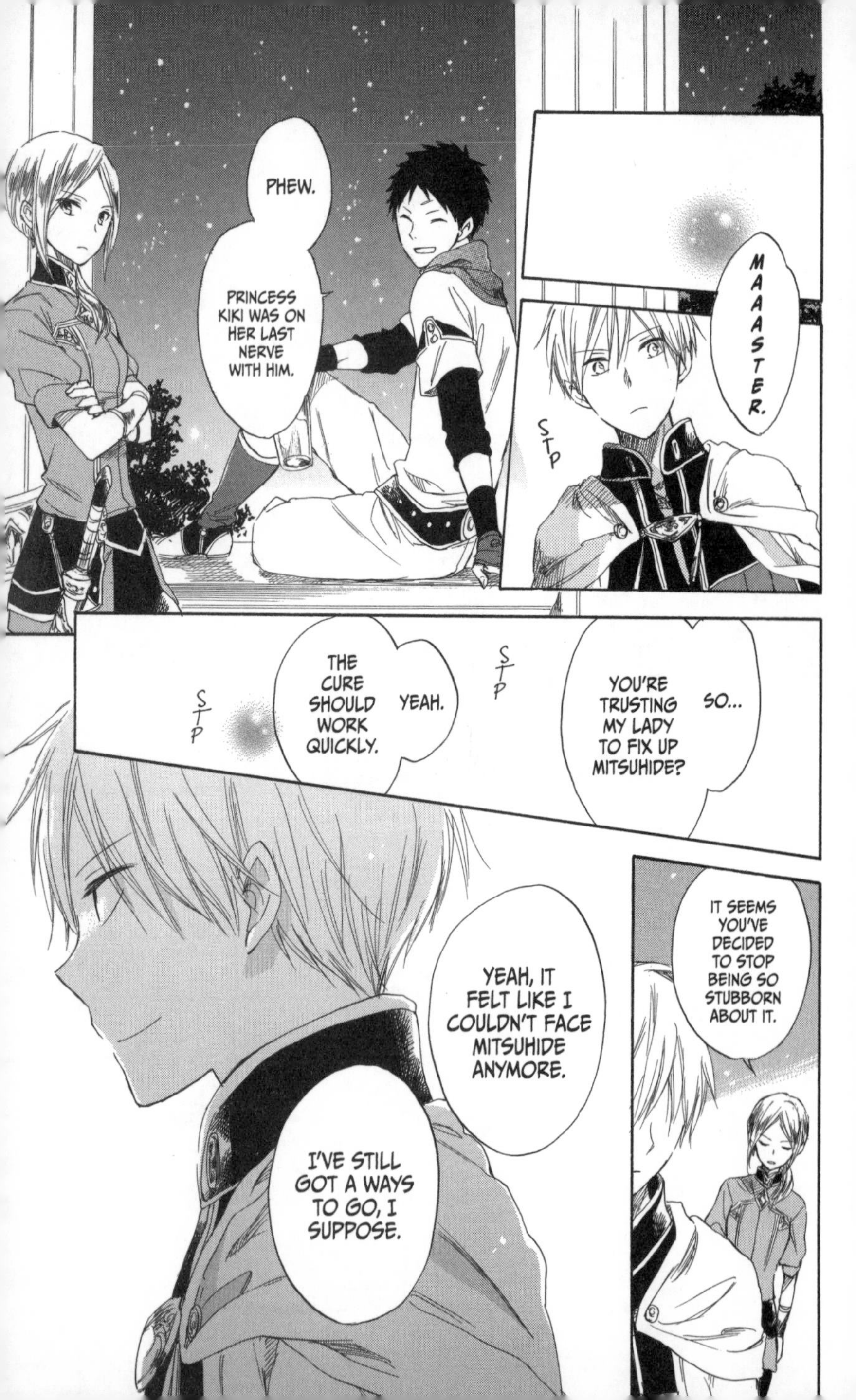
MAAASTER.
STP
PHEW.
PRINCESS KIKI WAS ON HER LAST NERVE WITH HIM.
SO...
YOU'RE TRUSTING MY LADY TO FIX UP MITSUHIDE?
STP
YEAH.
THE CURE SHOULD WORK QUICKLY.
STP
IT SEEMS YOU'VE DECIDED TO STOP BEING SO STUBBORN ABOUT IT.
YEAH, IT FELT LIKE I COULDN'T FACE MITSUHIDE ANYMORE.
I'VE STILL GOT A WAYS TO GO, I SUPPOSE.

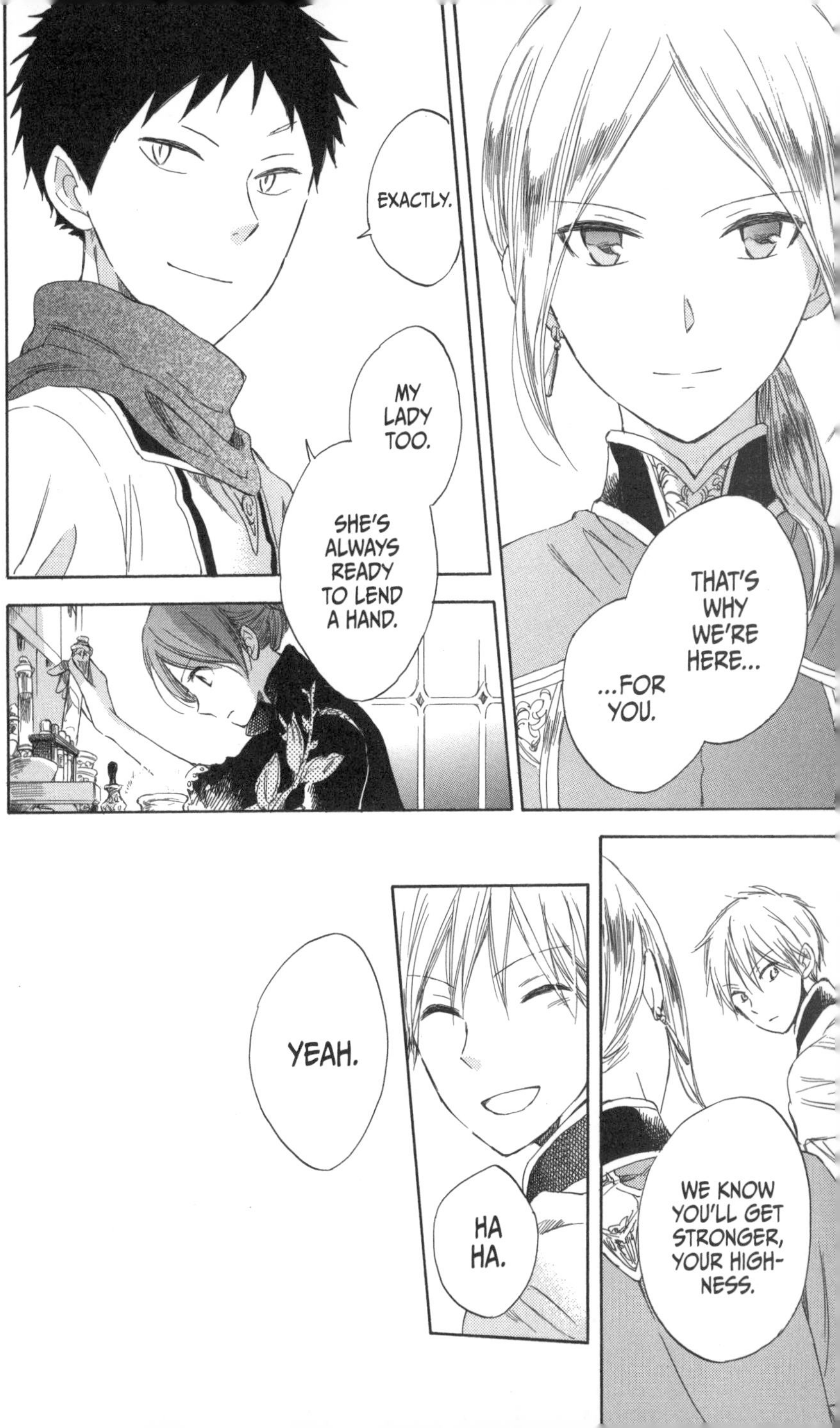
THAT'S WHY WE'RE HERE...
...FOR YOU.
EXACTLY.
MY LADY TOO.
SHE'S ALWAYS READY TO LEND A HAND.
WE KNOW YOU'LL GET STRONGER, YOUR HIGH-NESS.
YEAH.
HA HA.

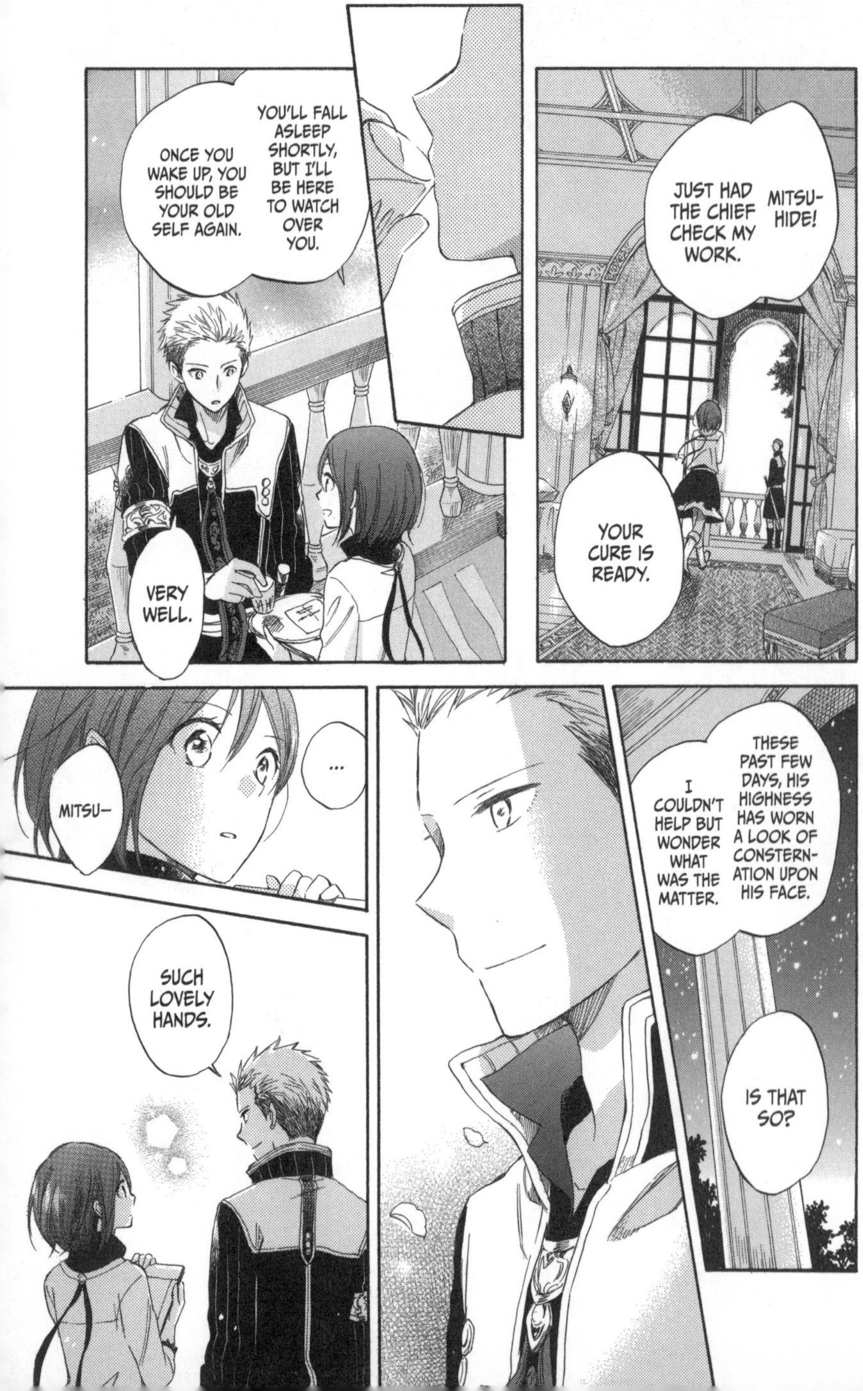
MITSU-HIDE!
JUST HAD THE CHIEF CHECK MY WORK.
YOUR CURE IS READY.
YOU'LL FALL ASLEEP SHORTLY, BUT I'LL BE HERE TO WATCH OVER YOU.
ONCE YOU WAKE UP, YOU SHOULD BE YOUR OLD SELF AGAIN.
VERY WELL.
THESE PAST FEW DAYS, HIS HIGHNESS HAS WORN A LOOK OF CONSTERN-ATION UPON HIS FACE.
I COULDN'T HELP BUT WONDER WHAT WAS THE MATTER.
IS THAT SO?
...
MITSU—
SUCH LOVELY HANDS.

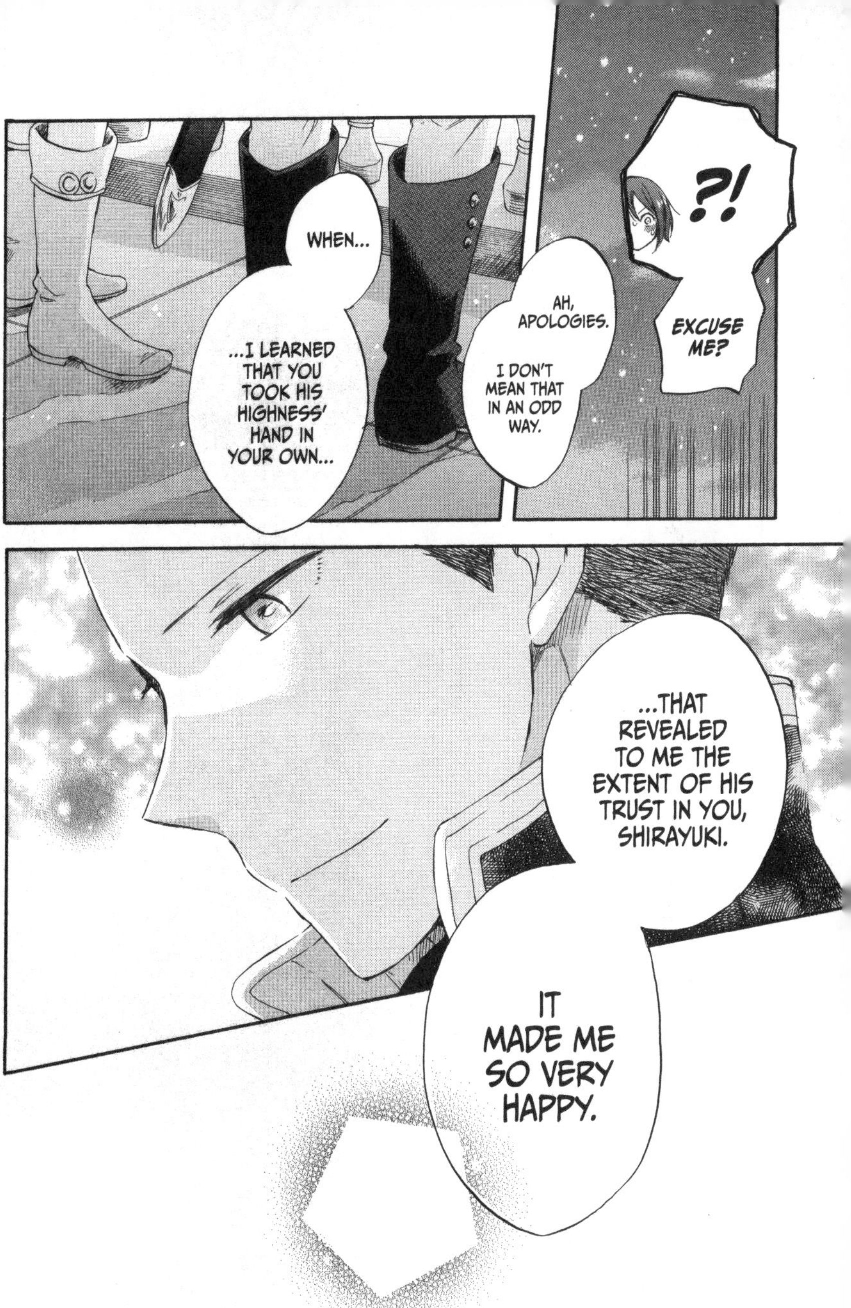
?!
EXCUSE ME?
AH, APOLOGIES.
I DON'T MEAN THAT IN AN ODD WAY.
WHEN...
...I LEARNED THAT YOU TOOK HIS HIGHNESS' HAND IN YOUR OWN...
...THAT REVEALED TO ME THE EXTENT OF HIS TRUST IN YOU, SHIRAYUKI.
IT MADE ME SO VERY HAPPY.

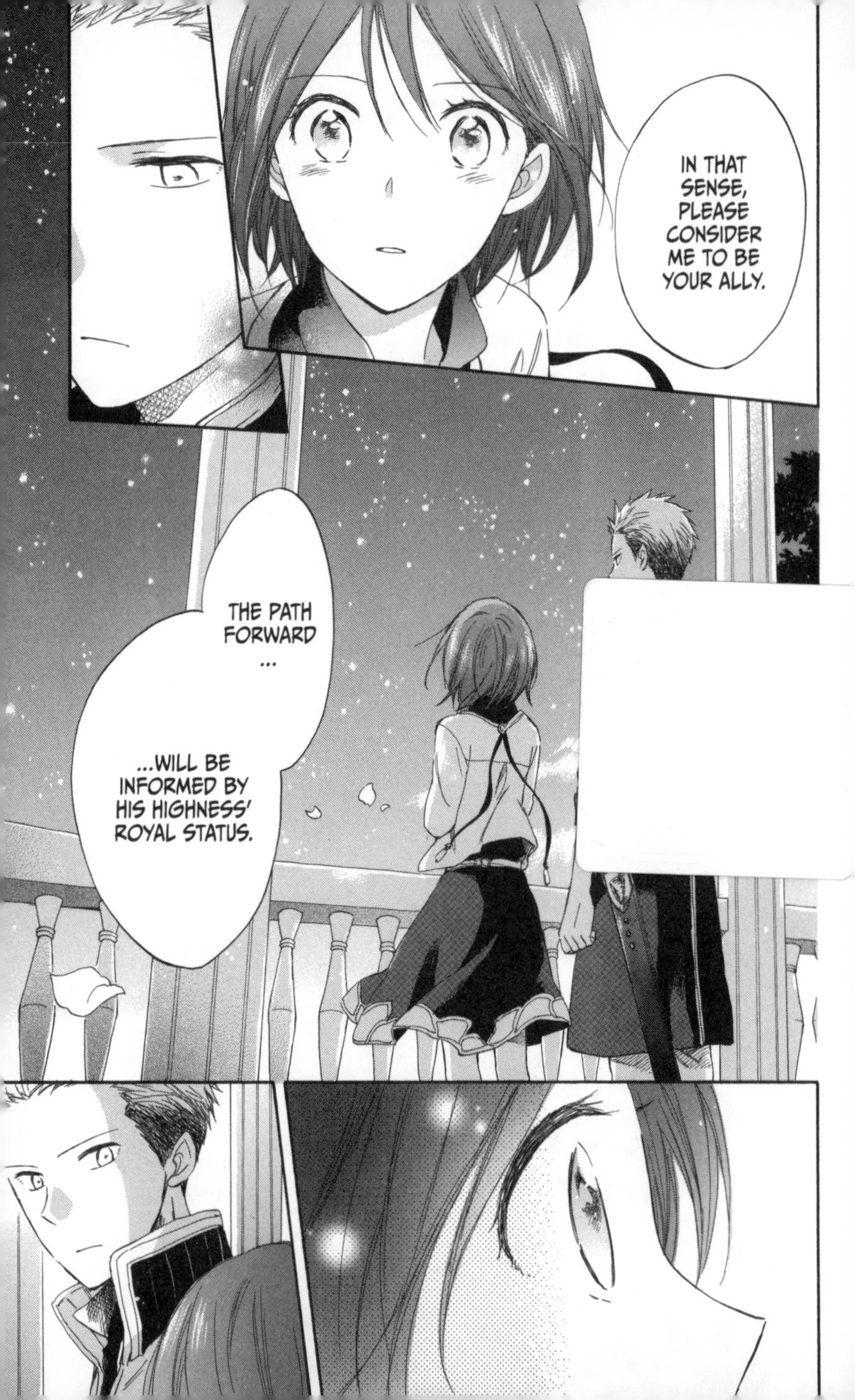
IN THAT SENSE, PLEASE CONSIDER ME TO BE YOUR ALLY.
THE PATH FORWARD ...
...WILL BE INFORMED BY HIS HIGHNESS' ROYAL STATUS.

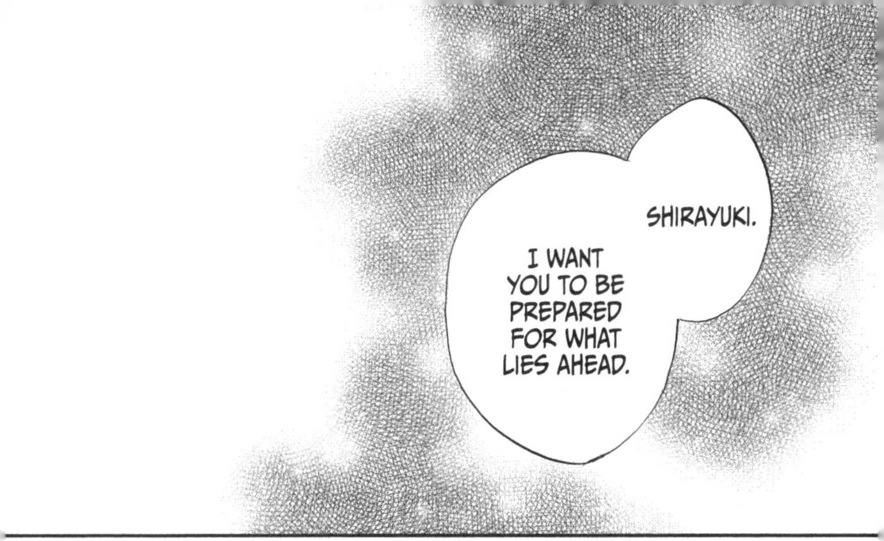
SHIRAYUKI.
I WANT YOU TO BE PREPARED FOR WHAT LIES AHEAD.

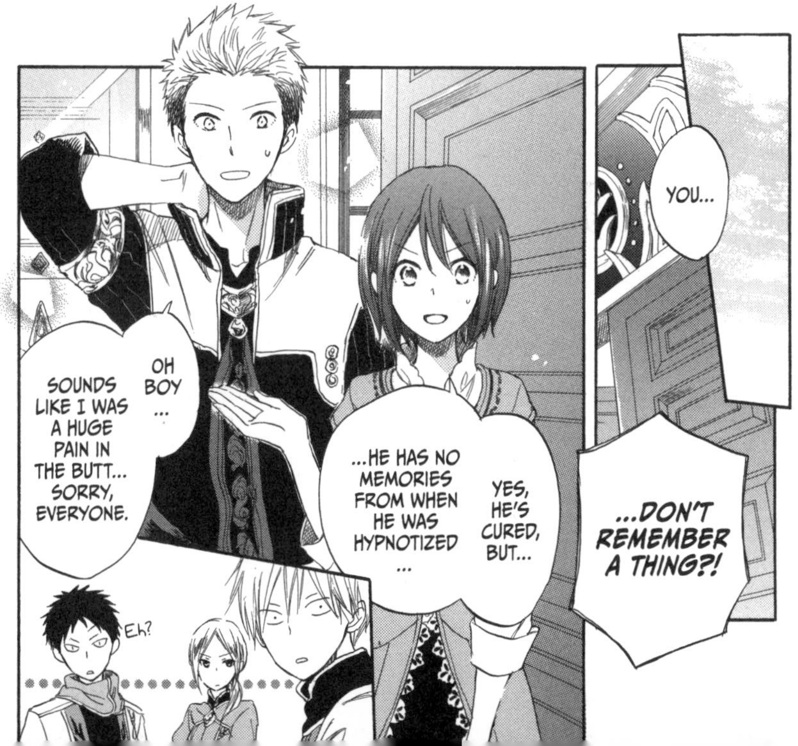
YOU...
...DON'T REMEMBER A THING?!
YES, HE'S CURED, BUT...
...HE HAS NO MEMORIES FROM WHEN HE WAS HYPNOTIZED...
OH BOY...
SOUNDS LIKE I WAS A HUGE PAIN IN THE BUTT... SORRY, EVERYONE.
Eh?

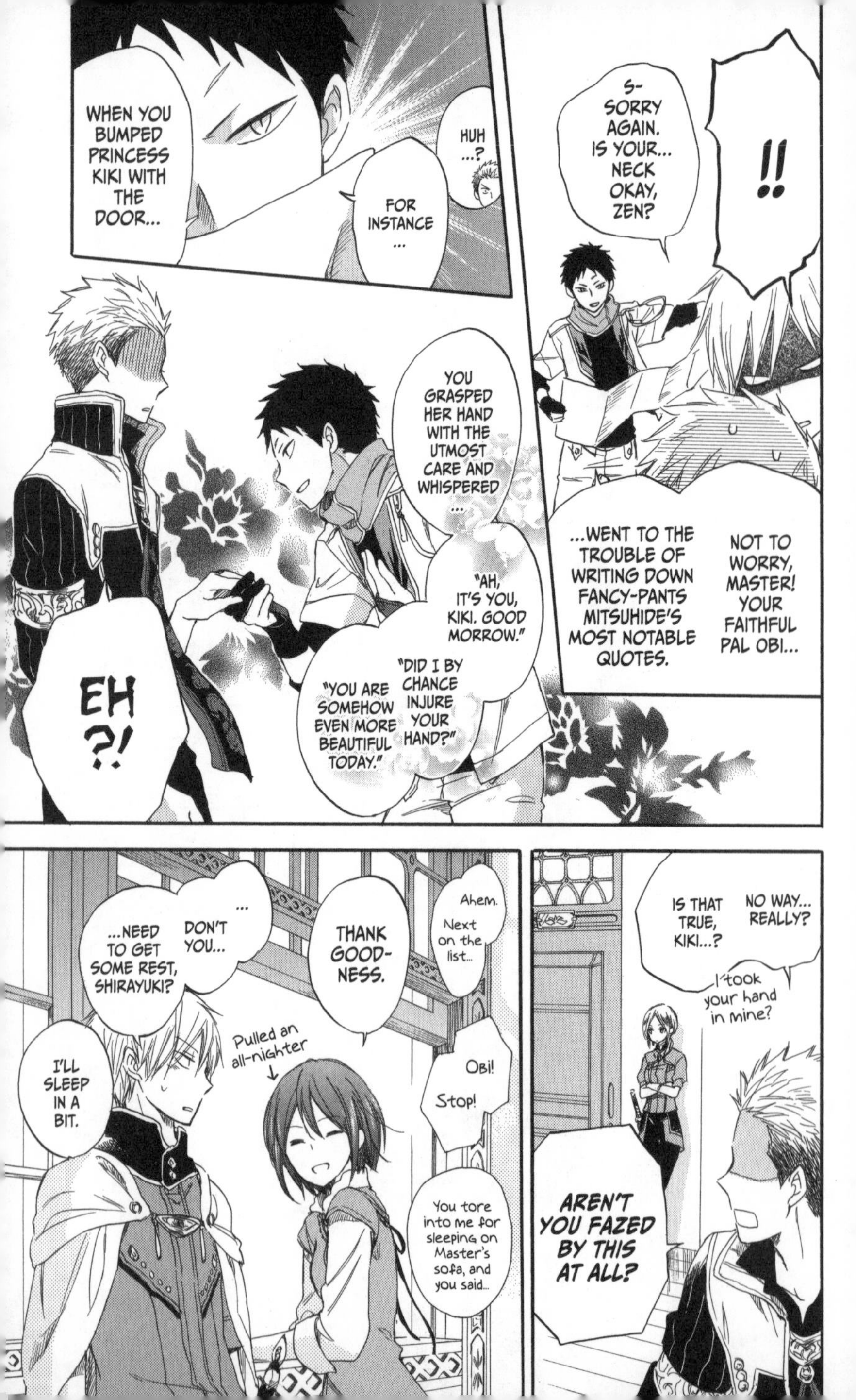
!!
S-SORRY AGAIN. IS YOUR... NECK OKAY, ZEN?
NOT TO WORRY, MASTER! YOUR FAITHFUL PAL OBI...
...WENT TO THE TROUBLE OF WRITING DOWN FANCY-PANTS MITSUHIDE'S MOST NOTABLE QUOTES.
HUH ...?
FOR INSTANCE ...
WHEN YOU BUMPED PRINCESS KIKI WITH THE DOOR...
YOU GRASPED HER HAND WITH THE UTMOST CARE AND WHISPERED ...
"AH, IT'S YOU, KIKI. GOOD MORROW."
"DID I BY CHANCE INJURE YOUR HAND?"
"YOU ARE SOMEHOW EVEN MORE BEAUTIFUL TODAY."
EH ?!
NO WAY... REALLY?
IS THAT TRUE, KIKI...?
I took your hand in mine?
AREN'T YOU FAZED BY THIS AT ALL?
Ahem. Next on the list...
THANK GOODNESS.
... DON'T YOU...
...NEED TO GET SOME REST, SHIRAYUKI?
Obi! Stop!
Pulled an all-nighter
You tore into me for sleeping on Master's sofa, and you said...
I'LL SLEEP IN A BIT.

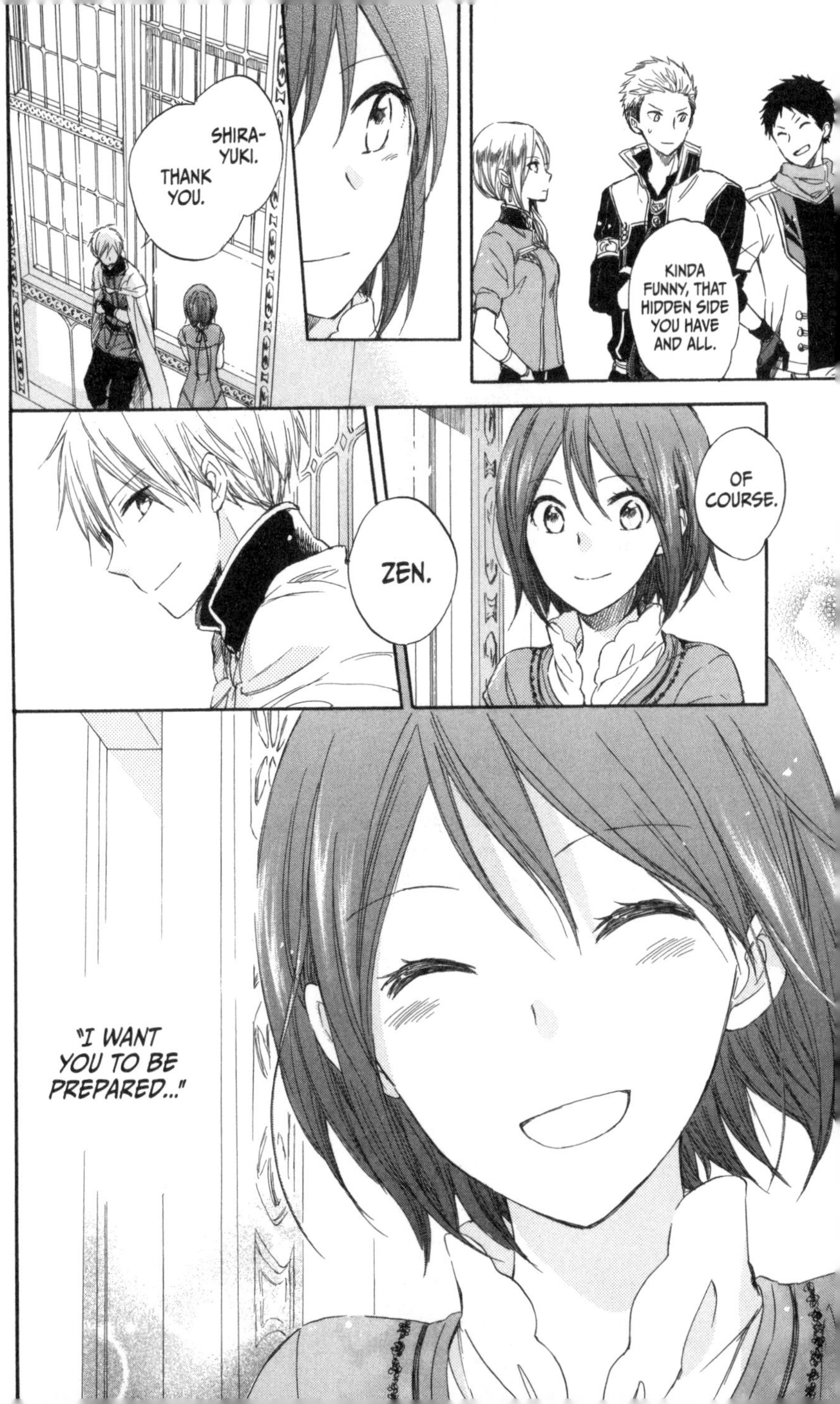
KINDA FUNNY, THAT HIDDEN SIDE YOU HAVE AND ALL.
SHIRA-YUKI.
THANK YOU.
OF COURSE.
ZEN.
"I WANT YOU TO BE PREPARED..."

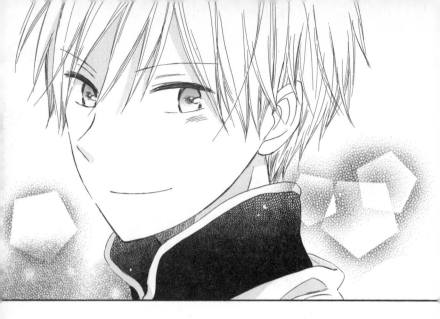

"IF, INDEED,
IT IS THE CASE
THAT YOU WISH
TO STAND BY
HIS SIDE..."

"...WHEREVER
HIS PATH
MAY LEAD."

Chapter 29

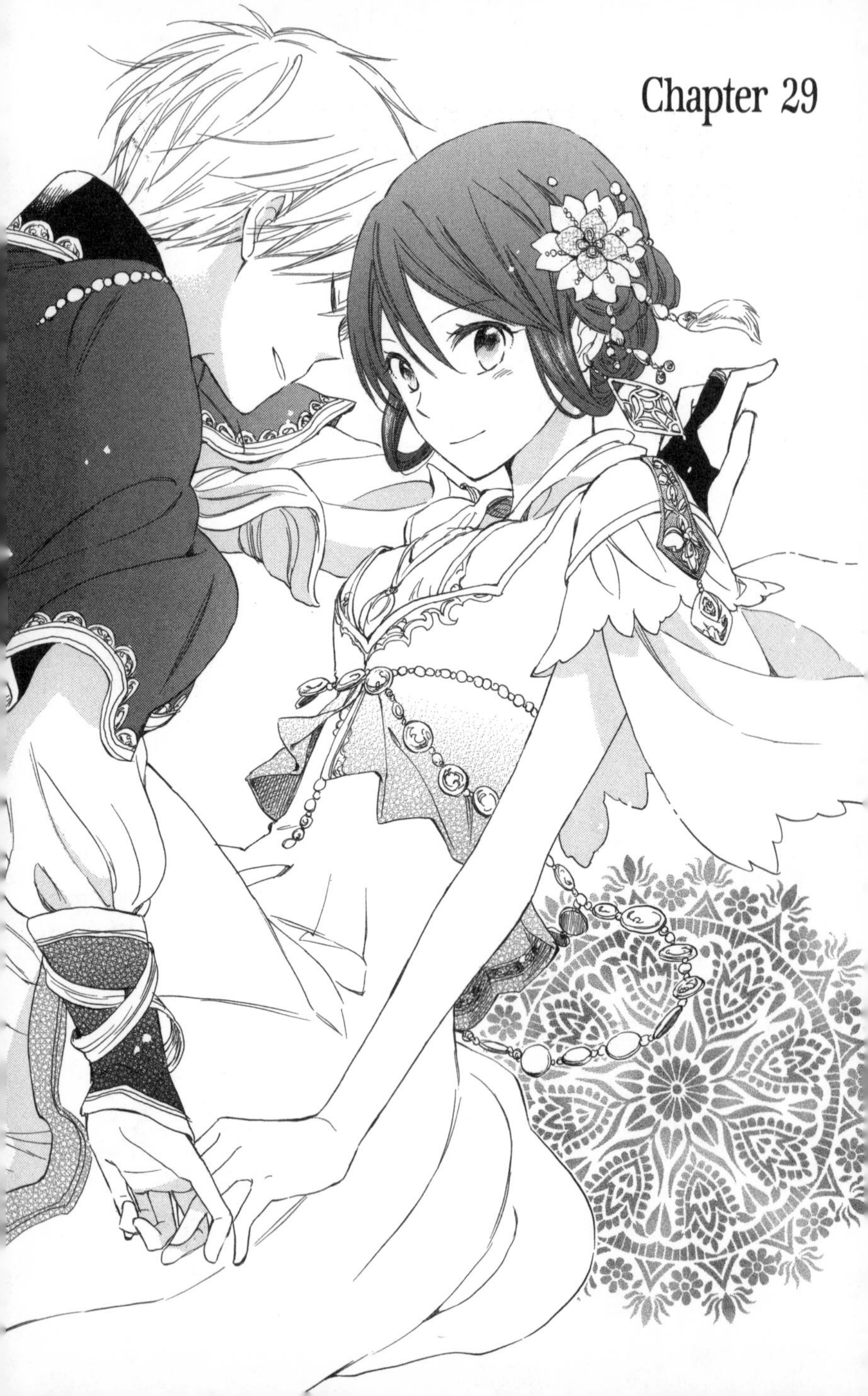

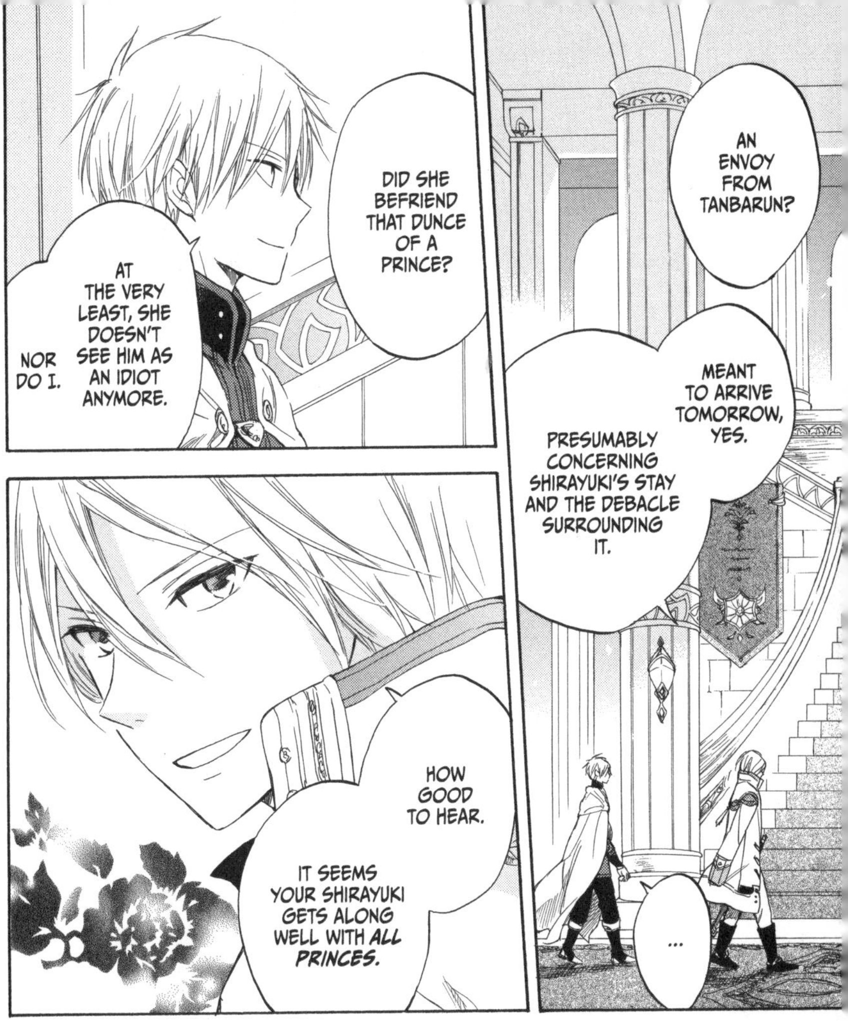
AN ENVOY FROM TANBARUN?
MEANT TO ARRIVE TOMORROW, YES.
PRESUMABLY CONCERNING SHIRAYUKI'S STAY AND THE DEBACLE SURROUNDING IT.
...
DID SHE BEFRIEND THAT DUNCE OF A PRINCE?
AT THE VERY LEAST, SHE DOESN'T SEE HIM AS AN IDIOT ANYMORE.
NOR DO I.
HOW GOOD TO HEAR.
IT SEEMS YOUR SHIRAYUKI GETS ALONG WELL WITH *ALL PRINCES.*

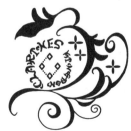

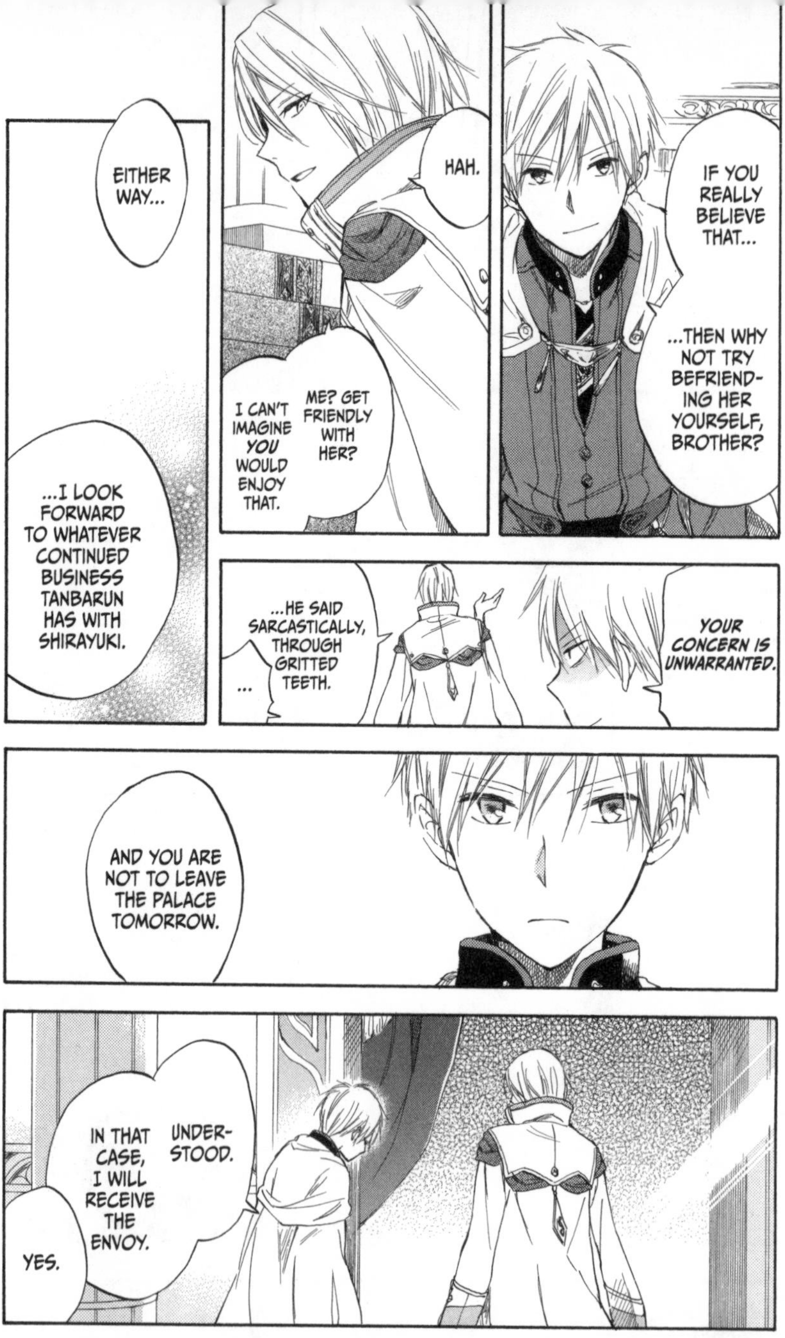
IF YOU REALLY BELIEVE THAT...
...THEN WHY NOT TRY BEFRIENDING HER YOURSELF, BROTHER?
HAH.
ME? GET FRIENDLY WITH HER?
I CAN'T IMAGINE *YOU* WOULD ENJOY THAT.
YOUR CONCERN IS UNWARRANTED.
...HE SAID SARCASTICALLY, THROUGH GRITTED TEETH.
...
EITHER WAY...
...I LOOK FORWARD TO WHATEVER CONTINUED BUSINESS TANBARUN HAS WITH SHIRAYUKI.
AND YOU ARE NOT TO LEAVE THE PALACE TOMORROW.
UNDERSTOOD.
IN THAT CASE, I WILL RECEIVE THE ENVOY.
YES.

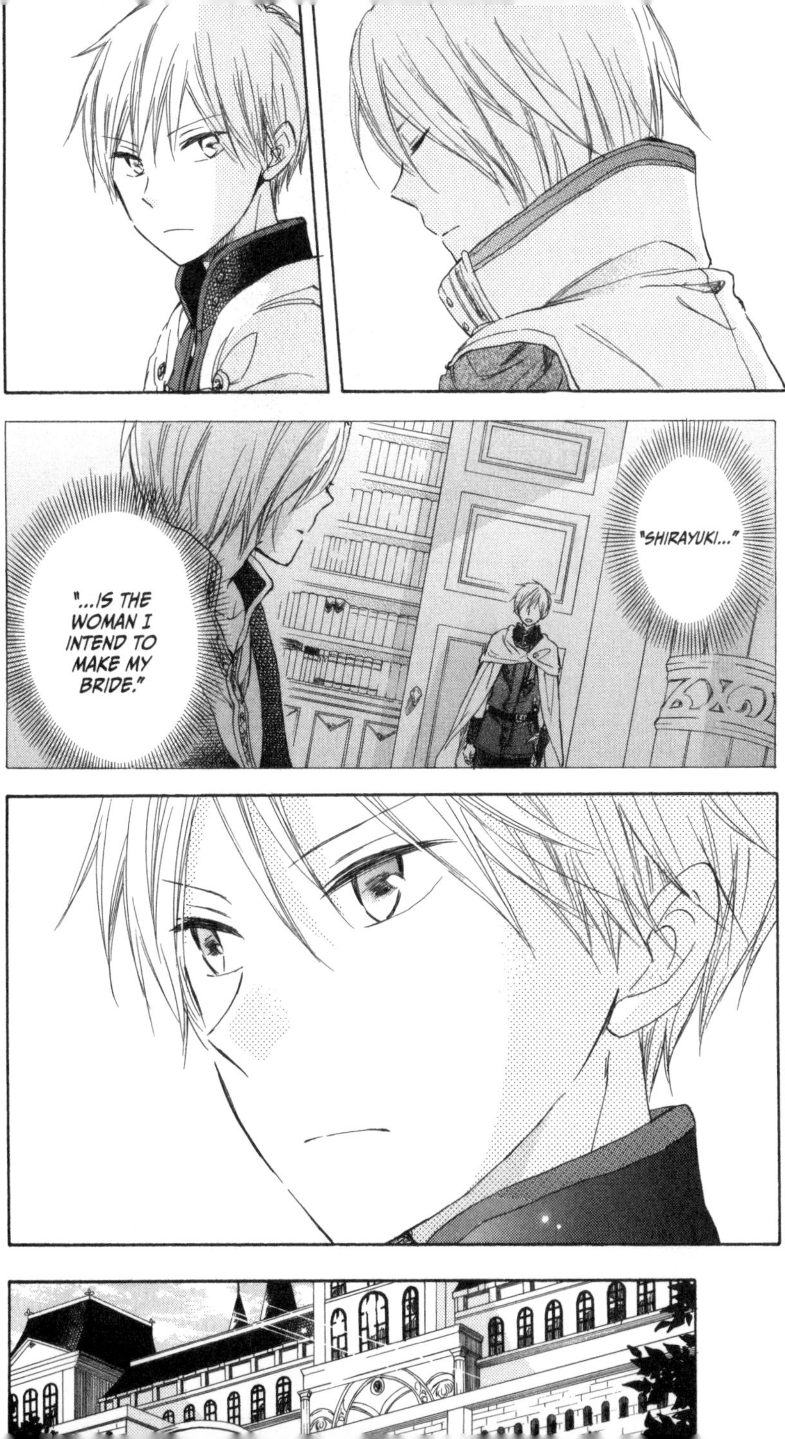
"SHIRAYUKI..."
"...IS THE WOMAN I INTEND TO MAKE MY BRIDE."

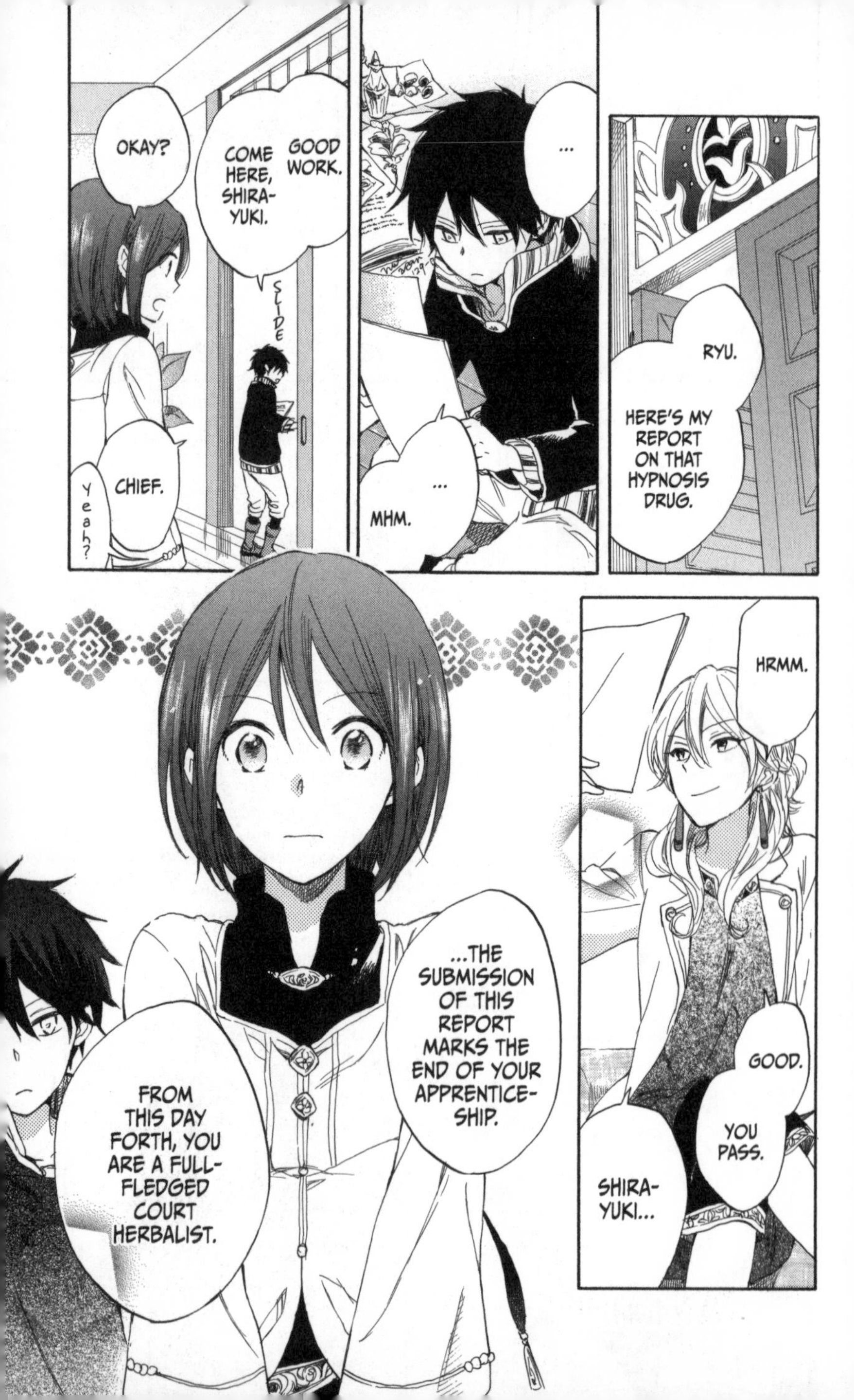
RYU.
HERE'S MY REPORT ON THAT HYPNOSIS DRUG.
...
...
MHM.
GOOD WORK.
COME HERE, SHIRA-YUKI.
SLIDE
OKAY?
CHIEF.
Yeah?
HRMM.
GOOD.
YOU PASS.
SHIRA-YUKI...
...THE SUBMISSION OF THIS REPORT MARKS THE END OF YOUR APPRENTICE-SHIP.
FROM THIS DAY FORTH, YOU ARE A FULL-FLEDGED COURT HERBALIST.

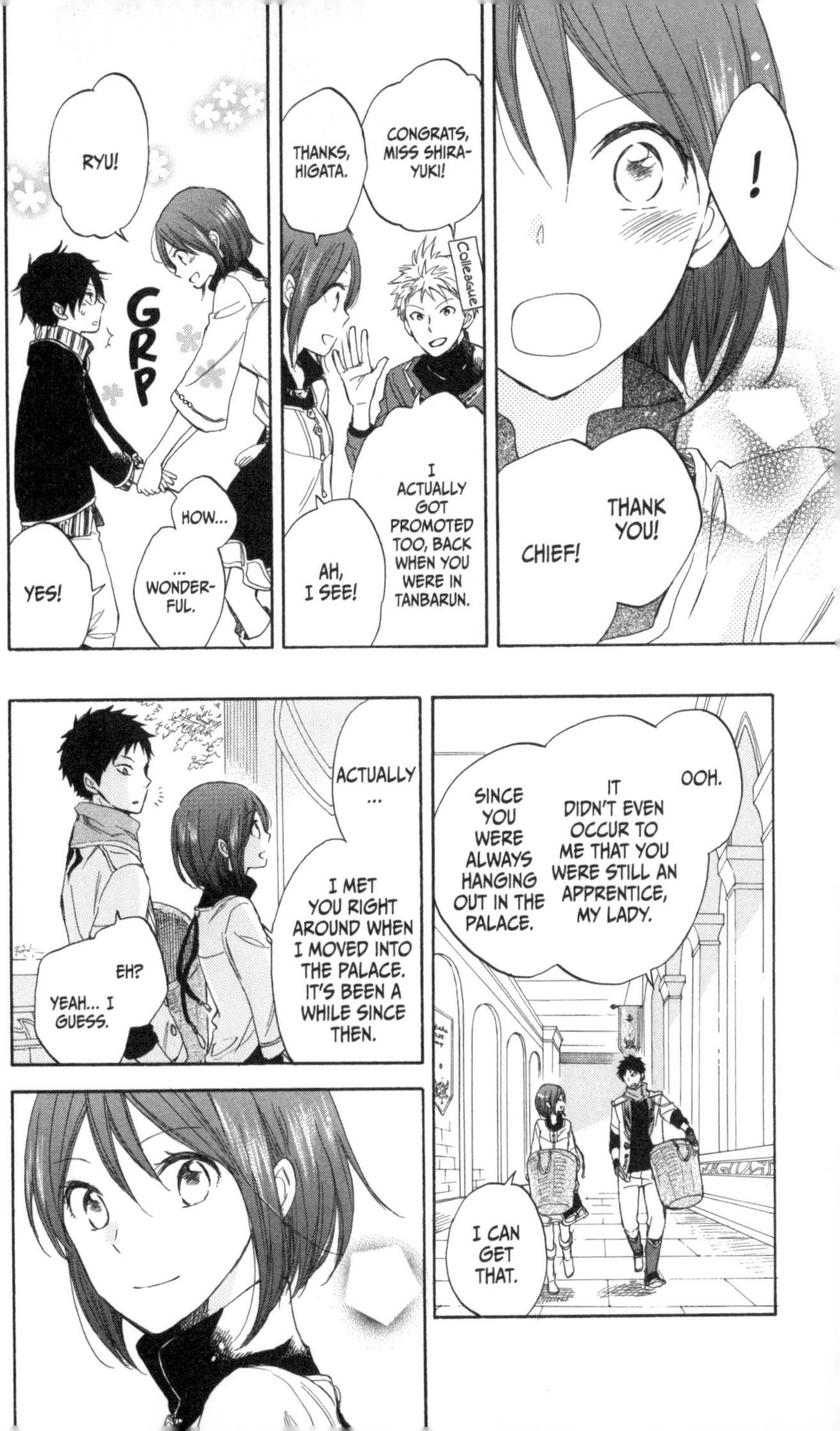
!
THANK YOU!
CHIEF!
CONGRATS, MISS SHIRA-YUKI!
THANKS, HIGATA.
Colleague
I ACTUALLY GOT PROMOTED TOO, BACK WHEN YOU WERE IN TANBARUN.
AH, I SEE!
RYU!
GRP
HOW...
... WONDER-FUL.
YES!
OOH.
IT DIDN'T EVEN OCCUR TO ME THAT YOU WERE STILL AN APPRENTICE, MY LADY.
SINCE YOU WERE ALWAYS HANGING OUT IN THE PALACE.
I CAN GET THAT.
ACTUALLY ...
I MET YOU RIGHT AROUND WHEN I MOVED INTO THE PALACE. IT'S BEEN A WHILE SINCE THEN.
EH?
YEAH... I GUESS.

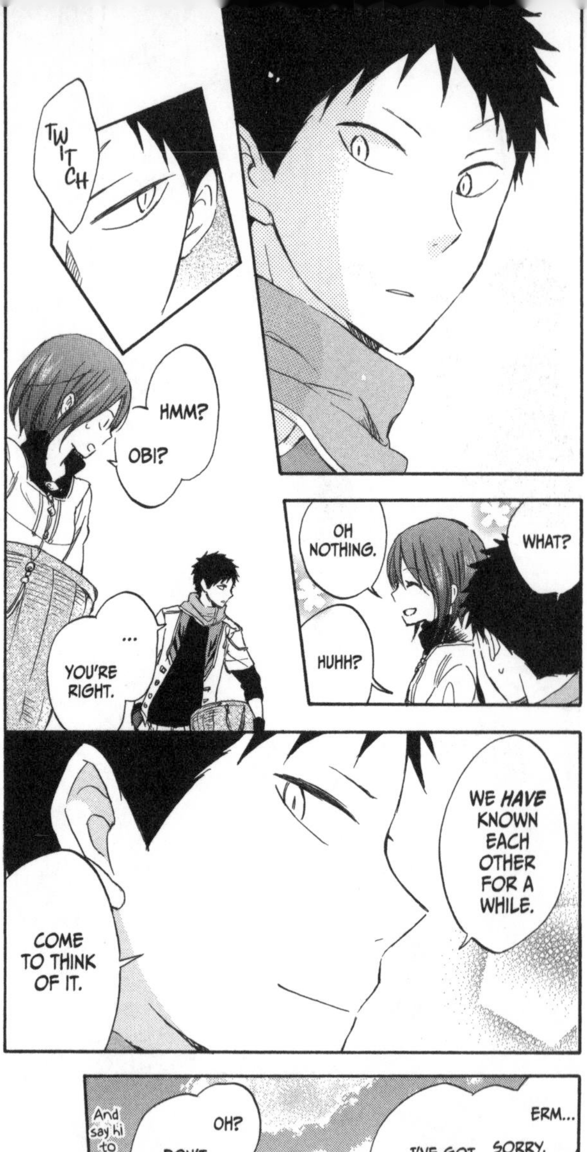
TWITCH
HMM?
OBI?
WHAT?
OH NOTHING.
HUHH?
... YOU'RE RIGHT.
WE HAVE KNOWN EACH OTHER FOR A WHILE.
COME TO THINK OF IT.
ERM...
SORRY, MY LADY.
I'VE GOT SOME BUSINESS WITH PRINCESS KIKI.
OH?
DON'T LET ME HOLD YOU UP.
And say hi to Kiki for me.

CHAPTER 28

Mitsuhide...

CHAPTER 29

I thought Izana would have a good laugh about the title Raj gave Shirayuki, so I'm glad I finally got to portray that scene.

If only Raj himself could've been in the scene. But no, I'm sure that back in Tanbarun, his little siblings are helping him grow, and Sakaki is mocking him all the while ("Ahem, no I am not"), and he's doing his best. Cheer up, Raj!

Don't you dare say that was my final appearance in the series!

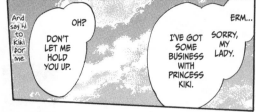

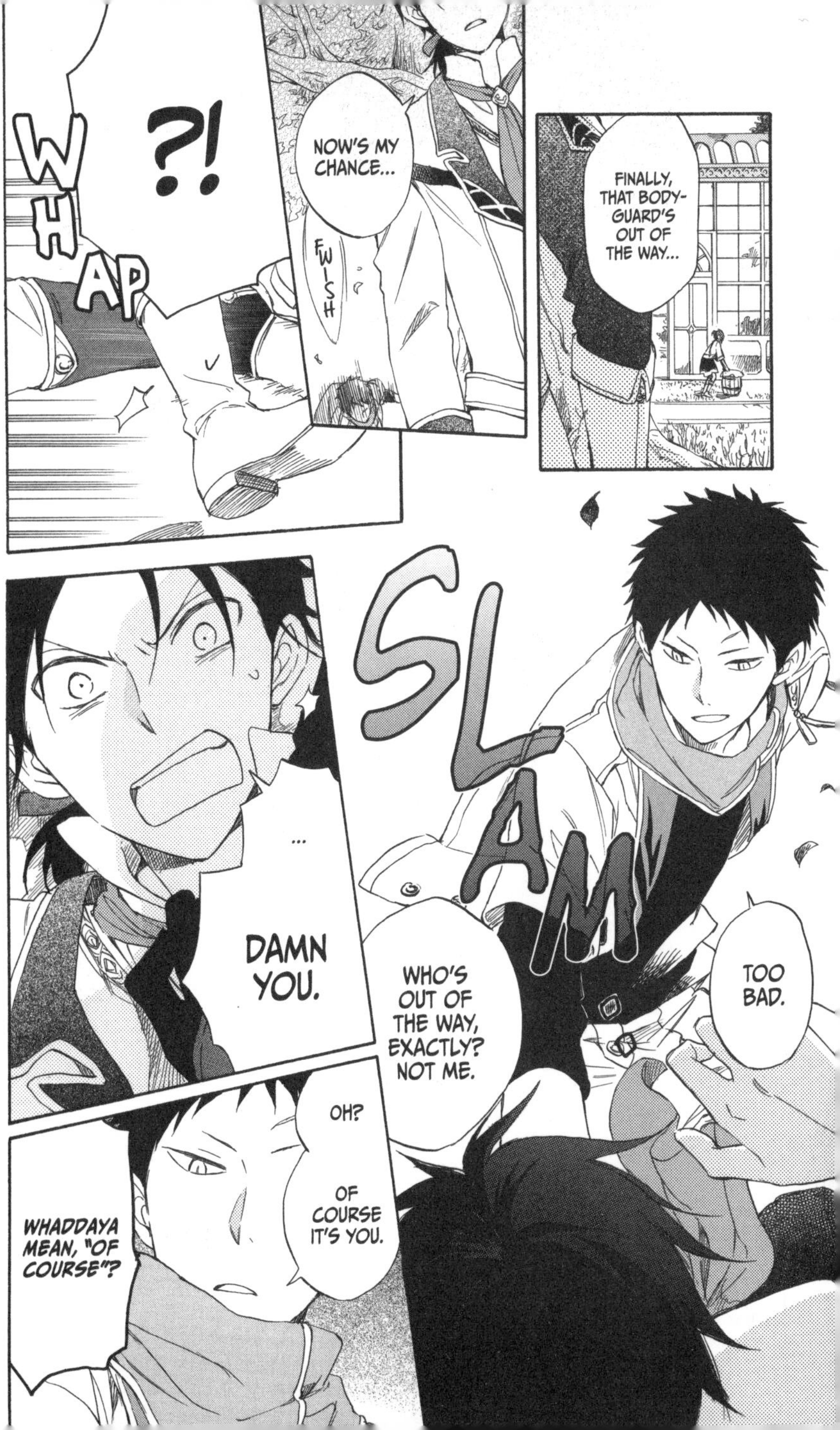
FINALLY, THAT BODY-GUARD'S OUT OF THE WAY...
NOW'S MY CHANCE...
FWISH
WHAP
?!
SLAM
TOO BAD.
WHO'S OUT OF THE WAY, EXACTLY? NOT ME.
...
DAMN YOU.
OH?
OF COURSE IT'S YOU.
WHADDAYA MEAN, "OF COURSE"?

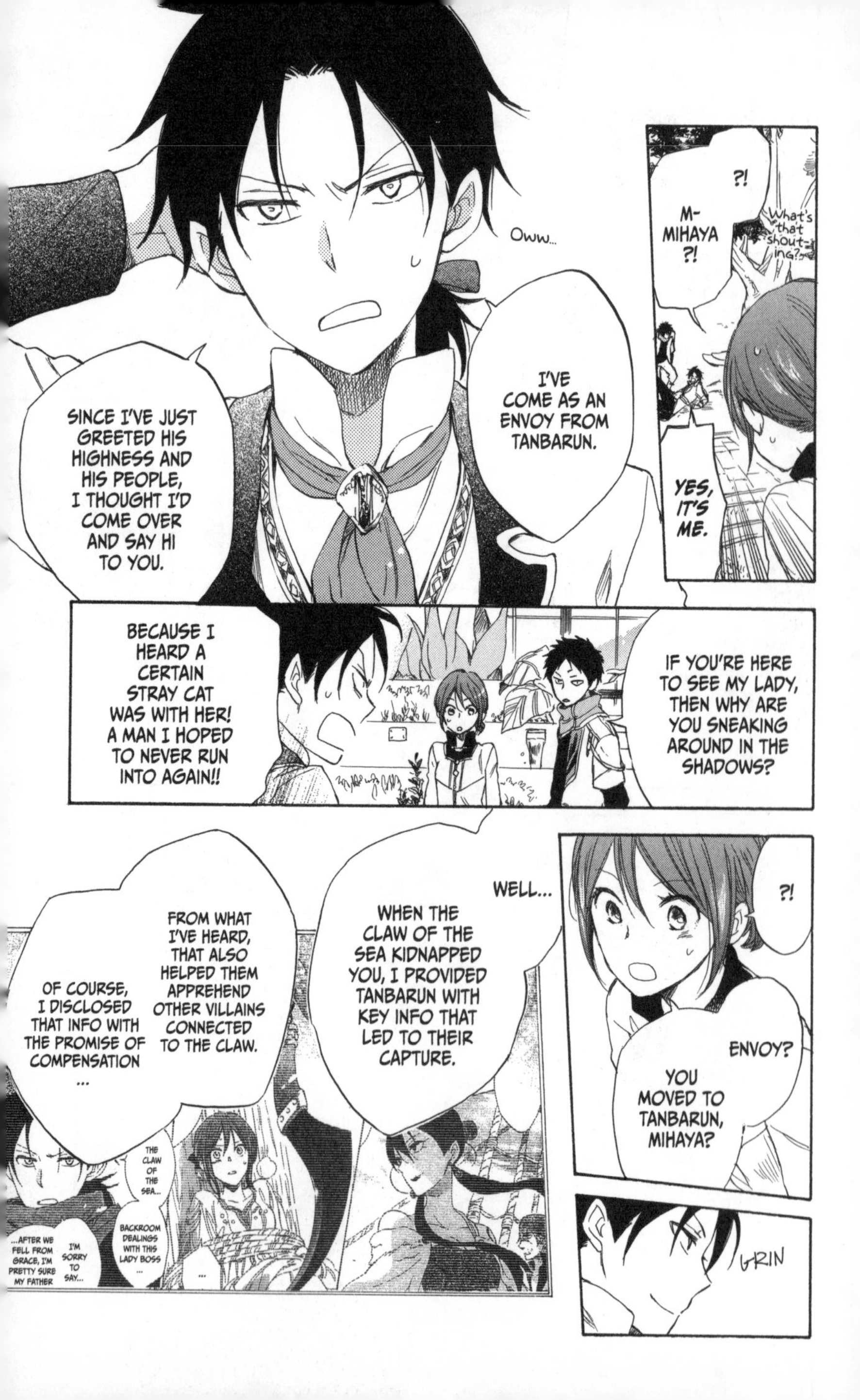
?!
M-MIHAYA?!
What's that shout-ing?
YES, IT'S ME.
Oww...
I'VE COME AS AN ENVOY FROM TANBARUN.
SINCE I'VE JUST GREETED HIS HIGHNESS AND HIS PEOPLE, I THOUGHT I'D COME OVER AND SAY HI TO YOU.
IF YOU'RE HERE TO SEE MY LADY, THEN WHY ARE YOU SNEAKING AROUND IN THE SHADOWS?
BECAUSE I HEARD A CERTAIN STRAY CAT WAS WITH HER! A MAN I HOPED TO NEVER RUN INTO AGAIN!!
?!
ENVOY?
YOU MOVED TO TANBARUN, MIHAYA?
GRIN
WELL...
WHEN THE CLAW OF THE SEA KIDNAPPED YOU, I PROVIDED TANBARUN WITH KEY INFO THAT LED TO THEIR CAPTURE.
FROM WHAT I'VE HEARD, THAT ALSO HELPED THEM APPREHEND OTHER VILLAINS CONNECTED TO THE CLAW.
OF COURSE, I DISCLOSED THAT INFO WITH THE PROMISE OF COMPENSATION ...
THE CLAW OF THE SEA...
BACKROOM DEALINGS WITH THIS LADY BOSS ...
...
I'M SORRY TO SAY...
...AFTER WE FELL FROM GRACE, I'M PRETTY SURE MY FATHER

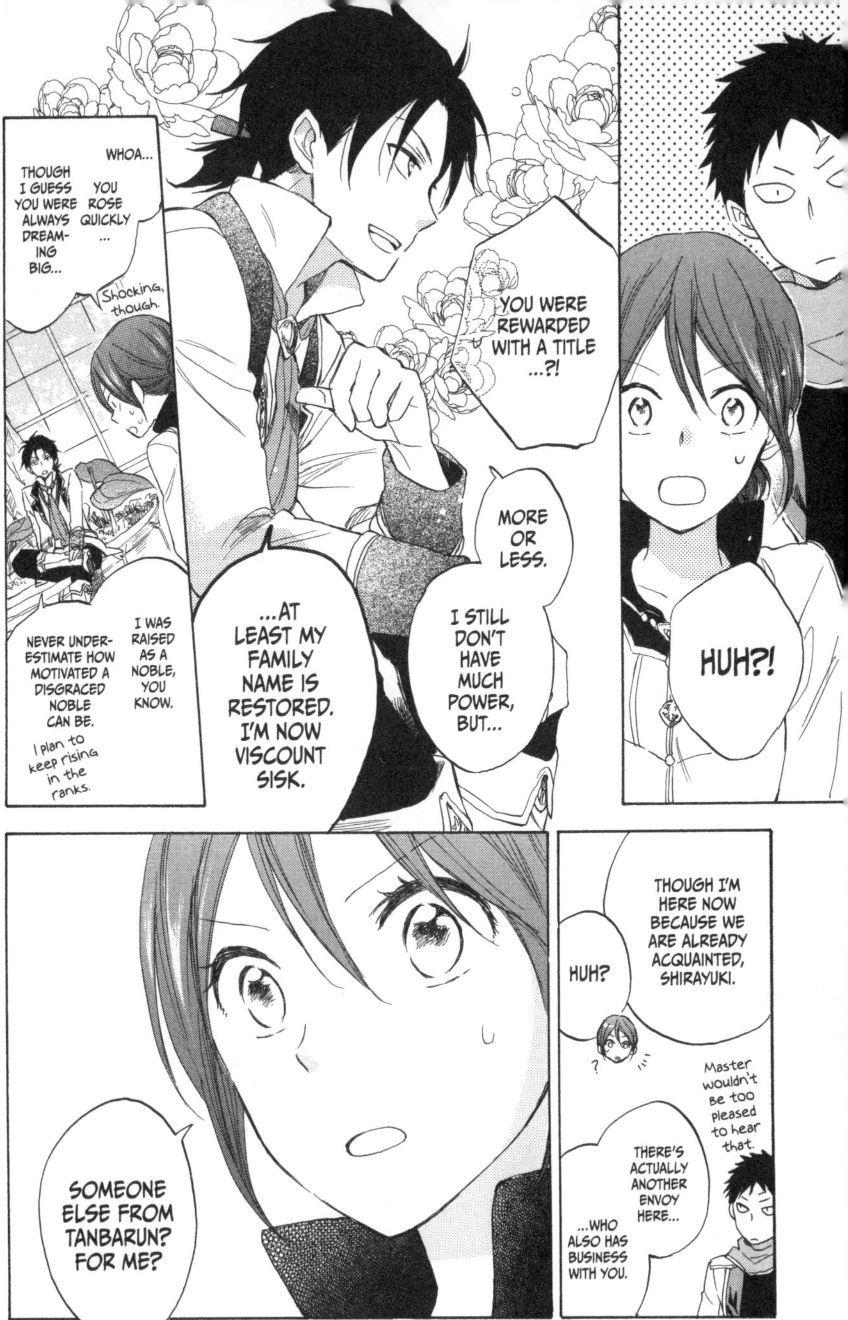
HUH?!
YOU WERE REWARDED WITH A TITLE ...?!
MORE OR LESS.
I STILL DON'T HAVE MUCH POWER, BUT...
...AT LEAST MY FAMILY NAME IS RESTORED. I'M NOW VISCOUNT SISK.
WHOA... YOU ROSE QUICKLY...
THOUGH I GUESS YOU WERE ALWAYS DREAMING BIG...
Shocking, though.
I WAS RAISED AS A NOBLE, YOU KNOW.
NEVER UNDERESTIMATE HOW MOTIVATED A DISGRACED NOBLE CAN BE.
I plan to keep rising in the ranks.
THOUGH I'M HERE NOW BECAUSE WE ARE ALREADY ACQUAINTED, SHIRAYUKI.
HUH?
?
THERE'S ACTUALLY ANOTHER ENVOY HERE...
...WHO ALSO HAS BUSINESS WITH YOU.
Master wouldn't be too pleased to hear that.
SOMEONE ELSE FROM TANBARUN? FOR ME?

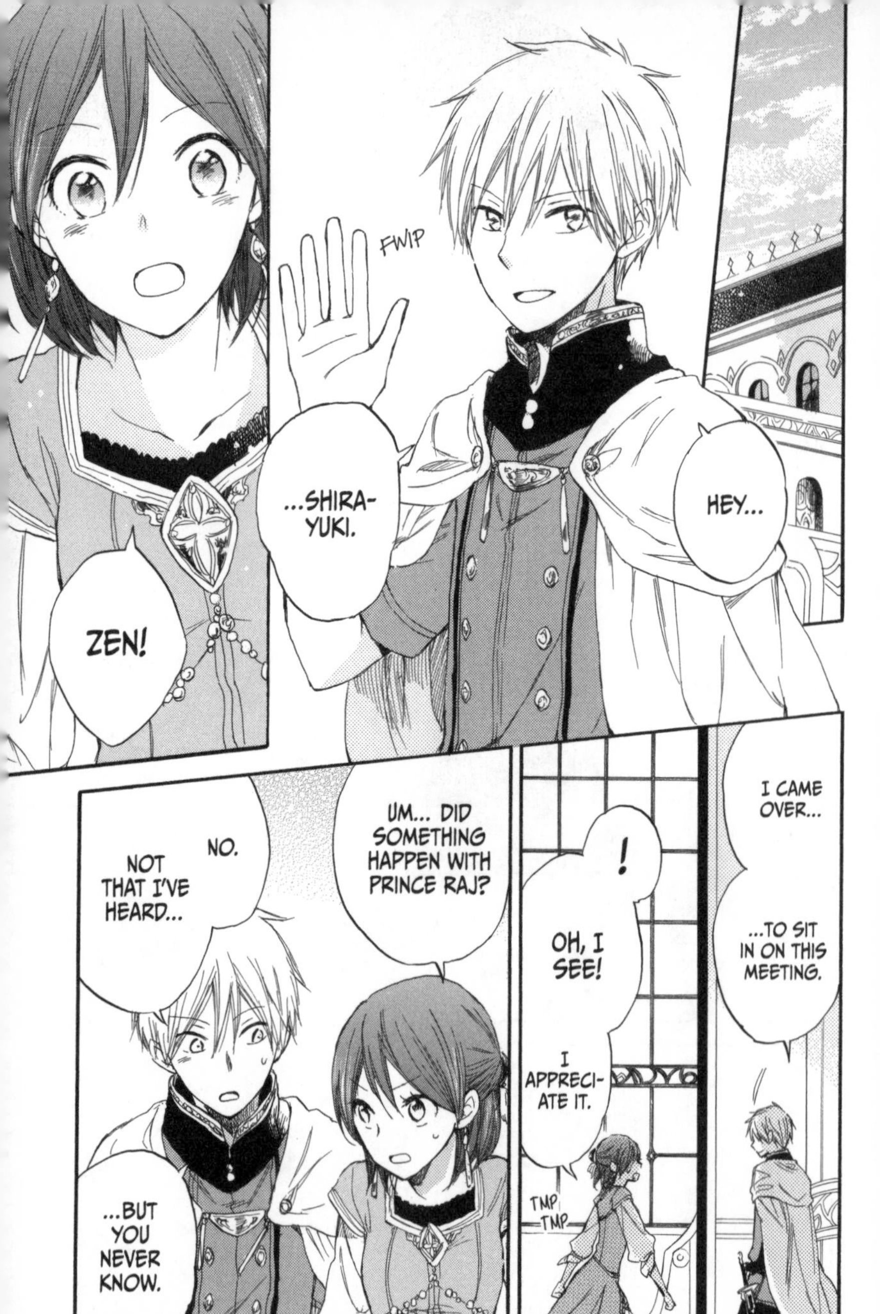
HEY...
FWIP
...SHIRA-YUKI.
ZEN!
I CAME OVER...
...TO SIT IN ON THIS MEETING.
!
OH, I SEE!
I APPRECI-ATE IT.
TMP TMP
UM... DID SOMETHING HAPPEN WITH PRINCE RAJ?
NO.
NOT THAT I'VE HEARD...
...BUT YOU NEVER KNOW.

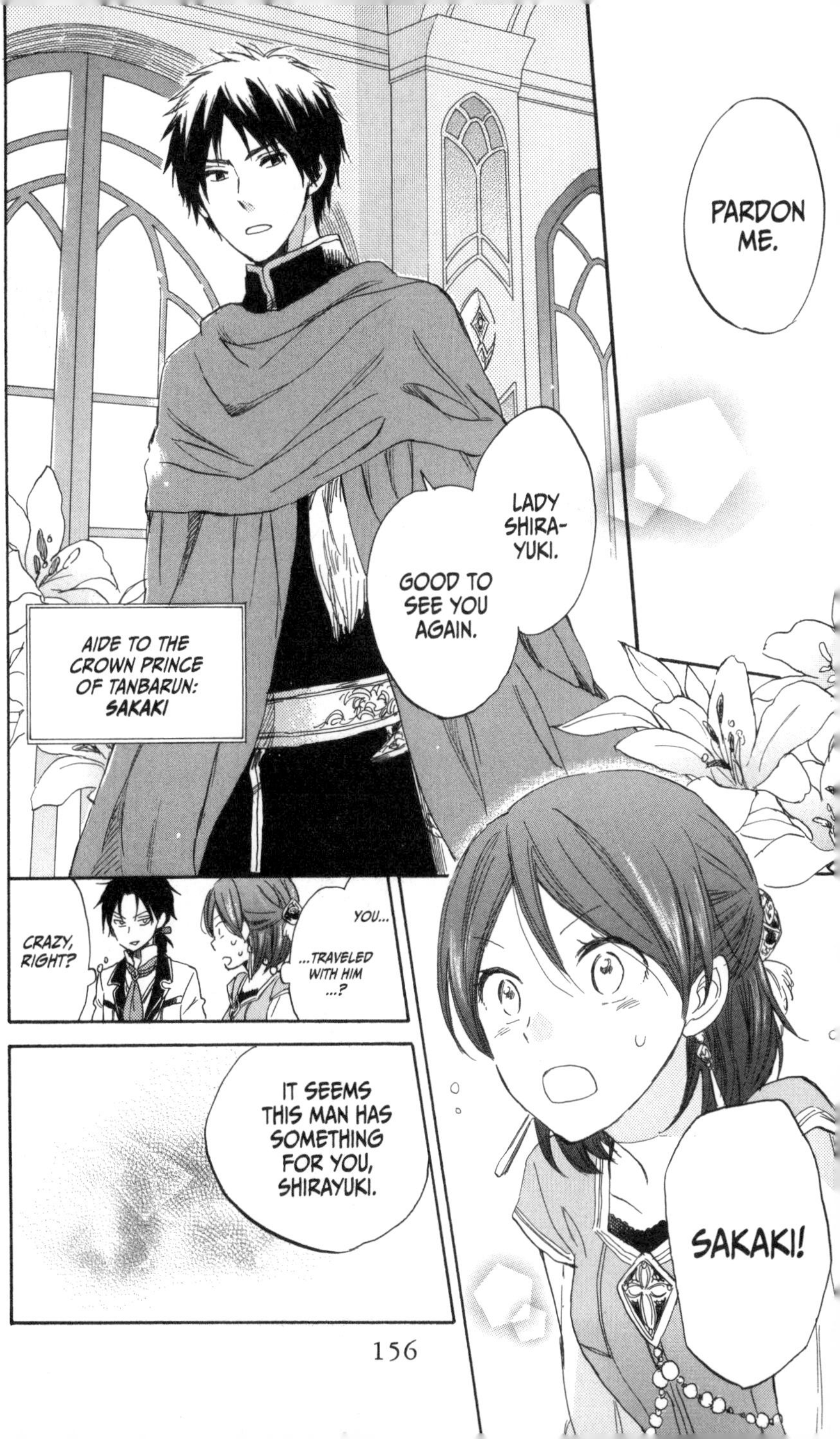
PARDON ME.
LADY SHIRA-YUKI.
GOOD TO SEE YOU AGAIN.
AIDE TO THE CROWN PRINCE OF TANBARUN: SAKAKI
SAKAKI!
YOU...
...TRAVELED WITH HIM ...?
CRAZY, RIGHT?
IT SEEMS THIS MAN HAS SOMETHING FOR YOU, SHIRAYUKI.

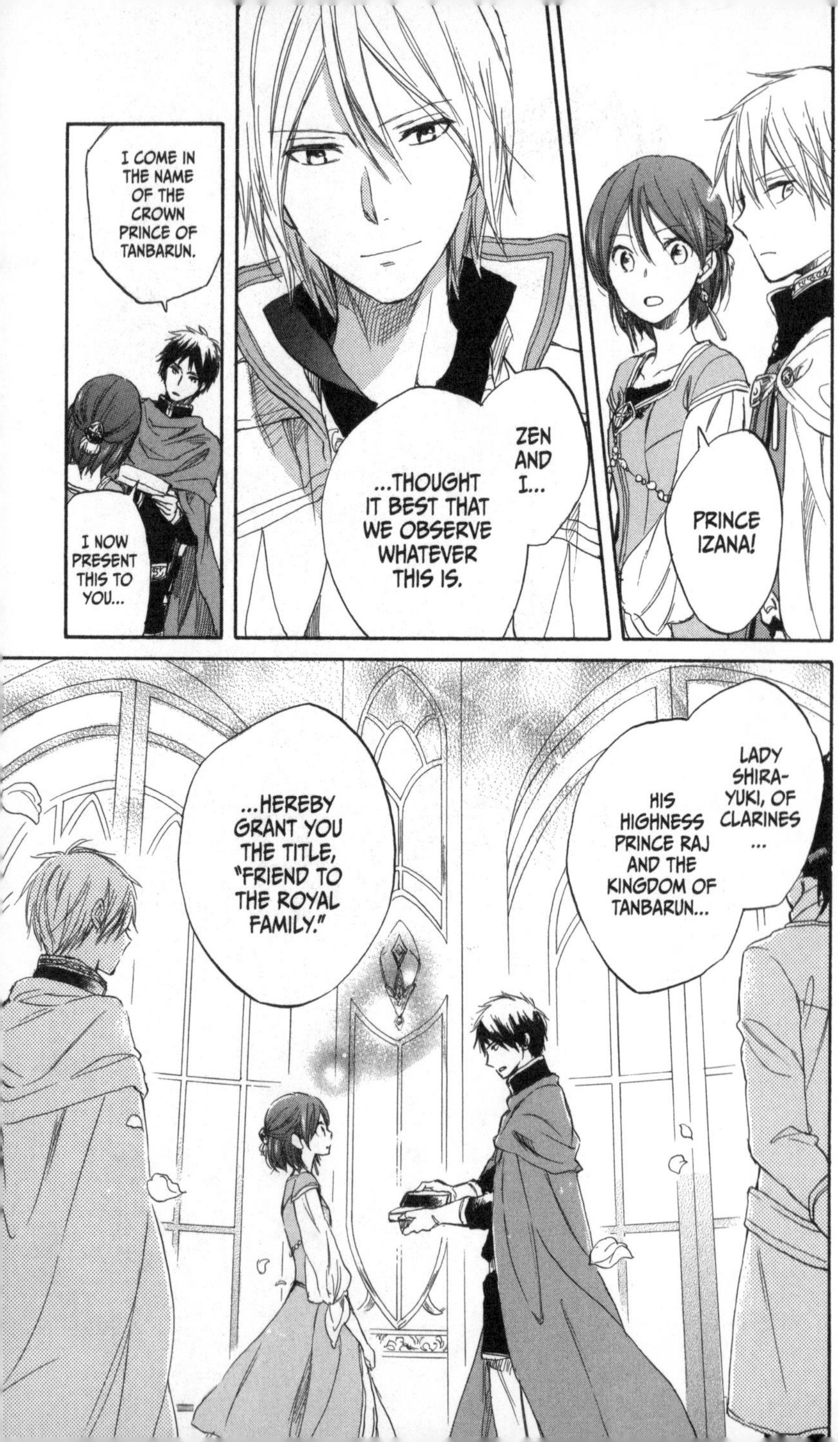
PRINCE IZANA!
ZEN AND I...
...THOUGHT IT BEST THAT WE OBSERVE WHATEVER THIS IS.
I COME IN THE NAME OF THE CROWN PRINCE OF TANBARUN.
I NOW PRESENT THIS TO YOU...
LADY SHIRAYUKI, OF CLARINES...
HIS HIGHNESS PRINCE RAJ AND THE KINGDOM OF TANBARUN...
...HEREBY GRANT YOU THE TITLE, "FRIEND TO THE ROYAL FAMILY."

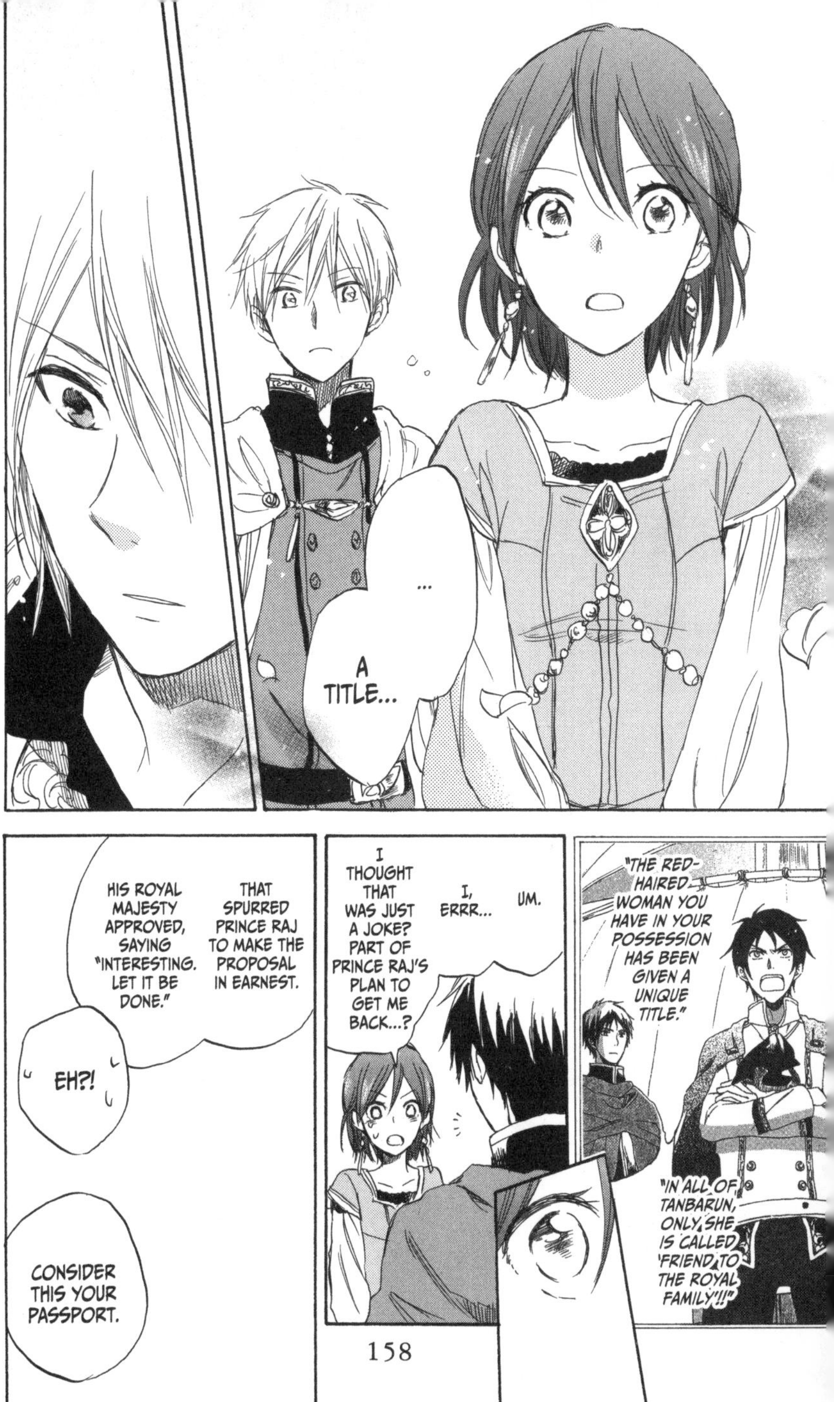
...
A TITLE...
"THE RED-HAIRED WOMAN YOU HAVE IN YOUR POSSESSION HAS BEEN GIVEN A UNIQUE TITLE."
"IN ALL OF TANBARUN, ONLY SHE IS CALLED 'FRIEND TO THE ROYAL FAMILY'!!"
UM.
I, ERRR...
I THOUGHT THAT WAS JUST A JOKE? PART OF PRINCE RAJ'S PLAN TO GET ME BACK...?
THAT SPURRED PRINCE RAJ TO MAKE THE PROPOSAL IN EARNEST.
HIS ROYAL MAJESTY APPROVED, SAYING "INTERESTING. LET IT BE DONE."
EH?!
CONSIDER THIS YOUR PASSPORT.

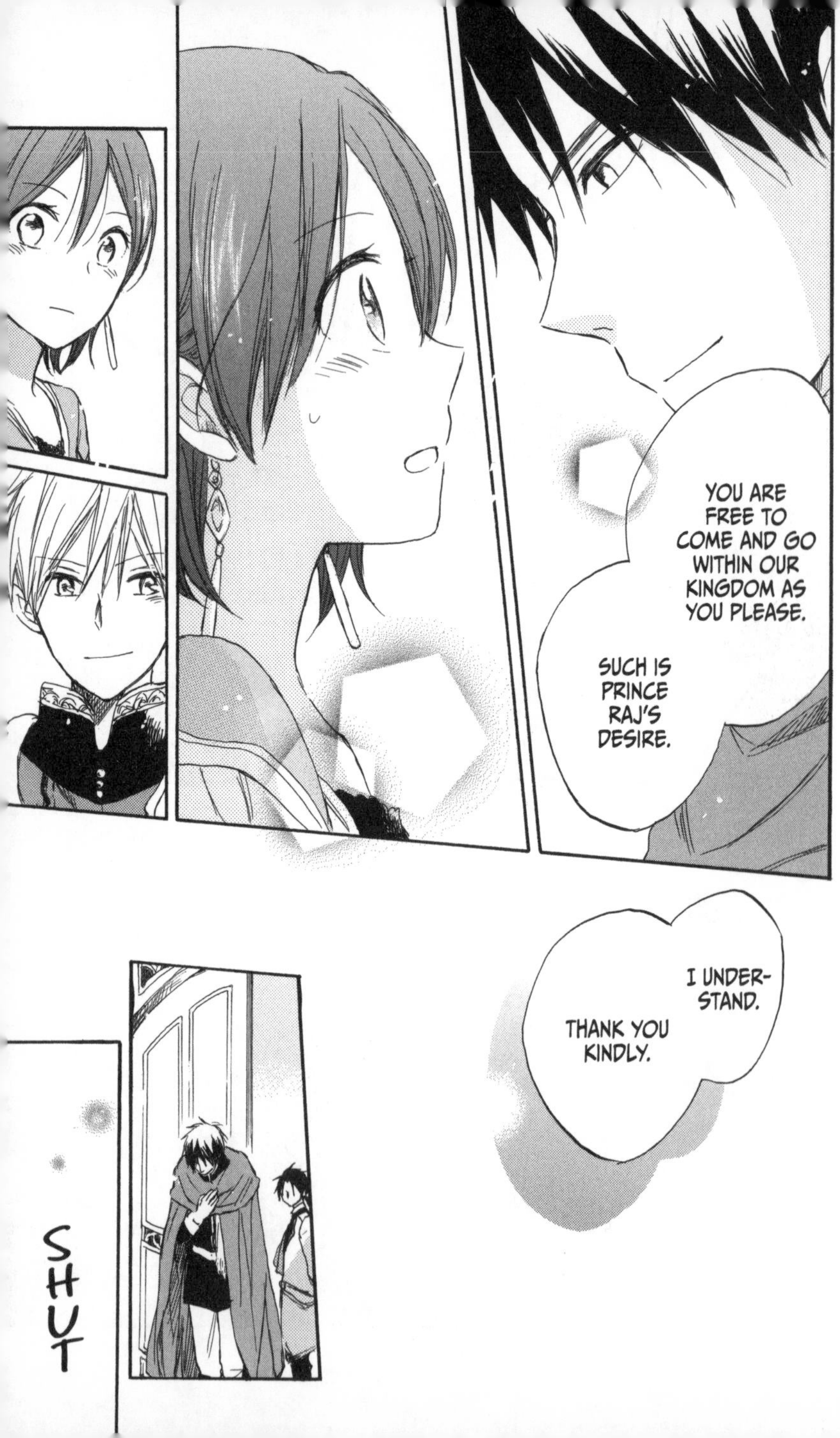
YOU ARE FREE TO COME AND GO WITHIN OUR KINGDOM AS YOU PLEASE.
SUCH IS PRINCE RAJ'S DESIRE.
I UNDER-STAND.
THANK YOU KINDLY.
SHUT

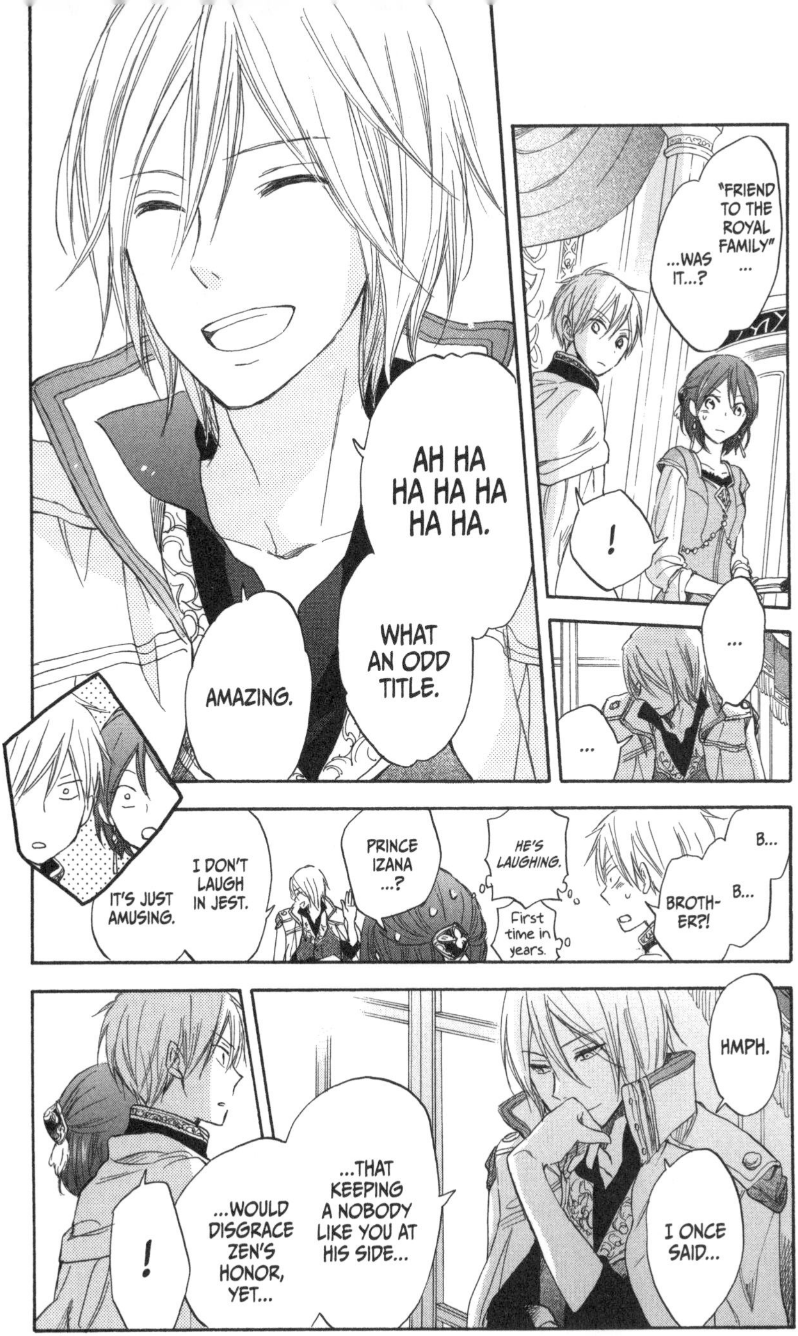
"FRIEND TO THE ROYAL FAMILY"...
...WAS IT...?
!
...
...
AH HA HA HA HA HA HA.
WHAT AN ODD TITLE.
AMAZING.
B... B... BROTHER?!
HE'S LAUGHING.
First time in years.
PRINCE IZANA...?
I DON'T LAUGH IN JEST.
IT'S JUST AMUSING.
HMPH.
I ONCE SAID...
...THAT KEEPING A NOBODY LIKE YOU AT HIS SIDE...
...WOULD DISGRACE ZEN'S HONOR, YET...
!

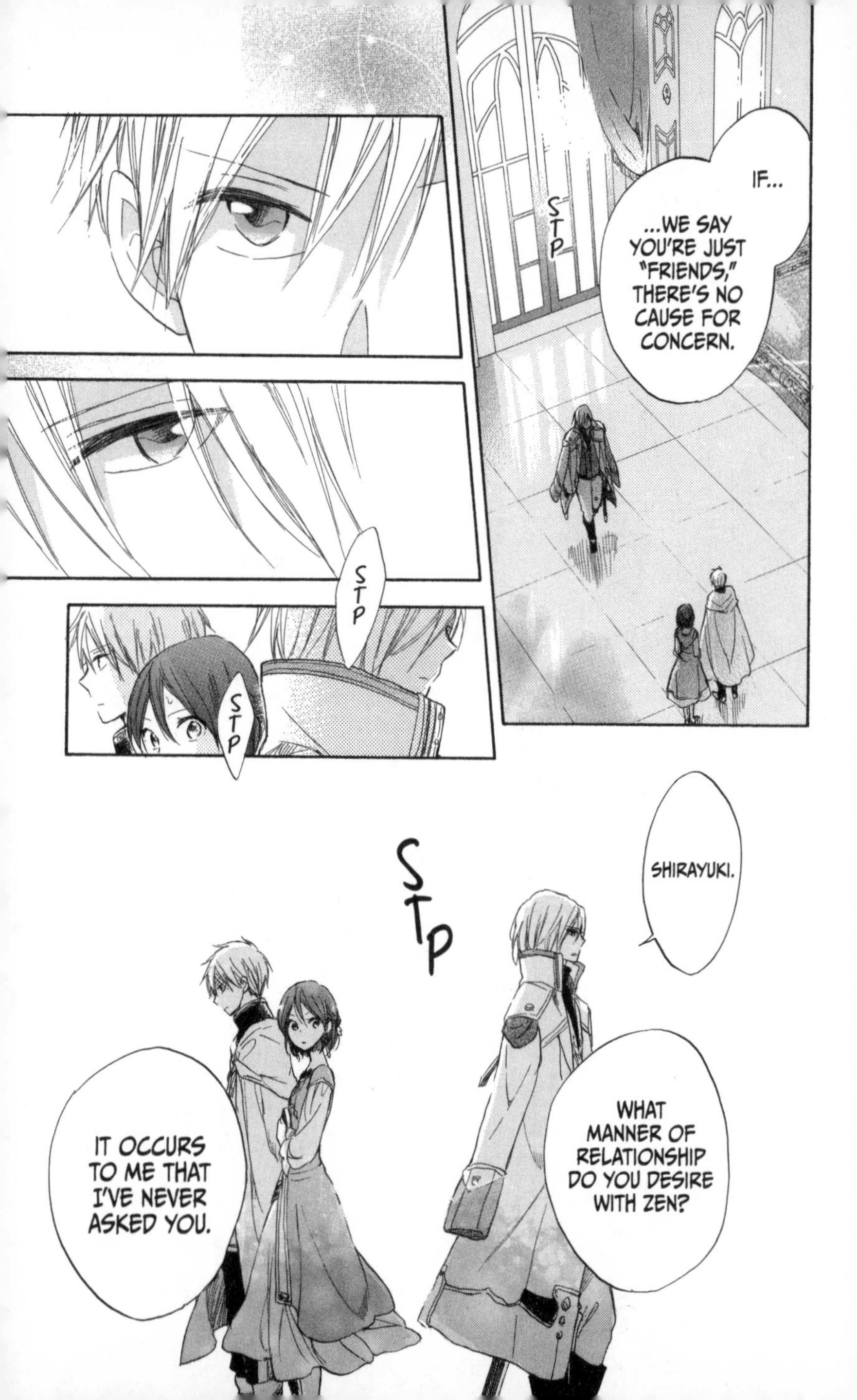
IF...
...WE SAY YOU'RE JUST "FRIENDS," THERE'S NO CAUSE FOR CONCERN.
STP
STP
STP
SHIRAYUKI.
STP
WHAT MANNER OF RELATIONSHIP DO YOU DESIRE WITH ZEN?
IT OCCURS TO ME THAT I'VE NEVER ASKED YOU.

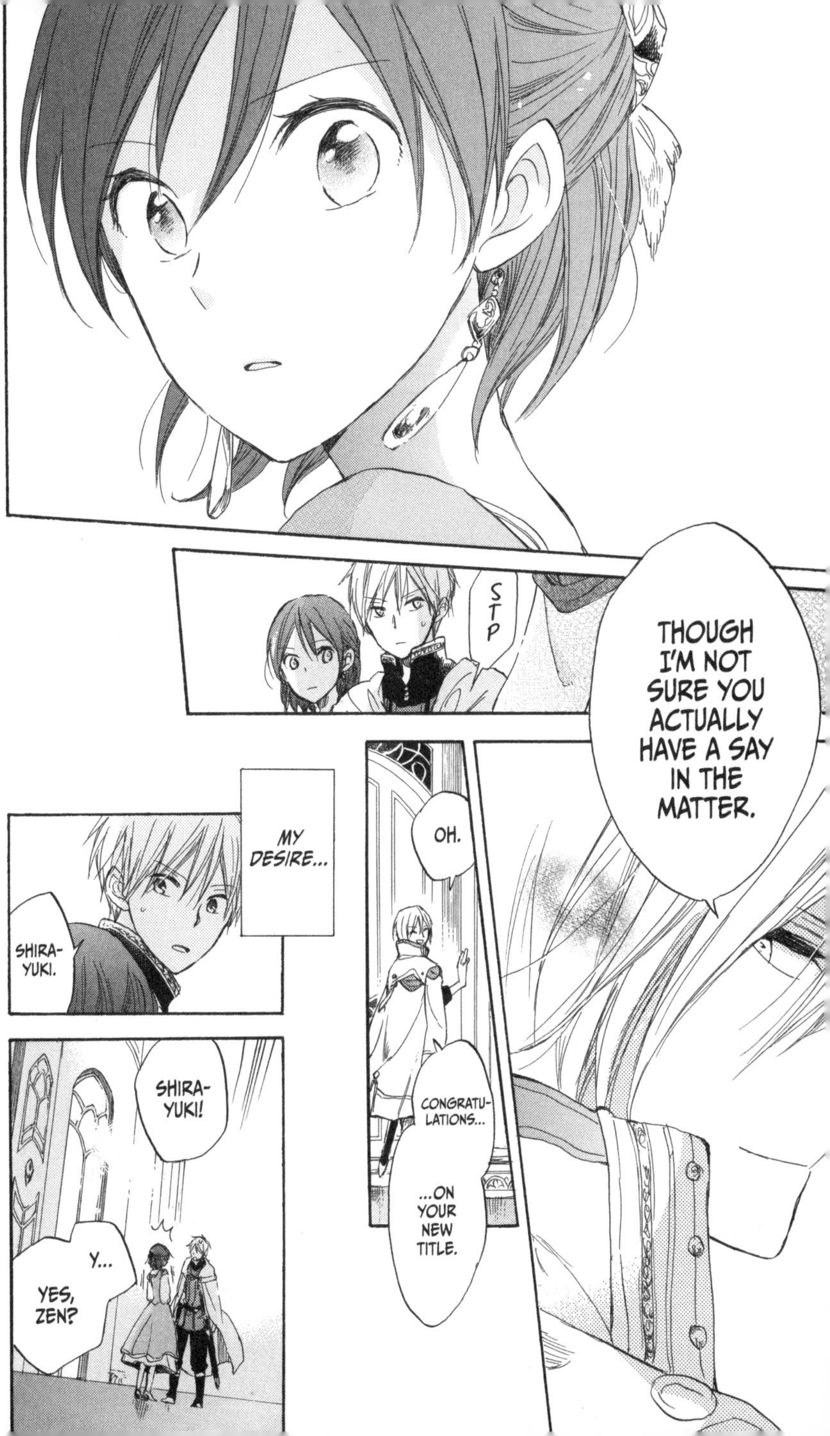
STP
THOUGH I'M NOT SURE YOU ACTUALLY HAVE A SAY IN THE MATTER.
OH.
CONGRATULATIONS...
...ON YOUR NEW TITLE.
MY DESIRE...
SHIRA-YUKI.
SHIRA-YUKI!
Y...
YES, ZEN?

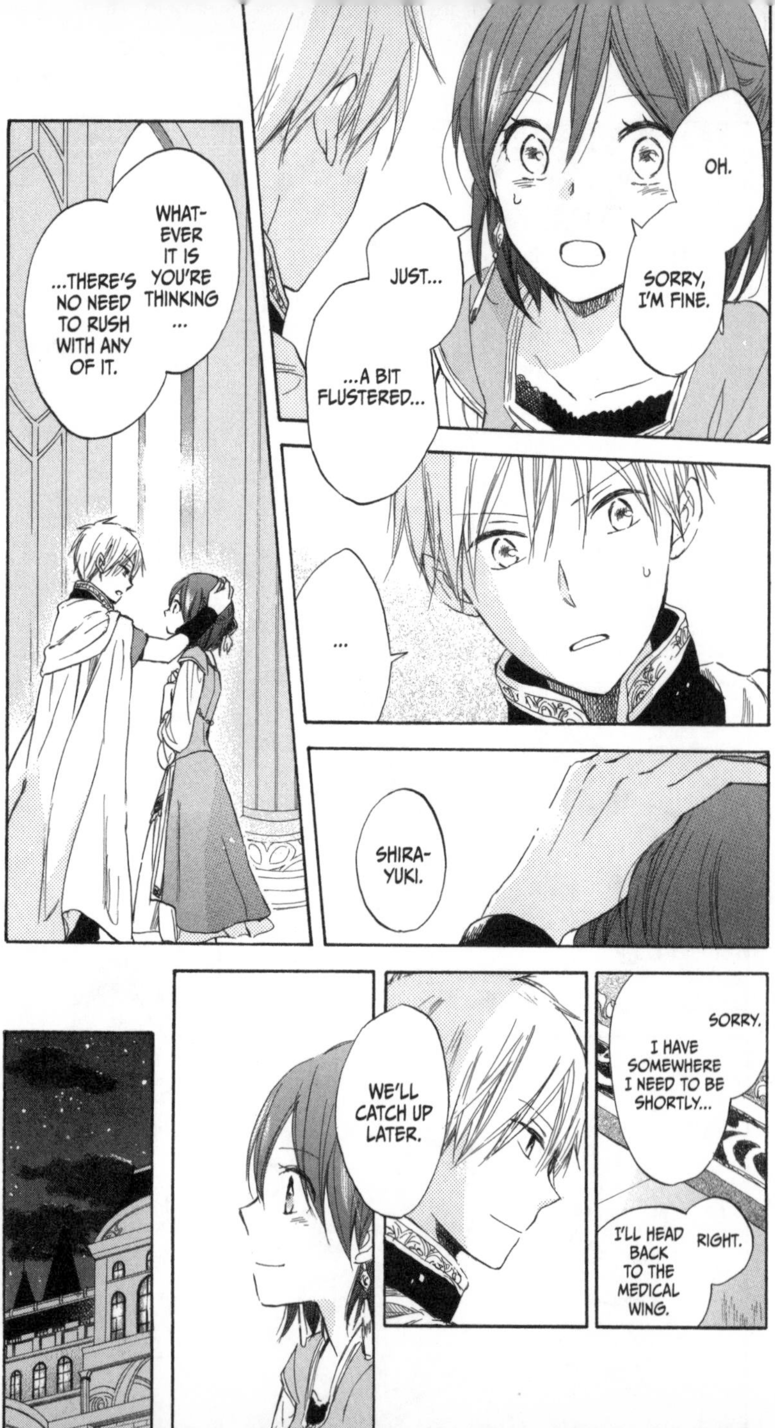
OH.
SORRY, I'M FINE.
JUST...
...A BIT FLUSTERED...
...
SHIRA-YUKI.
WHAT-EVER IT IS YOU'RE THINKING...
...THERE'S NO NEED TO RUSH WITH ANY OF IT.
SORRY.
I HAVE SOMEWHERE I NEED TO BE SHORTLY...
RIGHT.
I'LL HEAD BACK TO THE MEDICAL WING.
WE'LL CATCH UP LATER.

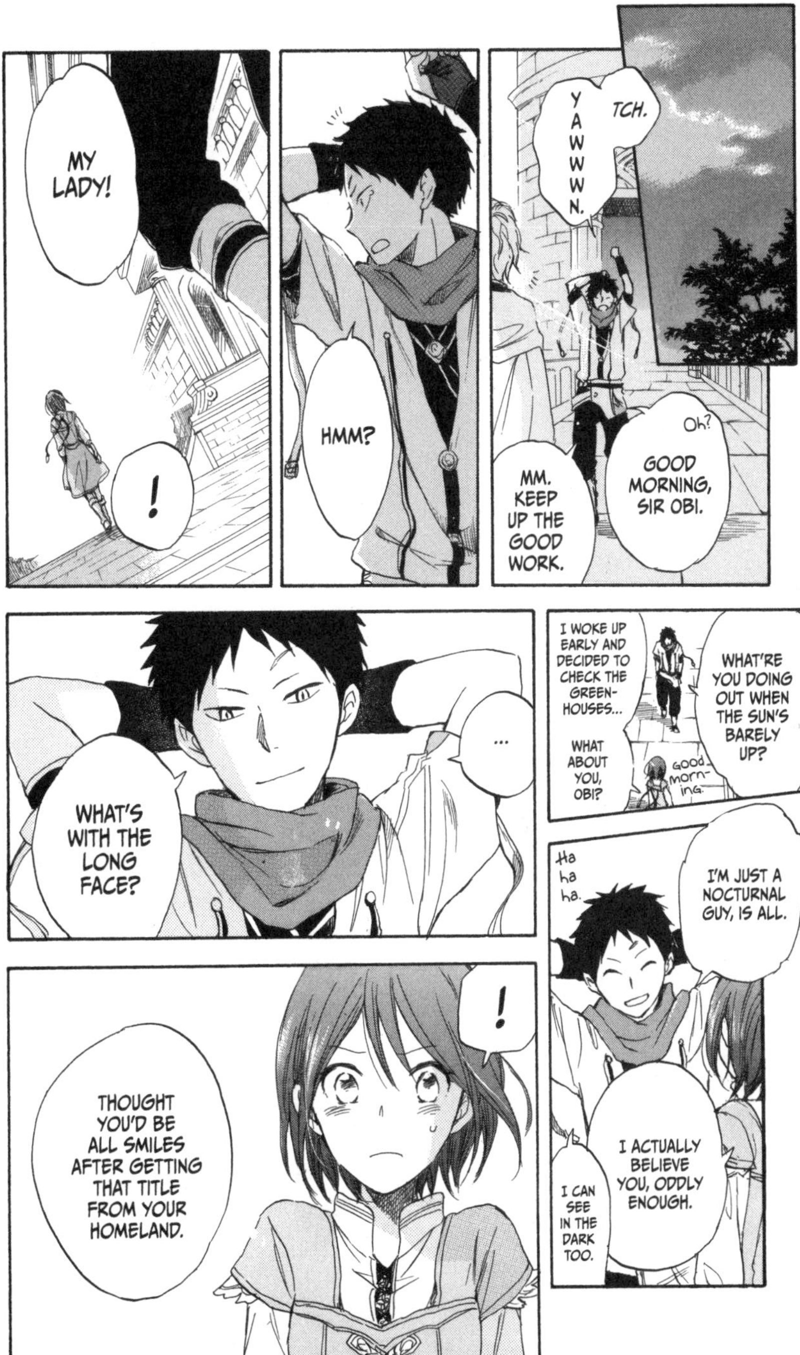
TCH.
YAWWWWN.
Oh?
GOOD MORNING, SIR OBI.
MM. KEEP UP THE GOOD WORK.
HMM?
MY LADY!
!
WHAT'RE YOU DOING OUT WHEN THE SUN'S BARELY UP?
Good morning.
I WOKE UP EARLY AND DECIDED TO CHECK THE GREEN-HOUSES...
WHAT ABOUT YOU, OBI?
I'M JUST A NOCTURNAL GUY, IS ALL.
Ha ha ha.
I ACTUALLY BELIEVE YOU, ODDLY ENOUGH.
I CAN SEE IN THE DARK TOO.
...
WHAT'S WITH THE LONG FACE?
!
THOUGHT YOU'D BE ALL SMILES AFTER GETTING THAT TITLE FROM YOUR HOMELAND.

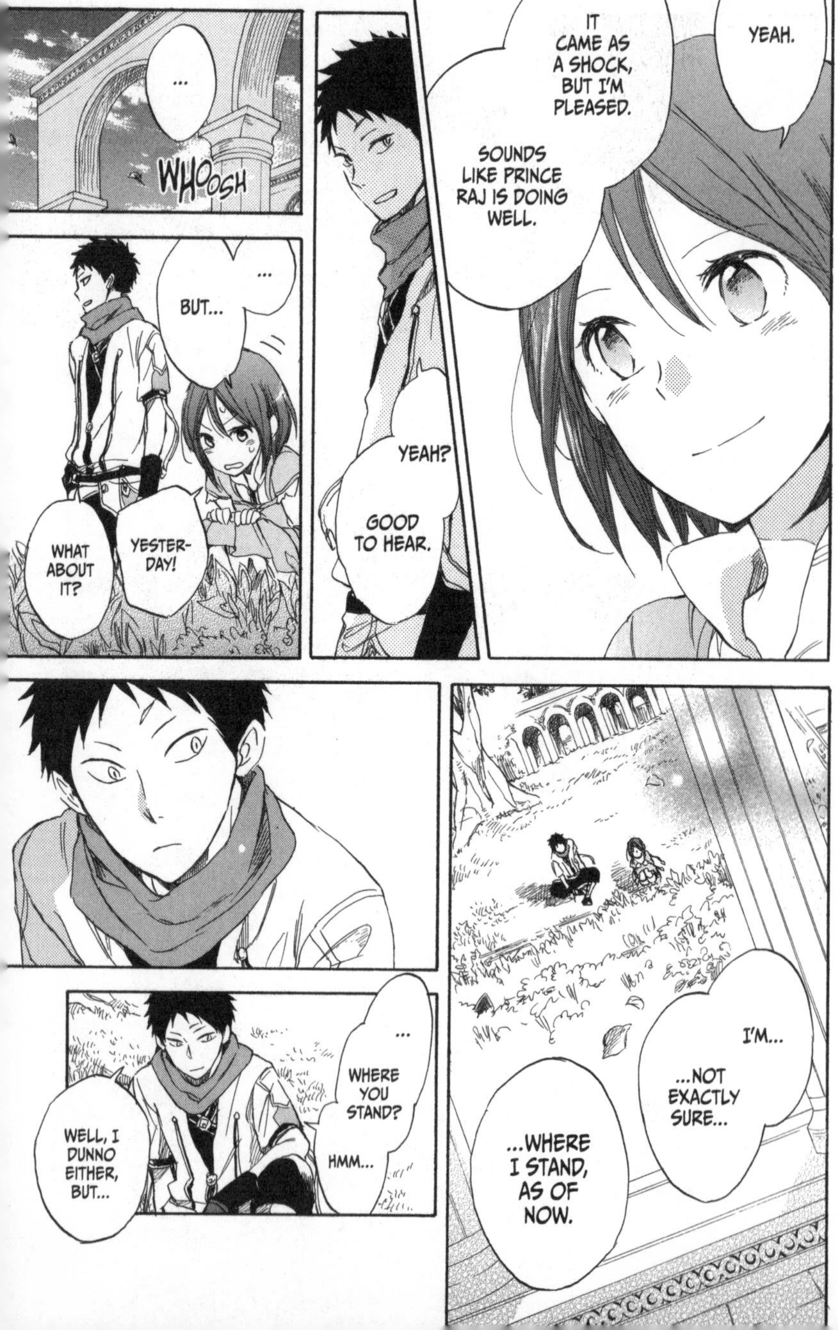
YEAH.
IT CAME AS A SHOCK, BUT I'M PLEASED.
SOUNDS LIKE PRINCE RAJ IS DOING WELL.
YEAH?
GOOD TO HEAR.
...
WHOOSH
...
BUT...
YESTER-DAY!
WHAT ABOUT IT?
I'M...
...NOT EXACTLY SURE...
...WHERE I STAND, AS OF NOW.
...
WHERE YOU STAND?
HMM...
WELL, I DUNNO EITHER, BUT...

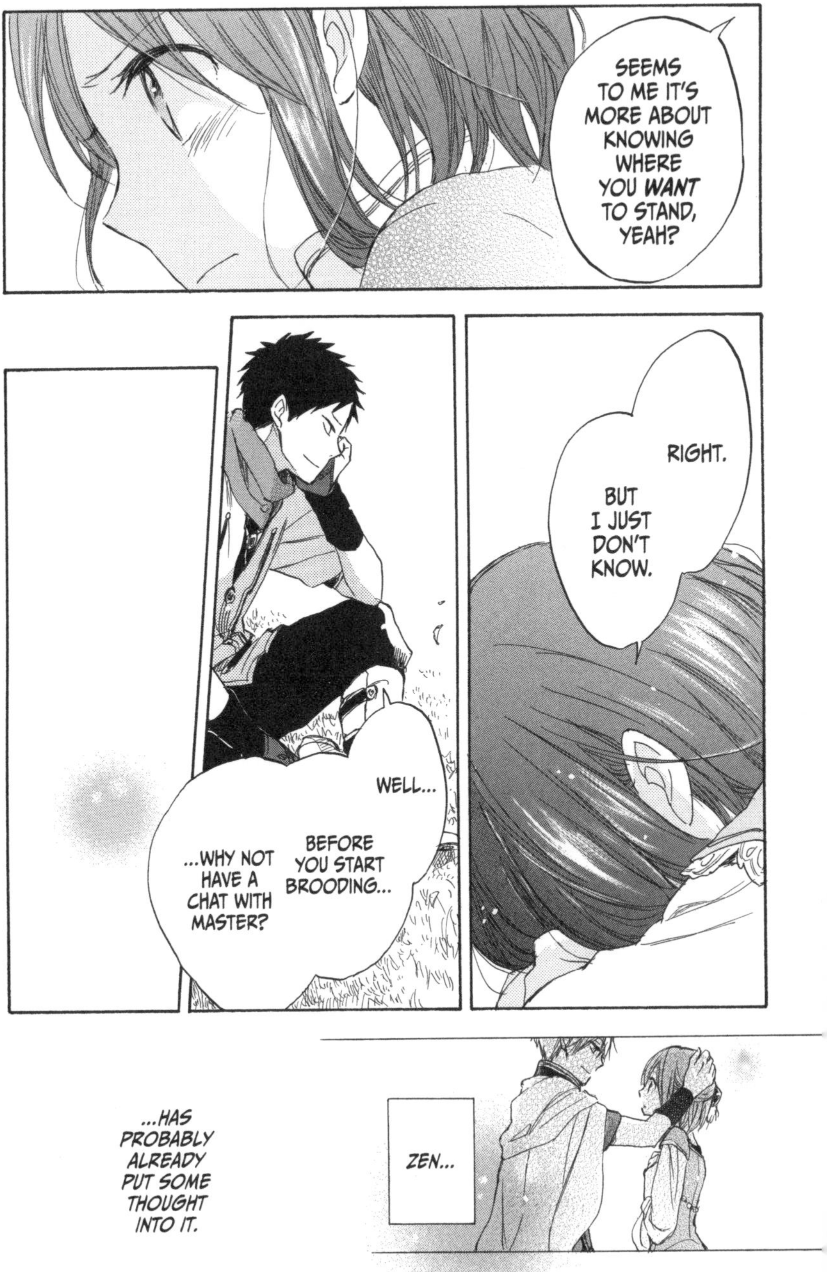
SEEMS TO ME IT'S MORE ABOUT KNOWING WHERE YOU *WANT* TO STAND, YEAH?
RIGHT.
BUT I JUST DON'T KNOW.
WELL...
BEFORE YOU START BROODING...
...WHY NOT HAVE A CHAT WITH MASTER?
ZEN...
...HAS PROBABLY ALREADY PUT SOME THOUGHT INTO IT.

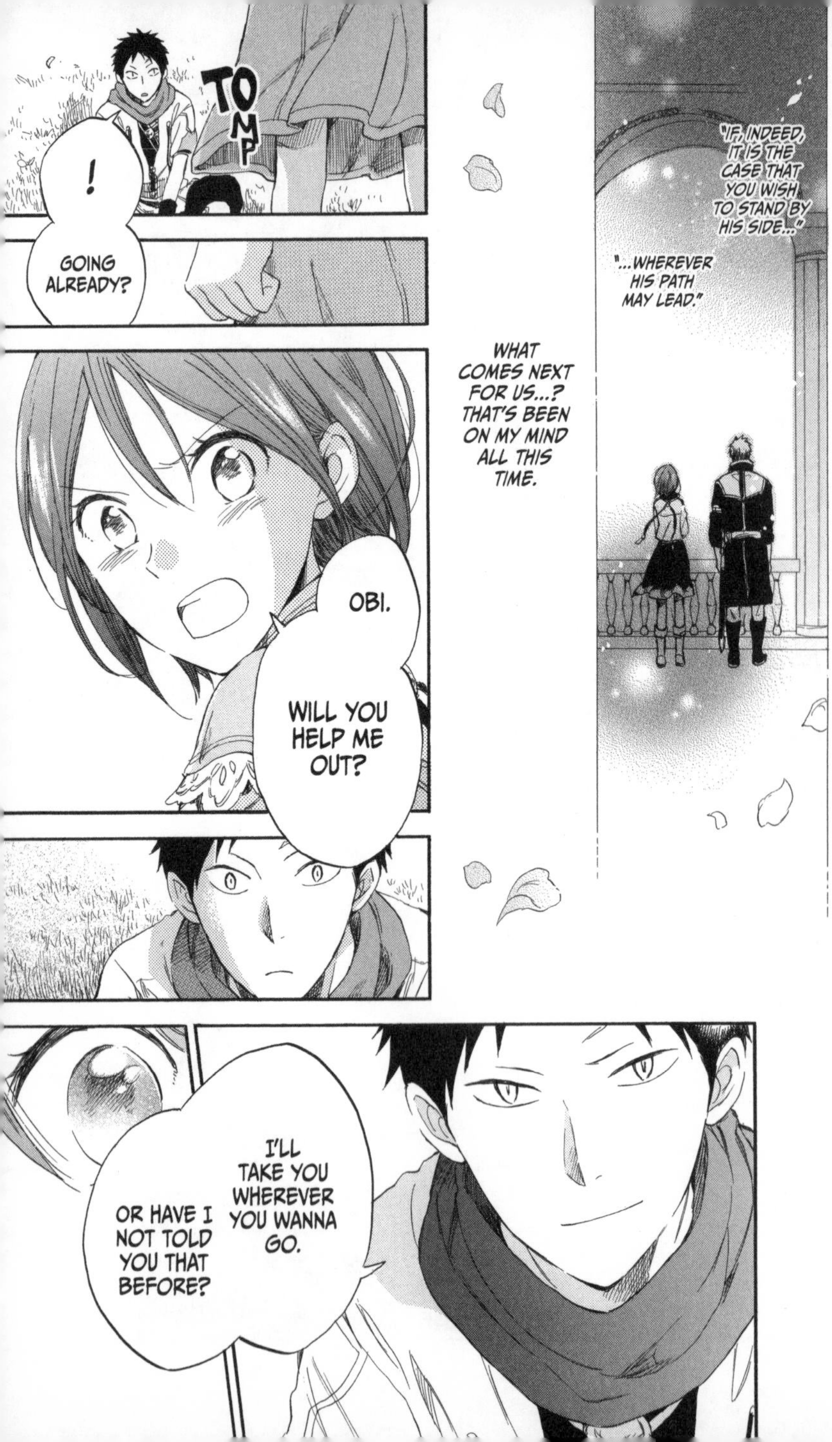
"IF, INDEED, IT IS THE CASE THAT YOU WISH TO STAND BY HIS SIDE..."
"...WHEREVER HIS PATH MAY LEAD."
WHAT COMES NEXT FOR US...? THAT'S BEEN ON MY MIND ALL THIS TIME.
TOMP
!
GOING ALREADY?
OBI.
WILL YOU HELP ME OUT?
I'LL TAKE YOU WHEREVER YOU WANNA GO.
OR HAVE I NOT TOLD YOU THAT BEFORE?

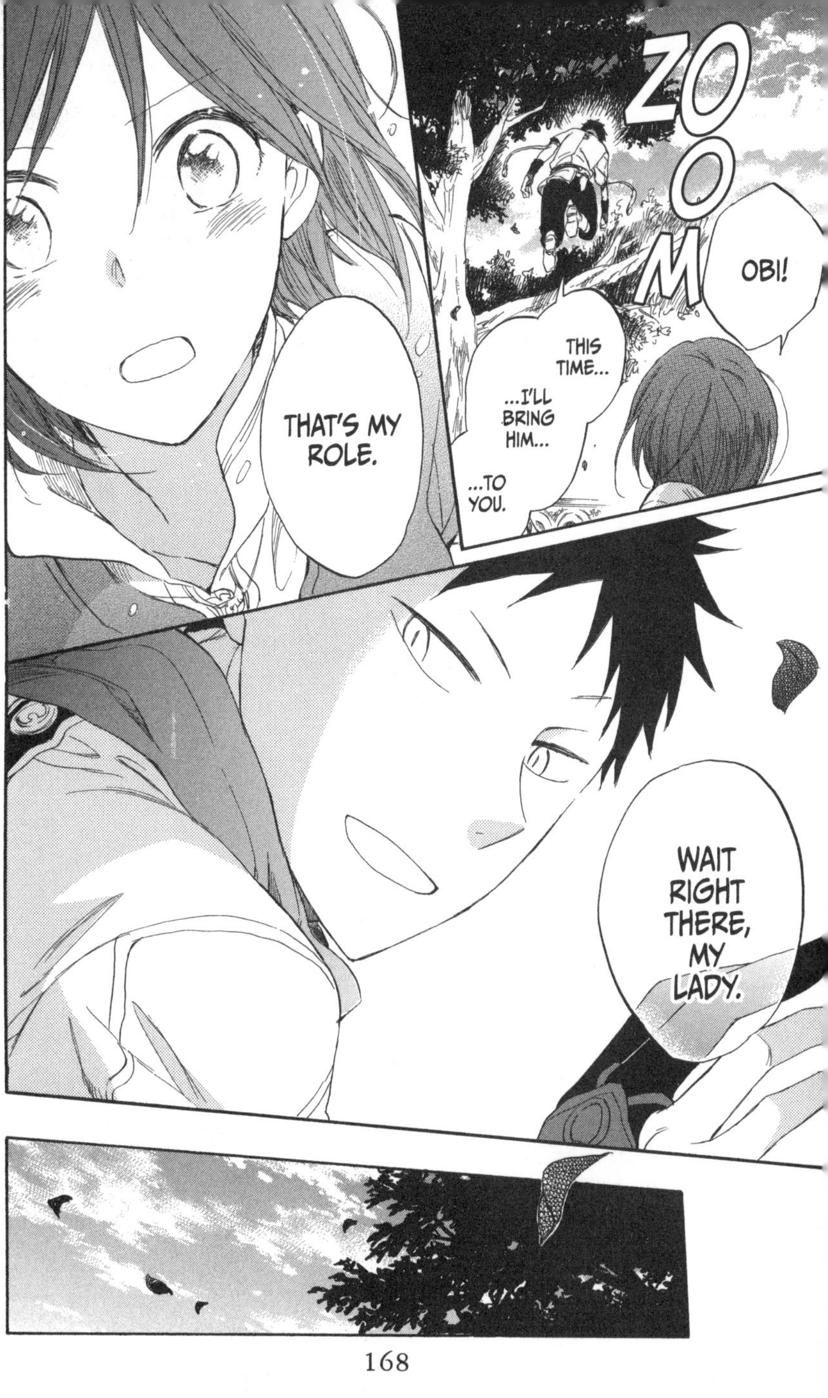
ZOOM
OBI!
THIS TIME...
...I'LL BRING HIM...
...TO YOU.
THAT'S MY ROLE.
WAIT RIGHT THERE, MY LADY.

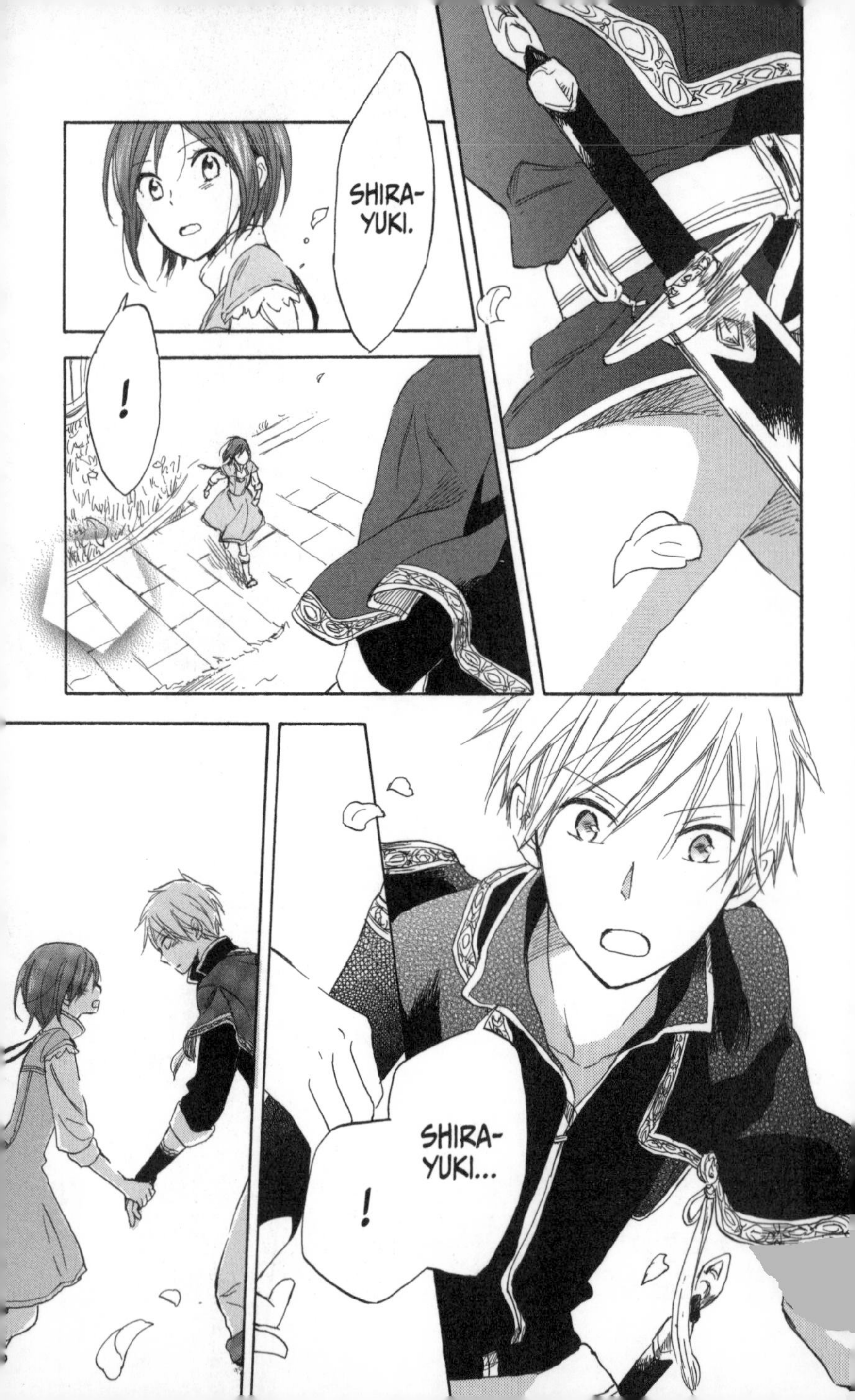
SHIRA-YUKI.
!
SHIRA-YUKI...
!

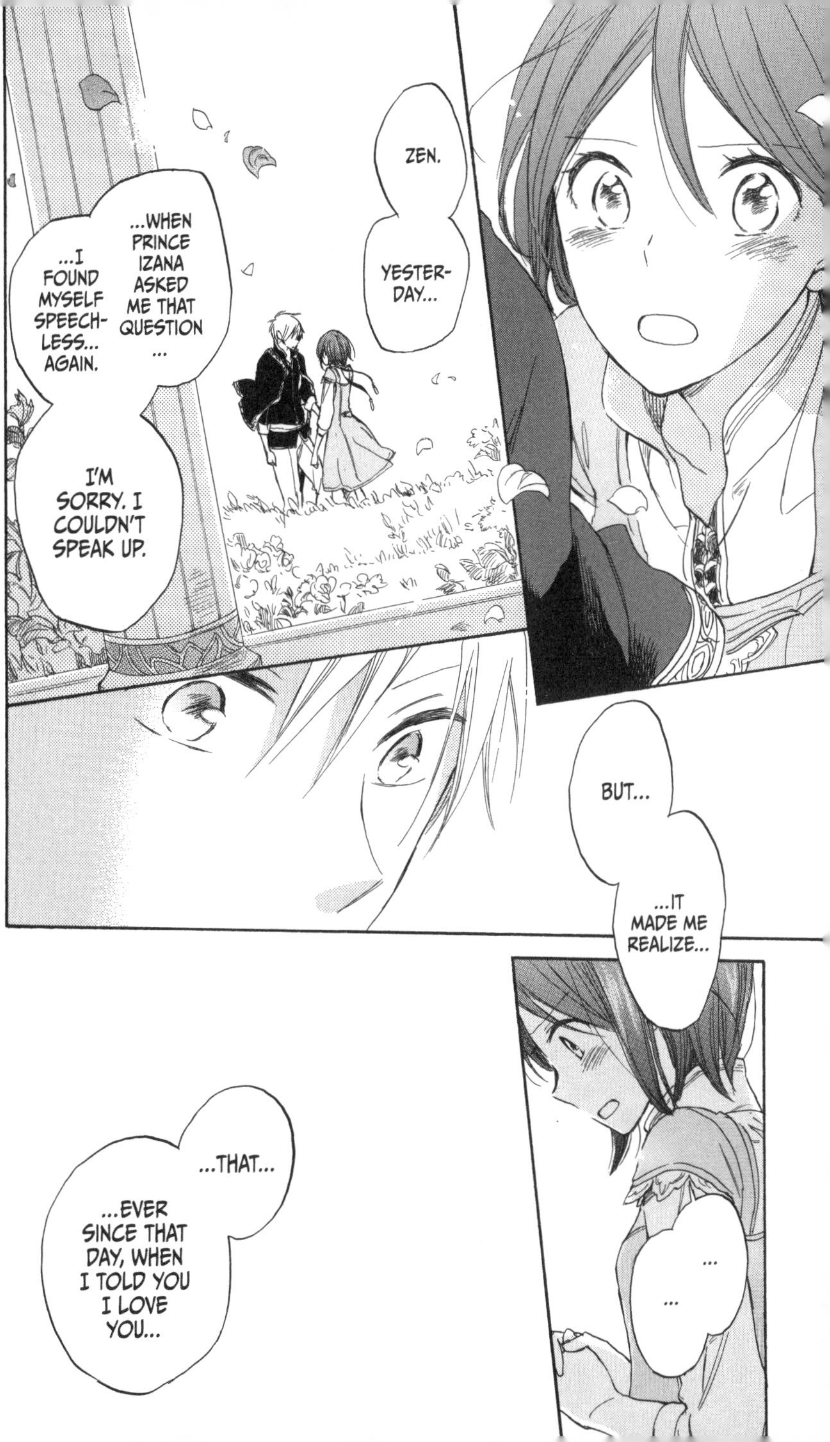
ZEN.
YESTER-DAY...
...WHEN PRINCE IZANA ASKED ME THAT QUESTION...
...I FOUND MYSELF SPEECH-LESS... AGAIN.
I'M SORRY. I COULDN'T SPEAK UP.
BUT...
...IT MADE ME REALIZE...
...THAT...
...EVER SINCE THAT DAY, WHEN I TOLD YOU I LOVE YOU...
... ...

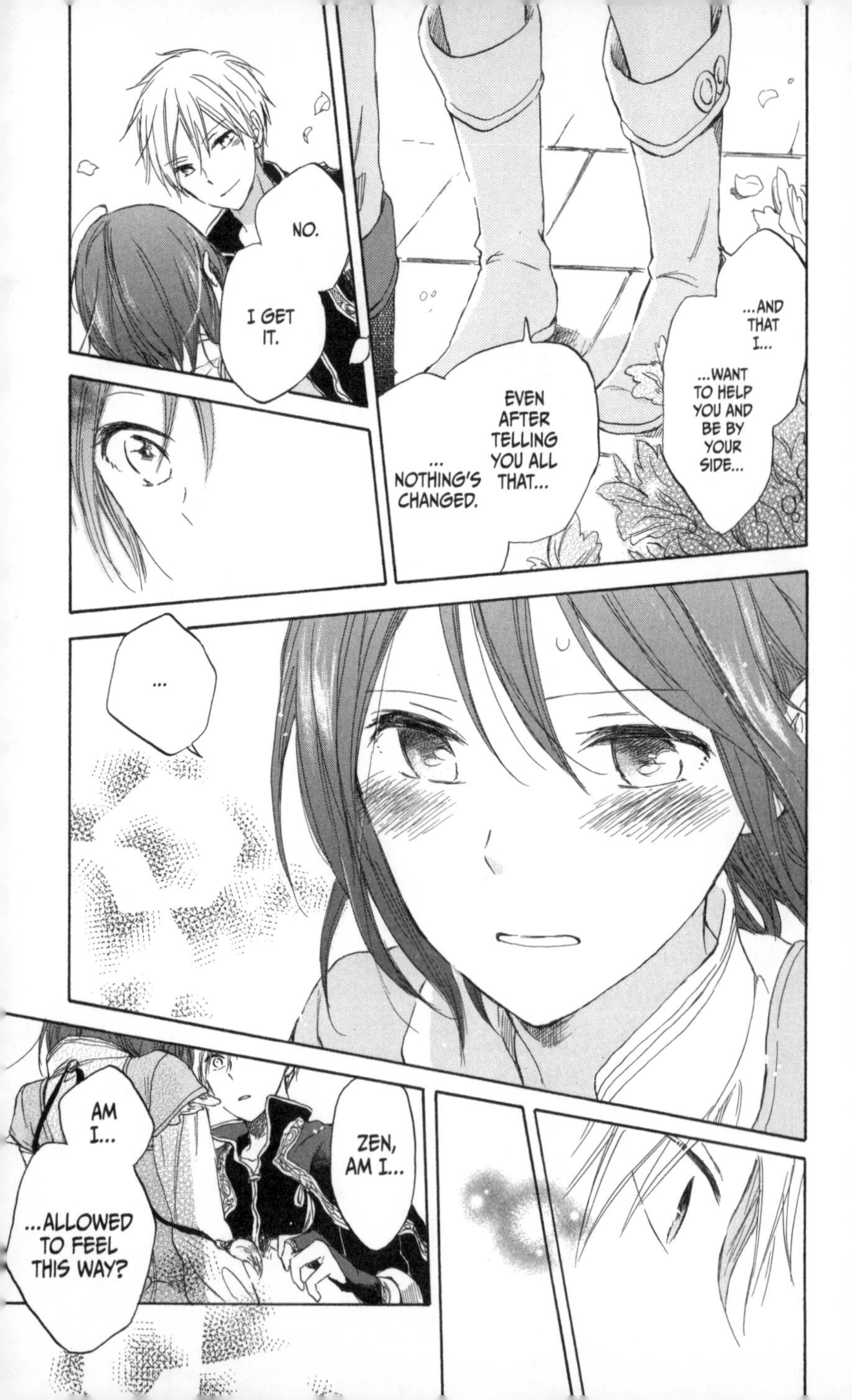
...AND THAT I...
...WANT TO HELP YOU AND BE BY YOUR SIDE...
EVEN AFTER TELLING YOU ALL THAT...
...NOTHING'S CHANGED.
NO.
I GET IT.
...
ZEN, AM I...
AM I...
...ALLOWED TO FEEL THIS WAY?

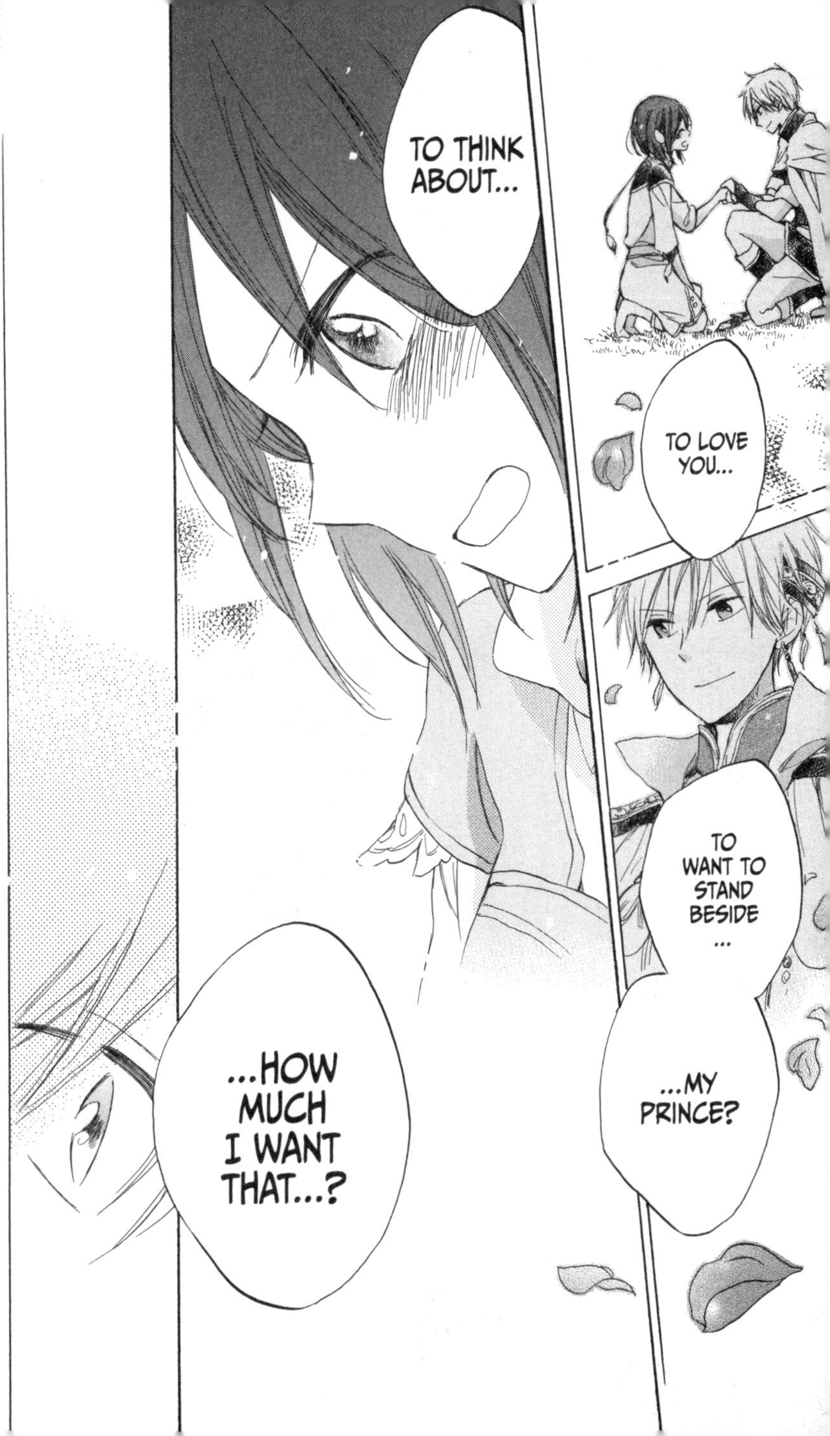
TO LOVE YOU...
TO WANT TO STAND BESIDE ...
...MY PRINCE?
TO THINK ABOUT...
...HOW MUCH I WANT THAT...?

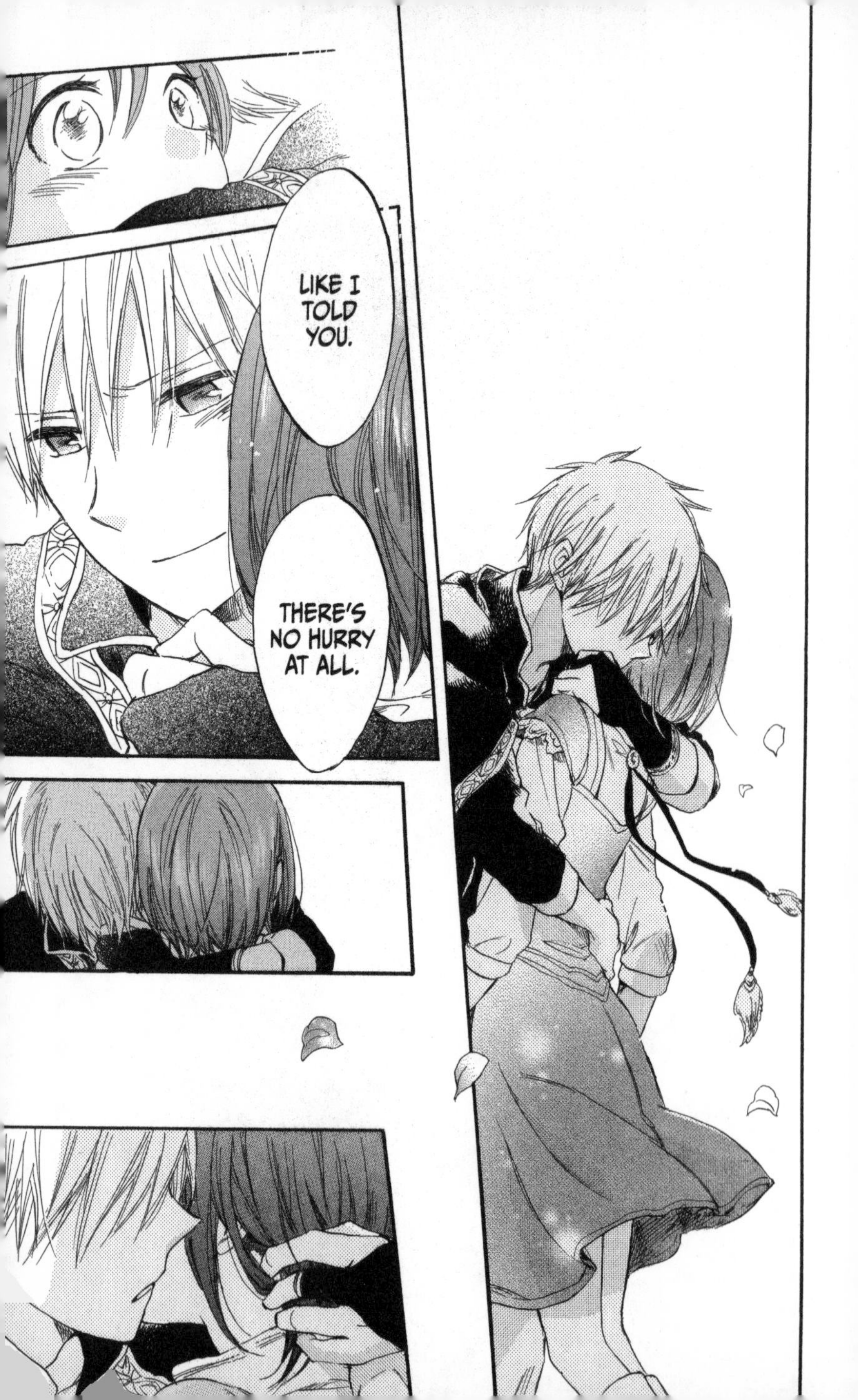
LIKE I TOLD YOU.
THERE'S NO HURRY AT ALL.

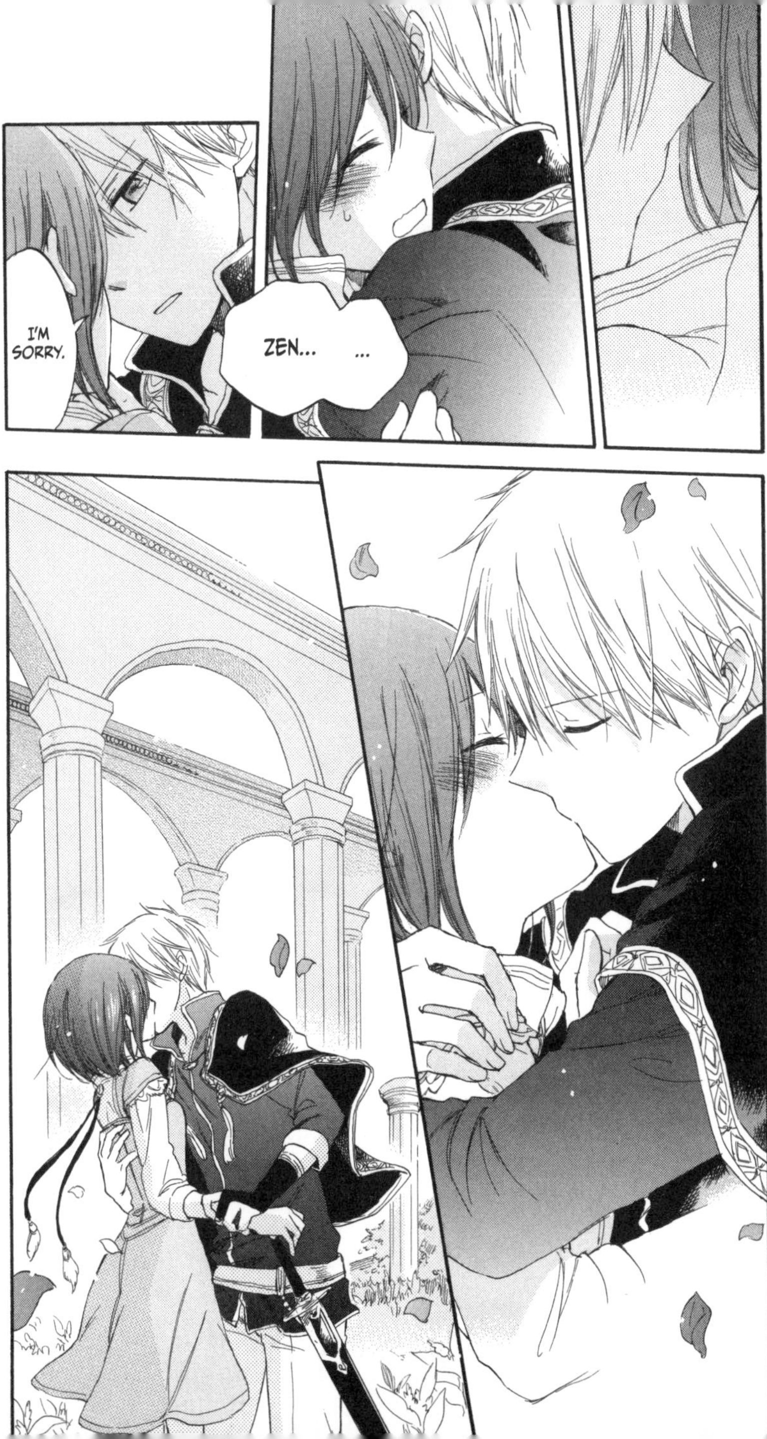
ZEN... ...
I'M SORRY.

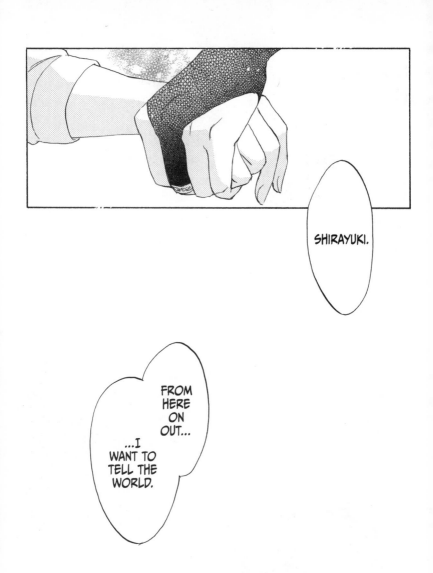

SHIRAYUKI.

FROM HERE ON OUT...

...I WANT TO TELL THE WORLD.

Snow White with the Red Hair
Vol. 7: End

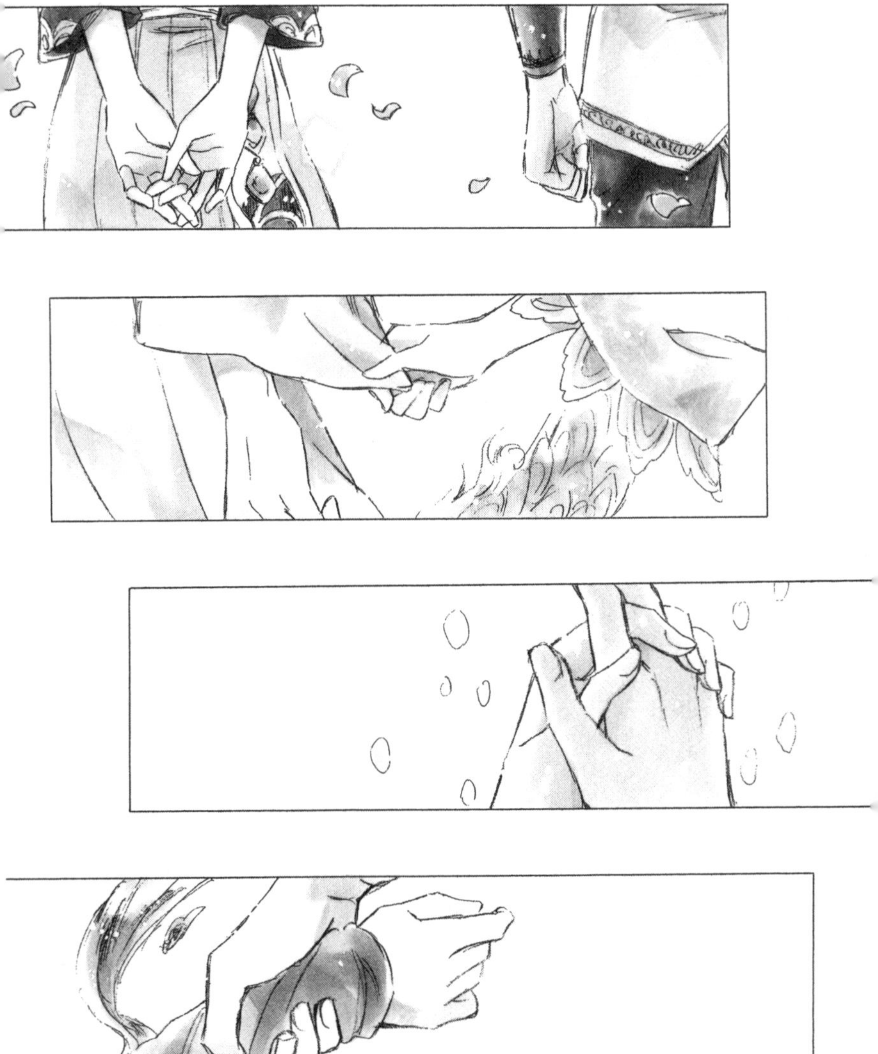

I finished my one-shot compilation
(Vahlia no Hanamuko).

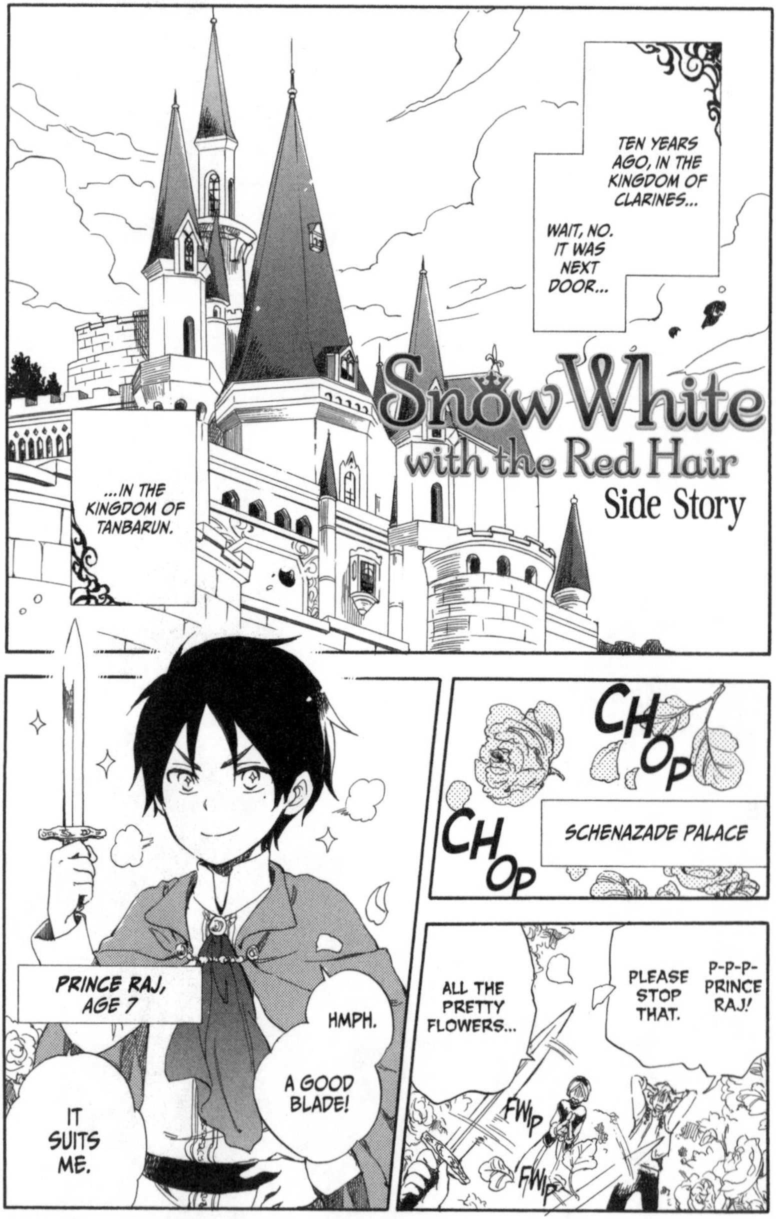
TEN YEARS AGO, IN THE KINGDOM OF CLARINES...
WAIT, NO. IT WAS NEXT DOOR...
Snow White with the Red Hair
Side Story
...IN THE KINGDOM OF TANBARUN.
CHOP
CHOP
SCHENAZADE PALACE
P-P-P-PRINCE RAJ!
PLEASE STOP THAT.
ALL THE PRETTY FLOWERS...
FWIP
FWIP
PRINCE RAJ, AGE 7
HMPH.
A GOOD BLADE!
IT SUITS ME.

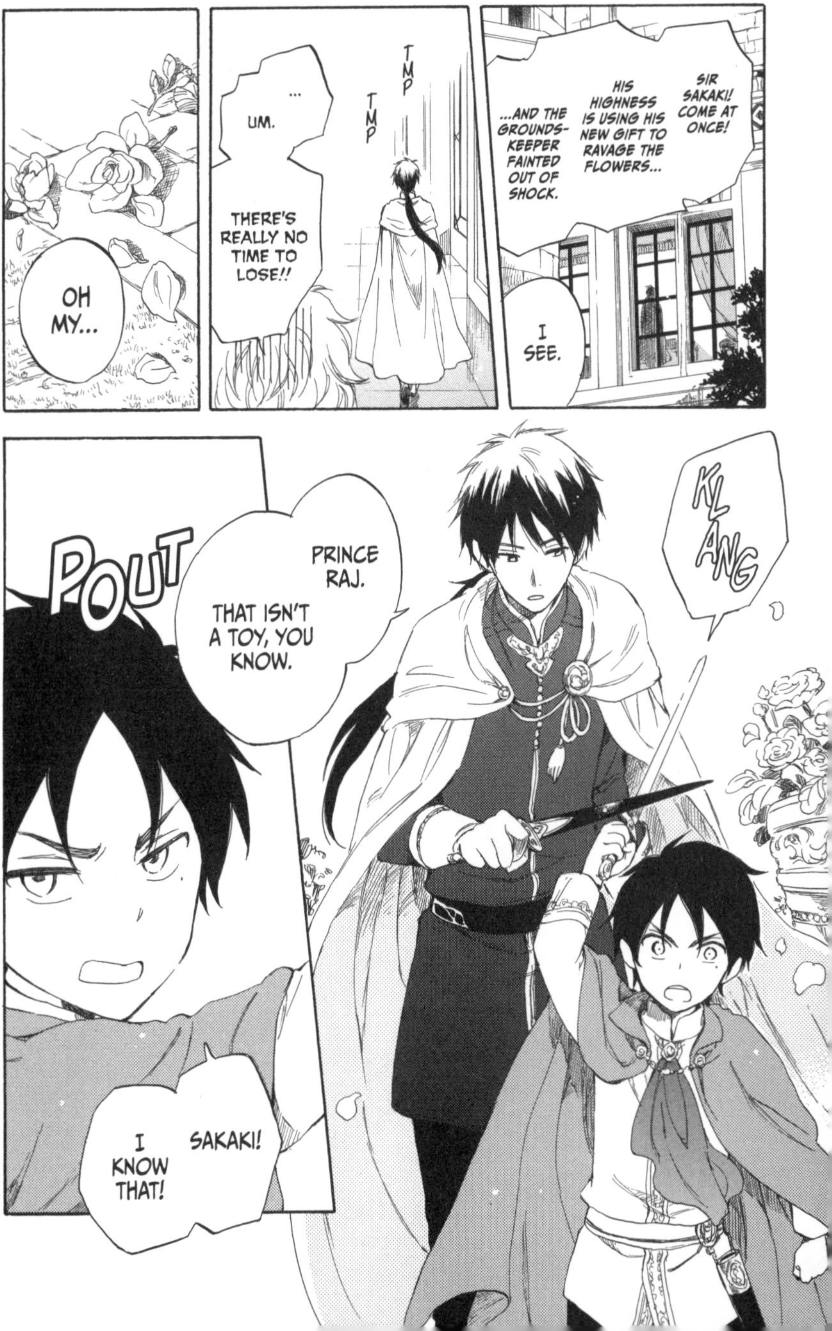
SIR SAKAKI! COME AT ONCE!
HIS HIGHNESS IS USING HIS NEW GIFT TO RAVAGE THE FLOWERS...
...AND THE GROUNDS-KEEPER FAINTED OUT OF SHOCK.
I SEE.
TMP
TMP
...
UM.
THERE'S REALLY NO TIME TO LOSE!!
OH MY...
KLANG
PRINCE RAJ.
THAT ISN'T A TOY, YOU KNOW.
POUT
SAKAKI!
I KNOW THAT!

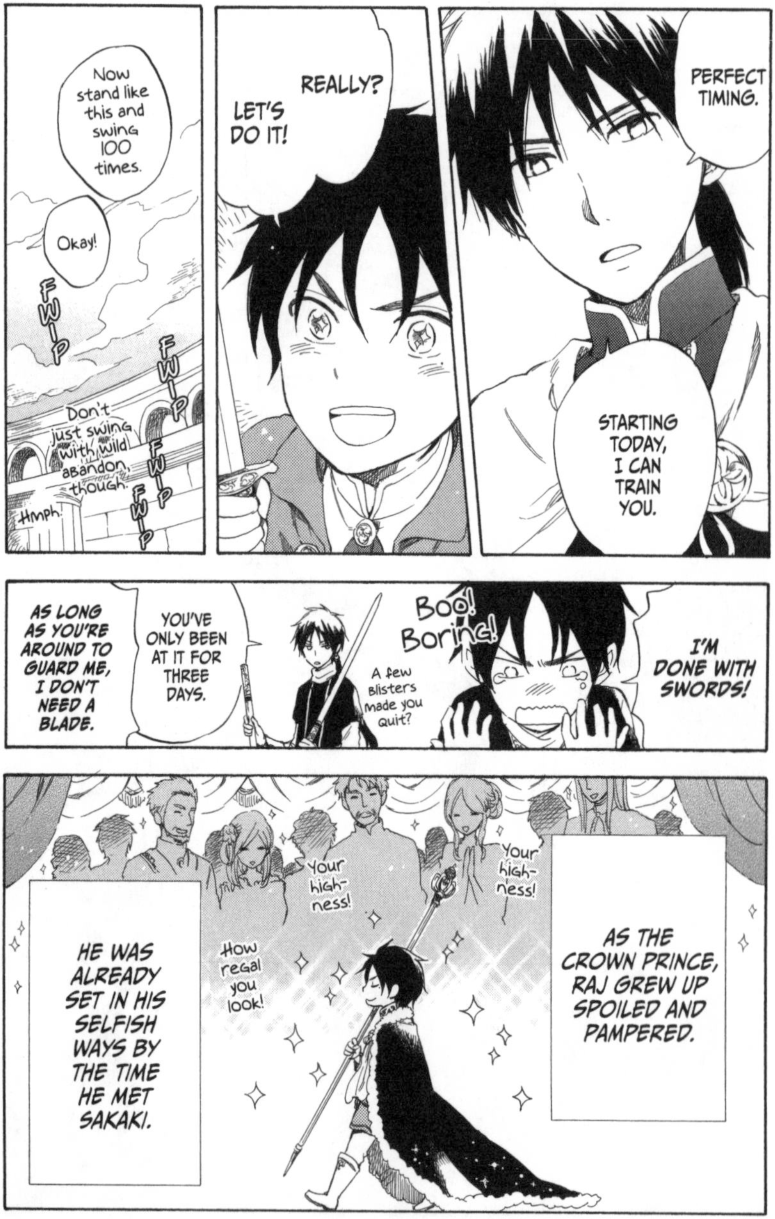
PERFECT TIMING.
STARTING TODAY, I CAN TRAIN YOU.
REALLY?
LET'S DO IT!
Now stand like this and swing 100 times.
Okay!
FWIP
FWIP
FWIP
FWIP
Don't just swing with wild abandon, though.
Hmph.
I'M DONE WITH SWORDS!
Boo! Boring!
A few blisters made you quit?
YOU'VE ONLY BEEN AT IT FOR THREE DAYS.
AS LONG AS YOU'RE AROUND TO GUARD ME, I DON'T NEED A BLADE.
AS THE CROWN PRINCE, RAJ GREW UP SPOILED AND PAMPERED.
Your highness!
Your highness!
How regal you look!
HE WAS ALREADY SET IN HIS SELFISH WAYS BY THE TIME HE MET SAKAKI.

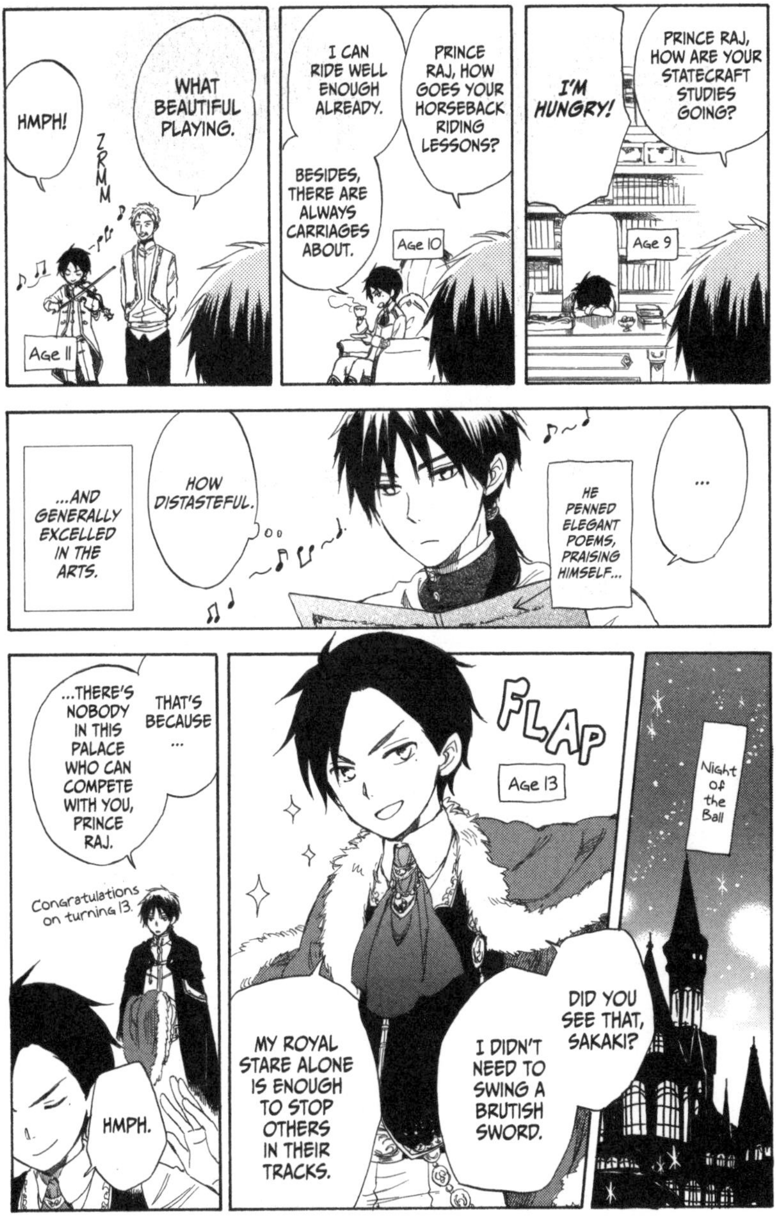
PRINCE RAJ, HOW ARE YOUR STATECRAFT STUDIES GOING?
I'M HUNGRY!
Age 9
PRINCE RAJ, HOW GOES YOUR HORSEBACK RIDING LESSONS?
I CAN RIDE WELL ENOUGH ALREADY.
Age 10
BESIDES, THERE ARE ALWAYS CARRIAGES ABOUT.
WHAT BEAUTIFUL PLAYING.
ZRMM
HMPH!
Age 11
...
HE PENNED ELEGANT POEMS, PRAISING HIMSELF...
HOW DISTASTEFUL.
...AND GENERALLY EXCELLED IN THE ARTS.
Night of the Ball
FLAP
Age 13
DID YOU SEE THAT, SAKAKI?
I DIDN'T NEED TO SWING A BRUTISH SWORD.
MY ROYAL STARE ALONE IS ENOUGH TO STOP OTHERS IN THEIR TRACKS.
THAT'S BECAUSE ...
...THERE'S NOBODY IN THIS PALACE WHO CAN COMPETE WITH YOU, PRINCE RAJ.
Congratulations on turning 13.
HMPH.

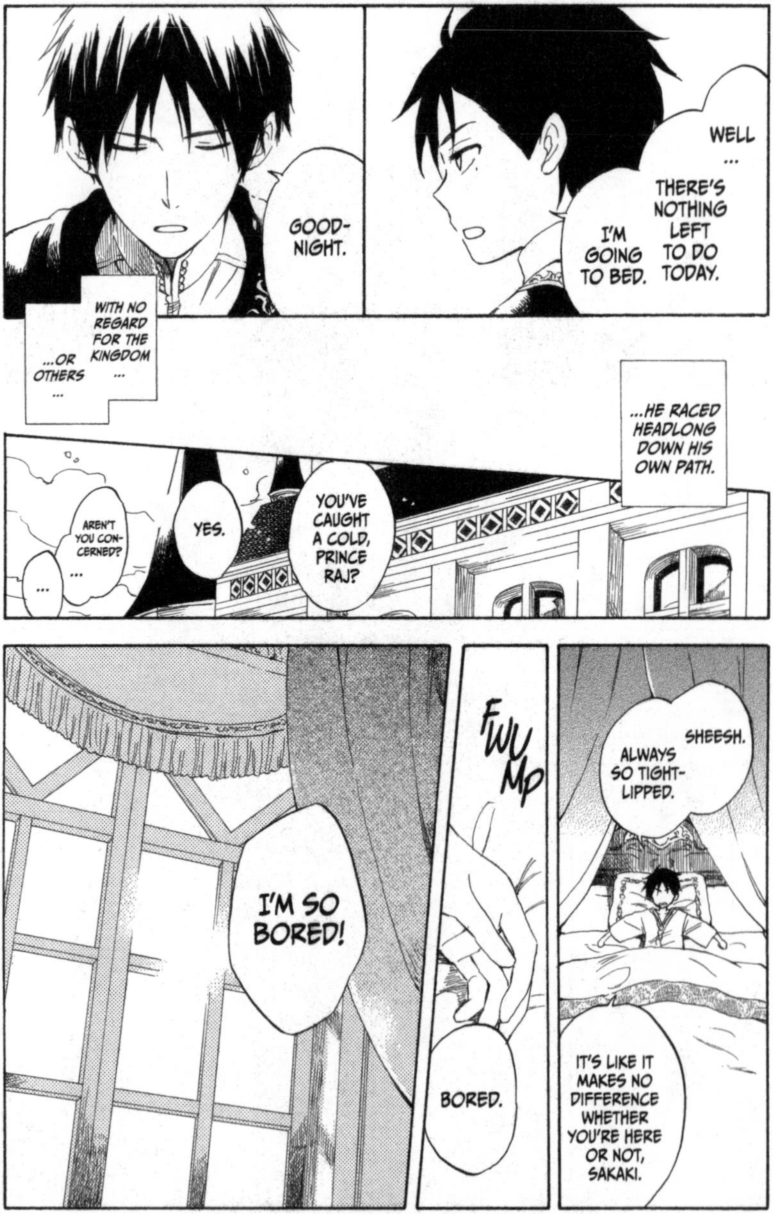
WELL ...
THERE'S NOTHING LEFT TO DO TODAY.
I'M GOING TO BED.
GOOD-NIGHT.
WITH NO REGARD FOR THE KINGDOM ...
...OR OTHERS ...
...HE RACED HEADLONG DOWN HIS OWN PATH.
YOU'VE CAUGHT A COLD, PRINCE RAJ?
YES.
AREN'T YOU CONCERNED?
...
...
SHEESH.
ALWAYS SO TIGHT-LIPPED.
IT'S LIKE IT MAKES NO DIFFERENCE WHETHER YOU'RE HERE OR NOT, SAKAKI.
FWUMP
BORED.
I'M SO BORED!

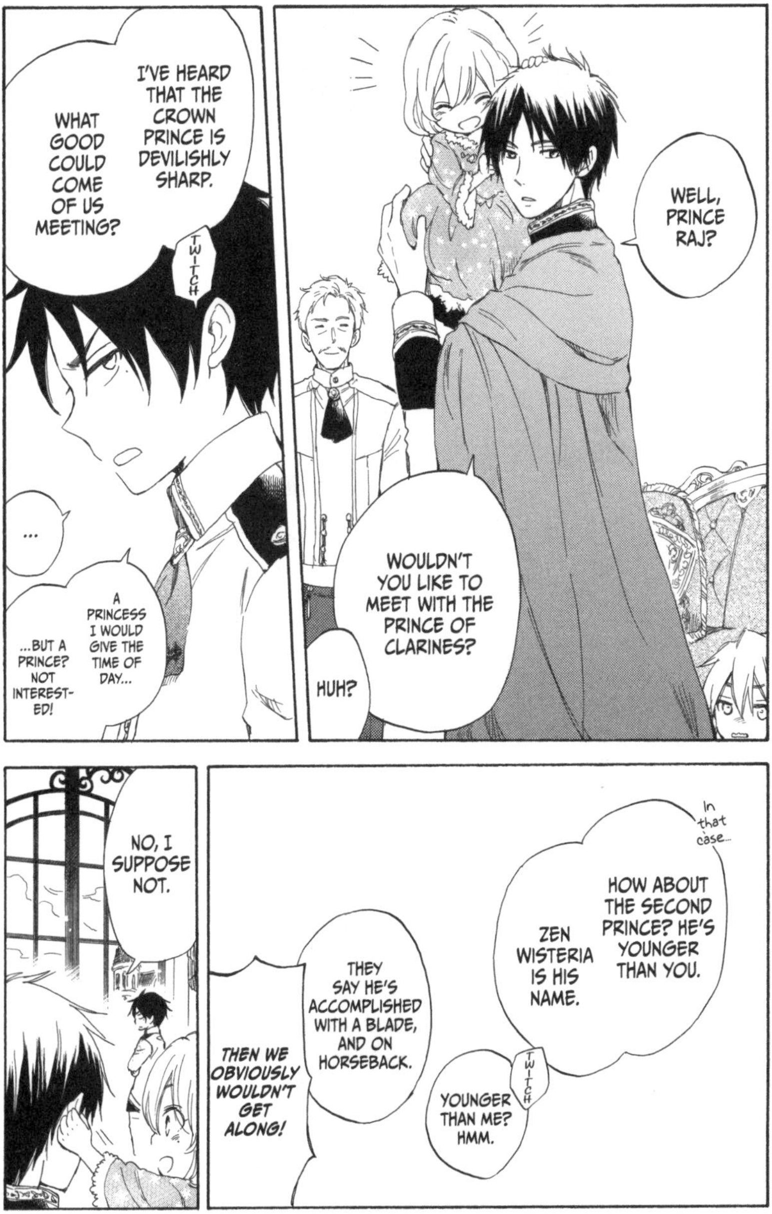
WELL, PRINCE RAJ?
WOULDN'T YOU LIKE TO MEET WITH THE PRINCE OF CLARINES?
HUH?
I'VE HEARD THAT THE CROWN PRINCE IS DEVILISHLY SHARP.
WHAT GOOD COULD COME OF US MEETING?
TWITCH
...
A PRINCESS I WOULD GIVE THE TIME OF DAY...
...BUT A PRINCE? NOT INTEREST-ED!
In that case...
HOW ABOUT THE SECOND PRINCE? HE'S YOUNGER THAN YOU.
ZEN WISTERIA IS HIS NAME.
TWITCH
YOUNGER THAN ME? HMM.
THEY SAY HE'S ACCOMPLISHED WITH A BLADE, AND ON HORSEBACK.
THEN WE OBVIOUSLY WOULDN'T GET ALONG!
NO, I SUPPOSE NOT.

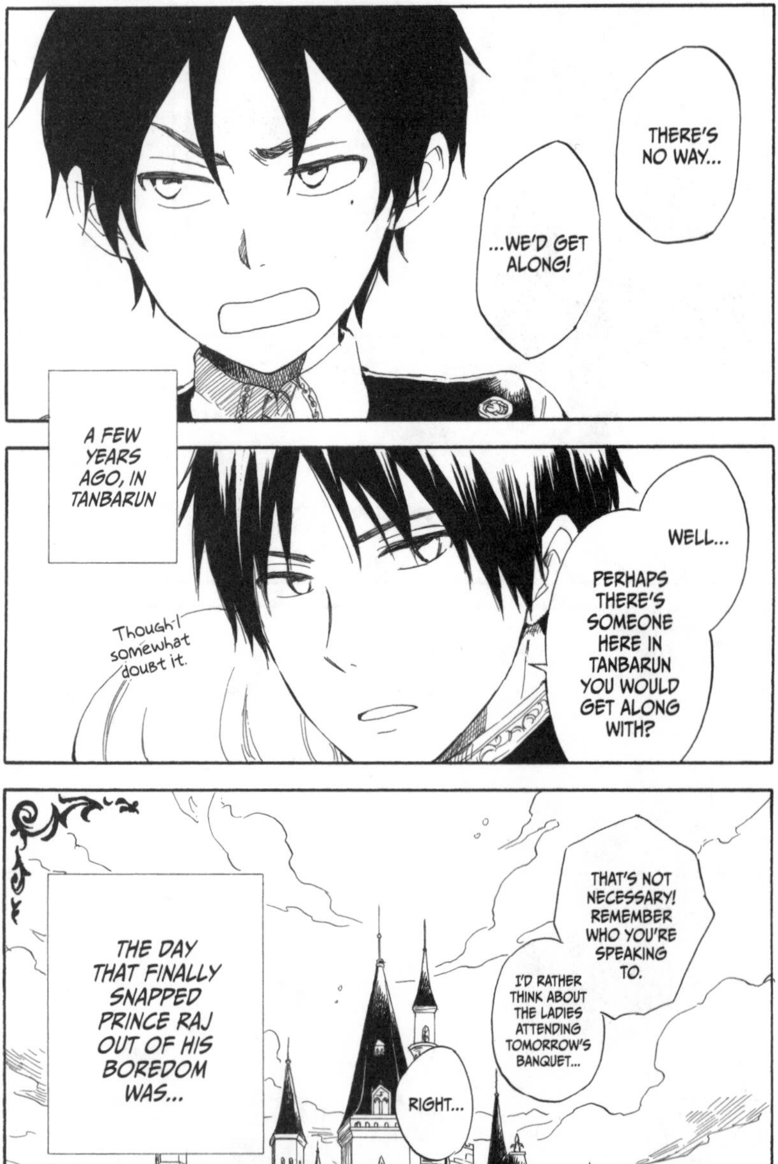
THERE'S NO WAY...
...WE'D GET ALONG!
A FEW YEARS AGO, IN TANBARUN
WELL...
PERHAPS THERE'S SOMEONE HERE IN TANBARUN YOU WOULD GET ALONG WITH?
Though I somewhat doubt it.
THAT'S NOT NECESSARY! REMEMBER WHO YOU'RE SPEAKING TO.
I'D RATHER THINK ABOUT THE LADIES ATTENDING TOMORROW'S BANQUET...
RIGHT...
THE DAY THAT FINALLY SNAPPED PRINCE RAJ OUT OF HIS BOREDOM WAS...

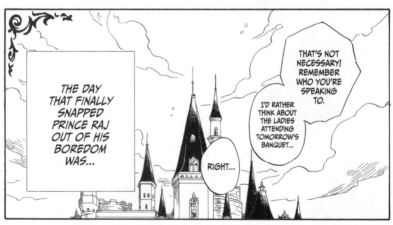

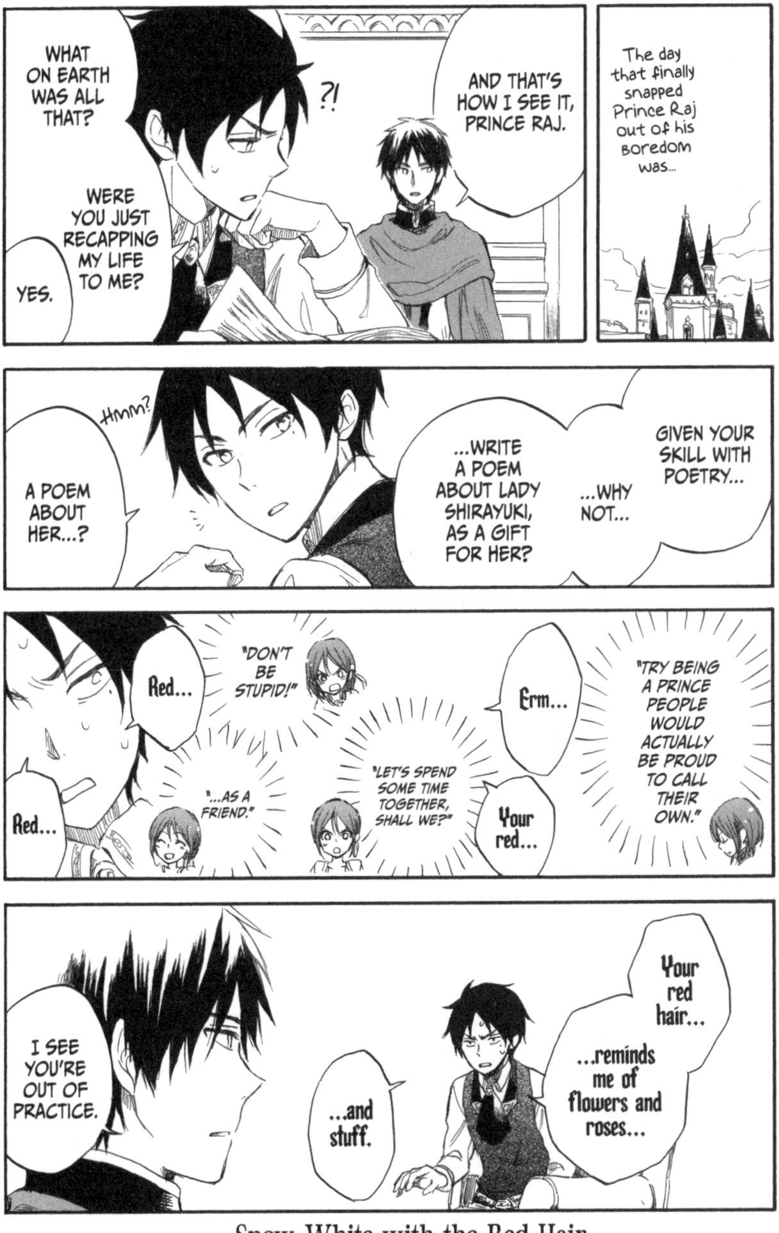
The day that finally snapped Prince Raj out of his boredom was...
AND THAT'S HOW I SEE IT, PRINCE RAJ.
?!
WHAT ON EARTH WAS ALL THAT?
WERE YOU JUST RECAPPING MY LIFE TO ME?
YES.
GIVEN YOUR SKILL WITH POETRY...
...WHY NOT...
...WRITE A POEM ABOUT LADY SHIRAYUKI, AS A GIFT FOR HER?
Hmm?
A POEM ABOUT HER...?
"TRY BEING A PRINCE PEOPLE WOULD ACTUALLY BE PROUD TO CALL THEIR OWN."
Erm...
Your red...
"LET'S SPEND SOME TIME TOGETHER, SHALL WE?"
"DON'T BE STUPID!"
Red...
"...AS A FRIEND."
Red...
Your red hair...
...reminds me of flowers and roses...
...and stuff.
I SEE YOU'RE OUT OF PRACTICE.

Snow White with the Red Hair
Side Story/End

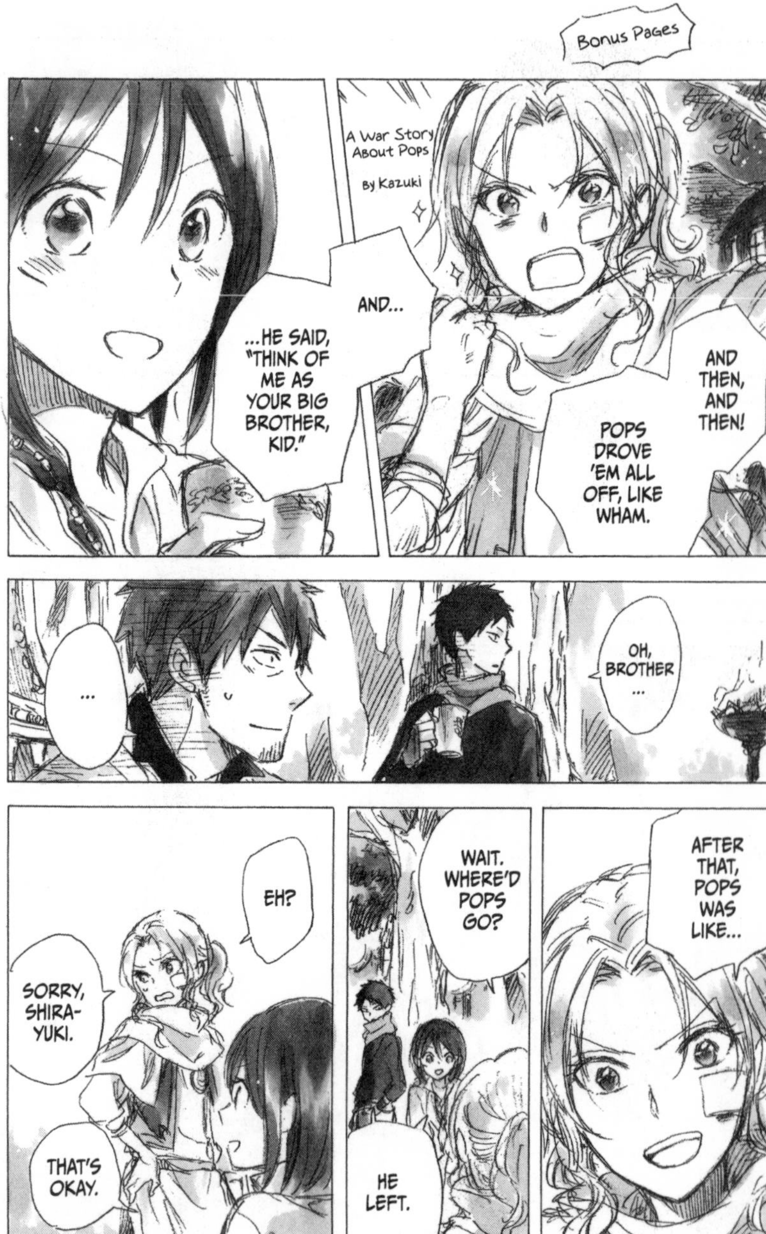
Bonus Pages
A War Story About Pops
By Kazuki
AND THEN, AND THEN!
POPS DROVE 'EM ALL OFF, LIKE WHAM.
AND...
...HE SAID, "THINK OF ME AS YOUR BIG BROTHER, KID."
OH, BROTHER ...
...
AFTER THAT, POPS WAS LIKE...
WAIT. WHERE'D POPS GO?
HE LEFT.
EH?
SORRY, SHIRA-YUKI.
THAT'S OKAY.

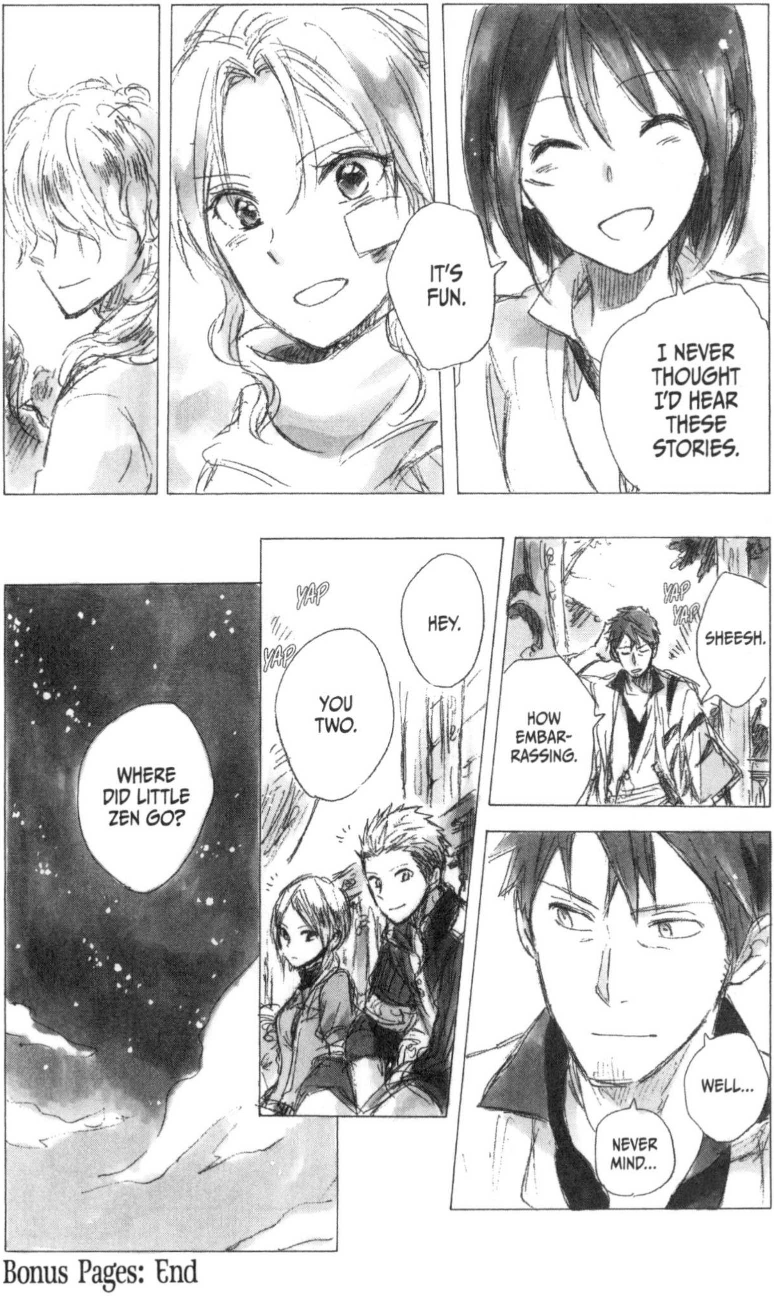
I NEVER THOUGHT I'D HEAR THESE STORIES.
IT'S FUN.
YAP YAP
SHEESH.
HOW EMBARRASSING.
WELL...
NEVER MIND...
YAP
HEY.
YAP
YOU TWO.
WHERE DID LITTLE ZEN GO?

Bonus Pages: End

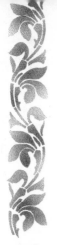

Big Thanks To:

-My editor

-The editorial staff at *LaLa*

-Yamashita-sama

-Everyone in Publishing/Sales

-Noro-sama

-My mother, big sister and father

-Everyone who sends in fan mail!

AND YOU!

-Sorata Akiduki

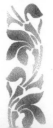

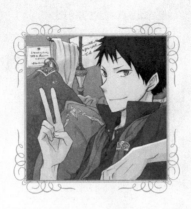

Sorata Akiduki was born on March 21 and is an accomplished shojo manga author. She made her debut in January 2002 with a one-shot titled "Utopia." Her previous works include *Vahlia no Hanamuko* (Vahlia's Bridegroom), *Seishun Kouryakubon* (Youth Strategy Guide) and *Natsu Yasumi Zero Zero Nichime* (00 Days of Summer Vacation). *Snow White with the Red Hair* began serialization in August 2006 in *LaLa DX* in Japan and has since moved to *LaLa*.

Snow White
with the Red Hair

SHOJO BEAT EDITION

STORY AND ART BY
Sorata Akiduki

TRANSLATION **Caleb Cook**
TOUCH-UP ART & LETTERING **Brandon Bovia**
DESIGN **Alice Lewis**
EDITOR **Karla Clark**

Akagami no Shirayukihime by Sorata Akiduki
© Sorata Akiduki 2012
All rights reserved.
First published in Japan in 2012 by HAKUSENSHA, Inc., Tokyo.
English language translation rights arranged with HAKUSENSHA, Inc., Tokyo.

The stories, characters and incidents mentioned
in this publication are entirely fictional.

Printed in Italy

Published by VIZ Media, LLC
P.O. Box 77010
San Francisco, CA 94107

10 9 8 7 6 5 4 3 2
First printing, May 2020
Second printing, August 2022

 MEDIA

viz.com   shojobeat.com

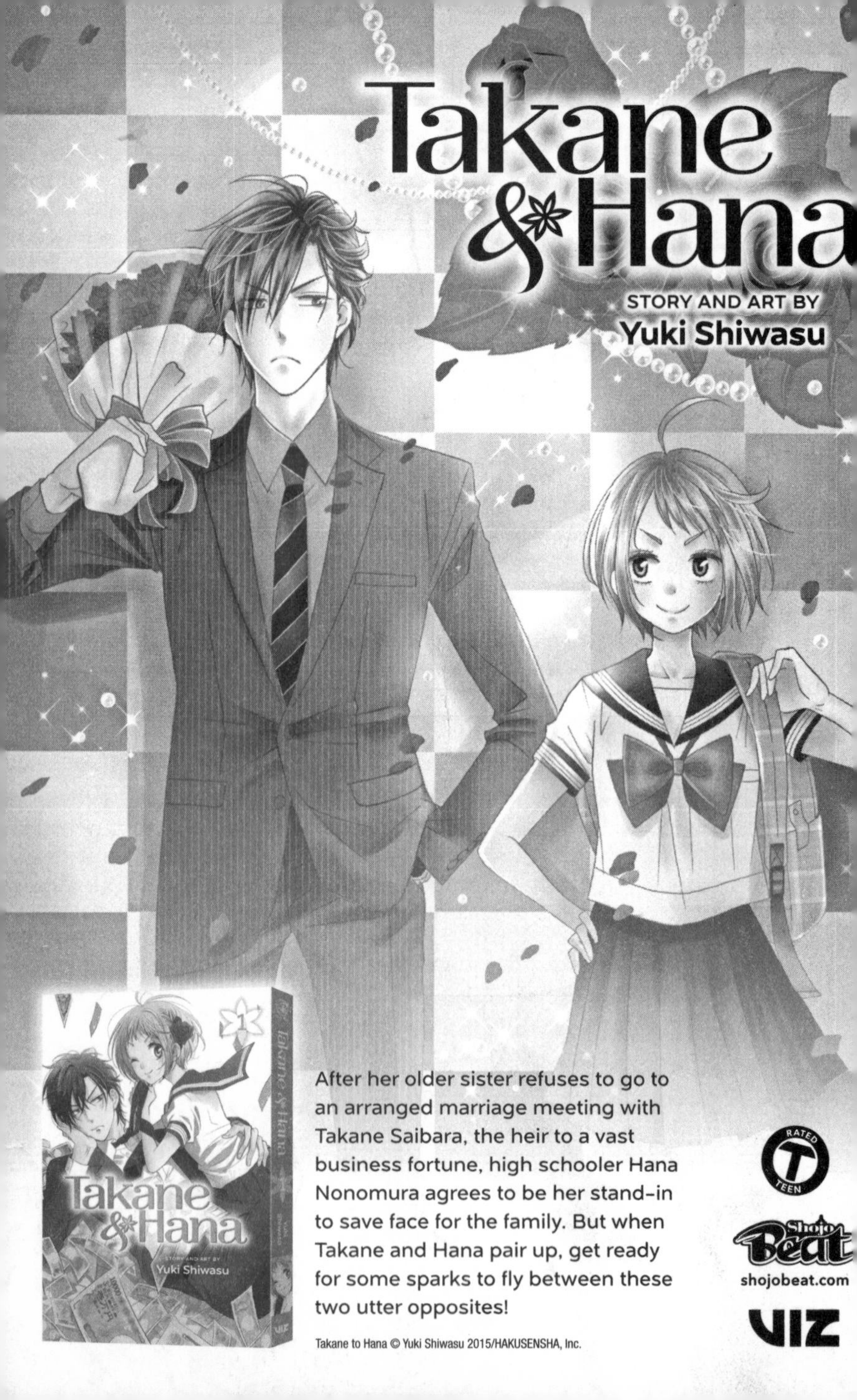
Takane & Hana
STORY AND ART BY
Yuki Shiwasu
1
Takane & Hana
STORY AND ART BY
Yuki Shiwasu
After her older sister refuses to go to an arranged marriage meeting with Takane Saibara, the heir to a vast business fortune, high schooler Hana Nonomura agrees to be her stand-in to save face for the family. But when Takane and Hana pair up, get ready for some sparks to fly between these two utter opposites!
RATED T TEEN
Shojo Beat
shojobeat.com
VIZ
Takane to Hana © Yuki Shiwasu 2015/HAKUSENSHA, Inc.

YOU'RE READING THE WRONG WAY!

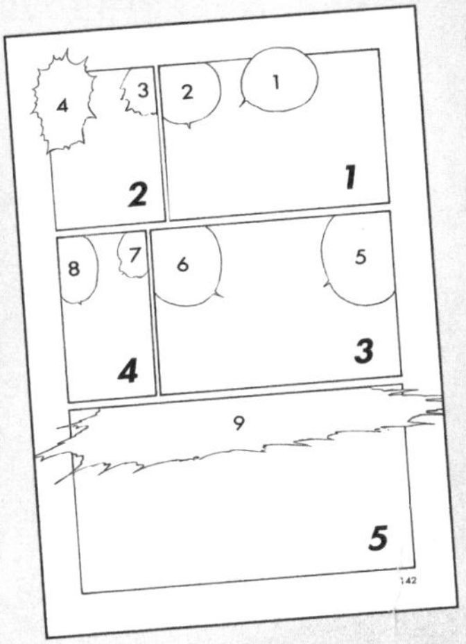

Snow White with the Red Hair reads from right to left, starting in the upper-right corner. Japanese is read from right to left, meaning that action, sound effects and word-balloon order are completely reversed from English order.

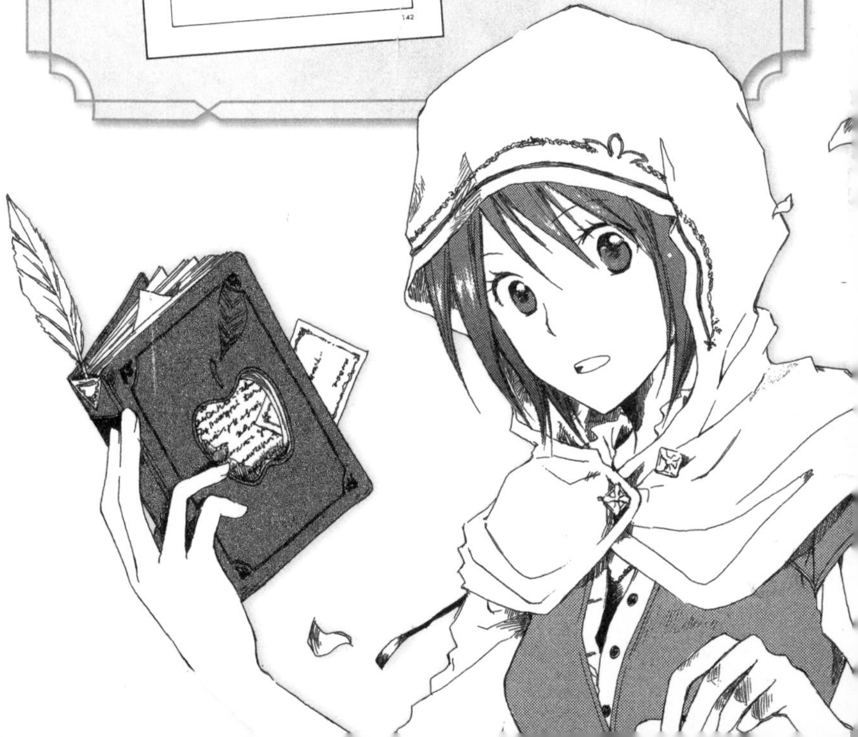